GUILT, SUFFERING, AND MEMORY

Guilt, Suffering, and Memory

GERMANY REMEMBERS ITS DEAD OF WORLD WAR II

Gilad Margalit

TRANSLATED BY
Haim Watzman

Indiana University Press
Bloomington & Indianapolis

This book is a publication of

Indiana University Press
601 North Morton Street
Bloomington, IN 47404-3797 USA

www.iupress.indiana.edu

Telephone orders 800-842-6796
Fax orders 812-855-7931
Orders by e-mail iuporder@indiana.edu

♾The paper used in this publication meets the minimum requirements of the American National Standard for Information Sciences—Permanence of Paper for Printed Library Materials, ANSI Z39.48-1992.

Manufactured in the United States of America

Library of Congress Cataloging-in-Publication Data

Margalit, Gilad.
[Ashmah, sevel ve-zikaron. English]
Guilt, suffering, and memory : Germany remembers its dead of World War II / Gilad Margalit ; translated by Haim Watzman.
p. cm.
Includes bibliographical references and index.
ISBN 978-0-253-35376-4 (cloth : alk. paper) — ISBN 978-0-253-22133-9 (pbk. : alk. paper) 1. Holocaust, Jewish (1939-1945)—Moral and ethical aspects. 2. Holocaust, Jewish (1939-1945)—Germany. 3. Memory—Social aspects. 4. Political culture—Germany. 5. Memory—Political aspects—Germany. 6. War memorials—Germany. 7. Death—History—20th century. 8. Germany—Politics and government. I. Title.
D804.3.M365713 2009
940.53'1—dc22

2009016443

1 2 3 4 5 15 14 13 12 11 10

To my wife, Vardit Gvuli,
and to my children,
Ili, Roni, Gaia, Gili, and Ruti

CONTENTS

ABBREVIATIONS

Press, Television, and Journals

ARD	Arbeitsgemeinschaft der Rundfunkanstalten	West German television Channel 1
DEFA	Deutsche Film AG	East Germany's main film producing company
FAZ	*Frankfurter Allgemeine Zeitung*	conservative daily newspaper
FR	*Frankfurter Rundschau*	left-liberal daily newspaper
ND	*Neues Deutschland*	organ of the *Linke,* previously of the Party of Democratic Socialist and the Socialist Unity Party
SZ	*Süddeutsche Zeitung*	liberal daily newspaper
TAZ	*Tageszeitung*	leftist daily newspaper, close to the Green Party
VfZ	*Vierteljahrsheft für Zeitgeschichte*	contemporary history quarterly
ZDF	Zweites Deutsches Fernsehen	West German television Channel 2

German and Foreign Archives

BA	Bundesarchiv	German federal archive
DRA	Deutsches Rundfunkarchiv	German radio archive
DVA	Deutsches Volksliedarchiv	German folksong archive
EVZ	Evangelisches Zentralarchiv	central archive of the Protestant Church, Berlin

HSTA	Hauptstaatsarchiv	central state archive
NL	Nachlaß	written remains
PRO	Public Records Office, London	
SAPMO	Die Stiftung Archiv der Parteien und Massenorganisationen der DDR	archive of GDR parties and mass organizations
STA	Staatsarchiv	state archive
StA	Stadtarchiv	city archive
StK	Staatskanzlei	State Chancellery of the German States
	Landeskirchliches Archiv	state church's archive
	Landesarchiv	state archive

The German States

BRD	Bundesrepublik Deutschland	
DDR	Deutsche Demokratische Republik	
FRG	Federal Republic of Germany	
GDR	German Democratic Republic	
HH	Hansestadt Hamburg	Hansatic city-state of Hamburg
SBZ	Sowjetische Besatzungszone	Soviet Occupation Zone (Germany)
	Bayern	Bavaria
	Niedersachsen	Lower Saxony
	Nordrhein-Westfalen	North-Rheine Westfalia

Parties and Organizations

BdV	Bund der Vertriebenen	Alliance of Expellees
BHE	Block der Heimatvertriebenen und Entrechteten	Bloc of Expellees and Disenfranchised
BvD	Bund der vertriebenen Deutschen	Alliance of Expelled Germans
BVN	Bund der Verfolgten des Naziregimes	Alliance of Victims of Nazi Persecution
CDU	Christlich Demokratische Union	Union Christian Democratic

CSU	Christlich Soziale Union	Christian Social Union
DP	Deutsche Partei	German Party
EKD	Evangelische Kirche in Deutschland	Protestant Church in Germany
FDJ	Freie Deutsche Jugend	Free German Youth (Communist youth movement)
FDP	Freie Demokratische Partei Deutschlands	Free Democrat Party of Germany (Liberals)
KPD	Kommunistische Partei Deutschlands	Communist Party of Germany
KPdSU	Komunistische Partei der Sowjetunion	Communist Party of the Soviet Union
NDPD	Nationaldemokratische Partei Deutschlands	National-Democratic Party of Germany (GDR)
NPD	Nationaldemokratische Partei Deutschlands	National Democratic Party of Germany (FRG)
OMGUS	Office of the Military Government of the United States	
PDS	Partei des Demokratischen Sozialismus	Party of Democratic Socialism
SED	Sozialistische Einheitspartei Deutschlands	Socialist Unity Party of Germany
SPD	Sozialdemokratische Partei Deutschlands	Social Democratic Party of Germany
VVN	Vereinigung Verfolgter des Naziregimes	Association of Victims of Nazi Persecution
WAV	Wirtschaftliche Aufbau Vereinigung	Economic Reconstruction Union
ZK	Zentralkommitee	Central Committee (in Communist Parties)

GUILT, SUFFERING, AND MEMORY

Introduction

In October 2002, Colonel Ernst Elbers, the new military attaché of the German embassy in Israel, sent out invitations for a memorial ceremony scheduled for November 17 at the cemetery adjacent to the Holy Family Hospital in Nazareth. The cemetery holds the remains of 416 German soldiers killed in action in Palestine during World War I.[1] The attaché wished to mark, in Israel, an official German memorial day, called the People's Day of Mourning (*Volkstrauertag*). Falling on the third Sunday of November and observed by the Federal Republic of Germany annually since 1952, it is a collective day of remembrance of German soldiers and civilians who died in the two world wars. The World War II dead include all soldiers who fell in battle in the service of any branch of the Nazi state's military—the Wehrmacht, the army proper; but also the SS, including members of the *Einsatzgruppen* (mobile killing squads operated by the SS during the war) and the Waffen SS (the SS's combat arm). The same memorial day is also dedicated to those killed by the Nazi regime, including German Jews murdered in the Holocaust, as well as opponents of the regime and other victims of Nazism. For more than fifty years, the Federal Republic of Germany has lowered its flags to half-staff on this day. Such ceremonies are held at military cemeteries around the world where German soldiers are buried, with the participation of members of Wehrmacht and SS veteran organizations—who in recent decades have dwindled with each year. Many Germans continue to call this memorial day by the name the day was given in the Third Reich, when it was instituted in memory of soldiers who had fallen in World War I—the Heroes' Memorial Day, or *Heldengedenktag.*

The German military attaché did not invite the Israel Defense Forces to send representatives. But several senior reserve officers who study World War I were astounded to receive invitations to a ceremony in memory of "the dead and missing of the two world wars." One of them, the military historian Yigal Shefi, notified Elbers that he refused to participate in "an event in honor of the dead of the Wehrmacht and other forces of the Nazi regime."[2]

When news of the invitation appeared in the Israeli newspaper *Ha'aretz*, tempers flared. The German attaché and the embassy's communications adviser, Reinhard Wiemer, offered convoluted explanations that sought to blur the nature of the ceremony and its essence. They sought to present in an acceptable way for a Jewish public the Federal Republic's official memorial policy regarding soldiers who had died serving in Hitler's army. The Federal Republic had, after all, been founded by the Western powers, as a democratic antithesis to the Nazi state. Yet this democracy also commemorates fallen soldiers who had participated in the slaughter of Europe's Jews.[3]

This minor scandal reveals the abyss between two concepts of national remembrance that grow out of two opposing experiences of the same events. In German memory, the period is that of the Nazi regime and World War II. In Jewish memory, it is that of the Holocaust (the Shoah). Germany's official designation of who is mourned on this memorial day includes soldiers who fell in battle, some of whom had previously served as hangmen, as well as German Jews murdered in the Holocaust (but not other European Jews annihilated by the Germans). To join the two is to utterly contradict Jewish memory of the Holocaust, which sees a huge difference between "those who shouted *Heil* and those who murmured *Shema Yisrael* [a daily prayer a Jew also recites when accepting martyrdom] at the hour of murder by Hitler's troopers," to quote Menachem Begin, who criticized the German concept of remembrance more than forty years ago.[4]

But only a minority of the German public today views this form of mourning, and People's Day of Mourning in particular, as a peculiar way of commemorating World War II, unfair as well as insulting to the memory of Nazi Germany's victims. Most of the German public is of one mind on the matter, believing that the official way of memorializing the war dead is fitting. They see it as an accurate reflection of the German experience of the war, as interpreted in hindsight and stored in the German collective memory since their nation's defeat in May 1945.

It is well known that the two Germanys, the democratic and the Communist, both established in 1949 on the ruins of the Third Reich, were bitter ideological rivals. But both regimes chose to view German soldiers who fell in battle as victims of the Nazis rather than Hitler's obedient servants. In the memorial tradition of Germany (as in that of other countries), the term "victims of war" was reserved for civilians killed during a war, not for soldiers who fell on the battlefield. But the shapers and agents of Germany's postwar memorial culture broadened the term to include German soldiers who died in the service of the Nazi regime's criminal enterprise. In East Germany, they were called "the victims of fascism and militarism," while West Germany included both German soldiers killed in action and German civilians slain during the two world wars. They were called "the victims of war and dictatorship."

Both rival states perceived the German soldiers killed in the war as a collective of victims. This choice implies a national attitude that absolves soldiers, across the board and to an unprecedented extent, for crimes they committed on the orders of the Nazi regime. It absolves them of responsibility for the atrocities in which they participated collectively, and in which no small number of them participated as individuals.

While this implicit absolution did not have sweeping legal ramifications, the fact is that the two Germanys brought only a handful of soldiers to trial for war crimes. Furthermore, the attitude contributed to the shaping of Germans' collective memory. It promoted a widespread trend in German historiography of the 1950s that regarded war crimes as exceptional rather than as the everyday experience of German soldiers, collectively exonerated German soldiers of war crimes and crimes against humanity, and depicted German soldiers as victims of the Nazi regime.[5] Traces of such an interpretation are still evident in some German historiography today, such as the tendency to minimize the number of soldiers who took part in Nazi crimes.[6]

When the Germans remember and memorialize their soldiers as victims of the war, they blur the unique criminality of Nazi war conduct. Cruelty and gratuitous violence were not restricted to the SS. The Wehrmacht was no less a central institution of the Nazi regime, and no less criminal. It implemented the Nazi criminal policy and was involved in war crimes and crimes against humanity, even if not every one of the millions of average Wehrmacht soldiers committed crimes himself.[7] The view of the soldier as victim derives, apparently, from Germany's difficulty in acknowledging the dimensions of its society's involvement in the regime's crimes. However, turning this common view into the official culture of memory in West Germany was a direct outcome of Cold War politics. The country's attitude is tantamount to rejecting the accusations made against German society by Western public opinion. But the same thinking was evident even earlier, during the war, when the first news of the crimes against civilians reached Germany. By portraying the soldiers as victims, Germans turned the private tragedy of the death of each individual German soldier who fell in battle into a universal tragedy.

This depiction of the soldier reflects a German perception and memory of World War II that differs significantly from the view taken by mainstream historiography, including history written in Germany itself since the 1980s, according to which the German conduct of the war was unlike any other fought in the West. The Nazi war, especially but not only against the Soviet Union, was, for Hitler, an ideological war of annihilation that the German army, driven by fervent racial hatred, implemented through a campaign of murder.[8] Yet German memory has portrayed the Nazi-indoctrinated soldier of World War II as if he were a World War I fighter motivated, according to the popular image, by a soldierly brotherhood that transcended the trenches.

The two Germanys were established on the basis of lessons learned from the Nazi past—each one, of course, in accordance with the ideological position of the bloc to which it adhered during the Cold War. Both were committed to anti-Nazi ideology and politics. The patterns of remembrance and memorialization of the war dead that the two countries instituted, however, produced a representation of the war entirely different from that which prevailed in the political blocs that each Germany's leaders sought to attach themselves.

This book presents and analyzes the background, causes, and circumstances that led to the consolidation and shaping of postwar Germany's unique concept of remembrance and memorialization of its World War II dead.

Germany classifies its war dead into a number of categories. This work primarily addresses soldiers killed in battle during World War II and civilians slain during the Allied bombings of German cities. There were 5.3 million servicemen killed or missing, while 400,000 civilians were victims of the bombings. A third category numbers about 500,000, comprising the civilian victims of the flight and expulsion from the German territories east of the Oder-Neisse line and from Sudetenland and other Eastern European countries.[9]

In the chapters that follow, I examine official memorial ceremonies for fallen soldiers and victims of the bombings, describe the memorials built in their memory, and provide an account of the various discourses on these dead—in the general public, in the media, and in art and culture—across German society.

The book focuses on the period of direct Allied rule over occupied Germany (1945–1949), and in particular on the first decade of the existence of the two German states, founded in 1949, at the height of the Cold War. This is the constitutive period for German war remembrance and memorialization. The book also looks at the links between the patterns of remembrance and memorialization chosen by the German states, and the tension between the discussion of German guilt for Nazi crimes (which began during the Nazi period) and that of suffering and the German sense of national victimhood during World War II.

It also examines central processes and trends that occurred in German remembrance and memorialization after this period, from the end of the Cold War until the beginning of the twenty-first century. The permeation of the Jewish Holocaust narrative into German public discourse characterized this period's changing memory of the past. Evident as early as the 1960s, it reached its climax in the 1980s and 1990s. I also look at how German patterns of remembrance and memorialization that crystallized during the two Germanys' seminal periods influenced German political culture after reunification in 1990, and at the current wave of preoccupation with national suffering and with German victims of World War II in united Germany.

Methodology

This work addresses historical, political, and cultural issues in post-1945 Germany. It is based on a variety of historical sources, among them documents in German government archives on the municipal, state (*Länder*), and federal (in West Germany) or central government (in East Germany) levels—as is common practice in political history. It also draws on a variety of literary, cinematic, artistic, and media sources, as is the practice in cultural history.

I use these latter works in a way fundamentally different from that used in the study of literature, art, and cinema. I do not analyze their artistic and esthetic qualities or related characteristics. This book examines the representation of the war and the Nazi past in these works, and the narratives within which they are interwoven. It focuses on an analysis of their meanings and symbolism for the perception of the war and the way in which German institutions and creative artists understood it in the postwar period. I also seek to follow the relevant implications these works have for how the broader public understands the past.

Issues of memory occupy a large part of this book. I must, therefore, briefly address the study of this issue in historical research. Memory is often presented as the opposite of forgetting. But an individual's and nation's memory of the past, and all the more so the official memories that states adopt with regard to problematic periods in their recent history, are constructed and interpreted presentations of the past that contain within them no small amount of forgetting, in both the passive and active sense.[10] Beyond the existing differences and variety among the memories of individuals and of certain groups within German society, it is possible to locate certain patterns that appear in the memories of individuals and groups. It is therefore possible to speak, with some element of generalization, about the existence of ruling narratives of the Nazi regime and the war in German public memory and discourse. So, for example, Peter Fritzsche stresses the sentimental nature of the popular view of the past in Germany, where the Germans appear as victims and their history is presented as a tragedy.[11] The nation's official shapers and agents of memory, among them politicians, historians, artists, and writers, as well as social institutions, choose, consciously or not, to emphasize certain aspects and play down, or even dispense with, other parts of the past. They do so on the basis of the psychological, social, and political needs that motivate them to interpret the past in the specific way they have chosen. These memories are formulated as a narrative (in German, an *Erzälung*). The narrative weaves the details and facts of historical events into a story that grants them meaning. Members of the ruling elite are usually the shapers of the representations of historical events from the nation's recent past into the nation-state's official memory. The nature and contents of the memory are, of course, shaped to fit their interests, and what they see as the national interest. Yet many citizens have their own memories of this time, which the elites cannot ignore. If the elites' "constructed memory" of the recent past entirely contradicts the personal and collective memories of most of the country's citizens, or their psychological and social needs, the citizens will see the official memory as false. The official memory must therefore contain certain elements of individual and group memories of Nazism and the war.

The remembrance of the national past is a social construction, which the memories of large numbers of individuals play a part in creating. As such, it is not just a tool that serves the ruling elite of the nation-state, nor is it an autonomous and isolated creation of an individual.

These narratives of the past appear in a wide range of forms, in journalistic, historical, literary, or cinematic formulations, in analytical, didactic, homiletic, or artistic styles. They are also conveyed by nonverbal symbols, familiar to the society they serve—memorials, posters, and works of art. Understanding these forms of artistic expression requires iconographic and typological analysis. This work also uses the findings of public opinion polls. All these sources reveal how German society and its elites have preferred to see and depict "the victims of the war and the dictatorship."

Obviously, these representations are not a blueprint of the past as it was. It contains the interpretation of that past by the shapers of the national memory.

The writing of contemporary history is an important field that contributes to shaping memory, but at the same time it is also influenced by memory. Under the influence of the study of literature, the dominant national narratives that aspire to offer an exclusive and comprehensive (and in fact an ideological) interpretation of the past are called "master narratives." These have been sharply criticized because of their "imperial" pretension to present the events of the past as they allegedly were. In response, there have been calls to liberate the national past from the yoke of these official interpretations of the nation's past.[12] And indeed, in comparison with the way the Nazi past was addressed in the 1950s, recent decades have seen German historians break free of the national master narrative; a variety of other narratives have replaced it.[13]

Nevertheless, some German historical narratives regarding the Nazis and the war tend to share attitudes that distinguish them from non-German narratives of the same events.[14] This is not surprising, given that memory and historiography are not dichotomous categories. Indeed, especially during the Federal Republic's first decade, the great majority of German historians viewed themselves as servants of the people and felt obligated to foster their nation's rehabilitation following its defeat.[15] This phenomenon was apparent in East Germany as well, although with different emphases, and because of the totalitarian nature of that state it continued until the fall of the Communist regime. The common wisdom in Germany and the world today regarding the role of the historian is entirely different, however. This view proclaims that the historian should strive to be independent of the national collective and master narratives, and that his duty is to the truth and nothing else (excepting historians who accept postmodern premises). It has also been the approach of historians since ancient times.

Even the second generation of German historians who engaged in empirical research on the Nazis and the war since the early 1950s and 1960s came from what has been called the Hitler youth generation, or the *Flakhelfergeneration*—the generation of teenagers who helped anti-aircraft batteries in the cities.[16] In other words, they were born at the end of the 1920s and the beginning of the 1930s, and were too young to have been drafted into the army before the Third Reich's defeat. These historians tended to differentiate between memory and history. They believed they possessed sensible and sober methods that were the only means for determining historical truth. These methods were, they claimed, superior to memory, especially the memories of Jewish victims, which were perceived as biased and as depicting the Nazi past in a mythical light, and according to moralistic judgment.[17] Today in Germany there is more awareness of the difficulties and limitations that face a historian who chooses to study events in the recent past of his own nation. Things are not entirely different in the Jewish world, as Jewish history is so tragically interwoven in modern German history.

This work does not focus only on manifestly historiographic issues. It also discusses the political culture's public use of the Nazi and war past, by various means and for a variety of purposes. I therefore apply a general term to this broad area of interest, one accepted in the German discourse of remembrance and memorialization: the culture of memory, that is, the entire range of social preoccupation with the past.[18]

Acknowledgments

This book is based on research conducted in Germany from 2001 through 2003, with the aid of a generous grant from the Alexander von Humboldt Foundation, and in the summer of 2004, with the assistance of a grant from the Friedrich Ebert Foundation. I thank these foundations for their assistance.

I am grateful also to the Volksbund organization and its representative, especially Thomas Gliem of the organization's Kassel Center, for the considerable assistance he extended me, and for allowing me to use the organization's archives. I wish to thank the head of the organization's Hamburg chapter, Mr. Rüdiger Tittel, who acquainted me with the "war graves" in Ohlsdorf Cemetery in his city. I also owe a great deal to the Hamburger Institut für Sozialforschung (the Hamburg Institute for Social Research) and its staff, and especially to my friends Dr. Ulrich Bielefeld and Professor Michael Wildt for the assistance they provided when I was in the Hanseatic city; as well as to Dr. Katherin Hoffmann-Curtius and Dr. Arie Hartog, the curator of the Gerhard Marcks house in the city of Bremen; to Dr. Christian Groh and Mrs. Hede Mettler of Pfortzheim for their help; to Mrs. Barbara Boock of the German folksong archive in Freiburg; to Mrs. Elisabeth Fendl and Dr. Felicitas Drobek of the Johannes Künzig Institute for the study of East German folklore in Freiburg; and to Mr. Klaus Mohr and Mrs. Emily Wiebe of the German Sudeten archive in Munich. I am also grateful to Mr. Joachim Edelblut and Mr. Bernhard Klein of the archive of the *Frankfurter Rundschau* newspaper in Frankfurt. Special thanks go to my friend Professor Robert G. Moeller of the University of California, Irvine. Our virtual conversations accompanied important stages of writing this book and fertilized my ideas, even if we disagreed about various issues. Later, he read the English manuscript and his wise and intriguing comments contributed immensely to the book. I also wish to thank the Bahat Prize committee at the University of Haifa for granting me its prize, and to the University of Haifa's publishing house for issuing the Hebrew version of this book. Finally, I wish to express my heartfelt thanks to Haim Watzman, who has translated the book into English, and who invested a great deal of thought and labor in my manuscript.

GILAD MARGALIT
BERLIN, SEPTEMBER 2008

1

Coping with Guilt: The Germans and the Nazi Past

That a nation must accept collective responsibility for the actions of its members, in particular for crimes committed at the order of the country's leaders, was not at all a foreign concept for many Germans. Acceptance of such national responsibility has roots in Christian theology, according to which God may punish an entire nation for the sins of individuals. Despite the secularizing processes that large portions of German society had undergone, Christian perceptions and ethics still ran deep in German consciousness during and after World War II.

A few weeks after the war's end, at the end of May 1945, a Dr. Kottman, of the local Catholic church in Rotenburg, wrote to his priests: "As Christians, we know that the entire nation shares guilt and bears sin, even with regard to crimes of which we did not know, not to speak of the fact that we did not want them and did not commit them."[1]

The bishop of Münster, Cardinal Clemens August von Galen, decreed in several of his sermons that the horrible war was a divine punishment for the peoples of Europe who had abandoned God and prostrated themselves before technology and man.[2] According to this view, God punished all Europe's inhabitants collectively for sins committed since the beginning of the enlightenment and secularization, visiting his wrath even on those who had remained faithful to him.

This religious view of the Christian community's collective responsibility for its members persisted into the secular national period. The view characteristic of modern nationalism, that the members of the nation have a duty of solidarity, bound them also into mutual responsibility for their nation's actions and misdeeds, and certainly for crimes committed in the name of the nation and on the orders of its leaders.

At the end of World War I, the victorious Allies maintained that Germany bore sole responsibility for the outbreak of the war. Many Germans were insulted by this accusation, seeing it as a stain on the nation as a whole. Then as well, most Germans did not feel guilty of starting the war. Rather, they viewed themselves as victims of global circumstances. The political right and extreme right largely blamed their political rivals, especially the left and the Jews, for "stabbing the nation in the back" in 1918. (In this view, Germany's vast army was not defeated at the front. The enemy within—that is, the left and the Jews—fomented antigovernment mutinies by soldiers and rebellions by citizens, and these made Germany lose the war.) The accusers, of course, did not see any problem in blaming all Jews for bringing on defeat. That the entire Jewish people stood convicted of crucifying the Messiah was a fundamental tenet of European Christian culture. By the 1840s, this concept had been secularized into antisemitic claims made throughout Europe, on the right and the left, accusing the Jews of responsibility for the ills of modernization and what was called "Manchesterism." The slogan "The Jew is guilty" (*Der Jud' ist schuld*) was used by the Nazis even before they came to power, and they did not abandon it after their defeat in 1945.

Guilt feelings regarding specific groups persecuted by the regime—the Jews first and foremost—began to spread through German society while the war was still in progress, in the wake of rumors and information on atrocities committed by German forces at the orders of the national leadership. These human feelings increased after the war, when the dimensions of the crimes were made public. A free public discourse on German society's responsibility and guilt for Nazi atrocities now began. This discourse became a prominent element of German political culture in the early years after the defeat of the Nazi regime. Even when it faded, when the political climate changed under the force of the Cold War at the end of the 1940s, its impact was still evident, especially in West German political culture. The feelings of guilt that many Germans felt for Nazi crimes did not grow out of a policy of "reeducation" and the de-Nazification pursued by the Allies who defeated Germany in 1945, as was argued by Barbro Eberan,[3] and were not a fabrication by the German press that was established under Allied license (*Lizenzpresse*), as extreme right-wing groups in German claimed then and claim today.

The Crystallization of Germany's Consciousness of Guilt

What did the German public know about the crimes being committed by German soldiers and security personnel in the territories the Wehrmacht occupied during the war? Since late summer 1941, rumors and information about mass executions of defenseless women, children, and elderly people reached world Jewish organizations and Allied governments that were fighting Germany.[4] From the time of the Allies' declaration of December 17, 1942, about the systematic extermination of the Jews in the areas of German occupation in Eastern Europe, this information was reported on German-language radio, in broadcasts aimed at and received by the German populace.[5]

However, the German public also had its own sources of information. Wehrmacht troops and the members of other forces on the eastern front were forbidden to speak about the atrocities being committed in the occupied areas. But soldiers nevertheless passed on rumors and up-to-date information to their families and friends at home. They reported a wide range of horrors, including the mass slaughter of Jews, in letters they sent home shortly after being involved in or witnessing such crimes.[6] In a number of cases, they photographed the atrocities.[7] A significant number of Germans thus knew in real time that their country's armed forces were killing innocent civilians at the bidding and with the blessing of the German state.[8]

In a public opinion poll conducted in 1961 by the Allensbach Institute, 32 percent of those thirty years old and up said that they had heard of the extermination of the Jews before the war's end.[9] Given that this was an incendiary question, it is reasonable to assume that some interviewees who claimed they had not heard did not answer honestly. In other words, considerably more than a third of Germany's populace probably knew about these crimes while the war was still in progress. Further evidence comes from reports written by Nazi Party and state authorities about the German public's mood and views regarding the murder of the Jews. These reports, collected by Otto Dov Kulka and Eberhard Jäckel in a monumental project, demonstrate that there was considerable public knowledge about the fate of the Jews. This contradicts the picture presented in the past by prominent German public figures and historians.[10]

Even though the crimes committed by German armed forces, particularly the systematic destruction of European Jewry, were a state secret, prior to the war Hitler himself spoke publicly about the fate awaiting the Jews. On January 30, 1939, during a speech in the Reichstag, he prophesized: "If international money Jewry succeeds in and outside Europe in plunging the nations into a world war, the result will not be the Bolshevization of the world and the victory of the Jews, but the destruction of the Jewish race in Europe."

During the war, the Nazi dictator repeated this threat publicly on a number of occasions, at a time when the extermination of European Jewry was already a routine operation in Eastern Europe.[11] Other Nazi leaders also addressed the murder of the Jews during the war. In an article in his newspaper *Das Reich* on November 16, 1941, headlined "The Jews are Guilty" (*Die Juden sind schuld*), the Nazi propaganda minister, Joseph Goebbels, wrote that "Hitler's prophecy of January 30, 1939, is being put into practice," and that the Jews "will be destroyed in a gradual process." Goebbels again took up the subject in 1943.[12]

Hans Mommsen has argued that these pronouncements of Hitler were simply threats made to the Allies and did not really indicate an intention to eliminate the Jews. But even if we accept his claim, there is no doubt that by the end of the war many Germans who heard these speeches viewed them in retrospect to have been explicit statements of intent to murder the Jews, not empty threats.[13] This impression amplified the sense of shared guilt.

The rumors and information about the crimes being committed by German forces at the front led some Germans to fear revenge. Many documents from 1943 from all parts of the Reich, collected in Kulka and Jäckel's book, show that such fears were common in the German public after the defeat at Stalingrad and the declining likelihood of a German victory.[14] For example, the SD (the SS's security service) office in Schwabach, south of Nuremberg, reported on December 23, 1942:

> One of the major factors in the current unrest among people connected to the Church and among the villagers, is based on reports from Russia on the execution and extermination of Jews. These reports often cause fear and anxiety in this sector. Many villagers are doubtful of our victory. In their opinion, if the Jews return to Germany, they will wreak a horrible revenge on us.[15]

Alongside those, like the citizens of Schwabach, who criticized German policy for practical reasons, there were religious figures and groups who condemned Hitler's policies on theological-ethical grounds. Culpability for the atrocities, they charged, lay not just with their perpetrators and the Nazi regime, but with all Germans. They would be punished by heaven for the crimes their countrymen committed at the bidding of the regime.

The statements made during the Third Reich by German church leaders, both Catholic and Protestant, about the crimes their countrymen committed are very similar to the concept of divine accusation and retribution found in a letter sent in August 1943 to Cardinal Adolph Bertram by an anonymous Polish Jew. Bertram was the Catholic archbishop of Breslau and the chairman of the conference of Catholic bishops in Fulda. The desperate Jew wrote to him:

> I wish to cry out before you that in the General government [the part of Nazi-occupied Poland that was not annexed to the German Reich] four million Jews have been murdered so far, is that known to you? Every German, yourself including, bears guilt [*haben schuld*] for this mass crime. The almighty God will not exempt this nation from punishment. The German people who produced Satan will disappear with him.[16]

On August 3, 1941, in his famous sermon in a Münster church on the euthanasia program (the murder of disabled Germans) and the expulsion of church officials by the Nazis, Bishop von Galen made a similar point, although he did not refer to the Jews. He compared Nazi Germany to biblical Jerusalem, the city whose people transgressed all God's commands and who refused to follow Jesus, who had warned them and called on them in vain to repent. Therefore Christ grieved for the city, knowing that God's judgment would be the total destruction of Jerusalem. Von Galen warned the Reich authorities and the Germans: "God must and will inflict just punishment upon all those who, like the thankless Jerusalem, oppose their wishes to those of God."[17]

The Protestant bishop of Wurttemberg, Theophil Wurm, used similar language in his secret appeals to Reich authorities. In a letter he sent in December 1941 to the department of church affairs, he protested the murder of the mentally ill in the framework of the euthanasia program, as well as the mass murders in the eastern territories:

> This gross violation [the murder of the mentally ill] of the principle of the sanctity of life, which has been recognized in penal law up until now, alongside the rumors of mass murder in the east, have made God-fearing people fear that there will be a day when God will take retribution against Germany.

This position was not restricted to these two bishops.[18] The Nazi Party bureau documented similar warnings from clergymen in northern Germany: "If these acts of murder do not bring bitter retribution upon us then there is no longer any divine justice! The German nation has taken upon itself such a blood guilt that it should not expect mercy and absolution."[19]

When the war's tide turned, some German priests and ministers told their flocks that the defeat at Stalingrad in early 1943 was divine punishment imposed on the Germans because of their treatment of the Russians, Jews, and Poles.[20] Other Germans offered similar explanations of the destruction and injury caused by the heavy British and American bombings of German cities.[21] For example, the damage caused to the Cologne Cathedral by Allied bombers in the summer of 1943 or to the city of Schweinfurt was seen as divine punishment for the synagogues burned on Kristallnacht in 1938.[22]

Guilt was not felt only in religious circles. It could be found in a wide variety of social strata. Helmuth James Graf von Moltke, an opponent of the Nazi regime and a co-conspirator against Hitler in the plot of July 20, 1944, wrote to his wife at the end of August 1941: "The blood guilt [*Blutschuld*] will not be atoned during our lives and will never be forgotten."[23]

A heavy sense of guilt gradually seeped into the consciousness of influential German groups and public figures. It even penetrated the Nazi party, although we may assume that such opposition was exceptional within the party before Germany's defeat seemed certain. Sarah Gordon cites the case of a party member sentenced to death for having said that no one any longer believed in victory and that "by murdering a million Jews we have taken a heavy burden on our shoulders."[24]

As defeat approached, there was an increasing tendency among the Nazi leadership to speak, in a variety of forums, about the extermination of the Jews—one example being Himmler's speech in Posen in October 1943.[25] The intention was to broaden the circle that was party to both the secret and the guilt, and to give the message to a wide segment of German society that they too, in the eyes of the Allies, were complicit in war crimes. Consequently, they had no choice but to continue to fight loyally for the Nazi regime.[26] This Nazi strategy not only increased anxiety about the future, but also amplified the sense of guilt, and even of remorse, that already pervaded some parts of German society. This feeling can even be found in the letters Wehrmacht soldiers wrote toward the end of the war. For example, H.P. wrote to his family in October 1944: "The treatment of the Jews and the Poles—the former even before the war, and both peoples during it—was not only a critical political error, but also a human injustice that will increasingly weigh on the German people's conscience."[27] Not all the German clergy participated in this guilt narrative, however. There were still many priests who supported the official Nazi line.[28]

In other words, a discourse of guilt had begun to crystallize in Nazi Germany even as the war was in progress, especially when the chances for the notorious "final victory" began to seem less promising. This discourse was very much like that conducted outside Germany, among the Allies and among the Nazis' Jewish victims. This discourse recognized, even if only implicitly, that the moral guilt was not restricted to those who actually committed crimes, but lay also on every German who remained silent in the face of atrocities, who stood aside and did nothing.

With regard to the crimes of the Wehrmacht and SS forces, the Germans were most aware of the Jewish victims. Indeed, the murder of the Jews seems to have occupied a special place in German consciousness during the Nazi years, even though, in their total war against the Soviet Union, the Germans killed more than 16 million Soviet civilians and at least 8 million Red Army soldiers, far greater than the number of Jews slaughtered. Nevertheless, the Soviet deaths did not bear the same significance for Germans.[29] The Nazis presented their persecutions of the Jews from 1933 onward, including the massacres of Jews during the war, as acts of self-defense in the face of Jewish plots to destroy the Germans. But this attempt to legitimize the offenses was not completely successful in penetrating German consciousness.

The special significance of the crimes against the Jews in the consciousness of many Germans undoubtedly derived from the exceptional position the Jews and Judaism had in Christianity, and from the centrality of the Jewish issue in Nazi propaganda. These feelings were amplified among that broad swath of the German public that, though they partly accepted the Nazi theory about an international Jewish conspiracy against

Figure 1. "They are beating him . . . ," charcoal drawing from the series *The Passion*, by Otto Pankok. (Otto Pankok Museum, Haus Esselt, Hünxe-Drevenack)

the Germans, had reservations about the Nazis' program of mass murder. At the time, after all, there was no Jewish state at war with Germany. Unlike Soviet civilians, the Jews looked like innocent victims of deplorable racist persecution, not belligerents in an armed conflict.[30] Crimes committed by German forces against the Soviet population were, in fact, a posteriori, presented and justified as measures of defense vis-à-vis a ruthless Soviet partisans' campaign. Only ardent Nazis could accept such apologetics regarding the atrocities against the Jews. It is highly doubtful that it could have convinced non-Nazis.

In Christian culture, the iconic symbol of the innocent victim is the crucified Jesus. The German artist Otto Pankok was the first to choose this iconography, in his series *The Passion* of 1933–34, to protest the persecution of the Jews. Pankok deliberately drew Jesus with stereotypical Jewish features and his persecutors as Aryans.

From this point onward the motif became a common one in prewar and postwar antifascist art in Germany and the entire West.[31] It portrayed the persecution of the Jews as the passion of Christ, and later labeled the archetypical place of their murder, Auschwitz, as Golgotha.[32] In 1937, in response to Nazi antisemitic acts, figures of crucified Jews first appeared in the work of Marc Chagall. In 1943, he painted his famous *White Crucifixion*, depicting a Jewish figure, wrapped in a prayer shawl, crucified on the background of a village in which a pogrom rages.[33]

Martin Niemöller, one of the leaders of the Confessing Church (*Bekennende Kirche*) during the Third Reich period, gave clear expression to this concept of guilt as it appeared in the Protestant Church in a series of speeches throughout Germany in 1946. He called on his audiences to acknowledge that they had sinned. In one speech he referred to Jews who had been incarcerated in concentration camps in 1938, after Kristallnacht, as images of the tormented Christ:

> And when I was returned to Oranienburg, [and I saw] the endless march of thousands of Jews on foot, I was shocked. But I did not see then, and perhaps I did not want to see, that this was my Lord and Redeemer (*Mein Herr und Heiland*) trudging there along the Way of the Cross, a thousand and ten thousand times—to suffering and death.[34]

One could assume that many German Protestants did not remain untouched by such preaching.

Public Discussion of the "Guilt Question" in Postwar West Germany

On December 17, 1942, the British government promulgated the official Allied declaration about the Nazis' extermination of Jews.[35] From that point onward, public opinion in the free world—often in opposition to their governments, and like the Jewish community—viewed the German people as a whole, not just the Nazis, as responsible for the crimes.[36]

For the Nazi leadership, the mass murder of the Jews was an integral part of the war and its goals. Hitler and his tyrannical regime were popular in Germany. It is hardly surprising, then, that public opinion in the West and various elements among the Allies assumed that the German people as a whole unreservedly supported the policies of the Nazi regime, and that the German nation and Hitler's regime were one and the same.[37] This presumption in fact accepted, without qualification, Nazi propaganda's claim of German popular support for the regime,[38] and thus the Allies were able to present the strategic bombing of German civilian targets not only as an important component in the war to crush Nazi aggression and as a means of fomenting rebellion against Hitler, but also as retribution for the way Hitler's popular regime conducted the war. The German novelist Thomas Mann, living in exile in California, voiced this view in a speech in April 1942 that was beamed to Germany by the BBC. Mann, referring to the bombing of his home city of Lübbeck on March 29, 1942, accused the German people as a whole, not just the Nazis:

> In the recent British attack on Hitlerland, Lübbeck's Old City was hit. It touches me. It is the city of my father. The raid hit the port of Travemünde, the war industries there, but fire also broke out in the city. The thought that the Church of Mary, the wonderful Renaissance-style city hall, or the shipping company's hall were damaged is not at all nice for me. But think of Coventry [a British city the Germans bombed in 1940–41], and I have no opposition to the lesson that [Nazi Germany] pay for its deeds.[39]

It was not just intellectuals like Mann who spoke this way. In a memorandum sent to British Prime Minister Winston Churchill in June 1942, General Władislaw Sikorski, the prime minister of the Polish government in exile in London, demanded bombing on a large scale of non-military targets in Germany in reprisal against the cruelty of the Germans against Poles and Jews. The Czechoslovakian foreign minister in exile also demanded the bombing of German villages as a revenge for the massacre in the village Lidice in June 1942. Although Churchill was inclined to agree and proposed that when Berlin was bombed, pamphlets be disseminated stating that the attack was in retribution for the persecution of Poles and Jews, all these proposals were rejected for diplomatic and practical reasons.[40]

The representatives of the governments in exile and Churchill were seeking to grant public and official force to the position Mann had earlier expressed—that the bombing of Germany's cities was in fact collective punishment imposed on the German people for the crimes committed by its armed forces, on the orders of a leadership that had been chosen by a majority of Germans.

Under the influence of this way of thinking, the Allied military administrations instituted a de-Nazification and reeducation program for the German population in their zones of occupation. As part of it, they disseminated among the Germans information about the extent of the Nazi regime's crimes against the Jews and others, and accused all Germans of bearing collective responsibility for the atrocities. In the summer of 1945, the U.S. and British military administrations in Germany circulated posters headlined, "These Appalling Acts: Your Fault!" (*Diese Schandetaten: Eure Schuld!*). Alongside photographs of piles of bodies and of emaciated survivors of concentration camps, the following text appeared:

> For twelve years the Nazi criminals tortured, robbed, and murdered millions of Europeans; hangmen under Hitler's thumb incited against men, women, and children and tortured them to death, just because they were Jews, Czechs, Russians, Poles, or Frenchmen. You watched and you remained silent. Even the Allies' toughest soldiers could not hide their revulsion and shock at the site of the gassed, incinerated, and wasted bodies of the victims of the concentration camps.
>
> According to German reports, at Buchenwald 50,000 human beings were burned, shot, and hanged. At Belsen, British forces found torture chambers, crematoria, gallows, and whipping posts. Thirty thousand people were murdered there. Uncounted political detainees and prisoners, in numbers unprecedented in all of human history, were the victims at Gardlegen, Nordhausen, Ohrdruf, Erla, Mauthausen, and Vaihingen. You watched and did not lift a finger. Why did you not awaken German conscience by protesting or crying out? That is your great guilt. You share responsibility for these brutal crimes!

The Allies thus charged the German people with not taking action against the slaughter, rather than with direct involvement—the same accusation that no small number of Germans voiced. The Allies made a clear distinction between those who were criminally liable and those who bore moral responsibility for the Nazis' rise to power, not protesting the regime's crimes.[41] Immediately subsequent to Germany's defeat in 1945, the Allies addressed Nazi atrocities as crimes against humanity, not explicitly identifying Jews but victims of all nations. This approach was also promulgated by the Association of Victims of Nazi Persecution (known by its German acronym, VVN) and in East Germany generally following its founding in 1949: the generic image of the "victim of fascism" was a universal one that emphasized the antifascist fighters incarcerated in the concentration camps, and also included the Jews as victims of Nazism among many others. But as the Cold War began and the VVN metamorphosed into a Communist organization, this same image fell from grace in West Germany. In particular, from the late 1950s onward, the Jews became the archetypal victims of the Nazis in the Federal Republic.

The military administrations also conveyed this message to the German population through the cinema. They screened documentary films on Nazi atrocities, one example being the film *Death Mills* (*Todesmühlen*). But the Allies reached the conclusion that didactic films were not an effective instrument, and by spring 1946 they abandoned this approach.[42]

After the war, as the German public received information about the atrocities committed by Germans from all walks of society, feelings of guilt, shame, and shock spread. These emotions were expressed in a swelling public discourse at the beginning of the summer of 1945. Saul Padover, a Jewish officer in the U.S. Army stationed in Aachen in 1944–45, testified to the pervasiveness of this sense of guilt among Germans at the time:

> There seems to prevail a strange sense of guilt about the Jews, an uneasy feeling and frequently an open admission, that a great wrong has been committed. There is also a fear of revenge and a dread of hearing the worst about the horrors that have been inflicted on the Jews in Poland. The Germans simply dare not face the awful truth.[43]

At the instigation of the Allies and of a minority in the German public, the guilt discourse turned into a vibrant public debate immediately after Germany's surrender in 1945. The Communist Party (KPD) was the only party in occupied Germany that accepted the concept of collective guilt. In a public statement its Central Committee issued in June 1945, the issues of guilt and responsibility predominated. It assigned primary guilt to the Nazis, the generals, and "their imperialist employers, the master of the large banks and industrial concerns, Krupp, Röchling, Poensgen, and Siemens." Nevertheless, it did not ignore the guilt of larger strata of

German society: "Not only Hitler is guilty of crimes committed against humanity. Some of the guilt is borne also by the ten million Germans who in 1932 voted for Hitler in free elections, even though we, the Communists, warned: 'Whoever votes Hitler votes war!'"

Later, the Communist statement also assigned guilt to those Germans who supported the Nazi ideology, as well as to men and women who did nothing when the Nazis destroyed democracy and crushed the labor unions, and who did not resist when the regime arrested, persecuted, and murdered Germany's best young people.[44]

The same position was taken by the Socialist Unity Party (SED), established under Soviet compulsion in 1946 by the unification of the Social Democratic Party (SPD) and the much smaller Communist Party, in the Soviet occupation zone. In some areas of East German policy regarding the Nazi past, this position continued to find expression until the beginning of the 1950s. Only then, under the influence of the growing Cold War, did the concept of collective guilt make way for the concept that Germany's capitalists and warmongers in the West were alone guilty for the rise of the Nazis and their crimes, while the German people as a whole were innocent.[45]

The Guilt Debate in the Christian Churches

The German Protestant Church (EKD), in contrast with the German Catholic Church,[46] also contributed much to the postwar guilt discourse. Bishop Theophil Wurm of Wurttemberg, who would later head the EKD, spoke in the Stuttgart Theater on May 10, 1945, two days after the defeat of the Nazis. In his remarks, he expressed the common view in the Church, as well as in German society as a whole, regarding responsibility for the Nazi takeover of Germany and the subsequent war and destruction. Like the Catholic Cardinal Clemens August von Galen of Münster[47] and members of other churches, Wurm viewed Nazism as a product of the process of secularization, of man's growing distance from God, beginning in the Enlightenment. This process was augmented, in his view, by the economic crisis of the 1920s and especially 1929.

> Sadly, many who were fearful of economic crises and unemployment allowed themselves to be influenced by the new arrogant idolatry, and were seduced into denying the Christ and his church. . . . In the wake of this

> internal decline, whose roots lie in worldviews and heretical concepts of life from hundreds of years ago, which now reached its acme, an external destruction should have to come as well. . . . The needs of the time are not to complain and accuse, but to forgive and to help . . . to minister as much as possible to the wounds caused by the war.[48]

The implication is that Wurm did not think that a defeated Germany had to embark on a public and forthright discussion of responsibility and guilt for Nazism. In a letter he wrote to the world's Christians at the end of 1945, Wurm clearly seeks to minimize Nazism's uniqueness. He depicts the German nation as a passive victim of circumstances that were beyond its control. Wurm also stressed the suffering endured by the Germans during the war. According to Wurm, the Nazis rose to power because of the Versailles Treaty and the economic crisis:

> We seek to remind you that our nation also suffered through the terrifying years of merciless aerial bombardments, which caused huge losses. . . . Each nation has its own Jacobins,[49] who under certain conditions manage to come to power. These conditions were created in Germany because of the burden of war reparations and the associated mass unemployment, after World War I. . . . The belief in violence must be condemned not only among German politicians, but also among the Americans, the English, the French, and the Russians, and the demand for freedom of speech and thought, for freedom of religion and conscience, and for protection of the tranquil citizen's right to personal security, must include all countries now under the rule of the Allies. . . . We must not grumble before the Creator about why He allowed such a horrible thing to happen, but rather it is our desire to see in our abandonment of Him and the way of life [that He commanded] the profound reason for our suffering. Our slogan must therefore be: "Return to Christ, return to your brothers."[50]

This was the common wisdom in Germany at the time. As early as 1946, Moses Moskowitz, a Polish-born Jewish American army office, reported:

> Perhaps the most common mechanism by which the German masses avoid a sense of guilt for the fate of the first and most tragic victims of Nazism, the six million Jewish dead, is to convince themselves that they, too, have been victims of Nazism, and possibly in greater measure than any other people.[51]

Most of the German public was not interested in confronting the issues of responsibility and guilt for the Nazis' rise to power and the atrocities committed by Germans under the regime. Important Protestant clergymen spoke in opposition to this pervasive attitude. They called on their countrymen to grapple with various levels and aspects of guilt. There were not many such church figures, but the German media reported their positions extensively. The most prominent clergyman in the Protestant Church at the time who took a position opposing that of Wurm was Martin Niemöller, who had just been liberated from a concentration camp. A decorated German submarine commander during World War I, Niemöller was a nationalist who originally voted for the Nazi Party. But when Hitler sought to subordinate the Protestant Church to the state, Niemöller advocated the church's independence. He and Dietrich Bonhoeffer established a dissident body of ministers that eventually became the Confessing Church (*Die Bekennende Kirche*).[52] Because of his views and activities, Niemöller was put on trial, and in 1938 he was sent to a concentration camp. American forces liberated him from Dachau at the end of the war. Prior to the convention at which the German Protestant Church reconstituted itself after the war, held in Treysa in August 1945, Niemöller demanded that Wurm[53] and the church leadership express contrition:

> We stand on the brink of total chaos, and perhaps within it. We must ask how we got here. Our plight does not derive from our having been beaten in the war; who of us would have wished for our victory? Had we won the war, where would we be now? . . . Neither does our present situation [derive], first and foremost, from our nation's and the Nazis' guilt; how they could have walked a path that was unknown to them; they simply believed that they were on the right path! No, the real guilt lies on the church! Because only it knew that the chosen road would lead to devastation. And it did not warn our nation. It did not reveal the injustice taking place, or did this for the first time after all was over. Thus the Confessing Church bears an especially large portion of the guilt. Because it saw with the height of clarity what was going to happen and develop. It even spoke of this, but it tired and feared man more than the living God. That is how catastrophe came upon all of us and swept us into the heart of the storm. But we, the church, must beat our chests and confess, we are guilty, we are guilty, we are most guilty! This is what we must say today to our people and to Christianity, that we did not stand before them as pious and righteous people.[54]

Niemöller's uncompromising demand that the Germans acknowledge their sins attributed the greatest guilt to the opponents of Nazism in the

Confessing Church, one of whose leaders he was. Their culpability was that they, who discerned the evil and criminal nature of the Nazi regime, did not do what their Christian faith required them to do: to act as martyrs, in emulation of Jesus Christ, to sacrifice their lives on the altar of faith, justice, and truth.

> I again ask myself, what would have happened if, in 1933, or in 1934—and it was not impossible—14,000 Protestant ministers and all the Protestant communities then in Germany had defended the truth unto death? . . . I can surmise that 30,000–40,000 Protestant Christians might have given up their lives. But I can also surmise that we would have saved the lives of 30 or 40 million human beings, the price that we have paid today.[55]

Niemöller saw in the failure of most clergymen to act this way a denial of the Lord and Redeemer.

In addition to the demands of Niemöller and his colleagues in the Confessing Church, the occupation authorities and the World Council of Protestant Churches expected and pressured the recently reorganized German Protestant Church to issue an official declaration on the issue of guilt. This led to such a declaration in October 1945. After considerable misgivings and debates in which substantial opposition was expressed, the country's Protestant leaders issued an official statement, which became publicly known as the Confession of Guilt (*Die Schuld Bekenntnis*). Its wording was a compromise between the positions of different factions in the Protestant Church's leadership. Yet even those who feared that such an admission of guilt would legitimize punishment of and retribution against the German people under the occupation regime recognized that such a statement was necessary:

> We know we share with our people: not only a large community of suffering, but also in solidarity of guilt. In great pain we say: infinite suffering was brought through us on many lands and peoples.[56] We hereby declare, in the name of the entire Church, words that we have spoken frequently before our congregations: for long years we struggled in the name of Jesus Christ against the spirit that found its horrible expression in the tyrannical National Socialist regime. However, we accuse ourselves of not having displayed greater courage, we did not pray with greater devotion, we did not believe with greater joy, we did not love with greater passion.

This part of the Confession of Guilt, nowhere in which is there any reference to the murder of the Jews, is balanced by the last part of the document, which sharply criticized postwar Allied policy toward Germany, without naming the Allies explicitly:

> We put our trust in God, that through the common rite, the spirit of peace and love will again come to reign and overcome *the spirit of force and vengeance that again seek to become prodigious today* [i.e., after the downfall of the Nazis; emphasis added] throughout the world; in that alone may anguished humanity find succor.[57]

German clergymen, both Protestant and Catholic, and secular German aid organizations viewed the transfer of Germans from Eastern Europe under the terms of the Potsdam agreements as causing "the annihilation of a large part of the German nation." This position is expressed in their letters to officials in the Allied military administrations during the summer and autumn of 1945.[58]

Despite the demands of clergymen like Niemöller and the theologian Karl Barth, the declaration's language regarding German guilt was oblique.[59] It does not take the German people to task. Nevertheless, it produced a controversy among clergymen and their congregations, who were an integral part of the German public.[60] Some bishops who signed it did not support its wording wholeheartedly. Bishop Hanns Lilje, one of the signers, wrote in November 1945 to an anonymous woman (who had apparently expressed her astonishment at his and the church's position) that the document was a clarification of the church's position, not a political document, and that it was not intended for the public.[61]

On top of the expulsion of millions of Germans remaining in former German territories now incorporated into Poland, from Czechoslovakia and Hungary in accordance with the decisions made by the Allies at Potsdam, came a harsh postwar famine, exacerbated by the harsh winter of 1946–47. Both these events produced a change in German thinking about confessing guilt. Many felt a need to state that the crimes committed against the Germans were "equal and even harsher than those committed by the Nazis."[62] Circumstances seemed to confirm the arguments made by the opponents of the church declaration during the discussions that preceded its formulation.[63] Some of the Protestant bishops who signed the Stuttgart declaration had reservations about it during the two years after the war, given the harsh course of events. But this is not evidence that German society's sense of guilt had dissipated. The position taken by these bishops was a practical one—they felt that under the political circumstances of the times, German churches, institutions, and organizations should not acknowledge guilt publicly, because doing so might grant legitimacy to acts that the Germans saw as punishment and revenge against the German people—such as the transfer of Germans from the east and its implications, the de-Nazification program, and the trials of German soldiers and Nazi officials on charges of war crimes and crimes against humanity.[64] For example, the theologian Hans Asmussen, among the leaders of the Protestant Church, wrote in April 1947:

> The Church's confession in Stuttgart was the worst sort of foolishness [*die größte Dumheit*] at this time, since given our guilt it is permissible to commit against us, the Germans, the [deeds] that they despise, criticize, and punish us [for having committed]. . . .
>
> The Stuttgart declaration of contrition was a sincere text. Even today it is still of far-reaching significance to state, in the face of what we have done, that we acknowledge the significance of our crimes.[65]

In a talk he gave in Schwäbische Gemünd in August 1947, Asmussen further fleshed out his position:

> In reference to the whole, we must recognize that we assumed that the Stuttgart declaration [would have a corresponding] response. I do not at all anticipate any further discussion of the Stuttgart declaration, if no change begins on decisive points. That is, so far, it has not brought absolution in its wake. All contrition declared, in its Christian sense, brings atonement. [If] I say to my brother, I have sinned against him, he must tell me if he has forgiven me. If the congregation or its shepherd has declared in its name that it has sinned, that declaration must bring divine absolution, that will comfort those who express contrition.[66]

Asmussen thus criticized the confession of guilt because of what he interpreted as its political implications, and because his hope that it would lead to absolution of the Germans by the world's nations was unfulfilled. His critique does not, then, deny German guilt. Neither does he categorically reject the declaration's moral significance. Yet, despite some reservations, Asmussen does not hesitate to equate, implicitly, the jailing of Nazi criminals by the Allies to the Nazis' treatment of its victims in concentration camps:

> Neither of us is so blind as not to discern the fundamental differences between the Auschwitz concentration camp and the detention camps in

> Ludwigsburg. However, we cannot but see that at present it is not sufficient just to talk about the detention camp at Ludwigsburg, but rather we must speak about many other things, of which our knowledge and insight is greater and deeper than our knowledge of the German concentration camp was in 1934.[67]

Grievances about the treatment of captured German soldiers, comparing Allied POW camps to Nazi concentration camps, were common in Church correspondence with the Allied military administrations.[68]

But even Niemöller, who in his 1946 sermons still told his countrymen to confess their sins and ask, as he did, "Where were you, Minister Martin Niemöller, where were you in 1933 when people were already being burned here [at Dachau]?"[69] Like many others in the Church, he understood guilt to be primarily a theological issue, rather than a political one. The guilt of Germany's Christians was centered, according to Niemöller, on their denial of God and His Messiah. A speech he delivered at Kaiserslautern in April 1946 on the tasks then facing the church reflects his view:

> And the same rule holds for all human suffering I encounter today. There is no distinction between a Jew and a German who has lost a leg, who limps down the street, nothing. Both of them are victims of my denial. My denial of Jesus Christ. And I want to say to him: Dear German brother! Forgive me for my cowardice, for my sacrilege. Forgive me, the confessing minister, for my alienation.
>
> This is how the question of guilt looks from a Christian point of view. This guilt seeks to be public, to be visible, and to bear witness. For we must [receive] not only God's absolution, but also learn once more that we, as human beings, must forgive and find forgiveness for the guilt among us.[70]

For Niemöller, then, contrition is intended first and foremost to lead to divine absolution and reconciliation among human beings and nations.[71] Purgation of guilt does not depend on political actions to right injustice, as was demanded by, for example, the philosopher Karl Jaspers in *The Question of German Guilt,* published in 1946, and which is discussed later in this chapter.[72]

Niemöller's own sermons and actions (in particular his opposition to de-Nazification in his capacity, after 1947, as the president of the German Protestant Church and his advocacy of clemency for Nazi criminals)[73] display tension between the Christian approach to absolution and comfort that Wurm expressed in his speech at the Stuttgart Theater at the end of the war, and the demand for contrition. At Third Advent in the winter of 1945, Niemöller preached in Büdingen on the prophet Isaiah's words "Comfort, comfort my people" (Isaiah 40:1–11), in which the prophet says that Israel has been punished for its sins and will now be forgiven:

> We hear this Sunday the scriptural lesson: "Comfort, comfort my people! It is the voice of your God; speak tenderly to Jerusalem and tell her this, that she has fulfilled her term of bondage, that her penalty is paid; she has received at the Lord's hand double measure for all her sins." This is the great plight of our time, dear congregation, that we have become so homeless. It began during the war that lies behind us.

Niemöller enumerated the details of Germany's agony, so as to portray the destruction of Germany as divine punishment for the country's sins. In other words, he encouraged his flock to believe that Germany had paid a "double measure" for its crimes.[74] This theological stance was consistent with his political position, expressed in an interview he granted to an American army chaplain at the end of the war. Niemöller told his interlocutor that the Allies should not punish the German nation for the war, because "God has already taken his due from it; its young people and old people have died on the front and in the rear. Its cities and villages have been utterly ruined . . . and their hopes and beliefs have been shattered."[75] This sermon of comfort does not stand out as a singular instance. Christian ideas of atonement, forgiveness, and comfort ran through others of his sermons and the sermons of his colleagues in those years.

But even Niemöller's ambiguous position on the issue of guilt was perceived as far-reaching by the German public at the time. His appearances elicited anger and criticism. The public responded to the issue of guilt in a number of ways. Only a tiny minority fully accepted the thesis of collective guilt. The thinking of most Germans in the postwar years ranged from categorical rejection of the demand that they acknowledge their guilt to an attitude that was full of contradictions. This attitude recognized, on the cognitive level, collective German responsibility for Hitler's rise to power, and the accountability of the Germans (as opposed to the Nazi regime) for crimes. But it reflected difficulty in drawing, on the emotional level, the inevitable personal conclusions. Many Germans recognized their own and their nation's political responsibility for the atrocities, but at the same time they viewed themselves, especially on the emotional level, as innocent victims of the Nazi regime, the war, and the occupiers, and they felt that they had been done an injustice.

Karl Jaspers on the Question of Guilt

The Nazi regime stripped the philosopher Karl Jaspers of his professorship at the University of Heidelberg and forbade him to publish articles and books, because his wife was Jewish. Yet Jaspers remained in Germany throughout the war. After the defeat, he devoted a series of lectures at the university during the winter semester of 1945–46 to the issue of guilt. The fact that he addressed the issue at all was exceptional—his colleagues at this and other German universities avoided it.[76] However, his position for all intents and purposes was rather ambivalent regarding the responsibility of the German society, as a collective body, for Nazi crimes.

In his lectures, Jaspers maintained that every German was indubitably guilty in some way.[77] Nevertheless, he denied the fact that large numbers of Germans had been deeply involved in the Nazis' crimes. At the end of October 1945 he responded to a pessimistic article by the anti-Nazi Norwegian author Sigrid Undset, a Nobel laureate in literature, published in the Allied German-language newspaper *Die Neue Zeitung*. Undset wrote that there were two obstacles to the reeducation of the Germans. One was the German conceptual world and the other was the Germans' actions during the war. She addressed the involvement of millions of German fathers in atrocities against civilians in the occupied lands, and the extensive involvement of average Germans in dispossession and plunder in Europe, as well as in the murder of the Jews and the theft of their property. The victimized nations could never forget these deeds, she asserted.[78]

Jaspers responded:

> I am skeptical that there are millions of German children whose fathers participated in acts of cruelty against civilians, women, and children in Russia, Poland, Yugoslavia, Greece, France, and Norway. True, millions bore arms in the army, but the atrocities were committed by a small number of criminals. It is common sense that a decisive majority would not have been capable [of committing such crimes].[79]

Jaspers's skepticism was not based on any empirical data or informed estimate. He stated what he wished to be true. It could not be, he reasoned, that a normal, upstanding person could carry out orders to commit atrocities. Only a small group of criminals were involved. Hitler and his accomplices were a tiny minority of a few tens of thousands of people among millions of Germans.[80]

In his book *The Question of German Guilt,* he distinguished between four types of culpability. Each, he said, had an appropriate forum:

1. Criminal culpability derives from the commission of crimes. The courts are the appropriate forum for investigating this type of guilt, in a legal proceeding, according to the rules of criminal procedure and in keeping with the law.
2. Political guilt is the outcome of the actions of statesmen and the state's elected officials. All citizens of the state share responsibility for the leadership's actions. The appropriate forum for addressing this sort of guilt is the military governments of the victorious powers, guided by political prudence and the accepted norms of natural law and the law of nations.
3. Moral culpability, in Jaspers's view, is a special category covering political and military actions that an individual carries out under orders. Jaspers maintained that even if an order is enforced by blackmail or terror, these are not extenuating circumstances. The individual remains morally responsible for such actions. The forum for determining moral guilt is the human conscience, "and in communication with my friends and intimates who are lovingly concerned about my soul."

   The Nuremberg trials thus created an important precedent. It established that war crimes are not only the responsibility of the state; the individual who commits them is also criminally culpable. But Jaspers, like many others in Germany, sought to remove such violations perpetrated by soldiers and by others not only from the authority of the court but also from the arena of public and political debate. This question was to be left in the hands of the individual, to be worked out on his own. Such an individual accounting might take place, but in practice, in the reality of Germany at that time, it was more likely to be pushed into a corner and never dealt with at all.
4. Metaphysical guilt is a universal category with its source in the brotherhood of all human beings and human solidarity, under which every person is responsible for all acts of injustice in the world, especially for crimes committed in his presence or with his knowledge. If I fail to do whatever I can to prevent them, I too am guilty. If I was present at the murder of others without risking my life to prevent it, I feel guilty in a way not adequately conceivable either legally, politically or morally. Heaven is the forum for clarifying this guilt. It is a forum over which there is no public oversight.

   The discussion is thus diverted from its concrete public and political contexts.[81]

The division of guilt into Jaspers's categories narrows the area of criminality and entirely dissolves the concept of guilt that took form in German society during the war itself, as well as the concept of collective guilt as understood by the Allies. Jaspers goes far beyond understanding extenuating circumstances for the failure of Germans to do anything to halt the crimes, or even protest them. He gives prominence to those Germans who opposed such crimes, but who, in fear of their lives, did not go out into the streets to defend the victims. Incidents "that elicit disgrace and shame," such as Kristallnacht, made them fell helpless. Jaspers implies that Germans did not lift a finger to help the Jews because they feared that they too would be exterminated. But he ignores the enthusiastic support that the Nazis received from a not insignificant portion of the German public. He makes no mention of how some Germans rejoiced in the Jews' misfortune on Kristallnacht, a fact that testifies to unreserved popular support for the regime and its criminal actions by at least part of the population.[82] On the one hand, he grants the concept of guilt for Nazi crimes a universal dimension, which entirely blurs its meaning. By this reasoning, some victims in theory are culpable, since they did not sacrifice their lives to prevent the murder of another person. The different forums for clarifying guilt also undermine the authority to accuse and demand moral and political accountability from German society, from the public sphere. Channeling guilt into "individual conscience," lacking any public and political depth, calls into question whether the issue of guilt will be scrutinized in a true and just way.

Jaspers further states in his book:

> It is nonsensical, too, to lay moral guilt to a people as a whole. There is no such thing as a national character extending to every single member of a nation. . . . Morally one can judge the individual only, never a group. The mentality which considers, characterizes and judges people collectively is very widespread. Such characterizations—as of the Germans, the British—never fit generic conceptions under which the individual human being might be classified, but are type conceptions to which they may more or less correspond. This confusion, of the generic with the typological conception, marks the thinking in collective groups—*the* Germans, *the* British, *the* Norwegians, *the* Jews, and so forth. . . . That something fits in with the typological conception must not mislead us that we have covered every individual through such general characterization. For centuries this mentality has fostered hatred among nations and

> communities. Unfortunately natural to a majority of people, it has been most viciously applied and drilled into the heads with propaganda by the National-Socialists. It was as though there no longer were human beings, just those collective groups.[83]

Jaspers discounted entirely the concrete guilt reflected in the broad German public support for Nazism with its aggressive policies and of the deep involvement of the German society in Nazi crimes. Beyond this, he also distorted the meaning of the concept of collective guilt as used by the Allies in the summer of 1945. This concept, according the Jaspers, consists of no more than a stereotype used against every individual German, holding him accountable for crimes committed by a small number of individuals. Jaspers compares (if only implicitly) this thesis of collective guilt to Nazi antisemitism and racism. Later, Theodor Heuss, the first president of the Federal Republic, would make explicit use of this claim. Analyzing Jaspers's theory of guilt, Peter Reichel determines that Jaspers was "a classic child of his time" (*ein Kind seiner Zeit*) who "prepared for the people of his country an additional list of absolving claims."[84]

The Germans Cope with Guilt

Within a short time after the war, German leaders and ordinary citizens from all over the political spectrum, perhaps unable to acknowledge their accountability, let alone guilt, seemed to shift responsibility for the actions of the Nazi regime. Rather than perceive Nazi atrocities as unique crimes committed by representatives of Germany against Jews and others, especially Soviet citizens, Poles, and Gypsies, the crimes were viewed as having been perpetrated by a tyrannical regime against some of its own citizens and those of other countries. Or, alternately, they were simply one component of a brutal war in which the distinctions between front and rear, persecutor and persecuted, were entirely obscured.[85] This tendency to shift guilt was common in Germany after the defeat. Niemöller himself referred to it in several lectures and sermons he gave at the beginning of 1946:

> No one in our German nature wants to take on guilt. Everyone shunts it off to someone else. A member of the [Nazi] Party says: I was just a small cog, Mr. Ortsgruppenleiter [a local, low-ranking Nazi official], you bear the guilt. And he repeats [his underling's excuse] and says: I didn't inflict any suffering on anyone, I only obeyed orders. You from the Gestapo. You

> should take the guilt upon yourselves. But they don't want it either, and in the end the guilt lands on Himmler and Hitler. They are the principal sinners. They can't pass the guilt on, even though they tried to do so before their deaths.[86]

The notion that the Nazi leadership and SS bore sole responsibility for all atrocities, while Germany's elites were innocent, was adopted as the founding myth of the Federal Republic. It finds expression in early German historiography as well.[87] It was adopted by Germans in the face of the lacuna between their cognitive and emotional attitudes to the issue of complicity. After the war, German society had a difficult time acknowledging that war crimes were committed not only by SS men but also by large numbers of Wehrmacht soldiers. The Wehrmacht, after all, was the largest German public organization during the war, in which some 19 million Germans of all walks of life served, including doctors, scientists, and intellectuals.

Moses Moskowitz, the American intelligence officer who spoke with Germans during the initial months after the war, received the impression that there was no sense that the defeated country's citizenry felt guilt or remorse, nor was there a spirit of penitence. To explain this, he suggested comparing this prevailing mood to the position of "a parent sheltering a wayward son who has terrorized his neighbors, and this parent has accepted the proceeds of his son's crimes." Moskowitz seems to have seen this reaction as a defensive strategy of rejection, concealing up a profound sense of guilt.[88] In the articles written in 1946, both Moskowitz and his fellow officer in the American military administration, Morris Janowitz, cite the lack of a sense of guilt among the German public. Individuals either tried to minimize their guilt or explicitly deny any guilt at all, they wrote. But their descriptions imply, in fact, that they refer only to the answers of their interviewees and not to their feelings. I tend to interpret these answers and that position as a strategy of rejecting guilt, which actually testifies to the existence of guilt feelings among the interview subjects.[89] Indeed, a different picture arises from what Germans were writing at the time, and from other empirical evidence.

Years after the war's end, many Germans continued to deny that their soldiers committed crimes during the war. A public opinion poll conducted by the Allensbach Institute in August 1953 asked subjects: "Do you think that there is cause to attribute to German soldiers in World

Do you think that there is cause to attribute to German soldiers in World War II any guilt regarding their behavior in the occupied territories?

	% men	% women	% total
No	60	51	55
Partially	24	18	21
Yes	7	5	6
Don't know	9	26	18

War II any guilt regarding their behavior in the occupied territories?" The responses are shown in the table. Helmut Dubiel maintains that Germans' obsessive denial of collective guilt after 1945—an accusation that he claims the Allies never made, or more precisely made for only a short time in 1945—actually testifies to the existence of a profound sense of guilt for crimes committed during the war.[90]

Germans stridently rejected the charge that many knew, or could have known something, about the crimes being committed in the concentration camps and the front. Such a claim is, of course, a precondition for establishing a foundation of collective guilt. Yet this denial can also be seen as a strategy of rejecting guilt. Julius Posener, a German Jew who served as a British officer in occupied Germany in 1945–46, wrote:

> The question of to what extent they knew remains hazy, despite [the reports of the atrocities]. All the private conversations I have conducted have invariably begun with the ingenuous assertion: "But just believe me, we didn't know a thing about all that, not a thing."

Posener continues:

> No. The lack of knowledge was not complete, and that can be learned immediately from the second defensive statement that always comes after the first, according to which the individual was unable to act, because had he done something, he would immediately have been sent to a concentration camp.[91] The response to that really discomfits them—that is, either or. Either they didn't know about the terror of the camps, in which case it would have been possible to speak without fear against the regime's tyranny and persecution, which they did know about, and even at the risk of being sent at least once to one of "those sanatoriums"; or in fact, and this seems more reasonable to us, they knew, or at least they had a clear notion of what was going on in those places.[92]

The testimony of Germans who reject collective guilt fails to offer resounding proof that there was not recognition of guilt (let alone feelings of guilt and shame for the crimes). A public opinion poll conducted by the military administration in April 1947 buttresses this claim: 63 percent believed that the Germans bore at least partial blame for the deeds of the Hitler regime, because of their support for it. And 59 percent of the adult population agreed with the statement that Germany had tortured and murdered millions of defenseless Europeans.[93]

As knowledge of the Nazi crimes spread, and as understanding of the depth of guilt increased, so did the difficulty of acknowledging it. Many Germans denied responsibility for the fate of their abused and humiliated Jewish neighbors (not just by the regime—many individuals looted Jewish property).[94] They also refused to acknowledge their compatriots' responsibility for serious crimes during the war. But their personal memories, and the knowledge that accumulated regarding the fate of their Jewish neighbors, made them feel guilty.

A firm rejection of every demand to accept guilt or responsibility is not necessarily evidence of pro-Nazi politics, even though there were certainly Nazi sympathizers among those who rejected all guilt. Such sympathy is evident in the following letter of protest, which reeks of antisemitism. The anonymous writer sent it to the Protestant Church at the end of October 1945, in the wake of the Stuttgart resolution:

> I am an integral part of the German nation. But neither I nor my fellow Germans feel that we bear any guilt from the war! . . . To speak of me or of the Germans as guilty is idiocy, just as it would be if church councils in other countries would want to speak about the war guilt of their nations. Neither I nor the German people is guilty of the war, just as other nations are not guilty. It is rather those powerful few international inciters who bear the guilt, the warmongers who may be found in *every* country, not just from 1914 or 1939, but throughout the ages, to the extent that we can follow the course of history.[95]

The language used by the writer—"international inciters" and "warmongers"—is the same used by Nazi propaganda as synonyms for international Jewry. Because the conspiracy is built into the writer's conceptual world, the subject of guilt is, for him, also a component of the anti-German plot.

But it was not just Nazis who refused to acknowledge guilt, who played down the dimensions of German society's cooperation with the Nazi regime, and which blurred the motives behind it. Even among anti-Nazis who went into exile, only a minority believed that the German people as a whole bore any sort of responsibility for the Nazi phenomenon and the atrocities committed under its regime.[96] Thomas Mann, who went into exile in the United States, complained in his letters to Agnes Meyer in March and April 1945 about "the patriotic madness pervasive among the exiles." Mann claimed that most other exiles thought that anyone who argued that Nazism had deep roots in the German nation and character was a traitor.[97] The exiles, who intended to return to their fatherland, were of the opinion that even if the great majority of Germans voted for Hitler and supported his policies, they did not do so out of profound belief in the correctness of Nazi ideology. They were rather seduced by the Nazis, or supported them out of fear or opportunism. For the most part they rejected the other possibility suggested by Mann, that many Germans supported the regime and its policies out of ideological conviction and enthusiasm for Hitler.

As we have seen, even the two Germans who, both inside and outside Germany, were most identified with opening up a public discussion of guilt after the war, Martin Niemöller and Karl Jaspers, diverted the question of guilt away from its concrete, specific social and political context into the abstract areas of theology and metaphysics, thus dulling its sting and mitigating its severity.

After 1945, most Germans had difficulty giving explicit expression to the sense of guilt that lay within them regarding the crimes against Jews and others committed during the Nazi period. But at the margins of their political culture, there have been some expressions and manifestations of acknowledging a sense of heavy guilt since 1945. Some quantitative data also points to the dimensions of these feelings in German society.

The German Wish for Atonement

Profound remorse and a sincere desire to atone for the horrible injustice done to the Jews found explicit expression primarily in relatively small circles of both the Protestant and Catholic Churches. But the impulse toward atonement also could be seen daily and routinely in broad circles of the public. This was reflected in a desire to do service for Jews, or to aid a Jewish neighbor who had returned from a concentration camp.[98]

An early expression of guilt feelings and the wish to atone appears in Thomas Middlebrook's account of the bombing of Hamburg in 1943, in which more than 40,000 people were killed. The author quotes an anonymous woman who was an eyewitness:

> When I was at the home of friends, after being bombed out, someone said over breakfast, "This is the punishment for our attack on Coventry," and a teacher colleague of mine, a woman of very noble principles, said to me, later, "I shouldn't really say this but I felt a wild joy during those heavy British raids. That was the punishment for our crimes against the Jews." I could only agree with her.

Middlebrook notes that such thinking during the war was confined to a small minority of the German public,[99] and it is plausible that he is correct. Nevertheless, the tenor of the testimony is that of satisfaction. The German people are physically atoning for the injustice Germans inflicted on the Jews of Europe and the inhabitants of Britain. German suffering during the war is perceived here as collective punishment for Germany's crimes. This is a position very similar to that taken by Thomas Mann in his BBC talk on the bombing of his home city of Lübbeck. There are few sources that testify to thinking much like this in Germany itself during and after the war. One of the early expressions of a wish for atonement in German literature can be found in *Das Brandopfer* (The Burnt Offering), published by the author and Protestant clergyman Albrecht Goes in 1954. The story's protagonist is Margarete Walker, a German butcher responsible for selling meat to the persecuted Jews who remained in her city. Walker learns about her clients and their fate. She is shocked when one of her Jewish customers, Mrs. Zalewsky, who is in the final months of pregnancy, gives her the carriage and diapers she has prepared for her baby. She will not need them, Mrs. Zalewsky tells Walker.

> If that is the case, that a woman expecting a baby must give away her carriage, because she has been condemned to death for no reason together with her unborn child, if that is the way of the world, then there is no repair for the world any longer and it will never regain its balance. And, actually, nothing else is any longer possible except this: that all be purged—by fire.[100]

That same evening, Allied planes bomb the city. Walker remains in her blazing apartment and seeks to sacrifice herself as a biblical burnt offering, burned on the altar. But a Jew, expelled from a public bomb shelter because of the yellow Star of David on his coat, sees her through the window as she goes up in flames, and saves her. "He did not accept it," Walker says to the Jew who saves her. "Accept what?" I [her Jewish savior] asked. "The burnt offering." "Who?" "God did not accept it."[101]

In this fictional story, Goes addresses the wish for atonement and redemption he feels within himself in artistic guise pervaded by a profound religious reverence or piety vis-à-vis the Nazis' crimes. Margaret Walker's atonement bears a clear element of *imitatio Christi* (imitation of Jesus' agonies, ending with his crucifixion). However, this imitation of the Christian savior goes beyond Christ's example—he was executed, whereas Walker tries to kill herself. Walker in fact imitates the suffering of the persecuted Jews, consciously choosing a horrifying suicide, the dread of which will ostensibly atone for the horrible deaths of the Jews at the hands of the Nazis. Goes, a Protestant minister, chooses to portray his protagonist's exemplary attempt at atonement as a suicide. This is astonishing, because it is not consistent with Christian strictures. The choice may have grown out of an unconscious feeling of this Protestant priest that there is no normative Christian way to atone for such reprehensible crimes. Auschwitz poses an unbearable theological burden for the believing Christian in Germany. Apparently, he felt that the solution offered by Martin Niemöller in 1946—remorse and public contrition—was not sufficient.

Another less dramatic demonstration of remorse was the initiative of Lothar Kreyssig, a member of the Confessing Church during the Third Reich. At a Protestant synod in Berlin in April 1958, Kreyssig called for the establishment of a Sign and Atonement youth organization (*Aktion Sühnezeichen*). Its members would spend a year doing humanitarian and other work in Israel, Poland, and Russia, the lands of the peoples most harmed by the Nazis, as atonement for the crimes of the German people:

> We Germans instigated World War II. Just for that we are guilty more than others for [causing] untold suffering to humanity: in a criminal act of rebellion against God, Germans killed millions of Jews. And even those of us, the survivors, who did not want this, did not do enough to prevent it.[102]

Konrad Weiss, a member of Sign and Atonement, took part in a pilgrimage to Auschwitz organized by the group in 1965. In his biography of Kreyssig, he offered a broader exegesis of German guilt. His inspiration may have been the guilt that traditional Christianity attributed to the Jews as a collective for the sins of their fathers, who ostensibly crucified Jesus. The same was true of Auschwitz—this sin of the fathers would haunt Germans for many generations to come.

"Those days in Auschwitz changed me. I understood what it meant to be a German. What responsibility our fathers' guilt has placed upon us and upon many generations after us."[103] The term "collective responsibility" (*Verantwortung*) had appeared in German political discourse by the summer of 1945 as a gentler alternative for the concept of collective guilt promoted by the Allies. Advocates of this maintained that the German people bore no guilt whatsoever. However, just as a son whose father has gone bankrupt bears responsibility for his father's deeds, so the German people were responsible for the actions of their countrymen.[104] The term became the official formulation of the political leadership of West Germany regarding the crimes against the Jews.

The findings of the only quantitative study that sought to estimate the extent of guilt feelings in West Germany show that young people of the educated class born between the end of the 1960s and the mid-1970s had internalized something of the sensibilities of Goes and Weiss. In 1989, Konrad Brendler examined the feelings of 1,130 German high school and university students about the Holocaust. Of those questioned, 65 percent felt shame when the Holocaust was mentioned. Furthermore, 41 percent felt guilt, even though they had not committed the crimes.[105] Of course, it is hardly possible to use this sample to deduce the feelings of the population at large that same year, and even less valid to take it as an indication of how the population felt about the issue in previous years. Nevertheless, in my view the findings reveal something of the profound sense of guilt that a large proportion of the educated German strata feels, sometimes without even being conscious of it. In June 2002, the newsweekly *Der Spiegel* published a survey on shame—a category close to guilt—about the Holocaust. Of those polled, 86 percent responded that they feel personal shame about German crimes against the Jewish people. Only 75 percent felt this way in December 1991. These results point out that such feelings are widespread throughout German society.

In the 1980s and 1990s, the number of German children bearing Jewish names increased. This may also be an expression, perhaps an unconscious one, of guilt feelings involving Jews. In particular, Germans are naming their daughters Sarah. During the Third Reich, Jewish women who bore German names were forced to add "Sarah" as a second name. In 1988–1989 it was the second most popular name for German girls.[106]

A small number of Germans determined to seek atonement went even farther. Their identification with the persecuted Jews moved them to join their fate to that of the ethnic group the Nazis had tried to annihilate—they converted to Judaism. In some cases, they were rebuked by both Jews and Germans for doing so.[107]

But it is far more common for Germans to have difficulty acknowledging guilt and responsibility for the Nazis' crimes. The postwar cultivation of a sense of German suffering and victimization has intensified this difficulty.

2

Remembering National Suffering in World War II

Germany's suffering has been a central motif in the ideology of *völkisch* (populist-nationalist) circles in the Reich since the end of the nineteenth century. The conspiratorial *völkisch* view was that the Jews had striven, and continued to strive, to take over Germany and the entire world, subjugating and humiliating Christians in the process. The Jews' victim was variously represented. He could be a hard-working German farmer reduced to penury by the high interest his Jewish lender imposed on him, forcing him to forfeit his ancestral fields to his creditor. Or she might be a pure German lass preyed on by a Jewish seducer and villain. But after World War I this motif crystallized, among the nationalists, into a narrative of the Passion of Germany that had manifestly Christian overtones. Not all the versions of this narrative were overtly antisemitic. In some versions the Jewish role was played by other European peoples.

The Weimar Republic's social and economic ills, and the accusation by the victorious parties—embodied in the punitive reparations and territorial concessions mandated by the Versailles Treaty—that Germany bore sole responsibility for starting the Great War, exacerbated the conspiracy theory, adding bitterness and aggression. Consequently, the narrative became an attractive one not only for the extreme right, but also for Germans who denied that they were solely to blame for the conflagration of 1914–1918. Such was the view of many conservative Germans: their country and their countrymen, they believed, had been innocent victims of international forces and treacherous Germans who had conspired to humiliate and destroy the German state.[1] The national personification of Germany is the character of the sleepy German Michel, portrayed in caricatures of the time as an innocent victim unaware that his enemies are abusing and exploiting him.[2] Right-wing circles depicted Germany as a nation whose territorial integrity was under threat by its neighbors to the west and east, who were plotting to partition its territory.[3]

The Versailles Treaty's provisions seemed to confirm such suspicions. In the view of *völkisch* groups, the establishment of Slavic nation-states in Poland and Czechoslovakia that subsumed territories inhabited by ethnic Germans, partly on lands which had been ruled previously by the German-speaking Hapsburg dynasty and in part on land confiscated from the German Reich, violated German national rights. The new European order was seen as flouting the German right to self-determination, committing an outrageous injustice to the German people. Such discrimination against and persecution of the Germans was, they argued, a violation of the principles of the law of nations and paved the way for World War II.[4] In this view, the peace following World War I was merely an illusion that concealed an invisible struggle. Under these circumstances, Hitler justifiably began the war in order to redeem his people from servitude and humiliation.[5]

The famous radio play *German Passion 1933*,[6] written by Nazi Party member Richard Euringer, presents the essence of the *völkische Weltanschauung* of the time. The rape of German women by black soldiers of the French occupation army on the banks of the Rhine symbolized the despoiled, degraded German nation. The radio play depicted the German fatherland as wreckage pervaded by death, despair, distress, unemployment, and hunger. Instead of being glorified, Germany's war heroes were branded as criminals. The national culture had reached a state of collapse; Berlin was Sodom and Gomorrah. The play's protagonist was a dead soldier who set out to redeem Germany from its suffering. For Euringer, the ascendancy of the Nazis in 1933 symbolized the beginning of national redemption.[7]

From 1933 to the overthrow of the Nazis, this was the official explanation that the National-Socialist regime offered for global events. Anton Zischka, a pro-Nazi Austrian journalist and popular lecturer in the service of Nazi Germany during World War II who lived in Majorca and during the Third Reich, was the author of highly popular works published in Germany about raw materials and international politics and the Third World. He joined the Nazi Party in 1941. In September 1942, he wrote:

> On September 8, 1918, the English newspaper the *Weekly Dispatch* published . . . an article by P. W. Wille, emblazoned with the headline "The Huns of 1940." This essay investigated the effects of the British blockade of Germany, aimed at causing mass hunger. The author informs his readers that more than 750,000 Germans have died [as an outcome of the blockade], and he speculates regarding future implications of German starvation.

According to Zischka, Wille wrote: "Not only will tens of thousands of yet unborn Germans be physically inferior, but also thousands of Germans who have not yet been conceived."

Zischka also quoted the founder of the Boy Scouts, Lord Robert Baden-Powell, who predicted at the time of the Versailles armistice: "We should wait until 1940, in order to learn who had truly won the war." Zischka wrote that Baden-Powell followed this with the optimistic observation: "The whole weight of the blockade would be felt by criminal Germany only in the future." According to Zischka, Wille cited a certain Dr. Saleeby, who believed that "The German race will face annihilation . . . even if the birthrate remains constant, due to the blockade, by 1940 the German people will probably be physically degenerate. . . . Germany will have to pay a horrible price for having tried to be a great power."

Zischka sums up his proofs of the British plan to destroy the German race:

> It was . . . a long-range plan. The siege will not end when the war is over; Germany's enemies will leave it to starve far after 1918: German children were sentenced to be harmed. They had to prevent, by poverty and physical injury, any attempt at revenge. Hunger was to work against Germany just as it had in India and Egypt.[8]

Such paranoid interpretation of reality was not at that time an eccentric phenomenon in Germany. Hitler also construed World War II in a similar way. The Jew stood behind Germany's enemies, he said in a series of public addresses in early 1942. His explicit call for the extermination of the Jews of Europe (*Ausrottung*) was presented as a defensive action aimed at frustrating and preventing a murderous Jewish plot to destroy the German people, rape its women, and slaughter its children.[9] He continued to proclaim this view until the end of the war and his own death. For example, the order of the day for the Wehrmacht on New Year's Day 1945 read:

> The decisive significance for the world of the war that we are fighting today is clear to the German *Volk:* a merciless struggle for existence or nonexistence, that is, a struggle for life or death! Because the goal of the Jewish-international world conspiracy opposing us is the extermination of our *Volk.*[10]

Having supposedly comprehended the enemy's evil, criminal intention to destroy the country, the Nazis justified the use of the most ruthless means to ensure the existence and survival of the fatherland.

As the war turned against them, broad swaths of the German public wondered what had gone wrong with their Führer's "genius strategies." They found an explanation based in the traditional nationalist view, which became the official interpretation of global events during the Third Reich: the destruction, devastation, death, and defeat of World War II was a continuation of the saga of suffering and injustice that began decades earlier, on the eve of the First World War, if not before. Once again the German people were the victims of malevolent and barbaric enemies.

People who held this view, as well as a larger public that was exposed to and largely adopted it, disregarded Nazi Germany's international aggression and the huge public support the regime of terror enjoyed. They refused to acknowledge the enormity of the injustice and misery that Germany brought on all Europe's peoples, especially on the Jews and the nations of Eastern Europe.

The German Experience of Suffering and Victimization during World War II

When war broke out in the summer of 1914, the German public was hugely enthusiastic.[11] In September 1939, in contrast, the public squares did not fill up with joyous crowds. The horrible price exacted by World War I was still a living memory, and Germans did not want another conflict.[12] Nevertheless, Hitler's successful foreign policy brinkmanship during the 1930s, and the social welfare policies he pursued, made the Nazi regime extremely popular. Consequently, they also contributed to the fact that large sections of the public tended, despite their apprehensions about the war, to accept Nazi propaganda literally. They believed, in other words, that Germany had not sought hostilities. Its rivals forced it to go to fight, because they would not allow the Germans to live as a free people in their fatherland. A Nazi propaganda film of 1940 proudly displayed to the German public the devastation the Luftwaffe wreaked on the cities of Poland and in particular the capital, Warsaw, in September 1939. The destruction was presented as an apposite response to the "monstrous crime" committed by the Polish leadership by turning Warsaw into an armed fortress, and to the belligerence and deceit of British Prime Minister Neville Chamberlain: "Pay attention! This is what it looks like when the German Wehrmacht strikes!"[13]

But during the war, when the Allies retaliated against Germany and bombed its cities, the braggadocio gave way to cries of distress. Joseph Goebbels and other German propagandists described Allied war conduct as murderous and barbaric, criminal terrorism aimed not only at breaking the spirit of the freedom-loving German people but at exterminating Germany. They claimed that Allied terrorism did not spare women, old people, and children, nor Europe's centuries-old cultural assets.[14]

The American historian Michael Geyer emphasizes that "it is commonly overlooked that the notion of *Menschheitsverbrechen* (crimes against humanity) was in use by the Nazis long before it entered the Nuremberg trials through the back door."[15] Atrocities committed by a belligerent during a war against its own citizens in contrast to crimes committed against citizens of an enemy state were not defined as war crimes in the international law in force during World War II. As the war progressed, the Allies became concerned with the question how such acts could be criminalized and whether and how their perpetrators could be punished. It was not until the summer of 1945 that Allied legal advisers created the category of "crimes against humanity," with the purpose of providing a legal definition for these acts. However, this category was only ranked third, after crimes against peace and war crimes. The Holocaust was not a central issue in the cases tried before the military tribunal at Nuremberg.[16]

The war indeed struck hard at Germany's civilians. Heavy Allied bombing caused widespread destruction and killed hundreds of thousands of civilians, including the elderly, women, and children.[17] A couple of days after the bombing of Dresden, on February 20, 1945, a local propaganda broadcast this report:

> Dead soldiers, women, and children sprawl in the broad streets and squares. The larger part of the city that was hit was not in any sense a military target. This barbaric and Satanic conduct of the war, which has

> emblazoned its banner with murder, terror, and crime, is entirely different from our own concept of conducting the war, and even total war in the true sense of the word. It is as far from our struggle and the life of our people as the sky is from the earth. This is murder! This is criminal! This is Satanic! It is not only a struggle against National Socialism, or against the party, or against the German leadership. This is simply an evil intention to annihilate the vitality of our entire people and its life.

Further on, the broadcast called on the population to persevere in the struggle, to harden itself, and not to lose its resolve.[18] This self-righteous and hypocritical Nazi propaganda, which entirely ignored the crimes committed on the orders of the Nazi regime, fostered and amplified the sense of victimhood and injustice that prevailed in Germany from the end of World War I.

During the war's final years, the collective experience shared by most of Germany's population, both regime sympathizers and those who had no great love for the Nazis, motivated some of the latter to adopt the Nazi view. In March 1944, Willy Brandt, later chancellor of West Germany, then a Social Democratic exile in Stockholm, wrote:

> The news that has come out of Germany recently is among the saddest I have ever heard. It is becoming evident that even people who had until recently resisted the pressure and propaganda of Nazism are now under the influence of the mood of national solidarity. I have [at] hand statements by radical workers to the effect that this war must be regarded as a war of national defense, because—as they see it—the enemy seeks the complete destruction of Germany. The air raids naturally also work both ways. It is even becoming evident in Berlin, where critical attitudes have been much more marked than in many other areas, that people are influenced by the general feeling that they are all in the same boat anyway and must make the best of a bad situation. Fear of the Russians is also an important factor.[19]

The following lines are taken from a composition written by Hedi R., a 14-year-old schoolgirl from Prenzlauer Berg in Berlin (in the Soviet zone of occupation) in 1946. She wrote it as part of a larger project of documenting the war experiences of the neighborhood's children. Hedi's experiences sitting in a bomb shelter during the Allied bombing of March 1945 reflect how a large part of the German public emotionally identified with this war narrative, and that these feelings did not dim in their memory even after the regime's collapse:

> The small children entwined their little arms around the necks of their mothers and buried their fear-stricken faces in their mothers' coats. The mothers petted the toddlers' heads with trembling hands. Everyone thought only about himself and his closest relatives, everyone felt lonely and destitute; however, everybody had only one thought: hold on [*durchhalten*], be strong, and survive.[20]

Nazi propaganda presented the campaign against the Soviet Union as a defense of European civilization against Asiatic barbarian hordes threatening to flood and destroy Europe. Propaganda reports and the *Wochenschau,* the official Nazi weekly newsreel screened in cinemas before the feature film that showed the Red Army's westward thrust during the last months of the war,[21] focused on the destruction, devastation, looting, murder, and rape of German women inflicted by Red Army soldiers. Even those who did not personally experience the Soviet conquest understood the reports to be the fulfillment of Goebbels's horrific threats about what would befall Germany if, God forbid, it surrendered.

During the initial weeks after the Soviet conquest, first in East Prussia and later even to the west of the Oder-Neisse Rivers' line, large numbers of German women, young and old, were ravaged; widely circulated but probably unfounded assessments spoke of a million acts of rape.[22] After the very early period of occupation, this shameful and terrible phenomenon was rigorously suppressed by the officers of the Red Army. Undoubtedly, the assaults left deep emotional scars on the women involved, but a large part of the public perceived rape not only as a private trauma suffered by not a few women, but also as a symbol of the state of the German nation.[23] The nationalist writer Ernst Jünger even went so far as to see mass rape as a tactic that sought to debilitate the willpower of disarmed Germans.[24]

The Nazi propaganda evoked deep anxiety. Many Germans killed themselves out of fear of what might happen. This trauma, and the heavy price paid in life and property, made the Germans even readier to accept Nazi propaganda as an accurate portrayal of the war. It left them with bitter feelings about their conquerors, especially the Soviets. Some of this bitterness became part of German collective memory.[25]

Not only propaganda but valid information as well amplified fears that civilians would be hurt. At the end of the war, the Nazi regime evacuated populations close to the battlefields in the Reich's eastern territories. Not all the evacuees were sent west in trains or on ships on the Baltic

Sea. Many made their way on foot, or in long caravans of horse-drawn wagons. The bitter cold of the winter of 1945 took many lives, especially infants, children, and the elderly. The refugees were joined by millions of other Germans in flight from the Red Army and the war. (According to the estimates of the historian Theodor Schieder, some 5 million Germans were evacuated or fled.)[26] As Poland and later Czechoslovakia were liberated by the Allies, sporadic deportations of Germans began from these countries (the so-called "wild expulsion"). At the Potsdam conference, in the summer of 1945, the Allies decided to deport most of the Germans who yet remained in Poland, Czechoslovakia, and Hungary. The governments of these countries carried out this decision, although only about half the German population was expelled from Hungary. Yugoslavia also expelled her German population. Millions of Germans were deported, and they joined the others who had been evacuated or fled during the last stages of the war.

Expellee organizations today tally between 12 and 15 million German refugees but, peculiarly, they count the offspring of deportees as refugees as well.[27] Ingo Haar, on the other hand, claims that only between 7 and 10 million Germans were uprooted from their homes and the lands where they had lived for generations. Death statistics for those who fled as well as for the evacuations and deportations—some were killed out of revenge, but most died because of the harsh conditions of the winter of 1945—are controversial, ranging from 100,000 to 500,000 (probably much nearer the higher figure). The official historiography of the Federal Republic on this subject claimed that their numbers amounted to somewhere between 200,000 and 2 million.[28] Since the 1950s, common estimates spoke of millions, and right-wing circles and expellee organizations continue to cite such numbers today. The extreme right even held that the German dead amounted to 6 million, a symbolic total that recalled the number of Jews murdered by the Nazis in the Holocaust.[29] The political establishment and West German public preferred, after defeat, to ignore the evacuation initiated by the Nazi regime and to focus on the term "flight and deportation" (*Flucht und Vertreibung*).

These German refugees were absorbed, not without difficulties and despite their being rejected by a part of West German society,[30] into the Allied zones of occupation in Germany.[31] Their proportion of the population throughout Germany was relatively high, and they could be distinguished by their unfamiliar dialect and their poverty. Most of them reached West Germany (especially Bavaria, Lower Saxony, and Schleswig-Holstein), but their presence was also tangible in the Soviet zone, where they made up about a quarter of the population. In the state of Mecklenburg–West Pomerania they constituted 40 percent of the inhabitants. This was the highest proportion of refugees anywhere in the German states.[32]

In the Federal Republic, ethnic German refugees and displaced persons from the eastern territories were collectively defined as expellees (*Vertriebene*), a term that emphasizes the terrible injustice inflicted on these people.[33] In East Germany, they were called "new settlers" (*Umsiedler*). In any case, they all perceived their fate and their expulsion from their homes as a criminal injustice motivated by hate, a vindictive act against an innocent German population by the countries of Europe. This uncritical view of the circumstances of the expulsion was expressed in the following lines sung by ethnic Germans from Hungary (*Donauschwaben*), who were driven out of their homes after the war and kept in a prison camp in the Soviet Union:

Our homeland we were forced to leave / *Unser Heimat müssen wir verlassen*
Why? We know well / *Und warum, das wissen wir ja gut;*
All the nations around hate us / *Alle Völker um uns her nur hassen,*
The blame is therefore in our blood./ *Schuld daran ist bloß nur unser Blut.*

Another verse of the song also expresses disregard for historical reality and for German responsibility for expulsions from the east:

Our sons and fathers fell / *Unser Söhne und Väter sind gefallen*
For our dear fatherland / *Für ihr teures Vaterland;*
They fought and spilled their blood / *Sie kämpften und bluteten,*
But they are called criminals / *Doch Verbrecher warden sie genannt*[34]

Another song written and sung by this group offers a different explanation for the suffering of the ethnic Germans (*Volksdeutsche*), one interwoven with racist Nazi ideology. The song tells how the Slavic peoples hounded and murdered ethnic Germans:

Simply because we wanted to live our lives / *Nur weil unser Leben wir wollten gestalten*
In the German way, / *Gemäß unserer deutschen Art,*

Only because we wanted to maintain our German character, / *Nur weil unser Deutschtum wir wolten erhalten*
And to preserve the purity of our blood. / *Und rein unser Blut wir Bewahrt*[35]

In the first months after the collapse of the Reich in May 1945, a great majority of Germans felt a sense of national calamity.[36] Although the Germans doubtless felt relieved vis-à-vis the end of the belligerence which put an end to the Allied bombardments on German cities, there was no happiness at having been liberated from the Nazi dictatorship (except, of course, among those who had been Nazism's sworn opponents or victims). Overwhelmingly, the Germans, whatever their political attitudes, saw themselves as victims: victims of Hitler, who seduced them and brought disaster on them; victims of the war; and victims of the way the war had been conducted by the victorious Allies, who because of Nazi propaganda were perceived by the German public as vengeful and fierce.

A sermon given by Pastor Martin Niemöller plainly expresses this sense of a nationally shared suffering. Even people and groups that had been persecuted by the Nazis, like Niemöller himself and the Confessing Church, partook of this feeling, even if they did not explicitly blame the Allies for their fate:

> In the summer of 1945 I returned home: from imprisonment to freedom. After the joy of seeing [my loved ones] came the hour of comprehension, when it touched my soul that new empty holes had been torn open among those close to me during the final months of my imprisonment [in the concentration camp]. My beloved youngest daughter died within two days, my eldest son fell in the east, my third son was a prisoner of war in Russia.[37]

This bereavement over the loss of family and friends, alongside feelings of anxiety and uncertainty about the fate of missing or captured family members, was shared by many in Germany.

These common individual experiences crystallized into a German collective memory that was also assimilated by those who had not suffered such losses firsthand.

The research of Dorothee Wierling and Harald Welzer shows that this remembrance was passed on to subsequent generations through stories told by parents to their children and grandchildren.[38] The changes that the younger ones made to the stories, Welzer argues, blurred and distorted the crimes and atrocities that the war generation had committed, but did not mitigate at all the suffering and sense of victimhood that the older generation felt.[39]

Etched in this collective memory were the terror of nighttime bombardment of German cities, the flight from the Red Army as it dashed westward, the revenge its soldiers took on the civilian population, and the expulsions at the end of the war and its aftermath. All these were much more alive in the Germans' collective memory than was the deportation of their neighbors, Germany's Jewish citizens, to their deaths in the east and the plunder of their property by the Nazi Party and the public at large.

This trend was also apparent in the consolidation of the experiences of millions of German soldiers at the front into a collective memory. Here, too, the suffering and heroism of the soldiers in battle and in captivity took a more central place than the crimes they had committed previously. For them, the inhumanity and barbarity with which they treated subject populations, especially Slavs and Jews in Eastern Europe, paled by comparison with their own experiences.

More than 5 million German soldiers died in the war and in captivity.[40] During the final months, thousands of young boys were conscripted directly from their schools, often over their anxious parents' dismay, and were sent to be cannon fodder in the face of the advancing Allied forces. Between 2 and 3 million German soldiers were taken prisoner by the Soviets and incarcerated in POW camps. More than a million of them died. Repatriation was a slow process, however, and the last of those lucky enough to survive did not get home until 1955.

The huge suffering that the Germans caused themselves by putting the Nazis in power, supporting the criminal regime unreservedly, and cooperating as a society with Hitler's war aims not only made it difficult for them to acknowledge the great and terrible torment their country and people caused others in Europe. Their own suffering also served as a means of suppressing and rejecting any guilt they felt.

German Suffering as a Mechanism for Rejecting Guilt and Responsibility

The torment of the Germans during and after the war, and the template of nationalist interpretation that magnified their sense that they were victims of injustice, was accompanied by a profound sense of guilt that many had difficulty acknowledging. In 1950, Theodor Adorno and other scholars published a study on the difficulties that individual Germans had in coping with heavy feelings of guilt for the crimes of the Nazi period. Adorno and his colleagues argued that the increased preoccupation of individual Germans with their anguish during the war was a strategy for rejecting blame. The obsession with collective suffering reflected an attempt to shake free of the psychological pressure caused by the information that the Germans had committed crimes unprecedented in human history.[41]

The German public took refuge in a strategy of comparison—they made an analogy between the Jewish Holocaust and German suffering. To this end, they weighed the unique features of the Holocaust against the agonies experienced by the Germans. In this view, the Germans endured as much as the Jews, if not more.

A characteristic expression of this frame of mind can be found in a report of the American military government of occupied Germany (OMGUS) from November 1945: "For each Jew who died in a concentration camp, dozens of Germans were killed in the [Allied] bombing."[42] This false equivalency magnified German pain and discounted the horrors of the Holocaust. Furthermore, by divorcing German suffering from its source as the necessary product of Hitler's criminal policies and blaming it on allegedly criminal Allied conduct of the war, it implicitly equated the Allied war effort with the crimes committed by Hitler and the Nazi regime. A letter sent to Bishop Theophil Wurm, the president of the German Protestant Church (EKD), protesting statements made by Pastor Niemöller, also made the same analogy:

> What were the bombardments of Germany? Millions of people were annihilated. Look at Dresden, Hamburg, and Pforzheim. In the latter city, 35,000 Germans were killed in a single night [referring to February 23, 1945, on which some 18,000 civilians died].[43] Why does Niemöller not address the criminal guilt of the relevant nations? Mention of these events would wipe out the inflated numbers of concentration camp victims.[44]

Citizens who may have had Nazi backgrounds were not the only ones to articulate such beliefs. A broad national consensus in defeated Germany compared the Allied bombings and the expulsion of ethnic Germans from the eastern territories with the Holocaust. Proponents of this view ranged from Nazi leaders and administrators tried at Nuremburg such as Alfred Rosenberg, Einsatzgruppe D commander Otto Ohlendorf, and Admiral Karl Dönitz, who became the Reich's president after Hitler's suicide, to the philosopher Martin Heidegger, the nationalist novelist Ernst Jünger,[45] and the Catholic bishop of Bavaria, Cardinal Michael von Faulhaber.[46] Bishop Wurm of the Protestant Church regarded the expulsion of Germans from the east as tantamount to an attempt to annihilate part of the German people, a crime of the same magnitude as those against the Jews.[47] Even the conservative anti-Nazi émigré Volkmar von Zühlsdorff, who returned to Germany at the end of the war from exile in the United States, equated the Allied treatment of the Germans with the horrors of Auschwitz.

Zühlsdorff wrote to a Vienna-born older Jewish friend—the author Hermann Broch, who remained in America because he believed that exiled German Jews should not return to Germany:

> The ovens of Auschwitz have become the glowing fires of Hamburg and Dresden, of Berlin, Munich, Leipzig, Cologne, Essen, Dortmund, and Düsseldorf, of Frankfurt, Bremen, Stuttgart, Hanover, Nuremberg, Magdeburg, Mannheim, Karlsruhe, Augsburg, Lübbek, Regensburg, Kassel, Mainz, Aachen, Darmstadt, Bamberg, Offenbach, Würzburg, Bayreuth, Heilbrunn, and so falling down a whole array of German cities, millions of beaten and dispossessed, the terrors of Königsberg, Breslau, and the Sudetenland, and the gnawing hunger whose victims are now falling in flocks. . . . Dissipation, destruction, defeat through the merciless victor . . . has destroyed National Socialism and placed itself in that same spiritual image.[48]

The German historian Nicolas Berg commented: "It is impossible not to understand von Zühlsdorff's meaning as follows: 'The Jews experienced one Auschwitz, the Germans hundreds.'"[49]

Lutheran Bishop Hanns Lilje, among the leaders of the Protestant Church, quoted a protest he received after he and all the other Church's leaders signed the Stuttgart declaration. The letter refers to all three of the agonies that the Allies inflicted on Germany:

> How can such a declaration have been made without a parallel declaration on the part of foreign bishops, whose peoples also bear the same guilt for the events of recent years? I do not seek to prettify the events that took

> place during Hitler's rule in this country or outside the country, or to defend them, but the mass murder (*Massenmord*) by the enemy bombers, the suffering of our prisoners of war, the brutal deportation of our countrymen from the eastern areas robbed from us, and the likely demise of the nation (*Volkssterben*) seem to me worthy of at least the same measure of condemnation.[50]

A similar attitude characterizes the postwar literature of young German authors of the war generation. These were mostly former members of the Hitler Youth and had served as soldiers in the Wehrmacht. "The portrayal of Jewish figures in their works," writes literary scholar Hans-Joachim Hahn on the writings of Hans Werner Richter, Heinrich Böll, and Kurt Ziesel, "creates the impression that these authors found it difficult to acknowledge the agony of the Jews in the Holocaust and to regard them as victims. At times they feel obligated, ostensibly in the name of a universal ideal, to equate the fates of their Jewish and German protagonists. In some cases the latter had persecuted the Jews before they were killed." This literature "utterly expunges the differences between the Jewish victims of the Holocaust and German soldiers killed during the War."[51]

German society tended to ignore the fact that responsibility for their country's unprecedented crimes was not limited to the Nazi leadership and some members of the SS.[52] Millions of ordinary Germans collaborated with the regime and helped carry out Hitler's murderous policy throughout Europe, including Wehrmacht soldiers. The Nazi organs of power could hardly have accomplished their policies of persecution and murder without a German society obedient to their dictates and prepared to cooperate with mass murder.

The difficulty of coping with such enormous guilt amid mass German suffering led Catholic and Protestant officials to regard their countrymen not only as sinful, in the spirit of the Protestant Church's debate on guilt from 1945 onward (as discussed in chapter 1), but also as the innocent victims of catastrophic historical circumstances. World War I had ended in a humiliating defeat that enabled the victors to mistreat the losers. Suffering and hunger led to the rise of a dictatorship. Then came World War II, more terrible than its predecessor, which both sides had pursued in contradiction of Christian morality. And when the fighting was finally over, defeated Germany was again mistreated by its occupiers. This presentation of German history was combined with a political-ideological exegesis already widely accepted among nationalist circles in Germany years before 1945, in which the suffering of the Germans became sacramental.

These views found expression in the initial postwar years in opposition to and protest against the guilt discourse. Yet it also appeared independently—even characterizing, as we have seen, some of the sermons of Martin Niemöller, who is generally identified as one of its central spokesmen. Both churches began infusing the widespread narrative of German suffering with symbols steeped in religion and with meanings of a clear nationalist tinge, unknown in nationalist circles' previous incarnation. This renewed narrative, charged with Christianity, would spread to other parts of the public.

The Sanctification of German Suffering

The sermon delivered by the elderly Bishop von Galen of Münster on March 16, 1945, stated a commonly held theological position:

> Our agonies, like the agonies of so many good people who have never tasted sin, and like the agonies of Christ, are not simply punishment for sins and no more. Rather, they are also participation in His agonies. It atones for sins and contributes to the world's redemption, to the victory of life over death.[53]

Like von Galen, many other clergymen compared the fate of the German people to the passion of Jesus.

In his famous sermon on guilt, at the Emanuel church in Wuppertal in March 1946, Niemöller confessed his own guilt for not seeing (and not wishing to see) the cross-bearing Lord and Redeemer on his way to agony and death in each of the thousands of Jewish prisoners who were marched out of Berlin to the Sachsenhausen concentration camp after Kristallnacht. Niemöller thus framed the persecution of the Jews as a Passion. Later in the same sermon, Niemöller said: "Today Jesus walks among us as a refugee, as a man whose home was bombed, who does not know if his life has meaning, who wonders if he still finds meaning in the passing day."[54] And just as he framed the persecution of the Jews as a Passion, so he did with the suffering of the Germans.

At that time, there were but few in the Church who disputed this linkage. In a Good Friday sermon in 1947, the Protestant theologian Helmut

Thielicke referred to the common use of the term "German passion" and its connotations.[55] "By this term one means our fatherland's painful times, in which it suffers and is cast down onto the threshold of death." Thielicke expressed some reservations about the use of the phrase: "Our suffering derives from our guilt, while the crucified one on Golgotha bore not his own sins, but the guilt of his brothers." Nevertheless, he bestowed the Passion image on his countrymen. Thielicke presumed, though, that this contained a certain amount of dangerous self-pity that might deny the Germans the genuine fruit of expiation.[56]

Christian leaders found in their tradition other images of persecuted and suffering innocent people whose fate was comparable to that of the defeated German people. Pastor Rudolf Weckerling's radio sermon broadcast on the U.S. station in Berlin (RIAS) in October 1950 compared the Germans' suffering to that of Job. He extolled his countrymen's patience, for which heaven would eventually compensate them, as it had Job.[57]

Their flocks internalized these images.[58] Among the deportees from Eastern Europe, the Catholics in particular, another traditional Christian image was widespread alongside that of the passion—that of the Holy Family's flight to Egypt. The motif appeared frequently in *Königsteiner Rufe*, the journal of a Catholic institution, established in Königstein in the Taunus mountains in 1946, to help priests deported from the east. In the New Testament story, King Herod seeks to kill the baby Jesus after the Magi come to Jerusalem in search of the king of the Jews, whose star they saw in the east. When Herod is unable to find Jesus, he wrathfully orders the slaughter of all babies in Bethlehem and its environs (Matthew 2:1–18). Father Augustin Reimann, who was expelled from Czechoslovakia, wrote:

> We, too, were evicted from our homes by the order of the earthly powers. Something of Herod's cruelty is also present here. Because some of these powers would like to see the deaths of our children. But here, too, we have been guided by the providence of our father in heaven.[59]

The Protestant Church and Jewish Suffering

While prominent leaders of the Protestant Church accepted the widespread view of Germans' pain as a passion, they were reluctant, during the immediate postwar period, to take an unambiguous position on the murder of 6 million Jews at the hands of Germans—many of whom were

Protestants—or to criticize the Church's utter silence during the Holocaust. True, the subject was not a popular one, but the failure to take a stand about the genocide also had theological roots.

In 1947, a number of figures, both in the ecumenical council and missionaries who worked among the Jews, demanded that the Church assert itself on the Jewish question after years of silence. One of these was Otto von Harling, a member of the Church's chambers (*Kanzlei*) who was the son of a missionary to the Jews and the head of the Jewish Institute in Leipzig. He wrote to Martin Niemöller, who served at the time as the Church's president, that "everywhere I find agreement that if the church were to make a statement on the Jewish question in the form of the Stuttgart declaration, it would cause more damage than benefit."[60] After considerable discussion, the Church's Council of Brothers (*Brüderrat*) issued, in April 1948, "A Word on the Jewish Question (*Judenfrage*)." This document lacks any expression of remorse and simply restates the Church's dogma regarding the Jews:[61]

1. Since, in that the Son of God was born a Jew, Israel's election and destiny found their realization, the church must in principle oppose any other understanding, including Judaism's understanding that it bears or brings tidings of a general human idea or the world's redemption.
2. Since Israel crucified the savior, it rejected his election and mission. This created, at that time, the divine occurrence of the opposition of all men and peoples to the Messiah. We all share the guilt of Christ's crucifixion. For this reason, the Church refrains from branding the Jews as the only ones guilty of the crucifixion of the Messiah.
3. Israel's election was transferred from the Jews to the church of all nations, of Jews and of pagans, via and since the arrival of the Christ. The Christians of Israel and the gentiles are limbs of the Messiah's body and brothers to one another. Therefore, the church does not differentiate between Christians of Jewish origin and Christians of pagan origin. At the same time, the [Christian] community anticipates that Israel's lost children will again take the place reserved for them by God.
4. God's faithfulness has not abandoned Israel, despite its lack of faith and rejection [of the Christ]. The Christ was crucified and resurrected for the sake of Israel as well. This is Israel's hope after Golgotha. That God has delayed his judgment thus far is a sign of his patience. The church is guilty when it forgets or allows itself—for any reason—to forget this testimony to God's patience with Israel.

5. Israel under [God's] judgment is eternal proof of the truth and accomplishment of the divine word, and a constant warning by God to his congregation that God does not allow himself to be mocked. The mute moral of Jewish fate is for us a warning and for the Jews an admonition if they do not wish to convert to him, in which alone is their redemption placed.[62]

Three years after the Holocaust, the German Church had the temerity to imply in an official document that Hitler had served as God's scourge and that the Holocaust had been God's punishment for the Jews' refusal to acknowledge Jesus Christ. The Church maintained that the only redemption for the Jews was their acceptance of Christianity. In private conversations, Church leaders were still clearer on this point. Even Provost Heinrich Grüber, a member of the Confessing Church who headed an unofficial body that, during the Third Reich, helped "non-Aryan" Christians and others to flee Germany, and who had even been sent to a concentration camp because of this activity, held this view. As late as 1961 he stated that "it was God's will to send Adolf Hitler to annihilate the Jews of Europe."[63]

The Church's official position did not change until the Protestant synod in Berlin Weiβensee in April 1950. Apparently as a result of intervention by ecumenical officials and the American high commissioner, there was an attempt to revise the Church's position both theologically and morally. For the first time, the Church addressed the question of guilt and antisemitism:[64]

> We believe that God's promise to the people of Israel whom he chose remains in force even after the crucifixion of Jesus. We declare that we, in our idleness and our silence before the merciful God, bear part of the blame for the sacrilege committed against the Jews by members of our nation. We warn all Christians not to offset God's judgment on us Germans with what we did to the Jews; for in judgment the forgiveness of God seeks the penitents.
>
> We ask all Christians to abandon all antisemitism, to oppose it in every place it reappears, and to receive the Jews and Christian Jews in a spirit of brotherhood. We ask the Christian communities to take upon themselves the protection of Jewish cemeteries within their territories for as long as there is no one to care for them. We ask the merciful God quickly to bring the End of Days, when we, together with those of Israel that will accept redemption, will praise the victory of Jesus Christ.[65]

Even though the end of this declaration has a missionary ring to it, the document marks the beginning of a long and radical metamorphosis in German Protestant Church doctrine. This change, influenced by the theology of Karl Barth, for all intents and purposes recognized Judaism as a legitimate religion and abandoned old dogmas according to which God's promise and benevolence had been withdrawn from the Jews when they did not accept Jesus. The subject remained controversial in the Church, and only in 2000 did the synod in Braunschweig issue an amended declaration that criticized the Church's anti-Jewish tradition and its role in creating the atmosphere that led to the Holocaust. In the published document, the church renounced absolutely any aspiration to convert the Jews.

The church did not only portray German civilians who died in the war as victims. It did the same with regard to German soldiers, completely obscuring the political context of their deaths. The circumstances under which the war broke out and the way it was conducted—especially on the eastern front, where it was pursued as a war of annihilation against Jewish Bolshevism—was totally ignored. Churches throughout Germany—including in Communist East Germany—gave this visual expression after the war.

The War Dead as Christian Martyrs

Even the dissidents of the Confessing Church preferred to see fallen soldiers as having fallen for Christ and not for Hitler.[66] Their position reflects a very wide consensus that prevailed among the German churches after the war, expressed in the way these soldiers were commemorated within the churches. A relief of the crucified Christ was placed in a niche in the St. Marien Church in the center of Rostock in East Germany in the 1950s. Engraved on either side of the relief were two passages from the Gospel according to John. On one side was the verse: "For God so loved the world, that he gave his only Son, that whoever believes in him should not perish but have eternal life" (John 3:16). On the other was "Greater love has no one than this, that someone lay down his life for his friends" (John 15:13). On either side of the crucifix hung two oil paintings from 1947 by the artist Egon Tschirch (1889–1948). The image on the right side depicted the bombed-out ruins of downtown Rostock. Standing over the wreckage is

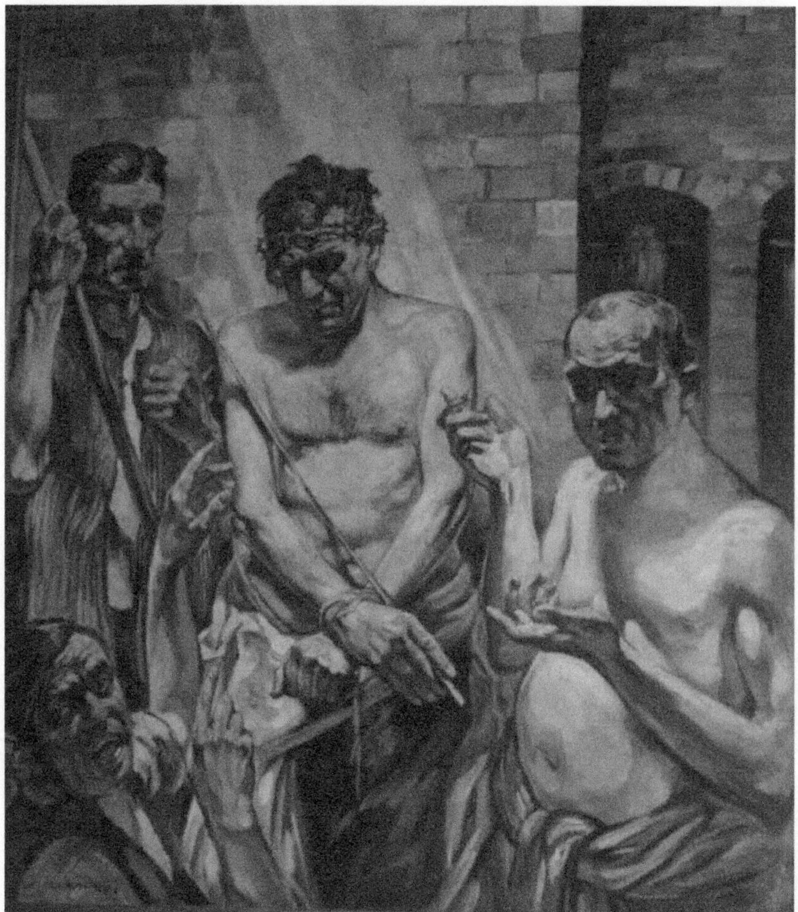

Figure 2. (*left, and above*), The St. Marien Church in Rostock—interior

the St. Marien Church, "as a sign of comfort and hope," as the caption at the painting's side states.

The painting on the other side of the crucified Christ shows a scene from the Passion: Jesus bound, with a crown of thorns, being led to Golgotha. A table stands before the crucifix, and engraved on it is the legend: "We remember today our dead." On the table is a book that records the names of the city's fallen and missing soldiers, and each day the book is opened to one of its pages.

On the opposing page is a drawing of a cross overlaying a triangle, a common gravestone symbol representing reconciliation between man

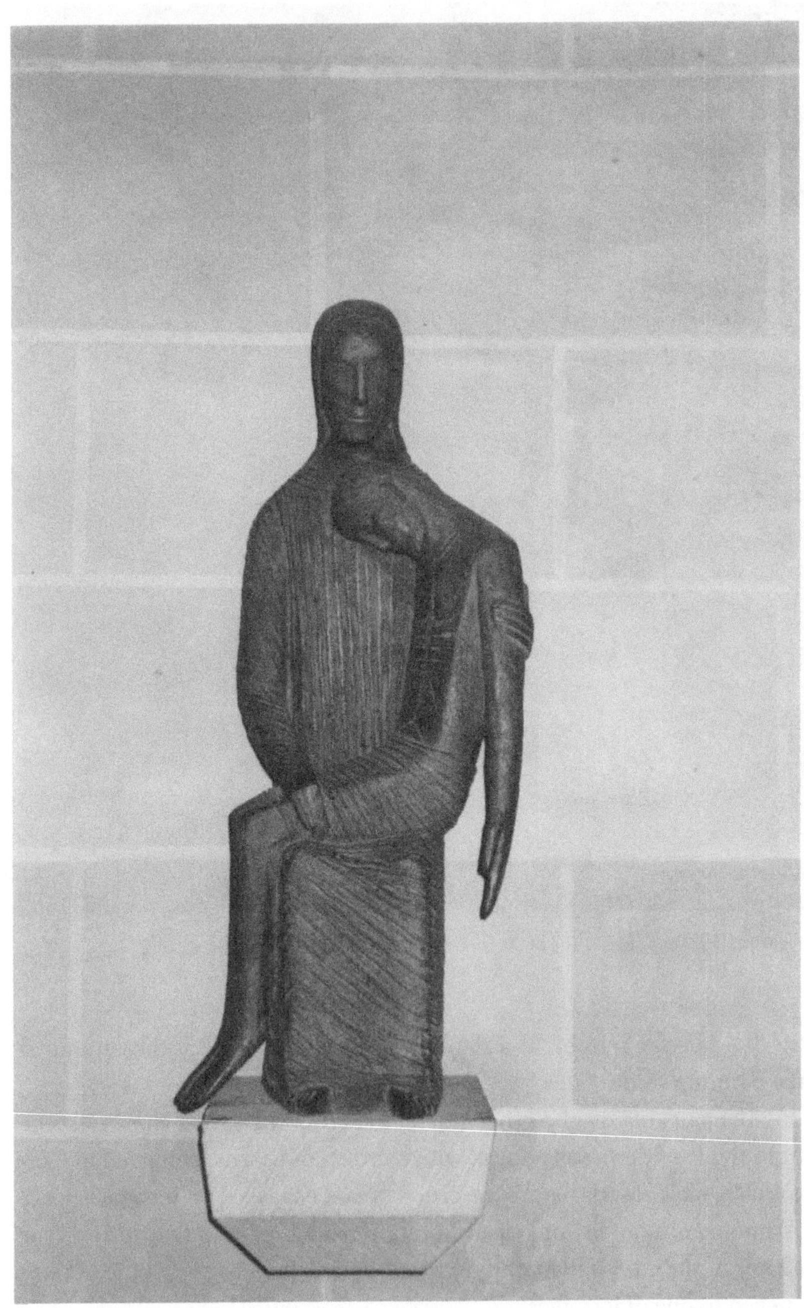

Figure 3. The Pietà at the Church in Münster, Berlin

and God. The city's fallen soldiers, and its civilians who died in the bombardments that are depicted in the painting of the devastated city, are like Jesus—innocent victims who endured agony and suffering—a passion.

This same motif was also widespread in West German Catholicism. An introduction to a booklet with the title "Conciliation at the Grave" (*Versöhnung über den Gräber*, a slogan of the Volksbund, discussed at length in the chapters that follow) has similar overtones. The booklet, which concerns the establishment of a proper cemetery for Wehrmacht dead in Belgium, was issued in 1955 by the Catholic publisher Kolping in Cologne. The introduction was by the Jesuit priest Theobald Rieth. Rieth opens with the quotation cited above: "Greater love has no one than this, that someone lay down his life for his friends." As far as he is concerned, that is the word of God and the final word on soldiers of all nations who fell in battle. Their deaths will be meaningless if the people for whom they sacrificed their lives do not offer their love. Otherwise, their deaths reflect nothing but a political power struggle, whose causes and circumstances no mortal can judge.[67] Here is an attempt to grant death in war an aura of holiness, while ignoring the political dimension and responsibility for the hostilities, which are presented as "beyond and hidden from human understanding."

This view of soldiers as martyrs found expression in other Catholic churches throughout Germany. Among the depictions of the Passion at the Church of Our Beloved Lady above the Waters (*Liebfrauen Überwasser*) in Münster stood a statue of the Pietà, Mary embracing the body of Jesus after his removal from the cross. Alongside the statue and the paintings is a book on a stone pedestal containing the names of soldiers who lost their lives in the war, with the dates of their births and deaths.

The Pietà is a frequent motif in central monuments in cemeteries established throughout Europe for German soldiers who died in World War II. In 1983, Memory Church in West Berlin installed, alongside a memorial plaque commemorating Protestant martyrs, a drawing with the title *The Madonna from Stalingrad*. The artist is Kurt Reuber, a surgeon who served in a Wehrmacht field hospital at Stalingrad and who died in Soviet captivity. Reuber, who was also a theologian, sketched the pic-

Figure 4. Kurt Reuber's *The Madonna from Stalingrad* (Courtesy Reuber's daughter, Ute Tolkmitt, and the Lutheran publisher LVH)

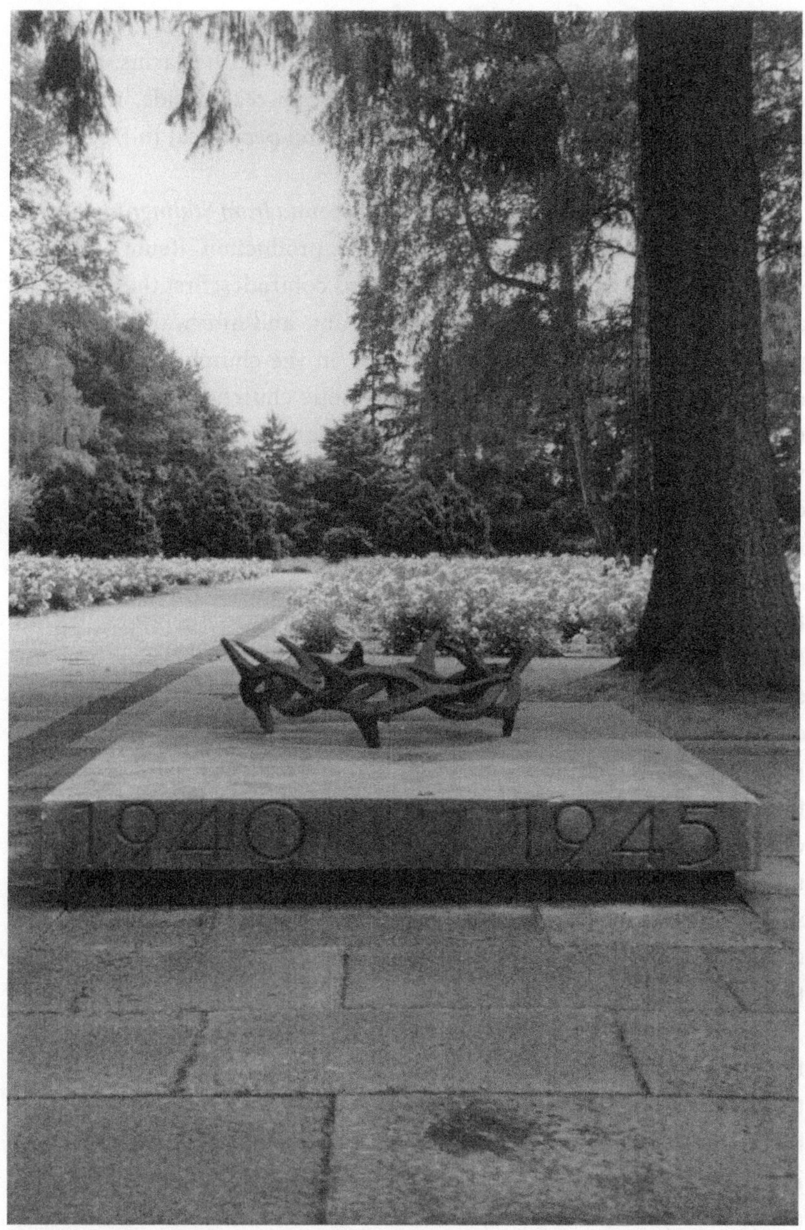

Figure 5. Egon Lissow's sculpture *The Crown of Thorns* at Ohlsdorf Cemetery

ture on the back of a Russian map in honor of Christmas 1942. The drawing shows the Madonna holding the child Jesus in her arms, and the words *Licht-Leben-Liebe* (light, life, love) inscribed alongside. The drawing first appeared on the cover of a Volksbund periodical in December 1952.

There is a connection between *The Madonna from Stalingrad,* its creator, and the dramatic circumstances of its production. Reuber was described as a martyr who gave his life for his comrades, first the wounded and dying Wehrmacht soldiers at the front, and afterward his fellow prisoners of war.[68] The drawing hanging in the church functions as a reliquary—a vessel found usually in Catholic churches, containing the remains or artifacts associated with a saint—for Germans who were killed in battle. The historical context of the tragic deaths of the surrounded soldiers grants *The Madonna from Stalingrad* the markers of a pietà, even if iconographically it is not one (but rather a Madonna and child). However, even the child in the drawing might appear to some as a dead child. It in fact represents the Germans who fell in Hitler's service. Their presentation as the victims of incalculable suffering elicits another Christian exegesis as well: their torment and death atones for their crimes and those of their comrades, just as the sacrifice of Jesus does for the sins of mankind. The placement of *The Madonna from Stalingrad,* with its Christian connotations, alongside the plaque for Protestant martyrs who were persecuted during the Nazi period, constitutes the creation of a model of visual memorialization that bears a message of Christian reconciliation between soldiers who represented the Nazi state and participated in the regime's crimes and those who fought against the regime and were murdered by the soldiers of these regime.

Such symbols were found not only in German churches. For example, the management of the Ohlsdorf Cemetery in Hamburg wished to honor the memories of civilian victims of the Allied bombardments who were buried there. In 1952, the artist Egon Lissow designed a bronze memorial in the form of the crown of thorns placed on Jesus's head as he was sent along his way of sorrows to his crucifixion.[69] This crown is also a common motif in many memorials to the expulsion from the east.[70] The obvious meaning, clear to any country with a Christian tradition like Germany's, is that the Allies sent the German people down the Via Dolorosa, and that the nation, like Jesus Christ, is sinless.

The Ruined Church Motif in the Landscape of Postwar German Memorialization

Many German churches, both Catholic and Protestant, that were damaged in the war have set aside a corner, sometimes even a chapel, in memory of the destruction of a house of prayer. A church building represents the Christian congregation. Prominently displaying wartime damage is tantamount to claiming that the Allied bombs were aimed at the Christian community. Numerous German churches were left in ruins, silent memorials of the war and, by implication, of German suffering.

East and West Germany dealt with this situation in similar ways, but for different reasons. In the GDR, the means and materials necessary for reconstructing the many devastated churches were lacking, and the Communists paid little attention to religion in general. In Rostock, for example, portions of the St. Nicholas Cathedral became apartment dwellings during the 1970s. Many churches were not reconstructed until after German reunification, the best known of which was the Church of Our Lady (*Frauenkirche*) in central Dresden. In Berlin, the ruins of the abbey of the Church of the Franciscan have been preserved as a remembrance site since 1951. In the late 1970s two sculptures, one a pieta (by Jürgen Pensow) and the other a mother and child, were erected in front of the ruins. And some churches, such as the Garnison Church in Potsdam, which symbolized the Prussian militaristic tradition, were demolished for political reasons.

In West Germany, at least two reconstructed churches showed the influence of Basil Spence's 1950 design of the rebuilt St. Michael's Cathedral in Coventry, which had been bombed during the German attack on the city in 1940. Spence had suggested keeping the ruins of the old cathedral there as a remembrance site and building a new cathedral alongside the ruins of the old. At the time, this was a most unconventional and daring architectonic concept.[71] The Kaiser Wilhelm Protestant Memory Church (*Gedächtnis Kirche*) in West Berlin is probably the best known of these structures. It was severely damaged in the Berlin bombardments of November 1943 and was not rebuilt. At the end of the 1950s, the architect Egon Eiermann won a competition for construction of a new church on the site. But when the public learned that the steeple of the wrecked church would be demolished, they protested. The local press urged on the protestors

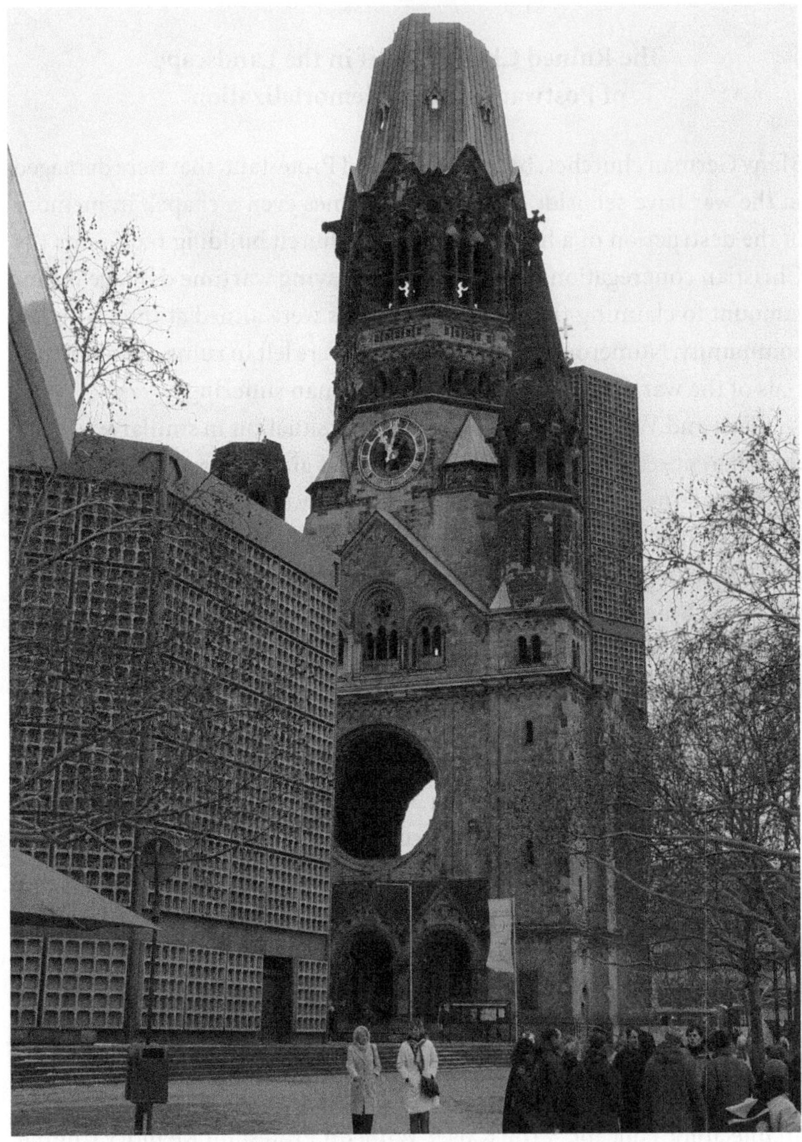

Figure 6. Kaiser Wilhelm's Memory Church in Berlin

and advocated leaving the ruined steeple "in the heart of Berlin."[72] In the end, Eiermann was persuaded that the steeple should remain in place, integrated into the new structure.[73] The steeple, he stressed, served as a memorial for the experiences of the war generation: "When all is said and done, there is no other structure like this ruin that can display to millions of human beings the grandeur and the suffering of their lives."[74]

The nave of the old church, topped by a scarred and ruined steeple, was preserved as a memorial hall (*Gedenkenhalle*). Since 1987, Berlin's Memory Church (which includes Eiermann's new church, constructed in the early 1960s, along with the ruins), serves also as an antiwar monument and a site calling for reconciliation between Germany and the nations it persecuted. A bronze plaque attached to the wall of the ruined steeple declares that the site has been left unrepaired "to bear witness to God's judgment on our people in the war years."[75] In other words, the consequences of the Nazis' belligerent policies is presented as divine judgment. The ruined building, bearing the scars of the war, constitutes a concrete expression of the suffering of the Germans and of their status as victims.

The Church of the Patron (Aegidien) in Hanover, the Church of St. Nicholas in Hamburg,[76] the Church of St. Alban in Cologne, and the Church of St. Christopher in Mainz also remained in ruins. The multiplicity of Coventry-like church ruins in the German urban landscape might express an unconscious notion that Germany, unlike Britain, had experienced many Coventries, implicitly competing with the message Spence wished to evoke with his design of St. Michael's. The architect Rudolf Schwarz, among the most important German church designers of the twentieth century, rehabilitated and rebuilt the structure adjacent to the ruined church in Cologne, the municipal hall dating from the Middle Ages known as the Gürzenich. Schwarz also seems to have been inspired by Spence's design in Coventry. He wrote that "the ruin warns that there is no end to the malice of the human heart." Did Schwarz mean the malice that led to war (Hitler)? Or was his intent the evil that destroyed the church (the Allied bombings)? It may well be that, like Bishop von Galen and many others in Germany, Schwarz meant the war in its entirety. If so, there is no essential difference between the Allies, who sought to end the war and put an end to the killing it engendered, and Nazi Germany, which sought to enslave and to murder.

Suffering, Victimization, and Reconciliation

Several German churches that preserved remains of their ruins as a symbol of German affliction established ties after the war with churches in

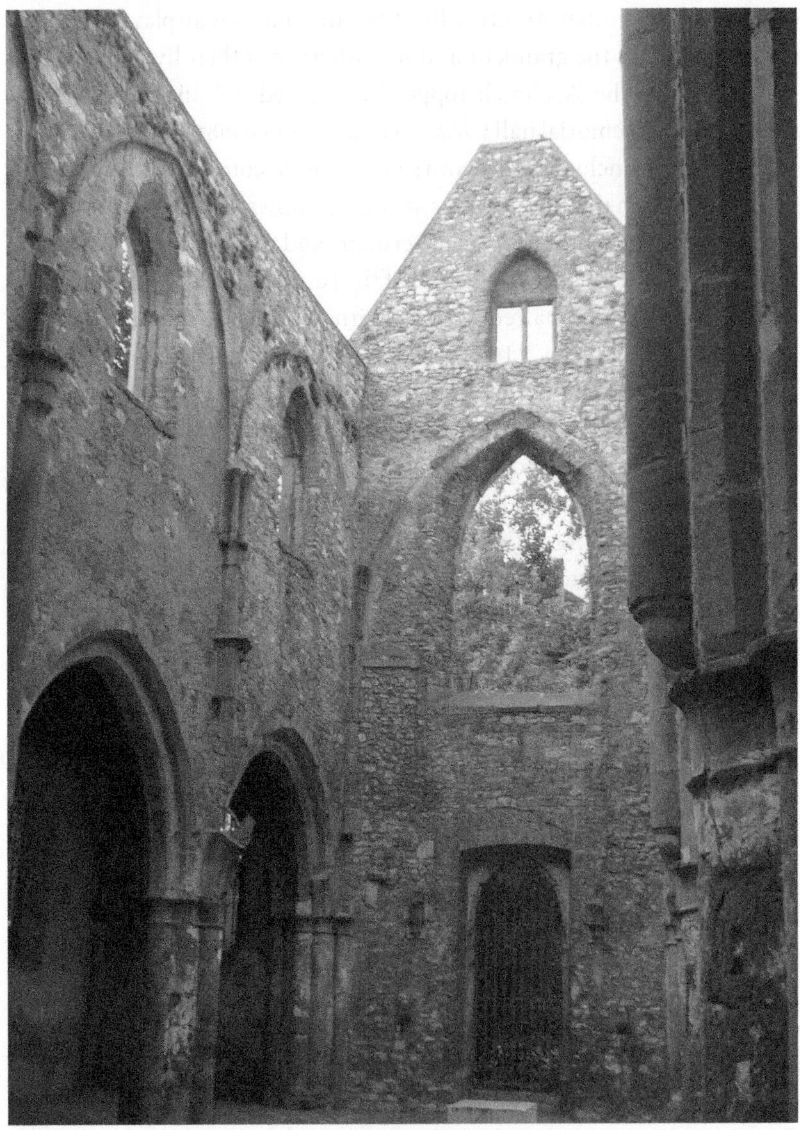

Figure 7. The ruined Church of St. Christopher in Mainz

countries that Germany ravished during it. Suffering, it seems, was the foundation for reconciliation between former enemies, and it has been an undoubtedly important component in the German memory of the war, in both German states and in the united Germany today.

The Memory Church in Berlin installed a cross from the cathedral in Coventry, a British city bombed by the Germans, as well as a Russian Orthodox icon. Similar articles were placed as well: A copy of the Stalingrad Madonna was placed at the Millennium Chapel in St. Michael Cathedral at Coventry, for example. These sacred objects were donated to the church by "the Christians of these countries," and they were placed next to an icon of the crucified Christ that had previously stood in the old church and had been damaged in the Allied bombing. All these "teach about reconciliation through Jesus" (*weisen . . . auf die Versöhnung durch Jesus Christus hin*). Items from the cathedral in Coventry, such as a cross of nails and various plaques, appear in numerous German churches. In the Münster Cathedral, for example, a plaque reads, "Forgive one another as God in Christ forgave you," a clear expression of the Christian notion of reconciliation, which also appears in the sermons of Helmut Thielicke and Martin Niemöller.

These emblems of reconciliation in the ruined church, which seem to symbolize the suffering inflicted on Germany's Christian community by the Allies, indicate an ostensible equivalency between the suffering of Germany's civilian population and that of the British and Russians during the war.

In a pastoral epistle issued in 1943 by the Catholic Council of Bishops in Fulda to its congregations, the writer lamented that the war was not being conducted as a knightly contest. Its conduct was merciless and barbarian, not sparing the lives of women and children, nor houses of God.[77] Despite its criticism of the German prosecution of the war, this balancing of the two sides is characteristic of the Catholic Church's treatment of the issue after the conflagration as well—it ignores the unprecedented brutality of the Germans. Furthermore, it overlooks the fact that, for many of the Christians in England and Russia with whom the German Church seeks conciliation, Nazi Germany (and the Germans, who are taken to be the representatives of its legacy) is not perceived as an enemy occupying the same moral plane, as was the case in World War I. This attitude persisted in the Christian preaching of the German clergies after 1945. The basis of this delineation is Hitler's criminal conduct of the war, in particular with regard to Soviet civilians (against whom German forces fought a racist war of extermination, lacking any trace of legality or morality), and the crimes against humanity committed under the cover of the war, such as the genocide of European Jewry. Nothing the Allies and their armies did was in any way similar. It is this distinction, in the consciousness of the nations who were the targets of Hitler's aggression or who fought against it, that granted the combat against Nazi Germany a unique status, different from that of any other war. The war, in their view, was between the German nation, which was generally perceived as a belligerent collective, and those nations that became its victims. The broad public support for Hitler's belligerent foreign policy so long as the Germans were not called on to pay the bill was evidence bolstering this position, which attributed the same intentions to the Nazi regime and to the German people as a whole.[78] In this view the Germans, who bore collective responsibility for the suffering of the nations who were the victims of Nazi aggression, had to take the initiative in reconciliation and meet their demands and requirements. It was not a reconciliation between equals.

The memorialization concept of Berlin's Memory Church reflects the subjective point of view of the German populace during the war. The Germans focused on their own suffering and thus had difficulty seeing it as a direct result of the Allied response to Hitler's war. The reconciliation they sought was between two ostensibly equal sides, in effect denying Germany's war guilt. Of course, in the Anglican Church at the end of the war and in 1965 among the Catholic bishops of Poland, there were those who responded to German Christians' calls for reconciliation.[79] But there were many Russians, Poles, and Britons who did not.[80] Such calls for reconciliation may simply have been perceived as an expression of the German public's profound need to be free of what it sensed to be its heavy burden of guilt, borne out of an awareness that there is no equivalence between German and Allied actions during the war, and certainly none between the experiences of ordinary Germans and of Europe's Jews at the time. Since 1945, the Germans have gradually become aware that the crimes its citizens committed in their name were unique and not comparable to the Allies' war policies.

Even though, since 1945, a majority of Germans have not been religious, it seems to me that the impression of Christian morality and conscience are still salient in many fundamental concepts in German culture. Even if German cultures of memory and memorialization of those harmed by the war are secular, they clearly adopt and integrate Christian models, motifs, and interpretations of guilt, suffering, reconciliation, and forgiveness. The Christian motif of suffering undoubtedly has great significance in the way individuals and large circles in German culture cope with their sense of guilt for the crimes of the Nazis. Indeed, many meanings are tied to this motif in German culture: in the traditional Christian view, national suffering is a means of atoning for guilt. In German nationalist tradition, however, this secularized motif served to establish and shape a German national community, and charged it with aggressive energy and an aspiration for revenge.

3

German Memory and Remembrance of the Dead from 1945 to the 1960s

Between World War II and the beginning of the Cold War, the German authorities, under the auspices of the Allied military governments, shaped an anti-Nazi policy of memory and memorialization. It adopted the point of view of Germans who opposed the Nazi regime, and honored the Nazis' victims and those who had fought against the Nazis.

The Third Reich's cult of the fallen had, in contrast, lionized sacrifice and death on the altar of the nation. Into this the regime subsumed civilian casualties, such as those killed in Allied bombings.

The postwar German authorities thus pondered the issue of how to publicly commemorate and memorialize those who fell in battle and others who lost their lives without awakening the demons of the all-too-recent past. Alongside the dominant trends of this period, other attitudes, sometimes contradictory, were widespread, and these sometimes affected local forms of commemoration. The establishment of two German states on the Reich's ruins opened the way to the consolidation of alternative cultures of commemoration and memorialization, shaped by the Cold War. Two factors made a major imprint: the anti-Nazi memory of the small group of Germans who opposed Hitler's Reich, and German national memory, constructed from the war experiences of the majority of Germans who had not opposed the regime and who at least partly adopted the official Nazi interpretation of those years. This memory reflected the contexts in which prominent circles in German society chose to understand the Nazi past and World War II. In this framework, a special place was reserved for German suffering during the war.

Official commemoration and memorialization policy after 1945 unequivocally denounced Nazi ideology and the murder of the Jews. It extolled the heroism of anti-Nazi fighters (the antifascist fighters in the Communist east, and the conspirators of July 20, 1944, in the democratic west). It also included some manifestations of explicit identification with the torment the Jews and others suffered at the hands of the Nazis.

However, in parallel to their official commitment to the anti-Nazi legacy, German postwar commemoration policies also reflected a certain loyalty to a different German legacy, one that was definitely not anti-Nazi but rather understanding and uncritical of any number of aspects of co-operation between German society and the Nazi regime. It emphasized both the suffering endured by civilians during the war and the tragic heroism of soldiers. This approach was persistently and explicitly present in German political culture after 1945, even more so after the breakout of the Cold War and the consequent establishment of two German states in 1949.

These two heritages were woven into a kind of master narrative,[1] evident in the two official cultures of commemoration in the two states. The resulting German national narrative displayed understanding of the reality in which broad swaths of German society found themselves trapped during the Third Reich. The Jewish narratives of the Holocaust and the Anglo-Saxon narratives of the war were judgmental—the German people were regarded collectively as bearing political and moral responsibility for the crimes committed in their name. However, the two versions of this narrative (the Communist one of the GDR and the democratic one of the FRG) empathized with the predicament of the Reich's citizens and the morally problematic decisions they made regarding the Nazi regime and its crimes. In this narrative, not only the civilians killed in the war but also the fallen soldiers were victims of the war and the dictatorship, just as the Jews were. "The German Soldier" (the term they used to refer to all German soldiers, thus avoiding an unequivocal distinction between the Wehrmacht and the Waffen-SS) was not held to be collectively accountable for the crimes they committed; Hitler and the political leadership bore sole responsibility.[2] Germans did not regard the uniqueness of the Jewish genocide to be obscured by their narrative's equating of the slaughtered Jews with Germany's war dead and civilian casualties, or with the depiction of both the Holocaust and World War II as a kind of divine fate. In other words, this narrative implicitly diminished German responsibility for the crimes committed by the Nazi regime.

This chapter surveys and analyzes the manifestations of this master narrative—which I call the "reconciliation narrative"—in the official commemoration and memorialization policies instituted in the two German states. The narrative originated a few months after the end of the war in 1945. After the establishment of the two Germanys in 1949, its two variants mirrored the political cultures in the East and West.

The awakening of public discourse on the Holocaust in the Federal Republic beginning in the 1950s was largely a product of the Jewish Holocaust narrative's penetration into German discourse. The Jewish story entered German consciousness principally through literary and documentary works by Jews about their Holocaust experiences, written or translated into German, but also through the writings of German authors such as Albrecht Goes (mentioned in chapter 1). One of these was the poet Paul Celan's collection *Mohn und Gedächtnis* (Poppy and Remembrance), with its impressive "Death Fugue" (*Todesfuge*), which appeared in 1952. Another was the theatrical version of *The Diary of Anne Frank*, which Germans staged throughout the country in 1956, a year after the play's premiere.

From the late 1950s this awareness deepened, especially among the media[3] and the younger generation in West Germany,[4] and particularly after charges were leveled by East German propaganda and prosecutors against former Nazi criminals who were still active in the West German administration, including the legal and medical systems.[5] These exposés and the scandals they produced turned the Nazi past into a major topic of Cold War propaganda between the two Germanys and into a central weapon in their struggle for legitimization. The highest West German official whose Nazi past was exposed was the West German minister for the refugees and expellees, Theodor Oberländer.[6] In 1959 he was accused of involvement in the murder of Jews in Lvov in 1941. Oberländer and, at first, Chancellor Konrad Adenauer tried to portray the East German accusations as Communist slander, but in the end the former Nazi minister was forced to resign. A couple of years later, Oberländer's successor, Hans Krüger, was accused of having handed down death penalties in his capacity as a Nazi-era judge.[7] The fact that successive ministers for refugees and expellees, both central activists in the expellees organization and parties, were accused of involvement in Nazi crimes cast doubt on the reliability of the expellees' narrative of suffering, which had been continually equated with the suffering of the Jews and was an integral part of the official reconciliation narrative in West Germany.[8]

Another factor that contributed to deepening public preoccupation with the past was the wave of antisemitic graffiti, including swastikas, which began in Cologne in the winter of 1959 (almost at the same time as the Oberländer scandal) and spread throughout the new republic. The Eichmann trial in Jerusalem and the Auschwitz trials in Frankfurt in the early 1960s, and their tremendous echoes in the German media, also played an important role in this process.

In the two decades that followed, an ever-increasing body of information about the Holocaust was presented to the public.[9] The Jewish narrative grew more pervasive, tarnishing the reconciliation narrative and pushing it out of the central position it had occupied in West Germany's political culture during the first postwar decade. Nevertheless, this master narrative remained an important component of the commemoration policies of both German states in the years that followed.

The Reconciliation Narrative in East Germany

In February 1942, Stalin said: "It would be absurd to identify Hitler's gang with the German people, or with the German state. History teaches that Hitlers come and go, but the German people and the German state remain."[10] The Soviets and the German Communists used Marxist tools to analyze the phenomenon of fascism. They maintained that its principal causes were the capitalist system and German financiers and industrialists. The distinction between "trust capitalists and Nazi criminals" and the German people, who were both seduced and terrorized by the Nazis, was a recurrent theme in the wartime speeches of Wilhelm Pieck, a veteran Communist Party leader and later the first president of the GDR, in his Soviet exile. Some of them were broadcasted to Nazi Germany.[11]

Thus, when the war ended, the USSR aimed to reeducate the German citizenry in their zone of occupation as well as transform its socioeconomic system. Only that, they believed, could prevent a resurgence of fascism. Indeed, the Soviet leadership and military administration acted on the basis of this Marxist analysis, as well as under the constraints of the circumstances they faced. Thus at the dawn of the Cold War, they allowed the German Communist Party and its successor, the Socialist Unity Party (SED), to institute a unique policy of commemoration. It addressed the German people's responsibility for allowing Hitler to gain power and for war to break out. But it also included reconciliatory aspects that were forgiving of the German people, and more in tune with the German collective memory of Nazism and the war. These motifs were less judgmental toward the German masses regarding their indirect responsibility for Nazi atrocities. Germans interviewed by Morris Janowitz in 1946 stressed that the broadcasts of Radio Berlin, a station sponsored by the Red Army, were "not so unfriendly to the German people" as were those of the BBC and Radio Luxemburg, which were sponsored by the Western Allies. Radio Berlin, they said, "drew a distinction between the guilty and those who merely stood by." In other words, they did not stress the German people's collective guilt and responsibility for Nazi crimes.[12]

At the end of the war, the Communist Party portrayed Wehrmacht commanders "[Wilhelm] Keitel, [Alfred] Jodl, and their collaborators [as] agents of reactionary militarism." This was the language, for example, of the first public appeal issued by the party's Central Committee on June 11, 1945. But this public document, like many others published by the party, refrained from explicitly censuring low-ranking Wehrmacht soldiers for their behavior during the war. This was the case even though such censure was implicit in the discussion of the German people's guilt in publications and speeches by functionaries of the Communist Party, and afterward by those of the SED, at least until the beginning of the Cold War.[13]

In early July 1945, the Communist Party newspaper *Deutsche Volkszeitung* reported on the decisions made at the first meeting of the Berlin City Council's Chief Committee for the Victims of Fascism (*Hauptausschuss "Opfer des Fascismus"*). The Committee acknowledged that millions of human beings had suffered under the Nazi regime. However, it restricted recognition as a victim of fascism, and the assistance that such status brought, only to Germans who had actively fought the regime. The Committee itemized the different categories of passive victims:

> The victims of fascism number in the millions: those who lost their homes and property; men who were forced to enlist and who were stationed in Hitler's battalions; those who were forced to give up their lives for Hitler's criminal war; the Jews who were persecuted and murdered as victims of

fascist racialist madness; Jehovah's Witnesses; and those who refused to work (defined as "work-shy" by the Nazis). But the category cannot be stretched this far.[14]

The Communist oligarchy in the Soviet zone of occupation indeed stressed the German people's role in Nazi crimes. But it preferred to view all Germans as having suffered under Nazi rule and during the war. It evinced the same attitude toward soldiers killed in action in Hitler's service. They, too, were victims, like the persecuted Jews, rather than Hitler's faithful servants who carried out his murderous policies.

Literature and film in the Soviet zone of occupation, and afterward in East Germany, seldom addressed the simple Wehrmacht soldier's responsibility and blame for atrocities in which he participated. Probably the only work published in East Germany that raised this issue, and in which the murderers are the protagonists, was Franz Fühmann's novella of 1955, *Kameraden* (Comrades). It concerns several Wehrmacht soldiers who unintentionally kill their commander's daughter and then try to cover up their crime. The novella addresses the distortion of the value of soldierly brotherhood in the Nazi army.[15]

In contrast, the Wehrmacht soldier was portrayed as the victim of fascism in Wolfgang Staudte's well-known 1946 film, *Die Mörder sind unter uns* (The Murderers among Us). The film recounts the love of a German solider, Dr. Hans Mertens, and a young woman, Susanne Wallner, who has returned from a concentration camp. Mertens was involved in the murder of civilians in Poland who were executed in retribution for an attack on German soldiers. The trauma he suffered as a result of this deed prevents him from returning to his work as a surgeon. It is not clear whether Mertens took an active role in the massacre or only abetted the crime. In any case, the vision of the slaughter haunts him and he reacts with a wall of indifference, cynicism, and even despair with life. Susanne was incarcerated for political reasons—her father was a Social Democrat. In the end, however, love is victorious. It overcomes the couple's difficulties, which grow out of the mental disturbance the doctor suffered as a result of the war. The acceptance and unconditional love of a Nazi victim for a traumatized Wehrmacht soldier heal and redeem the doctor's tortured soul. The message of Staudte's film was consistent with the position taken at the time by the Chief Committee for the Victims of Fascism and the Communist leadership. In parallel with preaching antifascism and condemning Nazism, Communists called for reconciliation between those harmed by the Nazi regime and the vast majority of the Germans who cooperated with it—even Wehrmacht soldiers like Hans Mertens who, despite their deeds, are perceived as victims of fascism.[16]

Even after twelve years of Nazi rule, the Communist Party adhered to the classic left-wing interpretation of the political development of capitalism and the fascist phenomenon. In this view, fascism was a device used by monopolistic capital to repress the German working masses, as the Comintern had stated in 1933.[17] The party's public declaration of June 11, 1945, and the SED's platform of April 1946 made this explicit.[18] The implication was that Hitler had been the representative of the German bourgeoisie, not an elected leader who had enjoyed broad popular support from all sectors of German society, including the working class.

Absolving low-ranking soldiers of responsibility for their actions, as did the declaration of the Chief Committee for the Victims of Fascism, was characteristic of the traditional outlook of the revolutionary workers' movements. In this view, one of the favorite methods by which reactionary regimes "tame" the masses is to coerce them into military service and send them into battle.[19] Implicit in this view is that soldiers are not personally responsible for their actions in the service of a reactionary regime. Many leaders of the SED, including Walter Ulbricht, Wilhelm Pieck, and Ernst Thälmann, the leader of the Communist Party during the Weimar Republic and the party's most prominent Communist martyr of the Nazi persecution, served in the Kaiser's army in World War I, even though they opposed the war politically. Thälmann deserted only at the end of the war.

However, application of the left's traditional view of the German soldiers of World War II completely ignores the utterly different nature of Nazi war conduct, especially in the war against the Soviet Union, as compared with the way German forces conducted themselves in World War I. Many of the millions of indoctrinated Wehrmacht troops who fought in World War II demonstrated Nazi convictions and absolute obedience and loyalty to their leadership, at a time that the army was deeply involved, in an unprecedented way, in committing war crimes and crimes against humanity.

The left's traditional view was not, however, the only factor that influenced the Communist leadership. In adopting this position, the Communists sought to gain the sympathy of the German public. After all, many men had served Hitler's criminal regime, and even more had supported the Führer. When the Communists formulated their commemoration policy, they had to take into account the prevailing mood in Germany. People there were alienated by anti-Nazi memorial practices and, consequently, by those who had decreed those practices—namely, the Communist state's political leaders, many of whom had been sent to concentration camps or exiled to the enemy countries that had later defeated Nazi Germany. In other words, the leadership needed to integrate itself with postwar German society, so it refrained from criticizing the behavior of low-ranking Wehrmacht soldiers during the war, who numbered millions in the GDR. While the SED's commemoration policy was unequivocally antifascist in character, it nevertheless included elements that clearly had their origin in the collective memory of millions of demobilized Wehrmacht soldiers and Nazi Party members.[20]

Dorothee Wierling's study stresses the central place of the German sense of victimhood in the consciousness of the Hitler Youth generation in East Germany, and that generation's conveyance of this sensibility to their children who were born in Communist Germany. She argues that these family memories, which stressed how parents and grandparents suffered during and especially at the end of war and afterward, occupied a larger space in the consciousness of the generation of 1949 than did the official antifascist memory of the heroes who had fought Nazism.[21] The work of Harald Welzer on the intergenerational transference of the war experience in the Federal Republic also points to the centrality of the sense of victimhood in the stories the war generation told to their children and grandchildren.[22]

The Communists intended to participate in the democratic process and thus needed to seek the good graces of the German voting public, especially given their ambition of keeping Germany united. As a consequence, the Communists had to find the means to persuade the residents of the American, British, and French zones of occupation that their position was the correct one. After the Austrian Communist Party's failure at the polls in the fall of 1945, the German Communists abstained, beginning in 1946, from taking too stringent an anti-Nazi line that might distance them from the masses of "nominal Nazis" (those who joined the Nazi Party for opportunistic rather than ideological reasons). In early January 1946, Wilhelm Pieck said in a speech in Halle:

> If we make distinctions in judging these criminals, and we are aware that with the help of socialist demagogy and repression the fascists were able to draw large parts of our people into the Nazi Party or associated organizations, we do so knowing that these masses have not been lost to our people. Rather, they need to be made aware how they were misled, and that it is their duty to work with us together, in a single front, to build our country.
>
> We tell them openly that they have greater responsibility [than others] for the fact that Hitler was able to carry out his crimes. But we do not espouse a permanent ban. We want these forces, who were simple party members, in other words "nominal Nazis." We wish to allow them to work at the front of our struggle, to prove themselves, and to again win trust.[23]

Pieck repeated these sentiments on several occasions, significantly toning down the collective guilt approach that had characterized the party's public declaration of June 1945.

The SED leadership began to integrate former Nazi Party members into public life. With the commencement of the Cold War, officials of the Soviet military administration began to do the same. In March 1948, the Soviet military administration halted de-Nazification proceedings in their zone of occupation. The Soviets acknowledged that "the Socialist Union Party is not the decisive political force in the Soviet zone of occupation, and that it has not become the true leader of the German people."[24] In June 1948, the SED leadership—in particular Walter Ulbricht's circle—and representatives of the Soviet military administration consulted with Stalin on the establishment of a new political framework. The National Front was to be an umbrella group of mass organizations and movements from all sectors of the public that would support the SED's pro-Soviet policies throughout Germany. According to the plan, the National Front would use German nationalist propaganda to gain broad popular support.[25] At the initiative of the Soviet military administration, the National Democratic Party of Germany (NDPD) was also established in the Soviet zone. Its goal was to enlist Wehrmacht veterans and former Nazis to help promote a pro-Soviet policy.[26]

In the first elections to the Bundestag in West Germany, in August 1949, the Communist Party suffered a painful beating, receiving only slightly more than five percent of the vote.[27] The results confirmed the assumption of the Soviet military administration and the Communist leadership in Moscow that only a nationalist propaganda line that would appeal to a much larger portion of the German public could motivate the masses to support the SED and its policies.

Some in the party leadership feared the adoption of nationalist messages, but that nevertheless is the direction the party took.[28] In November 1949, with the establishment of the German Democratic Republic in East Germany, its provisional parliament, the Volkskammer, enacted a law "on the measures of atonement and granting of civil rights to members of the Nazi Party and its supporters, and to officers of the fascist Wehrmacht."[29] Speaking to the Volkskammer, Walter Ulbricht, vice-chairman of the SED, justified the Communist regime's policy of integrating former Nazi Party members and Wehrmacht officers. "There is evidence," he maintained, "that these circles have recognized the mistakes of the past. Now they are devoting all their energies to building democracy."[30] Regarding the SED policy of exclusion of former SPD members and dissidents from its ranks, it was extremely generous in allowing former Nazis into its ranks: between eight and ten percent of its members at the beginning of the 1950s had belonged to the Nazi Party. The National Democratic Party (NDPD) had a similar, or perhaps smaller, level of former Nazis among its members.[31]

In the years 1949–1950, the anti-Western propaganda line leveled against the Federal Republic by East Germany and by the Communist Party in West Germany on foreign affairs and the question of Germany's future (the so-called *deutsche Frage*) had salient nationalist features. This Soviet-inspired propaganda was a blend of nationalist slogans condemning the West and general expressions of a desire for peace, German unification, and socialism. "Korea for the Koreans—Germany for the Germans (*Deutschland den Deutschen*)" was Wilhelm Pieck's cry when, as the Democratic Republic's president, he addressed the National Front's first national congress in August 1950.[32] This genuine *völkisch* and Nazi slogan also appeared in Martin Hellberg's prize-winning East German film of 1952, *Das verurteilte Dorf* (The Doomed Village),[33] in a scene in which farmers demonstrate against U.S. forces stationed in the Federal Republic. The phrase is even used today in extreme rightist and neo-Nazi circles, mostly against non-German immigrants who came as guest workers beginning in the late 1950s and still remain.

Similar slogans, such as "the struggle for the unity of German culture and against its degeneration and depreciation," or that condemn "cosmopolitan theories hostile to the people, against bourgeois objectivism and against American cultural barbarism," were no more than refurbished versions of images and metaphors from the Nazi past.[34] The campaign against Zionism and its "covert agents" in the early 1950s, which included purges, had a manifestly antisemitic character.[35]

A peculiar expression of these nationalist tendencies can be found in the surprising pronouncements of prominent representatives of East Germany's ruling party with regard to Wehrmacht veterans. The party was trying to mobilize them to support its cause. So, for example, in an article that appeared in 1952 in an anthology on the national question (the future of Germany), Albert Norden, a member of the Politburo of the SED Central Committee and one of the top men in the East German propaganda machine, wrote:

> We know that hundreds of thousands of German officers and NCOs in World War II believed with all their souls that they were going out into the [battle] field for the sake of Germany. [They believed] that they were sharing their soldiers' suffering and death on the front line. They had the courage to do this because they assumed that they were serving for the sake of the homeland [*Heimat*]. Their willingness to sacrifice was boundless: these men bled, thinking of the homeland until their last moment. The honorable German officer corps of 1914 to 1918 and of 1939 to 1945—and we are not referring to those whose hands drip innocent blood—believed, to the best of their awareness and conscience, that they were acting for Germany.[36]

This was not an official act of clearing the name of the German soldier, as in Chancellor Adenauer's speech to the Bundestag in Bonn at the beginning of the 1950s (discussed later in this chapter). Nevertheless, Norden's words are quite similar to the praise heaped on Germany's fallen troops of World War II by Theodor Heuss, the Federal Republic's first president, and other West German political figures at that time.[37]

Films and books produced in the Soviet zone of occupation and later in East Germany express the ruling party's position on the issue of integrating Wehrmacht veterans into public life. They depict the soldiers during the war, upon their return home afterward, or after spending time in Soviet POW camps (*Heimkehrer*) as passive. These soldiers never supported the Nazi regime or its ideology enthusiastically. In some of the works, the soldier who returns home tosses aside his passivity in the time of the Third Reich and promises to take an active, even aggressive position against fascism and its ally, capitalism, and in favor of socialism and peace. As Frank Biess emphasizes, antifascist commitment could be a truly redemptive moment for the returnees in the GDR.[38] Funk, the protagonist of *Die Rückkehr* (The Return), a story by Anna Seghers, is characteristic of this returning soldier:

> Up to this point, Funk took care to remain silent at every assembly. He was silent at assemblies of the Labor Front during Hitler's time. And when Free Germany [an organization established under the sponsorship of the German Communist Party in exile in the Soviet Union, in July 1943, which sought to enlist Wehrmacht POWs in support of Soviet policy and to call on their comrades to lay down their arms] convened an assembly in the POW camp, he didn't open his mouth. Now, so he thought, it's a little different. I'm free. He put his name down to speak.[39]

Heinz Weimann, the hero of Hellberg's film *The Doomed Village*, is a soldier who returns from Soviet captivity. Now, unlike in the past, he takes an active stance and leads the people of his village in their struggle against the Federal Republic authorities. The government seeks to evacuate the village and built a military airfield to serve U.S. forces. Weimann is arrested for his opposition to the evacuation. At his trial, he tells the judge: "I lost ten years of my life because of the war. Because then [during the Third Reich], there were not enough people who opposed the state's criminal power."[40]

Nevertheless, despite its policy of reconciliation and integration, and in contrast with the official memorial ceremonies for the war dead in the Federal Republic, East Germany never established a memorial day in memory of its fallen soldiers of World War II. In April 1950, the Ministry of the Interior ruled that "political monuments" would come under its sole purview, not that of other bodies. One purpose was to prevent the establishment of memorials to the fallen.[41] In November 1950, a high official in the Ministry of Popular Education (*Volksbildung*) in the state of Saxony-Anhalt by the name of Elchlepp stated that Wehrmacht dead should not be honored as heroes, and that no memorials (*Ehrenmaeler*) would be built for them. In guidelines he issued for his state's schools he wrote:

> Our soldiers were not heroes, because they did not fight to defend home, nor did they help realize lofty ideals for the sake of the nobility in man.

> ... The Soviet soldiers and their commanders are the heroes in the true sense of the word: they defended a homeland that was treacherously attacked.[42]

His was the official line. And, in fact, no Wehrmacht memorials were built in East Germany, with one exception (discussed at length below) at the Neue Wache in central Berlin. It was dedicated in 1960 as the German Democratic Republic's central site in honor of the victims of fascism and militarism, on the occasion of the fifteenth anniversary of the war's end.

The members of the Volksbund in Dresden[43] reported that the Communist state's authorities cared only for cemeteries where Red Army soldiers were buried. Wehrmacht plots were neglected. According to the Volksbund representatives in Dresden, anyone who looked after Wehrmacht graves during the Communist period was liable to be called in for questioning by the State Security Service (the Stasi).

The second largest World War II military cemetery in East Germany is located in Halbe in Brandenburg. It contains some 22,000 graves. A local pastor cared for them at his own initiative and with financial assistance from the Volksbund.[44]

According to central figures in the Communist oligarchy, Wehrmacht veterans were generally regarded as victims of Nazism, and former members of the Nazi Party who committed themselves to the SED's creed were accepted as penitents.[45] Paradoxically, however, they had a difficult time seeing the Jews, the Nazis' principal victims, as having suffered uniquely under fascism (even though they did not deny that the Jews had been persecuted). The first convention of the Chief Committee of the Victims of Fascism, on June 28, 1945, in Berlin, resolved that even though the Jews suffered, they were not "victims of fascism" because they did not fight the Nazis. They were the regime's passive victims. Therefore, the general welfare authorities were to care for Jewish Holocaust survivors, not the Chief Committee of the Victims of Fascism—which helped only those who actively opposed the Nazi regime. Only when the Jewish delegate Julius Meyer protested, along with church official Heinrich Grüber, was the decision changed. Even then, however, the revision was the result of political considerations rather than sincere recognition of Jewish suffering. At the end of September 1945, the organization amended its decision to state that "the Jews are also victims of fascism." However, prejudice did not disappear entirely.[46]

Figure 8. The memorial designed by Fritz Cremer at Buchenwald

This distinction between "victims" (*Opfer*) and "fighters" (*Kämpfer*) was part of the party's concept that the Communists had been Nazism's principal victims, whereas the persecution of the passive, mostly bourgeois Jews had been intended merely as a warning of what was to happen to the Communists.[47] German memorialization policy focused on fighters against fascism. They were perceived as the state's founding heroes. States and squares were named after them—especially after Ernst Thälmann.[48] Many memorials for those who fought fascism and for those who were incarcerated in the Nazi concentration camps for their political (usually Communist) convictions were erected in the German Democratic Republic.[49]

Toward the end of the 1950s, memorials and museums in honor of the Nazis' victims were built by the state on the sites of concentration camps in East Germany—Buchenwald, Sachsenhausen, and Ravensbrück. Next to the Buchenwald site, a kind of monumental secular temple was built in memory of the heroic struggle of the antifascist fighters.[50] It was a site of official pilgrimage and ceremonies in the GDR, and many young people have visited there. The Jewish victims were generally perceived as an integral part of the general class of the persecuted, and were not assigned prominent separate memorials.

At Buchenwald, a plaque with a Hebrew inscription was installed:

> Here were imprisoned, from November 1938 until February 1939, some 10,000 Jews: boys, men, and elderly. Six hundred of them were brutally murdered because of the criminal racism of the German fascists.

Official memorialization completely ignored other persecuted groups held in these camps, among them Sinti and Roma (Gypsies), homosexuals, and Jehovah's Witnesses.[51]

The first visual manifestation of the reconciliation narrative in East Germany was the design of the avenue at the Heidefriedhof Cemetery in Dresden (discussed in chapter 5). However, this memorial did not serve as a central place of commemoration in East Germany.

The country's central memorial for victims of fascism and militarism was at the Neue Wache, on Unter den Linden Avenue in central Berlin. It was a small neoclassical structure designed by the architect Karl Friedrich Schinkel in 1816–1818. Having served initially as the seat of the municipal guard, it later became a memorial to those German soldiers who fought Napoleon. At the end of the Weimar period, it was decided that the building would serve as a memorial to the dead of World War I. Its interior was redesigned by Heinrich Tessenow, who created a single interior space, opening a circular skylight in the ceiling that cast light onto a stone pillar in the center of the room. The pillar was adorned with a silver wreath of oak leaves. At the beginning of the Third Reich, the site became a central memorial (*Reichsehrenmal*) to heroes and played an important role in the Reich's Heroes' Memorial Day (*Heldengedenktag*) ceremony. These were large public observances graced by the presence of army and SS chiefs and the Führer, who placed wreaths on the site in memory of the dead. The building was destroyed during the war. The oak wreath disappeared (it was discovered in 1960 and is now located in the New-Cologne cemetery in Berlin).

In February 1949, representatives of the Free Democratic Youth (FDJ), the youth wing of the SED, proposed that the remains of the shattered building be demolished. They apparently believed that the structure was a typical symbol of Prussian militarism and its extension into the Nazi period, and therefore, like similar monuments such as the Berlin city palace (*Berliner Stadtschloss*) or the Garnison church at Potsdam, should be torn down. The proposal was rejected, partly because of public opposition.[52]

In August 1950, the Berlin City Council (*Magistrat*) proposed to build on the site a memorial to the victims of the wars against imperialism (*die Opfer der imperialistischen Kriege*). The municipal public works department quickly announced a competition for design of the structure. The call for designs implicitly sought to preserve the building's traditional function as a memorial to fallen soldiers, and to integrate that with the Communist worldview of the beginning of the Cold War.[53] The site's importance and the national significance of the decision seem to have led a higher-ranking body—the SED Central Committee's Secretariat—to take up the issue. The Secretariat rejected the proposal.[54] It may have been deterred by concern that it would perpetuate the Third Reich's cult of the fallen soldier.

In 1960, Mayor Friedrich Ebert placed before the city council the ruling party's proposal to build a memorial (*Mahnmal*) at the Neue Wache site to the victims of fascism and militarism. The rebuilt site would be presented to the citizenry on May 8, the fifteenth anniversary of the liberation from the Nazis. The proposal was accepted.[55] It combined the desire to establish a memorial to the victims of fascism in Berlin (proposed in the summer of 1949 but never carried out)[56] with the aspiration that the antifascist legacy be integrated with the German national tradition of the cult of the fallen soldier. The reconstruction of the site preserved the principal contours of the Tessnow building of the 1930s. An honor guard of the National People's Army (NVA) was stationed at the entrance, from the 1960s until the German Democratic Republic's demise. Its presence was a constant reminder of the continuity of the German military tradition and its intimate ties to this memorial site. In 1969, on East Germany's twentieth anniversary, the site was renovated by Lothar Kwasnitza. The ashes of an unknown Wehrmacht soldier, killed in battle in 1945 in the area of Görlitz, were interred there, along with those of an anonymous resistance fighter who had been imprisoned in a concentration camp and shot by an SS man in April 1945 in the area of Zittau. The ashes were covered with soil brought from World War II battlefields: Moscow, Leningrad, Stalingrad, Normandy, Monte Cassino, Narvik, Warsaw, Prague (Lidice and Dukla), and from Auschwitz, Mauthausen, Natzweiler, Theresienstadt, Dachau, Buchenwald, Sachsenhausen, Ravensbrück, and Dora-Mittelbau.[57] This imbued the memorial with a sacral character that had nationalist roots. The message it conveyed was that the blood of fallen soldiers sanctified the clods of earth it soaked. The symbolic mixing of soil from battlefields

Figure 9. The interior of Neue Wache, 1969 (Landesarchiv Berlin)

and concentration camps implied a brotherhood of blood between German soldiers slain in battle and the antifascist fighters incarcerated in the concentration camps. It proclaimed national reconciliation between the persecutors and the persecuted—the victims of the regime, represented by the antifascist tradition of the Communist oligarchy as having been politically persecuted, and the Wehrmacht soldier who died in battle and who personified the national German heritage of combat and the values associated with it. The redesign of the Neue Wache stressed the great similarity between the perception of the fallen soldiers as victims of Nazism in the cultures of memorialization and remembrance, both in Communist East Germany and in its democratic rival.

The Reconciliation Narrative in the Commemoration Policy of the Western Zones of Occupation and the Federal Republic

The reeducation policy pursued by the Allies in the Western zones of occupation accused the entire German people—sometimes explicitly, sometimes implicitly—of responsibility for Nazism and its crimes. Only infrequently, however, did the Germans respond with penitence and identification with the Nazis' victims, the Jews included, and their suffering. Only a small number defended the Nazi regime's treatment of the Jews. But many more claimed that the Jews' own behavior brought catastrophe upon themselves.[58]

The equation of German and Jewish suffering was more than just the conventional wisdom in neighborhood and village pubs. The German commemoration and memorial culture endorsed this claim in some places even during the Allied occupation, with the approval of the military administrations.

Take, for example, the case of Frankfurt. In April 1946, Germany's first post-Nazi memorial to the war dead was erected. It was dedicated to the soldiers who were slain in battle, to the civilians killed in the Allied bombings and, in addition, to the Nazi regime's victims—among them the German Jews.

In this case the memorial was not a new one. Instead, a monument that had been erected in 1920 to the military dead of World War I was restored. When the Nazis came to power in 1933, they removed the monument.

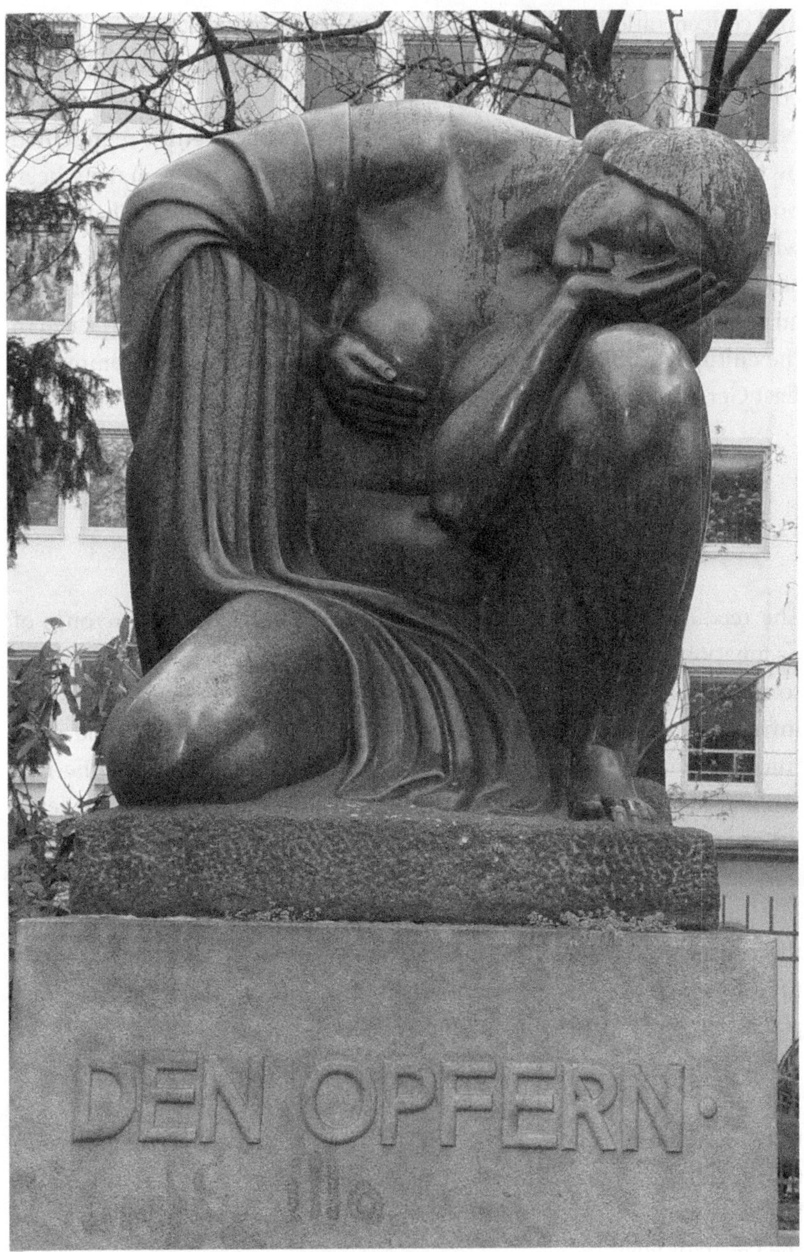

Figure 10. Benno Elkan's sculpture in Frankfurt

Its feminine character—a bare-breasted woman mourning her sons[59]—clashed with the new regime's nationalist cult of masculine heroism. Furthermore, the sculptor was a Jew, Benno Elkan, who left Germany soon after Hitler's ascendance to power in 1933 (he later designed the menorah erected outside Israel's Knesset building in Jerusalem).[60] Inscribed on the pedestal were the words "for the victims" (*den Opfern*). In December 1945, Frankfurt's Christian Democratic mayor, Dr. Kurt Blaum, who had been appointed by the American military administration, called for the reinstatement of Elkan's sculpture:

> I expect . . . that it will be dedicated to the memory of the victims of the two world wars and of the period of the Nazi regime. . . . Since the monument was originally erected for all the victims of World War I, it is likely to correspond with the notion of Frankfurt's citizens that from this point forward it will be dedicated to "all the victims," of all types, during the years 1914–1945. In this way we will also properly honor the artistic accomplishment of the sculptor, Benno Elkan.[61]

The sculpture was rededicated at a public ceremony on a most significant date—Holy Thursday (*Gründonnerstag*), the eve of Jesus's death. Dr. Blaum gave an address laying out his concept of commemoration. It became the prevailing concept in Germany, especially after the outbreak of the Cold War:

> Today we wish to dedicate this monument to all the victims who made sacrifices for Germany from 1914 to 1945, to those who lost their lives or their health at the front, during both world wars, or in the aerial bombings at home. But also for those who were sacrificed during the criminal era of the most brutal treatment of human beings, at a time when the murder of human beings in battle with the enemy was raised almost to a level of sanctity.[62]

Blaum's pointed criticism was aimed not only at the Nazis, but also at the Western Allies who had bombed Germany's cities. In his view, those who fought against Germany's civilians were no better morally than those responsible for the extermination of Europe's Jews.

Eberhard Beckmann, director of the municipal department of stages and concerts, spoke in the same spirit:

> The graves are too numerous to count: mass graves and piles of bones and cities of ash. They would not exist but for militarism and Nazism.

> Graves of Germans, for whom the irresponsible plans of the authorities and officials were fateful. The graves of Jews, who were good Germans, and precisely for that reason became the victims of coercive antisemitism, as did their brethren in faith in other countries. The graves of people of other nations, whose doom was sealed because of the cravings of a nation lacking room [to live].[63]

These formulations show that the reconciliation narrative, which placed all victims of the war and of Nazism in the same category (at least in Beckmann's version), viewed the German Jews massacred by the Nazis as having been persecuted, in fact, for being German, not for being Jewish. As such, they were an integral part of the German nation's victims, just like those who died in the Allied bombings. The latter, too, were killed for being German.

In September 1946, Dr. Curt Epstein, a senior Jewish official in the Interior Ministry of the state of Hesse (in January 1947 he was appointed the state's commissar in charge of Nazi victims), ordered the Frankfurt city council to allocate an appropriate space in the city center for the municipal office to care for those who had been persecuted for political, racial, or religious reasons—"perhaps on the square across from the opera house." On this site a monument to the victims of fascism would be erected, paid for by the office. The city council welcomed the idea and authorized the municipal administration to carry it out.[64]

The monument was indeed built, and dedicated in August 1947 in the presence of members of the Association of Victims of Nazi Persecution, but not in central Frankfurt and certainly not opposite the opera house, as Epstein anticipated, but rather in the small cemetery in the suburb of Nied.

The same was the case in Hamburg. At the beginning of the Cold War, the memorials to the victims of fascism that their advocates sought to erect in the middle of the city were banished to cemeteries and unfrequented places. The monument in Nied was desecrated in September 1949. Vandals painted a large swastika on it, along with the message: "We still live! Heil Hitler!"[65]

From the front, the structure indeed seems to commemorate the victims of fascism. However, a view from above reveals that one of its sections also bears an inscription for the victims of 1914–1945. In other words, the Nied monument, like Benno Elkan's memorial, is in fact dedicated to all victims, including German soldiers killed in the two world wars. This is

Figure 11. The monument in the Nied cemetery, near Frankfurt

Figure 12. The rotunda at the main cemetery in Frankfurt

not what the organizations of Nazi victims intended. Epstein's wish was finally realized in 1964, when a memorial for the victims of Nazi terror was erected at the northwestern stair tower of the Paulskirche, designed by the sculptor Hans Wimmer. The pedestal of Wimmer's sculpture bears the names of concentration and death camps.

In many communities in Germany, the names of the fallen of World War II were inscribed on plaques installed on World War I monuments. These memorials were thus rededicated to the dead of both wars. This was the case with several monuments, for example in the center of Hamburg, or in the rotunda designed by Paul Seiler in the military section of Frankfurt's main cemetery.

An approach that does not distinguish between persecutor and persecuted, and which views as martyrs all those who died in the war, was apparent in the debates over compensation laws. They were enacted, on the orders of the Allies, by West Germany's state legislatures. In 1949, only representatives of the left, especially the Communists, displayed any sense of duty to the victims of Nazism and identified with their fate. The

Christian Democrats (CDU) and the Liberals (FDP) tended not to support a privileged status for these victims, as opposed to other groups who suffered during the war—the millions of Germans expelled from their homes (*Vertriebene*) in Eastern Europe and German refugees and prisoners of war.[66] These politicians made no distinction between people persecuted by the Nazis and Germans who had suffered because of the war. In September 1949, when the Federal Republic was established, its top leaders also adopted this view. In the programmatic speech that Chancellor Adenauer gave when he presented his new government to the elected Bundestag, he implicitly compared German suffering in the war to the persecution of the Jews by the Nazis. Adenauer condemned the de-Nazification policy instituted by the Allies in occupied Germany. He did not believe, he said, "that there are still Germans prepared to persecute Jews and hate them simply because they are Jews. Today, however, Germans are being persecuted simply because they are Germans." As Robert G. Moeller stresses, the chancellor spoke of the POWs held in the Soviet Union and the refugees and expellees from the east "whose dead number in the millions," terminology that had been used in reference to the Nazi genocide of the Jews. One member of the Bundestag interrupted Adenauer with a shout of "Five million!"[67] Adenauer found no need to mention the victims of Nazism in his speech. That did not sit well with the leader of the Social Democrats, Kurt Schumacher, who spent the years of the Hitler regime in Nazi concentration camps.[68]

In this implicit equating of Nazism's Jewish victims with the various German victims of the war, Moeller identified a central feature of the identity policy pursued by the young Federal Republic.[69] Adenauer declared that his government had a duty to the German victims of the war, but refrained from relating in the same way to the Nazis' victims, the Jews in particular. The impression he gave was that the German government viewed aiding the German victims as more important than giving assistance to the non-German victims.[70] In retrospect, Adenauer would seek to portray his attitude to the Jewish (and Israeli) issue as growing solely out of moral considerations, and to claim that it was a guiding principle of his policies. That was indeed the Bonn government's official declared position. Yet the words he chose at the beginning of the 1950s refer explicitly to the practical factors that motivated his actions.[71] Adenauer rejected any "collective German guilt" for the murder of the Jews. And, as part of his historic declaration on the eve of the Jewish New Year of 1951 on his country's attitude toward the Jews, formulated in tough negotiations with Prime Minister David Ben-Gurion of Israel and Foreign Minister Moshe Sharett, he spoke only of "crimes committed in the name of the German people" and of German "collective responsibility" for what had happened.[72] In 1966, a short time before his death, he visited Israel, considered by many Germans to be the state representing the Jewish victims of the Holocaust. No longer chancellor nor seeking election, he had no need to tack toward his party's right flank.

"The Jewish people expect a clear sign that Germany recognizes the dreadful burden of its past," Israel's prime minister, Levi Eshkol, told him. "The Nazis killed no fewer Germans than it killed Jews,"[73] the elderly German statesman replied. In other words, Adenauer sought to blur the obvious distinction made by the victims and by Israeli public opinion, the distinction between "those who shouted *Heil* and those who murmured *Shema Yisrael* at the hour of murder by Hitler's troopers," to quote Menachem Begin's speech to the Knesset about what Adenauer said in Jerusalem.[74]

In a personal letter he wrote to a friend at the beginning of 1946, Adenauer was still severely critical of the German people, and his position on their guilt was not far removed from that of the Western Allies:

> The German people, as well as most of the bishops and clergymen, were in full agreement with the National-Socialist view. There was almost no opposition. They became addicted to enthusiastic integration [*gleichschalten*] [into the regime]. Here lies their guilt. As for the rest, people knew (even if they were not aware of everything that was happening in the concentration camps) that individual freedom and all principles of law had collapsed, that horrible atrocities were being committed in the concentration camps; that our Gestapo and SS and a part of our forces in Poland and Russia were committing unprecedented atrocities against the civilian population. The pogroms against the Jews in 1933 and 1938 took place in full view of the public. The murder of the hostages in France was published officially. It cannot be argued, then, that the public did not know that the National Socialist regime and army leadership were regularly and fundamentally violating natural law, the Hague covenant, and the most basic imperatives of humanity.[75]

That same year Adenauer spoke in a similar vein publicly. However, once he became the German chancellor at the beginning of the Cold War, his public pronouncements on these subjects changed completely.[76] He was influenced by the political need to play to his electorate and his coalition in the new atmosphere of the Cold War, and was also concerned about the radical right's political potential. The indictment of the German people was dropped; the status of the victims of Nazism was lowered a few notches; and the commemoration policy came to stress the German collective memory of the war years.

From the establishment of the Federal Republic in September 1949, a far-reaching consensus pervaded the Bundestag: the de-Nazification policy pursued by the Allies in occupied Germany had to be discarded. Both Adenauer's ruling Christian Democrats and Kurt Schumacher's opposition Social Democrats shared this view. Schumacher had, as noted, spent years in concentration camps, yet he and his party, like Adenauer and his party, supported sweeping amnesties for imprisoned and fugitive war criminals.[77] Schumacher reasoned that it was important to integrate the "little Nazis," as they were called, into the new Germany's political life, and that an effort should even be made to harness them to the Social Democratic struggle. Otherwise, they were liable to turn into a huge reservoir of detached persons who would eventually support an extremist anti-democratic movement.[78] As we have already seen, such a dichotomous view, differentiating between "little Nazis" and Nazi leaders, already existed during the war, in the Communist camp. The Social Democrats shared with Communists this leftist ideological interpretation that removed the real responsibility for Nazism and its crimes from the German people.

The amnesty laws were introduced by the German Party (DP) and the Free Democratic (Liberal) Party (FDP), which had active lobbies championing pardons for war criminals. They also advocated an energetic program of integration for Nazi sympathizers and for the reinstatement of government officials who had been ousted because of their Nazi pasts. In this, the Bundestag represented the greater part of the Federal Republic's population.[79] Norbert Frei attributes the across-the-board consensus to political calculations: "In the end, all the democratic parties knew they had to win their votes from a populace that in free and fair elections would have chosen Hitler by an overwhelming majority a mere decade earlier."[80]

In contrast with Chancellor Adenauer's cold and alienated position on the issue of Jewish victims and the memory of the Holocaust, President Heuss voiced an explicit moral commitment in a series of speeches he gave beginning in 1945. The awful crimes and injustices committed against the Jews should not be forgotten, he asserted. However, Heuss also rejected the concept of collective guilt that the Allies had promoted. In a speech given in November 1949 he declared: "The term 'collective punishment,' with all it implies, reflects a simplistic position, a kind of mirror image of the Nazis' treatment of the Jews, [according to which] it is sufficient that a person is a Jew for him to be marked as guilty." But, unlike Adenauer, he nevertheless maintained that "something like collective shame has grown since those days, and has remained. Hitler's greatest offense against us, and he committed many, was that he forced us into shame, because like him and his minions, we, too, bear the name German."[81]

After Heuss was elected, an attempt was made to depict him as a committed and brave anti-Nazi.[82] But this was hardly the case. He had not been an outstanding opponent of the Nazi regime. In fact, in March 1933, as a member of the Reichstag representing the State Party (*Staatspartei*), he voted in favor of the enabling law (*Ermächtigungsgesetz*) that allowed the Nazis to disregard parliament and dismantle democratic rule. Heuss also published, in 1940, cultural pieces and book reviews in *Das Reich,* a new Nazi weekly edited by the Nazi propaganda minister Joseph Goebbels.[83] Notwithstanding, as the Federal Republic's first president, Heuss contributed to the consolidation of a German collective memory of the Holocaust as a terrible crime and as Germany's moral nadir. In his speeches, he also criticized the ways in which the Germans had sought to mitigate their responsibility. "We knew," he declared in a speech he gave at Bergen-Belsen in 1952.[84] In a 1949 speech he said:

> We must not and may not forget a single thing: the Nuremberg laws, the yellow badge, the burning of the synagogues, the deportation of Jewish people abroad to misfortune and to death. This is a set of facts which we should not and must not forget, because we should not make it easy for ourselves![85]

In a number of his speeches, Heuss spoke of Jews he had known in Württemberg who were murdered by the Nazis, among them his friend Otto Hirsch, the head of the Jewish representative organization in Nazi

Germany (*Reichsvertretung der Juden in Deutschland*), who was murdered in Mauthausen. While the philosemitic tributes Heuss showered on Hirsch are embarrassing, and perhaps even jarring to Jewish ears, these speeches nevertheless put faces on the Jewish victims, without which they would have been for many Germans an anonymous mass bearing both traditional and Nazi antisemitic stereotypes.[86]

In 1950, war broke out between the two Koreas. On the one side were Communist forces, on the other United Nations forces, led by the United States. The Cold War intensified, and the Federal Republic's commemoration policy took a turn. The focuses switched from the Nazis' victims to the German soldiers who died in battle. Germany viewed the latter as victims of the war. The Federal Republic canceled the official memorial day for the victims of fascism that had been marked annually throughout Germany since September 1945. It now instituted a national memorial day "for all victims of the war." But this day in fact gave precedence to soldiers killed in action, not to the rest of the "victims of the dictatorship and the war." Portraying the German soldier as a patriot and a victim of Nazism—discussed at length in chapter 4—was a way of rehabilitating the German soldier, following the decision to rearm the Federal Republic and to integrate the West German state into the U.S.-led NATO alliance.[87]

With the advent of the Korean War and the arming of East Germany's "Barracked People's Police" (KVP), Adenauer proposed to the Americans in the summer of 1950 that the Federal Republic join the West's defensive alliance. This proposal followed previous informal consultations of the Adenauer administration with former Wehrmacht generals, with the consent of the Western Allies. Acceptance of the offer meant establishing a German army and rearming the country, in direct contradiction of the agreements on the demilitarization of Germany reached among the Allies at the end of the war.[88] Adenauer included in his proposal a demand that the Allies rehabilitate the Federal Republic's sovereignty and grant it complete independence from Allied rule. The foreign ministers of the Western powers accepted his offer, although the Allies were not prepared to fully pay the price that Adenauer demanded for founding a new German army, the Bundeswehr, and its integration into the Western defense alliance.[89]

Formation of the Bundeswehr began in October 1950. A group of generals, veterans of the Wehrmacht, gathered in secret (although with the agreement of the Allied high commissioners in West Germany) at the Himmerod Monastery in the Eifel Mountains.[90] The federal government instructed them to prepare a memorandum on the character of the new German army.

In their report, the generals claimed that "the slanders made during the last five years in many areas of the life of the individual and the country have systematically eaten away at the will to act resolutely against [our] enemies." Consequently, they demanded measures to transform public opinion at home and abroad: the release of Germans condemned as "war criminals" and "a cessation of all slander against the German soldier [a technical term that included SS units deployed in the framework of the Wehrmacht]." They also demanded that the federal government and the Bundestag announce an official apology (*Ehrenerklärung*) to the German soldier.[91]

U.S. General Dwight Eisenhower, supreme commander of NATO forces, was the first to respond to their demand. In a speech during a visit to Germany in January 1951 (the wording of which was apparently formulated in consultation with the Germans), he stated:

> In 1945 I believed "that the Wehrmacht, and especially the German officer corps, had been identical with Hitler and his exponents of the rule of force.... This conviction had been in error, for the German soldier had fought bravely and honorably for his homeland.
>
> As I told the Chancellor and some other German gentlemen with whom I had talked yesterday, there is a real difference between the regular German soldier and officer and Hitler and his criminal group.... For my part.[92]

In his war memoirs, however, published in 1948, Eisenhower presented a different picture of the German soldier and of the noxious fanaticism of the Waffen SS solders who were assigned to Wehrmacht units.[93]

In 1946, Adenauer, not yet chancellor but a prominent Christian Democratic politician, publicly condemned the German army's involvement in war crimes. Six years later, he changed his tune. In December 1952, he declared before the Bundestag:

> In the name of the federal government I wish to declare today, before this honorable house, that we all bear arms for our *volk* [and] recognize those who honorably fought on land, sea, and in the air, in the name of the glorious soldierly tradition. We are convinced that, the good reputation and

> great performance of the German soldier, despite all the outrageous acts committed in past years, have been vividly upheld in our nation's heart, and that they will also remain as such. It should be our mutual task to entwine the moral values of German soldierliness with [the values of] democracy. I am certain that we will accomplish the mission.[94]

The change that took place in the "politics of the past" (*Vergangenheitspolitik*, a term coined by the historian Norbert Frei to designate that element of West German politics pertaining to the Nazi period) with the establishment of the Federal Republic was consistent with the prevailing mood in Germany at that time, as well as later. At the end of the 1950s, Theodor Adorno characterized this mood as "wishing to turn the page and, if possible, wiping it from memory."[95]

Two events that occurred around this time in two small towns in the young Federal Republic drive home this widespread desire in both a colorful and blunt way. At the beginning of October 1951, the town of Stadtoldendorf in Lower Saxony held a festive ceremony at the local gas works for its 8,000 inhabitants. In the presence of Social-Democratic mayor Wilhelm Noske (originally a history teacher) and the members of the city council, all 600 de-Nazification files opened in the city during the period of the British military government were hurled into a fire. The files included a list of the townspeople who had belonged to the Nazi Party. Were that to fall into "the wrong hands," the atmosphere in the town would grow ugly, Noske maintained, since "every well-regarded person and official in town appears there." His town was the first in the Federal Republic "to draw a line on the past," he declared. To the press he said that the burning of the files should be seen as a service to peace and a step toward reconciliation. We must forget the past, he said, and direct our gaze forward and build the country anew.[96]

The second event took place at the end of October 1952 in Pforzheim, a city hit hard by the Allied bombings. Gottfried Leonhardt, a resident of the city and a Christian Democratic delegate in the Bundestag, gave a speech on Loyalty Day (*Tag der Treue*). In addition to demanding that the four powers (in particular the Western Allies) free their German POWs, he called on them to pardon imprisoned German war criminals.

> But if they do not wish to listen to us, we must then remember in particular the acts of violence as well as the acts of murder committed against

> the helpless among us, when they liberated us. . . . We were and are still prepared to forgive and forget and expunge the past; but the other side must do the same. Injustice does not justify injustice.[97]

These statements and actions, coming from both a member of the governing party and a member of the SPD opposition, were indicative of the mentality and political atmosphere in the new Federal Republic, at a time when Allied high commissioners still operated in the country.

Equation of the "crimes of the Allies" with Nazi atrocities and the view that the de-Nazification program and the imprisonment of war criminals were injustices were very common not only among the public at large, but also among the political leadership.[98] Konstantin von Neurath, Hitler's first foreign minister, had been sentenced in Nuremberg. When he was released from Spandau Prison in 1954 due to failing health, President Heuss himself publicly applauded the fact that "the martyrdom [*Martyrium*] of these years has come to an end for you."[99]

Public surveys quantify this mood: the proportion of Germans who believed that "judicial proceedings should not be pursued against Nazi criminals once some years have passed since the crimes were committed, and it is better to draw a line on the past," grew steadily from 34 percent in 1958 to 54 percent in 1963, and reached 67 percent in 1969.[100] No significant deviation from the latter number was evident in the 1990s.[101] However, since the 1960s a political majority in the Federal parliament (Bundestag) voted for the repeated extension of the statute of limitations (*Verjährungsfrist*) in 1965, 1969, and for the last time in 1979, when the statute of limitations for murder and genocide was totally abolished.[102]

The Federal Republic's attitudinal change regarding the Nazi past during the early 1950s can be seen also in how President Heuss addressed the Nazi past in official speeches he gave at commemoration ceremonies. In the heat of the propaganda war between the Eastern and Western blocs during the Cold War, West Germany, like its East German rival, used all means at its disposal. Its political leadership equated Nazi atrocities with the acts of its ideological nemesis. The Bonn leadership's highest priority was to delegitimize the rival Communist regime. Nevertheless, by drawing such an equivalence, West Germany's leadership was also responding to the wishes of the German public. It alleviated the pain of accepting the West's claim that the extermination of the Jews was a crime without equal in human history, one that cast a heavy pall over the German nation.

One of the handful of monuments erected in memory of the Jews who were injured and murdered by the Nazis was dedicated in West Germany in November 1952. President Heuss took part in the ceremony, which was conducted at the site of the Bergen-Belsen concentration camp. The memorial—an obelisk, wall, and memorial inscription—had been planned seven years previously by the British military government.[103]

In his speech, Heuss responded to a range of nationalist claims opposing the establishment of the memorial. Paradoxically, his self-righteous tone drew public attention to those very claims. "The obelisk is liable, like a thorn, to pierce the wounds that time is meant to heal," the opponents argued; "Best that the site be plowed under and its memory buried under cultivated fields." Heuss, for his part, maintained that the remains of the victims' flesh would never forget what had happened at this place. He also called on the Germans never to forget the offenses they had committed against their German Jewish compatriots during that shameful time.

Typically, Heuss focused only on the German-Jewish victims and disregarded the Jews of Eastern Europe. He referred to the accusations about the cruel treatment that the Soviets had meted out to the Germans it held during 1945–1946 in the concentration camps previously operated by the Nazis.[104] While he stated that "nothing changed there, except the emblems" (in other words, he equated the Soviets with the Nazis), Heuss stressed that the mistreatment of the Germans and the injustice done to them was not a reason to ignore the injustice done to the Jews.[105]

The president's speeches on Jewish subjects were, as always, directed also at the Jewish public and the international media. Consequently, the speeches referred solely to the Jewish victims. In contrast, references to the "Jewish issue" (the Holocaust) in speeches devoted to other subjects cast light on the place assigned to the Jewish victims, as opposed to the rest of the victims of the war and dictatorship, in West Germany's official memory.

In his speech at the dedication of a cemetery of the Wehrmacht dead in Weeze in the Lower Rhineland (*Niederrhein*) on September 10, 1950, as well as in his remarks at a similar ceremony in Hürtgen on August 17, 1952,

Heuss commented on the difference between Hitler's war and Germany's previous wars. The lives of those who were killed in the battles of the Rhine in 1944–1945 were sacrificed by others (implicitly, in the name of the goals of a cynical leadership), whereas in World War I soldiers sacrificed themselves for their homeland:

> Because by then the war was already lost. And many of those interred here knew that to be the case. And that is the tragic and disquieting feeling: they died of duty. We can thus only speak in gratitude and deference before the fate of the individual. Any other tone is forbidden. But the days of such soldierly conduct is past. Our country's doom can also be found in the mass graves of the night bombings, and in the ditches on the edges of the concentration camps.[106]

In Hürtgen, Heuss also emphasized the tragedy of the sacrifice of young soldiers by a regime whose only purpose was to delay an inevitable defeat. He also referred to the women and children killed in the Allied bombing of Hamburg, and stressed that all the war's dead should be remembered with reverence.[107]

The president voiced the same sentiments in other speeches as well. Heuss rejected the hero-worship characteristic of the World War I cult of the fallen and the Nazi hero cult. The soldiers had died a tragic death, he asserted. He was vague about the extensive involvement of Wehrmacht soldiers in war crimes. They were, he said, victims of "the fate of the nation," just like the civilians who died in the war and the targets of Nazi persecution, including the (German) Jews. Each of these three groups embodied the German national tragedy. Like Adenauer, Heuss used terms associated with the Holocaust to describe German suffering during the war. For example, in a speech he gave in May 1955 on the occasion of the departure of the Allied high commissioners and the expansion of the Federal Republic's sovereignty, Heuss addressed the defeat of the Third Reich on May 8, 1945. Against the "sense of liberation" of the Germans he juxtaposed the "military devastation" and the "annihilation [*Vernichtung*] of the German state and people's centuries of history." In 1949 Heuss had already stated that in 1945 the Germans "were redeemed and destroyed simultaneously."[108]

Norbert Frei noted that the president, who knew how to express himself incisively, expressed his contemporaries' ambivalent feelings about May 8, 1945.[109] This pattern could also be seen in the official Federal Republic commemorations of its war dead.

Gerhard Marcks and the Federal Republic's Concept of Commemoration

The sculptor Gerhard Marcks (1889–1981) was the embodiment of the Federal Republic's official commemoration concept, according to which all war dead were to be memorialized without distinction. The monuments he built throughout Germany from 1949 through the mid-1960s express this idea. His sculpture "The Angel of Death" (*Todesengel*), erected at the beginning of November 1949 in front of St. Mary's Church at the Capitol in Cologne, was the first memorial in the Federal Republic to be dedicated to "all victims of the war."

Marcks, who taught at the Bauhaus Academy in Dessau and was dismissed during the Third Reich, going into "internal exile" (remaining in Germany, but seldom taking part in public artistic activity), was, to the best of my knowledge, the first German artist to suggest the erection of a monument to all victims of the war. At the beginning of January 1946 he contacted Richard Strauss, who was the official responsible for art in the Central Administration for the People's Education in the Soviet zone of occupation. He sent Strauss two drafts of a proposal for the establishment of a 164-foot high cairn (*Totenhügel*) made of war debris from around the Reichstag. On the top would be a small chapel, and in front of that would be a statue of the Angel of Death. "It will be a kind of parallel to the mountain of the crucifixion [Golgotha], and will do well for Berlin."[110]

His proposal was rejected, which infuriated Marcks. In a letter to a friend in June 1946, he complained about artistic policy in the Soviet zone of occupation: "And those party monuments for the victims of fascism, who can really share in that? I'd happily erect a monument to all the dead (soldiers included!). But no—it won't be."[111]

Marcks, whose eldest son was killed in battle in 1943, maintained that war memorials should be dedicated to all the war dead, including those killed in military service. This view was unacceptable in the Soviet zone of occupation on the eve of the Cold War. At that time, memorials and plaques were dedicated only to those who had fought against fascism and had been persecuted by the Nazis. In 1947, the Hamburg Cultural Council asked him if he would be willing to design a monument to the Nazis' victims. Marcks said he was prepared to erect one "that will not be

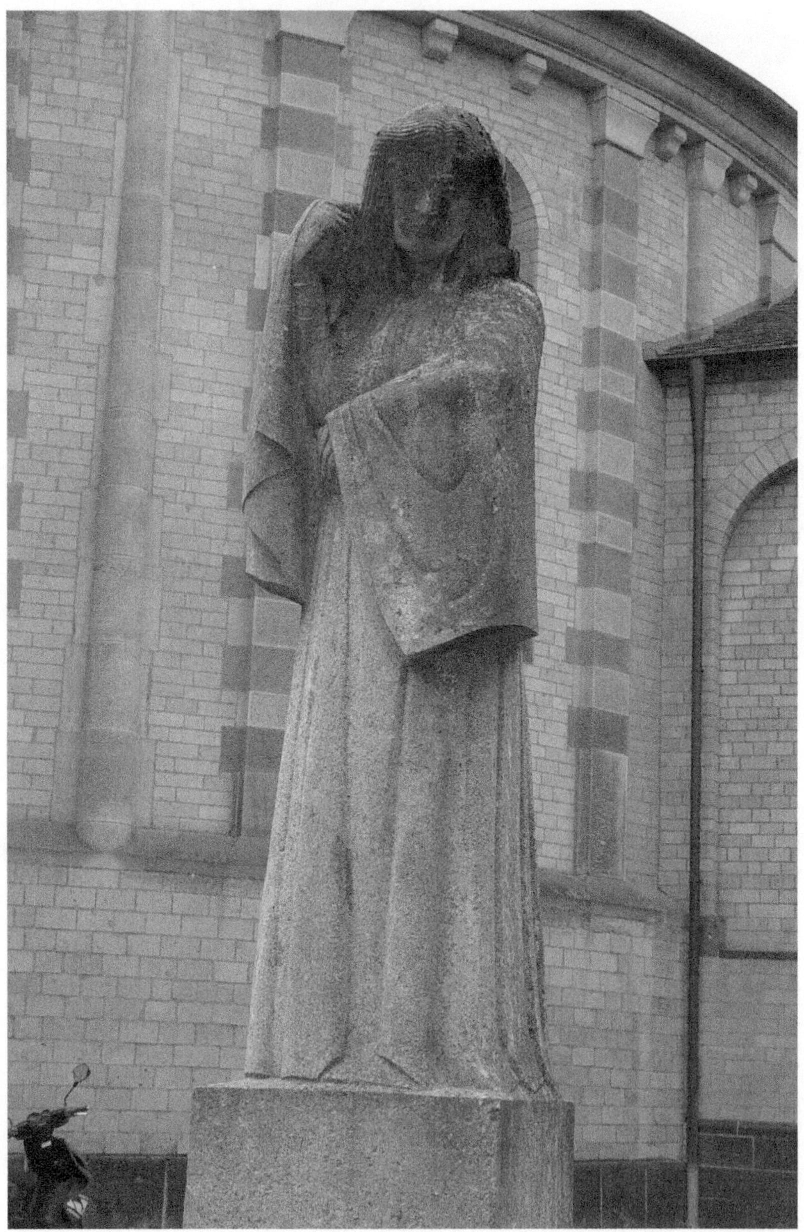

Figure 13. Gerhard Marcks's *Angel of Death,* Cologne

dedicated explicitly to those who died in the concentration camps, and as such serve a political idea, but will rather simply be a common monument for all victims of the Nazi regime, in other words, also for the victims of the war." By "victims of the war" Marcks meant to include soldiers.[112]

His offer was rejected by Hamburg, but in Cologne it found a ready ear. In a letter to his friend and fellow sculptor, Waldemar Grzimek, in 1947, after the latter city accepted a modified version of the design, Marcks wrote: "But there [in Berlin] they are incapable of separating art from politics—in other words [to erect a monument] for all the dead."[113] The Angel of Death sculpture was unveiled at the beginning of November 1949 in the courtyard of the Church of St. Mary at the capitol in Cologne, as a memorial (*Totenmal*) to the victims of the war and the Nazi regime. The inscription on the pedestal is "to [the memory of] the dead." A draft the Cologne municipality prepared for the speech of the mayor at the unveiling stated:[114]

> A host of the dead stands accusing before our eyes. Not only those who fell outside [i.e., soldiers], but also the workers for whom death's blow came in their workplaces; women, mothers and children, who died unnatural deaths in the ruins of our beloved city; those persecuted for political, racial, and religious reasons, who fell victim to racialist madness; the poorest and most stricken among us, whose death saved them from hunger and illness. Our thoughts at this hour are with them, all of them. And with them also are our hopes that the sacrifice they were forced to make will not be in vain. We remember with grief the dead, so that we may better serve the living and the generations to come, so that we may avert for them the suffering that we had to endure.[115]

Moritz Goldschmidt, the first chairman of the city's Jewish community, also spoke at the unveiling. He evoked the members of the community "who died solely because they had been born Jews" and stressed "that at this moment I do not wish to accuse anyone. Because in grief and death all are equal."[116] Goldschmidt undoubtedly spoke to Marcks's view, the prevalent one in Germany at the time.

The demand for memorials by Marcks grew. Following the monument in Cologne, his sculptures were erected "to all the dead" of the war in Mannheim in 1952 (*The Angel of Judgment Day*),[117] to all the victims and destruction of the war in Bochum (*The Old Woman in Mourning*)[118] in 1955, and in Osnabrück (*The Bound Man*), a sculpture dedicated also

Figure 14. Gerhard Marcks's *The Old Woman in Mourning,* Bochum (Courtesy of Mr. Arved von der Ropp, the son of the photographer Inge von der Ropp)

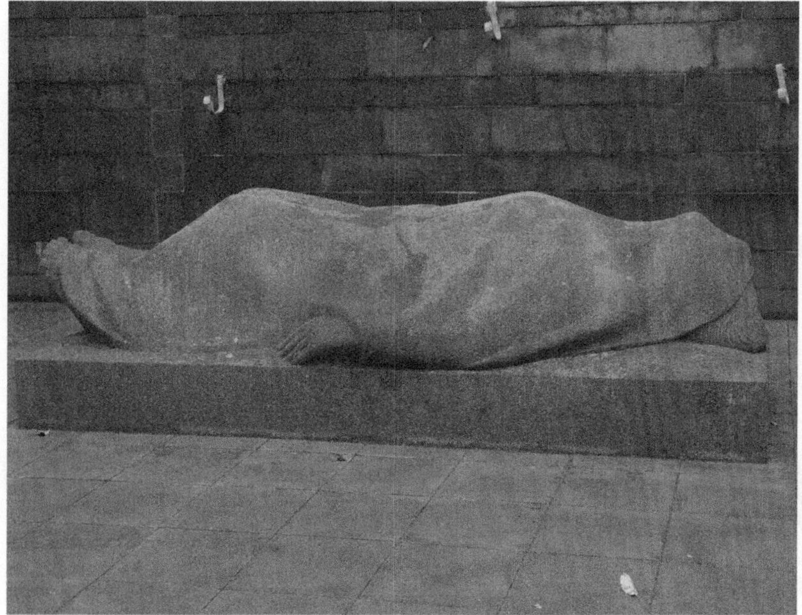

Figure 15. Marcks's sculpture in memory of the victims of the bombings in Mülheim

to the anti-Hitler conspirators of July 1944, as well as to the memory of those who rebelled against the Communist regime in East Germany on June 17, 1953. This inclusion of an event that was ostensibly detached from World War II and Nazism was characteristic of the Cold War period and the view common then that Nazi and Communist totalitarianism were equivalent.[119] Marcks also produced sculptures dedicated to specific groups of Nazi and war victims and soldiers who lost their lives. He fashioned a monument, dedicated to Germans killed in the Allied bombings, for the Ohlsdorf Cemetery in Hamburg in 1952, and another for the city of Mulheim in 1969.[120] His statue *Job* was installed in Frankfurt's main cemetery on the People's Day of Mourning in 1959 as a memorial to those persecuted by the Nazi dictatorship.[121] He designed a chapel dedicated to Claus Schenk von Stauffenberg and his fellow conspirators against Hitler in the July 20, 1944, plot, and other monuments to soldiers who fell in the war.[122] Marcks's artistic activity in this field made him one of the most important monument designers in West Germany's war commemoration and memorial culture of the 1950s.

Figure 16. Wallberg as seen from the main street of Pforzheim

His idea of a (Golgotha-like) memorial cairn, rejected in Berlin, came up for discussion in Stuttgart as well. In 1954, the office of the city's mayor proposed that the heap of the ruins of Birkenkopf, a neighborhood on a hill above the city, be made into a monument to the victims of tyranny, to soldiers who died in battle, and to the inhabitants of the city who were killed in the war. A large cross, then visible from every point in Stuttgart,

Figure 17. The monument to fallen soldiers in Ohlsdorf Cemetery, Hamburg

was installed on top of the hill. Cologne adopted the same idea, turning the pile of rubble in its central Herculeswiese (Hercules' meadow) (today called Herculesberg—Hercules' hill) into a monument to all those who had lost their lives during the war.[123] This concept has influenced commemoration projects to this day—a similar idea has gained support in recent years regarding the mound of ruins in Wallberg, which rise above the city of Pforzheim.[124]

During the Federal Republic's first decade, most public commemoration projects were dedicated to fallen German soldiers. Afterward came dedications to the civilian dead and to POWs who had not yet been released. The people persecuted by the Nazis were not, in general, honored with separate monuments, but were rather memorialized primarily in structures dedicated to "all the dead."

The two German states' respective cultures of commemoration and memorialization, dedicated to the victims of the war and of the Nazis and developed under the influence of the Cold War, were the products of different ideological views and bore different messages. Antifascism was the dominant component of official memorializing in East Germany. This culture condemned Nazism morally and politically, stressing the heroism of those who fought fascism and were thrown into concentration camps and sent to their deaths because of their political creed. Nazism was condemned as a matter of policy in West Germany as well, where it was seen as the ultimate moral degeneration and as the credo of a regime that had brought catastrophe on the German people. The democratic West's heroes of choice were the anti-Hitler conspirators of July 20, 1944, who were portrayed as anti-Nazis. Yet, despite this notable difference, there were also similarities in the basics of both countries' commemoration policy. These were expressed in the "reconciliation narrative," characterized by a Christian imprint that did not distinguish between Germans who were killed during the Nazi period for different reasons. All were victims, no matter what the circumstances in which they died. In the East, this narrative focused on civilian suffering under Allied bombings during the war. In the West, it focused on civilian suffering during the flight and expulsion of Germans from the eastern territories at the end of the war and during it aftermath, and to the heroism of the German soldier, especially those killed in battle, in the spirit of a German nationalist heritage dating back to the wars of liberation against Napoleon.

It is no coincidence that the reconciliation narrative was promoted by both German regimes. It derived from the similar political and historical realties of the rival states established on the ruins of the Third Reich, in the milieu of the Cold War. The desire to unite Germany peacefully, prevalent in the Communist camp as well as the Western one, required East Germany's unpopular Communist regime to seek the sympathy not only of his own citizens but also of public opinion in the free West. As a result, both German leaderships found themselves locked in a populist fight for the soul of the German people, and neither side hesitated to appeal to nationalist sentiments that were the bequest of the Nazis.

Despite the fundamental difference between the democratic state in the West and the dictatorship in the East, those holding power in both countries were in the minority with regard to their view of the Nazi past. East Germany was ruled by a small Communist elite under the protection of a foreign power. While the West's leaders were freely elected by the people (elections from which the Nazi Party was banned), they nevertheless resembled their rivals in the East in that most people's views of the Nazi past were at odds with those of the chancellor, his party, the president, and the Social Democratic opposition.

According to public opinion polls conducted by the U.S. and British military governments during the period of their direct rule, in 1945–1949, close to half the population maintained that Nazism had been "a good idea badly carried out." A British survey from April 1948 showed that SPD voters were no different: 47 percent of the men polled agreed with that statement, as did 59 percent of the women.[125] In his book *Hitlers Volksstaat* (Hitler's People's State), Götz Aly writes that the Reich paid the wives of Wehrmacht soldiers an allowance equal to 85 percent of their husbands' last net salary—almost double the amount that Britain and the United States paid the wives of their soldiers.[126]

This may explain the support both women and men expressed for the Nazi regime.

In 1951, a public opinion poll conducted by the Allensbach Institute and commissioned by the federal government asked, "When in this century was Germany's best period, in your opinion?" Forty-four percent answered, "the Third Reich," 43 percent "the empire period before the First World War," 7 percent "the Weimar Republic," and only 2 percent "the post-1945 period." When they were asked the contrary question, 80 percent answered that the postwar was Germany's worst period.[127]

Most of the inhabitants of both German states mourned for soldiers and civilians who died in the war. They did not mourn the Jews or those Germans who fought the Nazis. German men, more than women, tended to view those who had acted against the regime during the war as traitors rather than heroes—perhaps because so many of these men served in the army at the time.[128]

This situation motivated both the East and West German leaderships to seek to unite their heterogeneous populations, which still contained a considerable number of Nazi-oriented individuals and in which most disagreed with their leaders' politics regarding the immediate past. As part of their battle for public support at home and in the other German state, they sought to integrate their anti-Nazi ethos and memories (although in the West the ruling circle included not only anti-Nazis and non-Nazis such as Heuss, but also former Nazis such as Oberländer and the third chancellor Kurt Georg Kiesinger) with the larger public's perspective of the national German memory of the war. They engaged the collective memories of Wehrmacht soldiers and the millions of Germans who had favored the Nazis and Hitler by modulating the elements of that memory, using traditional Christian phraseology and gestures.[129] Bringing the German collective memory of the war into the framework of the reconciliation narrative of the two countries' commemoration policies made it possible for Germans in both states to identify with the respective official memory. It produced a legitimate and official framework for communing with German suffering during the war and with the tragic heroism of the Wehrmacht soldiers, who went on fighting in a campaign they knew was doomed from the start. This dedication was articulated as a sublime expression of love for their country, not as blind faith in the Führer and his racist Nazi ideology.

These memory cultures contributed to the preservation of certain elements of the Nazi portrayal of World War II in German collective memory, but at the same time attenuated its political virulence. By doing so, the political leaderships in both countries no doubt contributed to the slow and gradual process of estrangement of the Germans from Nazism. Yet they also legitimized certain components of the Nazi myth and the propagandistic portrayal of World War II that had been etched in the German collective memory during the Third Reich, adapting them to the Cold War and its terminology. Some of these have survived until the present. By stressing their victimization, the people could equate the German victim of the war with those that the regime persecuted, in particular the Jews. The slaughter of the Jews, and the guilt feelings it engendered, left a deep impression on the German psyche. Grouping together the people persecuted by the Nazis, Germany's wartime civilians, and soldiers who died on the battlefield as the victims of a tyrannical regime and a total war had the probably unintended value of blurring the distinctions among the dead and attenuating this sense of guilt.

4

Memorial Days in West Germany and Their Metamorphosis, 1945–2006

Memorial Days for Fallen Soldiers from the End of World War II to the Beginning of the Cold War

Heroes' Memorial Day was a legal holiday in the Third Reich, falling on March 16 or the Sunday closest to that date. It featured ceremonies organized by the Wehrmacht and the Nazi Party.[1] In 1946, the British military administration forbade it,[2] but the prohibition seems to have been in force only in the British zone. At the beginning of March 1946, the Soviet Zone's Council of Protestant Churches in Germany decided that it would permit an observance of Heroes' Memorial Day on Reminiscere Sunday (*Sonntag Reminiscere*) in the period of the Passiontide (the two weeks before Easter), as had been the custom during the Weimar period. In the years that followed, however, soldiers killed in battle were commemorated on the general memorial day for all the dead, held on the Sunday of the Dead (*Totensonntag*), the last Sunday before Advent.[3] This end-of-year memorial day had been decreed by King Friedrich Wilhelm III of Prussia in 1816, following the wars of liberation against Napoleon. The Protestant churches observed it, but the Catholic Church solemnized its war dead on All Saints Day (*Allerheiligen* or *Allerseelen*), November 1, observed by Catholic communities since the ninth century. This holiday derives from the belief that Jesus unites the dead and the living into a single living community.[4] However, these two memorial days were dedicated not just to those who had died in the war, but to the memory of all the dead.

The churches opposed the secular cast given to Reminiscere Sunday, which was based on a misconstrual of the term *Reminiscere* (the Latin imperative "remember"). The name came from the second clause of Psalms 25:7: "Remember thou me for Thy goodness' sake," a plea to God that He recall his mercies and goodness—not that mortals remember their dead.[5]

Neither German state (*Land*) instituted an alternative memorial day for their soldiers and civilians killed in the war. The tradition dating from the Weimar Republic of a National Day of Mourning (*Volkstrauertag*) on the sixth Sunday before Easter, known as Invocavit Sunday (*Sonntag Invocavit*), dedicated to the dead of World War I, was also abandoned. Its observance had never been mandated by law except in the state of Thuringia, which at the end of the Weimar period mandated a People's Day of Mourning on the fifth Sunday before Easter, Reminiscere Sunday. In accordance with their ideology, the Nazis transmogrified the People's Mourning Day into Heroes' Memorial Day (*Heldengedenktag*).[6] However, during the Third Reich, Protestant congregations, particularly those in rural regions, continued to observe the traditional Sunday of the Dead to commemorate their fallen soldiers.

In an effort to assert the primacy of Heroes' Memorial Day as the day of remembrance for World War I dead, the Nazis put an end to communal church observances of the traditional memorial days, changing them into individual and family days of remembrance. For example, in November 1942, the minister for church affairs issued a decree that prohibited reading the names of dead solders at memorial ceremonies in churches on these days. The ban, which was misunderstood by the public, roused the ire of congregations and the churches.[7]

After defeat, the large cities resumed observances of the traditional memorial days that the Nazis had annulled. In mid-November 1945, Kurt Sieveking, the Senatussyndikus (executive legal assistant to Hamburg's mayor) who in 1953 became mayor himself on the Christian Democratic ticket, received an internal memorandum proposing reinstatement of the Weimar model of commemoration. The anonymous author listed the sites at which the Hamburg senate used to lay wreaths on Heroes' Memorial Day, during the Third Reich and on the traditional Sunday of the Dead in the Weimar period. He proposed that on the latter day, wreaths be laid on the graves of German soldiers, including Jewish soldiers who had fought in the German army in World War I, and of British soldiers and civilians killed in the war. A decision would have to be made, he wrote, about whether also to lay wreaths on the graves of those who met their deaths in the concentration camps, as well as Russian slave laborers and the Allied soldiers buried in Ohlsdorf Cemetery. His proposal was accepted, with minor revisions. This proposal marks the paradigmatic turn from Nazi to democratic postwar commemoration patterns. Observances were held each year until the restoration of the People's Day of Mourning in November 1952, which fell a week before the Sunday of the Dead. From that year onward, the Hamburg senate laid its wreaths on all these graves on the new memorial day.[8]

The Volksbund was also, from 1946, in the western occupation zones, a vocal advocate of instituting a memorial day for World War II dead on the model of the Weimar People's Day of Mourning. The organization had been established in 1919 by figures from across the political spectrum to care for the graves of the World War I dead. In 1921 the authorities granted it exclusive authority over war graves. During the Weimar period, attempts were made to legislate the observance of the People's Day of Mourning, but official sanction was never achieved because of disputes among the parties about the date of the observance and because of bureaucratic delays.[9] Beginning in 1922, the Volksbund held its observances on Invocavit Sunday. The day was granted legal status in Thuringia in 1931 by Wilhelm Frick, the state's Nazi interior minister. It was observed on Reminiscere Sunday.

In the framework of the Nazis' *Gleichschaltung* ("bringing into line") policy, several party members were appointed to the Volksbund's board of directors. One of them was Martin Mutschmann, Gauleiter and Reichstatthalter (Reich commissioner) of Saxony. Interior Minister Frick drew up legislation designating Reminiscere Sunday as Heroes' Memorial Day. For years this Sunday had been observed, he said, as a memorial day for World War I dead and as a day of renewal for the German people.[10] However, relations between the Volksbund and the state soured during the war, as the former sought to protect its exclusive mandate against party and Wehrmacht encroachments.[11]

The monthly reports of the Volksbund's Hamburg branch during 1946–1947 indicate that the populace viewed it as an arm of the Nazi regime. Local party leaders pressured citizens to join the organization and contribute to its activity. After the war, in consequence, the public kept its distance from the Volksbund, even though the British military government sanctioned its activities in 1946. The organization had difficulty enlisting volunteers and, with the help of the authorities, worked to rehabilitate its image and its prerogatives.[12] The Hamburg branch's report of March 1946 indicates that the Volksbund sought to institute the Weimar period's People's Day of Mourning in the Hanseatic city, but the Protestant Church opposed the move. The report also states that wreaths were not laid on soldiers' graves on the People's Day of Mourning because Heroes' Memorial Day had not been officially recognized—the British military government forbade its observance. The Britons probably feared that such ceremonies might keep alive Nazi and militarist spirit among the Germans. For a long time, the Hamburg branch was unable to find any senior city figure to serve as its honorary president. Then, to the organization's surprise, the city's Social Democratic mayor, Max Brauer, offered himself. His appointment improved the organization's public image and helped it gain more financial resources.[13]

Memorial Day for the Victims of Fascism, 1945–1948

In June 1945, the Communist delegates to the council of the British zone of occupation proposed a Memorial Day for the Victims of Fascism (*Opfer des Fascismus*). Similar proposals were also submitted to the Berlin city council, and the first memorial day was set for September 8, 1945. The Christian Democratic delegates in Hamburg added a proposal for a day devoted to the memory of German war's victims (*Opfer des Krieges*—citizens killed in the war), since they were also victims of Nazism.[14] In 1946, the newly founded International Federation of Former Political Prisoners of the Nazi Regime (Fédération Internationale des Anciens Prisonniers Politiques-FIAPP) instituted a Victims of Fascism Day (*Tag der Opfer des Fascismus*) on the second Sunday of September. That same day, throughout Germany, memorial assemblies were held, arranged by the Association of Victims of Nazi Persecution (VVN), the organization that until 1948 represented Nazi victims across the political spectrum. All German states endorsed and helped fund the VVN's ceremonies held on this day. Representatives of all the country's political parties participated, conferring on the observances an official character.

In October 1945, a convention of former political prisoners (*ehemaliger politische Gefangener Komitee*) was held in Hamburg. The group that organized it would later be absorbed by the VVN. The delegates decided to hold a memorial week for the victims of Nazism at the end of that month. The discussions that preceded the week of mourning, and the speeches of politicians at its events, gave expression to the lessons of the Nazi past that were the basis of the German postwar culture of memory under the occupation of the Western Allies, prior to the foundation of the Federal Republic. At the opening of the convention, the head of the council of former political prisoners, Senator Franz Heitgres of the Communist Party, specified who was being remembered and the nonpartisan nature of the memorial week:

> We remember all victims of Nazism, all the war dead, all those who died in concentration camps, all those who were forced to sacrifice their lives in this time because of the policy that led to such chaos. The party representatives who participate in these convocations should recall the dead, and at the same time [they should] begin to gather together all those forces [that seek] to build a democratic Germany.[15]

Heitgres here reiterated Communist Party's principal approach, the same one evident in the Soviet zone of occupation in July 1945. His reference to "all the war dead" clearly meant that fallen German soldiers were to be considered "war dead." Nevertheless, in a memorial convocation speech he gave at the Hamburg Music Hall (Musikhalle) he stressed: "We wish . . . to kindle feelings of humanity and international solidarity, recognizing the comprehensive guilt of the German nation." In other words, broadening the range of those called victims did not, in his view, expunge the German people's political guilt for bringing Hitler to power and for supporting him. Heitgres spoke of the murder of millions, but did not mention Jews explicitly. Neither did Karl Meitmann, chairman of Hamburg's Social Democratic Party and a concentration camp veteran, refer to the Jews explicitly in his speech. He did, however, speak in detail about the atrocities committed by the Nazi regime, including beating prisoners to death, starvation, and gassings. He stressed that people "did not die here as an inescapable act of nature, nor did they fall here in a battle between one man and another. Here human beings were murdered, defenseless and helpless men, women, and children."

In a speech he gave at the cemetery, Friedrich Dettmann, another Hamburg Communist who then served as senator (minister) of health, cited the Jews first among the regime's victims, before anti-Nazi fighters, including Ernst Thälmann. "We remember you," he said. "We remember the millions of Jews from all the countries of Europe who were led to their deaths because of their race." Note that Dettmann referred to all the Jews targeted by the Nazis, not just the Jews of Germany. Most of Germany's other leaders at the time spoke only of Germany's Jews, and included them among the Germans persecuted by the Nazis: "We must rebuild, through disciplined work and sincere effort, all the destruction sown by the Nazis among the peoples of Europe in the name of Germany—because German workers and citizens did not fight Hitler sufficiently." In other words, Dettmann held all Germans, including the Nazis' sworn opponents, responsible. Hitler was able to take over Germany because they did not fight fascism with sufficient determination. They were therefore responsible for his catastrophic actions.

The speeches from the left indeed linked remembering the dead to responsibility and blame for the Nazis' rise to power. But they did not address the enthusiastic enlistment of many Germans in the Nazi Party, or the great popularity that Hitler and his regime enjoyed.[16] The speakers from the right and center did not address these issues at all. In their speeches, they portrayed the German people as the pawns of history between 1933 and 1945. In this view, the Germans were the Nazis' first victims. So claimed Rudolf Petersen, a Christian Democrat who was appointed mayor of Hamburg by the British in May 1945:

> The German people were despondent and miserable because of unemployment and inflation to the point that, because of German gullibility, they gave themselves over blindly to the hypnotic influence of a demagogue. And they were quickly drawn after him, against their will, like a hypnotized patient obeying authority.

Petersen went so far as to say that "only a few really knew the extent of the atrocities taking place on German soil." Nevertheless, the representatives of the right also expressed their respect and appreciation of the former political prisoners from all political movements. They had comprehended "before the German people did, that Nazism would lead to devastation."[17]

This consensus on the victims of fascism was also evident in the memorials built during this period. In July 1946, the Hamburg senate decided to construct the city's first monument to the victims of Nazi terror of all nations. But then a dispute broke out: former political prisoners wanted the structure to be built in the city's bustling center, perhaps facing city hall, while the city-state's planning division and some senators wanted it to be erected at the Ohlsdorf Cemetery in the city's north.[18]

At the end of 1947 it was decided to place the monument in the cemetery.[19] There is no way of knowing if there was a connection between the decision and the waning status of the political prisoners' organizations in the western zones of occupation. The Communists had always been the most prominent members of these groups, so when tensions between the Western and Eastern blocs intensified, the political prisoners' organizations lost their influence in the West. The monument, a fifty-foot-high tower containing burial urns, was designed by the engineer Heinz-Jürgen Ruscheweyh.

Up until 1948, the local governments in western Germany gave their sanction to the memorial ceremonies conducted by the VVN in September. "Our people must bow their heads in silent respect before the men who heroically strove to put an end to the German calamity. This is a debt of honor," declared the Hamburg senate and parliament (*Bürgerschaft*), which was controlled by the Social Democrats, in advance of Memorial Day for the Victims of Fascism in September 1947.[20] However, the Cold War broke out before construction of the monument was completed.

Political tension between the senate, chaired by the Social Democrat Max Brauer, and the pro-Communist VVN produced a personal rupture between the parties of the left. The result was that the monument was dedicated twice—first on May 3, 1949, by the senate, and five days later by the VVN.[21]

The culture of memory and commemoration that took form in Germany after 1945 was profoundly shaken by the Cold War. In 1948 the Communists took over the VVN; from then on it was subject to the central committee of the SED. Consequently, the Social Democratic leadership decided in May 1948 that members of the VVN could not be members of the SPD. But not all those who belonged to the SPD resigned immediately from the VVN. Philipp Auerbach, a Jewish community leader and

Figure 18. Monument to the Victims of Nazism, designed by Ruscheweyh, in the Ohlsdorf Cemetery, Hamburg

Bavaria's commissar for the victims of Nazism, did not obey his party's injunction. In October 1948, before he finally resigned from the organization, he argued that the VVN in Bavaria was nonpartisan, and that it included Christian Democrats and Liberals. While elsewhere in Germany Christian Democrats and members of other parties left the VVN in

1948, the Bavarians did not do so until May 1949.[22] The VVN subsequently began involving itself in the fiery political issues of the time, taking an uncompromising Communist Party line. It presented itself as representing the wishes and legacy of fascism's victims. This line, with its whiff of nationalism, found expression in the VVN's periodical *Die Tat,* which commenced publication in 1948.

Once the Cold War began, the VVN converted its ceremonies on Memorial Day for the Victims of Fascism into a forum for vilifying the West. In 1949, for example, the organization opposed establishment of the Federal Republic in the western zones of occupation, and in the early 1950s it campaigned against rearming Germany and its membership in NATO, virulently attacking the Adenauer administration.[23] In July 1951 the SED Central Committee ordered the VVN to play an active role in the Communist struggle against German rearmament.[24] In 1953 the SED dissolved the VVN in East Germany, similar to Stalinist purges against "Zionists" and cosmopolitanism.[25]

At the beginning of August 1948, Karl Kühne, of the Committee for Social Democratic Victims, wrote to Brauer, Hamburg's Social Democratic mayor, about commemorating members of the anti-Nazi underground. After the SPD's exit from the VVN, he wrote, his committee felt a duty to take responsibility for remembering German fighters against fascism. He asked that the senate transfer authority for conducting memorial ceremonies from the VVN to his committee. "For political reasons, we believe that the [SPD-controlled] senate should determine the structure of the celebrations and coordinate them with all the victims' organizations, including the VVN."

His request was not honored, but Brauer wanted the senate to conduct its own ceremony in parallel with the VVN's ceremony. In response, the VVN approached Senator Ludwig Hartenfels of the Liberal Party and asked him to arrange senate sponsorship for the VVN's September memorial ceremony.

Senatussyndikus Harder proposed holding the senate's memorial day on the Sunday of the Dead, but Social Democratic senators Heinrich Eisenbarth and Paul Nevermann objected. They argued that the senate's memorial ceremony should take place on the existing date that year, thus preserving its character. In the end it was decided to hold the ceremony in its established date at the cemetery. Furthermore, the senate's chancery would examine the possibility that the following year, 1949, the ceremony would be held on a different date.[26]

A few days after the Hamburg senate made its decision, the premier of Schleswig-Holstein, Hermann Lüdemann, like party chief Kurt Schumacher an anticommunist Social Democrat, sent a letter to the other premiers in the western zones of occupation. He notified them that, in his state, a Memorial Day for the Victims of Nazism and the War would be held that year on September 18 (rather than September 12, the day set by the VVN). He wrote that on this day, the people should be made aware that "those whom fascism murdered made the most sublime of all the sacrifices for democracy." In his opinion, this day should not look only to the past. It should be designed "as a popular democratic holiday that calls urgently for battle against any tyrannical regime and for full commitment to democracy." Lüdemann's implication was that the Communist regime was as oppressive as Nazism. He further proposed that all the states in the western zones of occupation adopt this day. Brauer responded that, in the future, Hamburg's ceremony would be held on the Sunday of the Dead. Thus, it could also serve as a day of remembrance for all who died in the war.[27]

The Cold War prompted the SPD's anticommunists to leave the VVN and to cease participation in the ceremonies it had organized since 1945. They organized alternative rites, but in the meantime they did not always enjoy support within their party.

Those who walked out of the VVN set up a number of other organizations. The first to leave were the Social Democrats, who in 1948 established, at their party's behest, the Working Group of Former Social Democratic Victims of the Nazis (*Arbeitsgemeinschaft ehemals verfolgter Sozialdemokraten*, or AvS). At the beginning of February 1950, Wilhelm Müller and Peter Luetsches, a Christian Democratic journalist from Düsseldorf, broke with the VVN and founded the Alliance of Victims of Nazi Persecution (*Bund der Verfolgten des Naziregimes*, or BVN), which was defined as a noncommunist organization. It had branches in West Berlin and in the cities of the British zone of occupation (Hamburg, Düsseldorf). Former members of the VVN also created the Alliance for Freedom and Law (*Bund für Freiheit und Recht*), in the framework of which two regional organizations worked independently: the Association for Freedom and Human Rights (*Verband für Freiheit und Menschenwürde e.V*) in Hesse, and the Council for Freedom and Law (*Landesrat für Freiheit und Recht*) in Bavaria.

The VVN's logo was a red triangle—the badge political prisoners in concentration camps had been forced to wear—against a background of blue and white stripes, reminiscent of the camp uniforms. The Alliance for Freedom and Law, in contrast, chose a globe as an expression of the organization's universal character, which went beyond the issue of Nazism. The new organization's structure also testified to its goals and philosophy. The Alliance had five divisions, three of which I refer to here: Political, Racial, and Religious Victims of Nazism (PVN); Political, Racial, and Religious Victims of Stalinism (PVSt); and the unit for the Study of Totalitarianism—Neo-Nazism–Stalinism–Anti-Semitism (VT). These new entities sought to create ceremonies for Nazi victims that would constitute a democratic and Western mirror image of the VVN's memorial day.

Just as the Communist organization combined its memorial work with an anti-Western political line, the Alliance and other anticommunist organizations combined their honoring of Nazism's victims with the pursuit of their own political agenda. Equating Stalinism with Nazism did more than censure Communism, in keeping with the theories of totalitarianism that became widespread after the war. It also downplayed the uniqueness of the Nazis' crimes.

Faced with the establishment of these alternative organizations, the VVN intensified its efforts in the summer of 1950, as its Memorial Day for the Victims of Fascism approached that September. At the beginning of July, after leaving the VVN, Philipp Auerbach—now president of the Reparations Office in Bavaria and member of the BVN—sent Hamburg mayor Max Brauer a "top secret" letter. Auerbach detailed the noncommunist organizations' efforts in advance of the memorial day. They would, he wrote, discard the term "victims of fascism" (with its Communist connotations) and replace it with "victims of Nazism," and stress that the day also honored those who still suffered in concentration camps in the lands under Soviet tyranny. The organizations' posters thus bore the slogan, "We remember the victims of brutality." Auerbach claimed that "the Communist VVN intends to misuse the memorial ceremonies for narrow partisan purposes, such as demonstrating against imperialist warmongers and other such slogans, in the spirit of Moscow jargon." He called on

Brauer to ensure that the authorities would not participate in the VVN ceremonies, which could be interpreted as assisting SED propaganda.[28]

In August 1950, the Alliance's action committee issued an official statement to all federal and local governments on the occasion of its Memorial Day for All Victims of Inhumanity (*Alle Opfer der Unmenschlichkeit*), scheduled for September 10. Under the heading "Fighting Brutality" it stated:

> Instead of remembering all the brave men and women who gave up their lives for freedom; instead of ardently opposing the renewed brutality in new concentration camps and new persecutions, the memorial ceremonies of the Association of Victims of the Nazi Regime exude a spirit of hatred, arrogance, and intolerance by giving anti-fascism a Stalinist cast.

The statement also claimed that the VVN took orders from the FIAPP, the Communist international organization of former concentration camp inmates, centered in Prague. In support of this allegation, the statement quoted an SED official, Franz Dahlem: "This year Memorial Day will be given the character of the international struggle for peace and against fascism." Consequently, the anticommunist Alliance of Nazi Regime Victims decided not to stand aloof. It planned memorial convocations in West Berlin, Hamburg, at Wuppertal in Düsseldorf, Bonn, Mainz, and Stuttgart. These convocations were to recount to the German people the balance of horror and the culpability of totalitarian systems of repression of Hitlerism and Stalinism.[29]

The West German federal, state, and local authorities indeed provided financial assistance to the anticommunist organizations. However, they did not replace the VVN's ceremonies with those of the democratic Alliance. Instead, they sought to formulate other models of memory and commemoration that would meet the needs and wishes of the majority of Germans.

West Germany Institutes Alternative Memorial Days

A short time after the Federal Republic was established in September 1949, a bill was introduced in the Bundestag proposing a German National Day of Mourning (*Nationaltrauertag*) in memory of the war dead. The measure was considered by the Bundestag's committees but never passed, because of doubts as to whether the federal parliament had the power to legislate on this matter.[30] Another proposal sought to create a special day of mourning for civilians killed in the war. Public bodies made similar requests. The draft laws were sent to the Bundestag's Internal Administration Committee, but differences of opinion in the panel kept the bills from being sent to the floor of the parliament.

Even after the Federal Republic was founded, the Volksbund continued to push for establishment of a People's Day of Mourning on Reminiscere Sunday, and it took this campaign to the national level. The Volksbund asked President Theodor Heuss to intervene. Heuss, who had been (together with Konrad Adenauer) one of the founders of the Volksbund in 1919, promised to do what he could to help reestablish the People's Day of Mourning. Cooperation between the organization and the federal government was institutionalized, and in 1950 a representative of the Volksbund was appointed liaison between the organization and the government in Bonn. On Reminiscere Sunday that same year—the day the People's Day of Mourning had been observed during the Weimar Republic—the Volksbund held, throughout Germany, ceremonies in honor of the dead of both world wars. The central rite for soldiers killed in battle was conducted at a special plenary session of the Bundestag, in the presence of President Heuss. For the Volksbund's leadership, this was an important step along the way to obtaining official status for its memorial day. The author of an article in the organization's periodical, "The People's Day of Mourning—Today Just Like 28 Years Ago," noted with satisfaction that the ceremony in the Bundestag building in Bonn reestablished a tradition that dated back to Reminiscere Sunday in 1922 when, for the first time, a ceremony for the war dead was held in the Reichstag building in Berlin.[31]

In May 1950, the Ministry of Labor, Agriculture, and the Economy in the state of Hesse wrote to the federal minister of the interior, Gustav Heinemann, requesting that the Memorial Day for the Victims of Fascism be postponed to the beginning of autumn. The letter explained that Hesse, the Rhine region, and Rhineland-Palatinate had centuries-old traditions of holding local celebrations and fairs on the second Sunday of September. Heinemann referred the matter to the coordinating office of the Interministerial Committee on Reparations, headed by Philipp Auerbach. He chose this committee because it included representatives of the large victims' organizations. (Among them was a representative of the Communist Association of Victims of the Nazi Regime, Dr. Marcel Frenkel, who, until he was suspended in 1951 because of his membership in pro-Soviet organizations, headed the Reparations Department of the state of North Rhine-Westphalia.) Nevertheless, it is astonishing that he referred the issue to a body responsible for coordinating reparations payments for the victims of Nazism. Perhaps he simply followed precedents from the Allied military administrations, when issues related to Nazi persecution were placed under the purview of the victims' organizations because of their political sensitivity.

The officials of the coordinating office rejected Hesse's request, recommending that the federal government prepare legislation that would establish the Memorial Day for the Victims of Fascism as a federal day of mourning throughout Germany. Heinemann acceded and, in June 1950, informed Hesse's Ministry of Labor, Agriculture, and the Economy that the memorial day would not be postponed, and furthermore that it might soon be mandated by federal law.[32] But Hesse did not give in, and asked that the question be placed on the agenda of the meeting of state interior ministers of the Federal Republic scheduled to convene in Berlin on July 17–18, 1950. At this meeting, the Hesse minister reiterated his request to change the date of the ceremonies. The interior ministers of Lower Saxony and Rhineland-Palatinate joined him.

The representative from Schleswig-Holstein, Dr. Galette, made a proposal with far-reaching implications for the Federal Republic's culture of memory and remembrance. Yet his arguments did not cite the Cold War and the struggle against the Communist VVN. According to Galette, Memorial Day for the Victims of Fascism had been observed in his state since 1948 on the basis of administrative orders and had never been legislated. Only a handful of people participated in the day's ceremonies. Only in one county or district (Kreis) was there active involvement by the inhabitants. The reason was that in that region the orders had been changed so that both Memorial Day for the Victims of Fascism and a memorial day for those who died in both world wars were observed on the same day. The representative from Schleswig-Holstein, where the Christian Democrats had just replaced the Social Democrats, proposed that

> five years after the war's end and the demise of Nazi regime, the time has now come to bridge the gap within the people and to unite the two memorial days. If that does not happen, the People's Day of Mourning will remain a Heroes' Memorial Day like that observed during the

> Nazi period. At bottom, the purpose is to honor those dead who loyally served their homeland and gave their best for it. Their good will and noble commitment should be venerated, and the great losses among the victims of fascism and those who died in the world wars should all be remembered. Schleswig-Holstein will thus act in accordance with the Volksbund's proposal to hold a joint memorial day as a People's Day of Mourning, and to win it official recognition in federal law during the year to come.

At the end of the discussion, the ministers voted on the question of whether to conduct a common day of mourning for the soldiers who had died in the world wars and for the victims of fascism. The representatives from Hesse, Lower Saxony, Rhineland-Palatinate, and Schleswig-Holstein voted in favor. Delegates from the other states abstained. None voted against.[33]

At another meeting of the state interior ministers on August 10, 1950, Heinemann called attention to the fact that the VVN intended to use the coming Memorial Day for the Victims of Fascism on September 10 to conduct demonstrations against the federal government and its policies. He claimed that "they intend to involve large Communist delegations from Eastern and Western Europe, in order to produce a revolutionary situation in West Germany." The interior ministers agreed that such provocations required a response. Heinemann proposed acceding to requests to observe a memorial day for all "who gave their lives for the highest good of humanity (*die ihr Leben für die höhren Güter der Menschheit gelassen habe*)." He suggested conducting a joint memorial day for the German people on September 3, 1950, stressing that

> the reflection about these dead, showing respect for whom is an expression of the people's fundamental character values, must not be exploited cynically for political purposes. It is therefore necessary that the honoring of these dead include the victims of the recent past. No distinction should be made between those who gave their lives (*ihr Leben hingegeben haben*) in bombings at home, or as soldiers, POWs, or political, racial, or religious [prisoners].[34]

In this view, there was no distinction between those persecuted by the Nazis and Hitler's soldiers who gave their lives in battle. All were victims "who gave their lives for the highest good of humanity." All were worthy of similar honor. Heinemann's position took one step further the position formulated in July 1945 by the Berlin City Council's Chief Committee for the Victims of Fascism.

A day after Heinemann made this statement, on August 11, 1950, the proposal was brought before the cabinet. Its ministers agreed that the days commemorating the ratification of the Basic Constitutional Law (*Grundgesetz*) and the war dead would be combined into a single observance. They proposed that this day be observed on the first Sunday of September. At the same time, Heinemann raised the subject with the leader of the Social Democratic opposition, Kurt Schumacher, who endorsed the proposal.[35] President Heuss opposed uniting the national day of mourning with the commemoration of the Basic Constitutional Law. He suggested holding a memorial day for all the war dead in March. During the early Weimar period, the People's Day of Mourning had been on Invocavit Sunday, the sixth Sunday before Eater. In 1926, it was moved to Reminiscere Sunday, one week earlier. The Volksbund favored the earlier date. Heuss wanted a separate day to commemorate the Basic Constitutional Law. In 1950, the National Memorial Day of the German People (*Nationaler Gedenktag des deutschen Volkes*) was observed on September 7, the anniversary of the Bundestag's first session (with the establishment of the Federal Republic in September 1949).[36] This day was observed throughout the Federal Republic.

In 1951, the federal Ministry of the Interior decided to act in the spirit of Heuss's suggestion and to detach the memorial day from Day of the Basic Constitutional Law. The ministry determined that "the central national people's memorial day" would continue to be held on its current date in September, but would focus on reestablishing a democratic order through the enactment of a Basic Constitutional Law. The war dead would be honored in a ceremony on a different date.[37] Representatives of bodies with an interest in the day—government officials, the churches, the Volksbund, and the Committee for Social Democratic Victims—convened in February 1952. They decided that the People's Day of Mourning would be observed on the second Sunday before First Advent in November. This was not the Volksbund's preference, but it agreed to the new date. However, this day's status was not anchored in legislation.[38]

In 1951, the Bavarian government acted to observe a War Victim's Day (*Tag der Opfer des Krieges*) on the Sunday of the Dead, which fell that year on October 30. Its decision stated that this day would be devoted to honoring the memory of those who died in both world wars, whether they were soldiers killed on the battlefield, civilians who lost their lives in the Allied bombings, or soldiers who died as POWs after the end of World War II.[39]

The announcement stressed that local communities had a duty to ensure that ceremonies were conducted properly, not exploited for nefarious purposes. It also stated that the Volksbund, the Association of War Injured, and the families of the dead could participate. Neither the VVN nor its anticommunist splinters were mentioned.

While the importance of the Cold War as a cause of these far-reaching changes in public memorial practices should not be underestimated, it should hardly be seen as the only factor in slighting the memory of the Nazis' victims in favor of soldiers and civilians who died in the war. Most Germans mourned only for the latter. Only a handful of West Germans advocated the elimination of an official memorial day for fallen soldiers (which the Nazis called Heroes' Memorial Day).[40] Whatever their political persuasions, most viewed the lack of such a day as an anomaly. When a German state with its own political culture would come into being, it was only natural that changes would occur in how it remembered its dead. The immediate postwar culture of memory and remembrance had been instituted under the tutelage of the Western occupying powers. It expressed a view of the war that was held only by a small anti-Nazi minority in German society at the time.

Using the victims of fascism as a device for scoring political points, principally in Communist propaganda of the Cold War, accelerated an inevitable process—they were pushed out of the consensus. During the first years after World War II, there had been general agreement in West Germany's political establishments regarding the political importance of honoring these victims in post-Nazi German society. But German soldiers and civilians who had died in the war soon displaced the victims in that consensus, including, of course, the Jews.

The federal government assigned the Volksbund to conduct the central memorial ceremonies of the People's Day of Mourning, excluding the anticommunist victims' organizations that had broken away from the VVN. This undoubtedly affected the character of the rite. The ceremonies arranged by organizations of political victims of the Nazis had, up until the Cold War, focused on the fate of those who fought the Nazis and others who were oppressed by the tyrannical regime. But the Federal Republic's leadership, in coordination with the Social Democratic opposition, chose to divert the focus from the victims, including the Jews and anti-Nazi fighters, and to emphasize instead the memory of those Germans who had suffered and died.

In 1952, the People's Day of Mourning was granted official status. The Federal Republic decided to honor the Nazis' victims, alongside the soldiers and civilians who lost their lives, on the second Sunday before First Advent.[41] In November, speaking before a special session of the Bundestag devoted to the People's Day of Mourning, President Heuss elucidated the new concept of remembrance:

> The stone markers and signposts multiply: this one is in memory of those killed in the bombings, this one lies on the edge of a concentration camp, and that one stands in a Jewish cemetery. Oh, heroism has passed on [a reference to the themes of the Heroes' Memorial Day of the Nazi period], it is simply immeasurable suffering. Here it was the result of *unrestrained technical power,* and there the result of *total moral disruption* [emphasis in the original]. And we stand mortified and aggrieved before these two stone witnesses. There will be those who will resent my calling these victims the victims of a single evil policy. But I know that the sincere soldier is at my side.[42]

Heuss implicitly rehearsed the reconciliation narrative, the German national account of the war that could be seen in East Germany's propaganda. It equated the Allies' attacks on German civilian targets ("unrestrained technical power") with the criminal acts of the Nazi regime ("total moral disruption") and analogized Nazism's Jewish victims to the Germans killed in battle. Such comparisons bore the imprint of the German nationalist view of the Allies' war conduct as evil and criminal, an element of Nazi propaganda during the war.

This "moral equivalence" shocked Jewish leaders, but it was not in their power to change it. Faced with this development, Karl Marx, the editor of the Jewish newspaper *Allgemeine Wochenzeitung der Juden in Deutschland,* had as early as November 1950 written to the Federal Republic's minister of justice, Thomas Dehler:

> I long ago ceased to believe that anyone [in the Bundestag] would propose a separate memorial time that would not be shared with the German war dead. However, it is impossible to expect that a Jewish representative will

> sit beside the family of an SS man who used to be a murderer of Jews and only afterward became a victim of the war.[43]

But even Dehler himself spoke in a similar fashion. For example, a year later, when he opened a working meeting with Jewish jurists in December 1951:

> One of my insights from the evil Nazi period is that everything the Germans did to the Jews got done to them in return. They deprived the Jews of their political freedom, and the German people lost its freedom; they took the Jews' lives, and millions of Germans lost their lives; they took away their property, and millions of Germans lost their property.[44]

Those persecuted for their political views also observed the rapid changes in the culture of memory and remembrance with a sense of repressed anger and helplessness.

Federal decisions that changed memorial practices were also manifested on the local scale. One example comes from the city of Mannheim. In his address in September 1948, on the occasion of Memorial Day for the Victims of Fascism, Dr. Hermann Heimerich took a position with far-reaching implications in those days: "We must admit that we feel disappointment that the great and painful sacrifice made has not received recompense and has not had the influence one should have expected, and which should be demanded." Later in his remarks, he expressed the hope that Germans would remember fascism's victims and the members of the resistance organizations and appreciate their lives and actions:

> But the way Germans live and the state of their country make it possible for them to disparage those who were murdered and those who fell [in battle]. The old fascism shows its face everywhere; it is easier for a veteran Nazi to get certain jobs than one persecuted by the Nazis for his political convictions or race. For example, Hjalmar Schacht [Hitler's economics minister in 1934–1937 and then the president of the Reichsbank until 1939], a servant of the Nazis, now enjoys . . . glory, as if he had saved the country.[45]

Mannheim can serve as an example of how the memorial culture changed on the local scale as the Cold War intensified. Up until 1948, Memorial Day for the Victims of Fascism was observed with a ceremony conducted jointly by the municipality and the VVN. In 1949, however, the city government revoked its sponsorship, and the rites were conducted solely by the Nazi victims' organizations.

In September 1949, the Social Democrats reinstalled Heimerich as mayor of Mannheim (he had served in that capacity from 1928 until he was deposed by the Nazis in 1933). On his return to office, he seemed to have changed his opinion on the memorial issue. Like other German Social Democrats, he had become alienated from the culture of memory and remembrance that he had spoken of so emotionally just two years previously. Only the Communists continued to give priority to the memory of the Nazis' victims. During a session of the Mannheim city council in August 1950, Heimerich said:

> I have before me a proposal from the Communist faction to install a plaque memorializing the citizens of Mannheim who were persecuted by the Nazis and who were executed by the Third Reich in Lechleiter Squre in the city. . . . I presented a somewhat different position on this issue, and expressed my opinion that we need to take more significant action here . . . to erect in an appropriate place in Mannheim a monument to those killed between 1939 and 1945, including the victims who lost their lives in the world war.

Georg Lechleiter had headed Mannheim's Communist underground. His comrades were captured and executed. Victoria Langendorf, a Communist member of the city council, was the widow of Rudolph, one of the executed members of Lechleiter's cell. She protested the mayor's intention of constructing a single memorial for members of the anti-Nazi underground and other Germans killed during the war:

> There is nevertheless an important difference between all those killed during the war and the active underground fighters who opposed Hitler staunchly, and who consciously led the struggle to topple the Hitler regime, for the sake of a better future.

She did not oppose erecting a monument to all who were killed in the war, but argued that those who died serving in the anti-Nazi resistance deserved their own memorial:

> We must say that there were in any case among [the war dead] people who enlisted enthusiastically in the war for Hitler, and who aspired to the precise opposite of what those who gave up their lives willingly aspired to. To volunteer freely for the war for Hitler is something different. In my opinion, the two cannot be connected.
>
> Heimerich responded:

> Even though it cannot be denied that the underground fighters performed especially worthy deeds, all were victims, whether they enthusiastically enlisted in the war or consciously gave up their lives. I believe that it is impossible to make such pedantic distinctions.

"It's not pedantic!" Langendorf replied.[46]

Her plea was to no avail. Ironically, in the milieu of the Cold War, German Social Democrats who supported the West perceived the pre–Cold War memorial culture in the West as representing a pro-Soviet political position they were duty-bound to oppose. Heimerich had no trouble pushing through a decision to build a common memorial for all the dead. At a meeting of the city's administrative committee devoted to this subject in June 1952, he responded to the renewed proposal of the VVN to install a plaque in Leichleiter Square. In response to a city council member named Locherer, who opposed Heimerich's view, stressing the exemplary nature of active resistance to the Nazis, Heimerich rejected the distinction and reiterated that "all these people were the victims of fascism and fell victim to the war connected to this regime." He argued that if a distinction were to be made between victims and anti-Nazi fighters, it would become a precedent that would produce demands to rehabilitate monuments to soldiers who died in World War I.[47]

The protests of the Jews and Communists were to no avail. The view of the People's Day of Mourning as a memorial for all the victims of the war and of Nazism remained in place. Nevertheless, speeches in the Bundestag on the People's Day of Mourning during the 1950s no longer equated the Jews killed in the Holocaust with Wehrmacht soldiers who were killed in action or with German civilians who died, as had President Heuss on the first People's Day of Mourning. They proclaimed the soldiers' heroism, their love of their homeland, and their self-sacrifice, and gave the day the character of a German national day of mourning.[48] Issues such as civil and political responsibility and the guilt for crimes and atrocities, which had been raised at ceremonies for Nazi victims up until the outbreak of the Cold War (even if not with great prominence), were simply ignored.

This phenomenon was all the more evident in ceremonies and convocations conducted in community and local frameworks throughout the Federal Republic during the 1950s. There the memory of fascism's victims, including Jews, was entirely absent. An exception was a speech by Max

Brauer, Hamburg's Social Democratic mayor, on the first People's Day of Mourning in 1952. He spoke about guilt and political responsibility for the rise of the Nazis, an issue that President Heuss had ignored in his speech to the Bundestag, just as other speakers did throughout the Federal Republic. At the beginning of his remarks he took up the subject of civilians who had been killed in the Allied bombings of Hamburg: "These 55,000 men, women, and children from Hamburg's civilian population were the victims of the total war that Hitler began, and which imposed immeasurable suffering on our people and on all brother peoples [*Brüdervölker*] in this world." Then he referred to the "war in the darkness" (*ein Krieg in Dunkeln*), no less bloody than the great killing fields or the horrible bombings, which erased the distinction between front and rear. Brauer meant the persecution of all political and religious opponents of the regime. He spoke in detail about the persecution of the Jews of Germany and in all of Europe. At the center of his speech he repeated his assertion of a few months previously, when he had dedicated a monument to the citizens of Hamburg killed in the bombings:

> Why did they die? Why were they sentenced to be torn from their families? From the survivors? . . . They were torn from us because we, with our own hands, gave up our independent free will. . . . They were cut off from us because the cooperation between nations was not sufficiently successful and sincere, and because we allowed racial hatred and prejudices to overwhelm us.[49]

But his contrition disappeared in subsequent speeches on the People's Day of Mourning. In 1958, the Volksbund's idea of reconciliation in the grave, and the aspiration for peace in the face of the specter of nuclear war, overwhelmed the demand to acknowledge guilt and assume responsibility.[50]

A more characteristic expression of the meaning of the People's Day of Mourning can be found in the report of the newspaper *Westdeutsche Allgemeine* in the city of Essen in 1952: "The memory of the war dead was commemorated yesterday at memorial sites. The soldiers, and the men, the women, and the children who fell at home (*Der in der Heimat gefallene*)." Not only is there no mention of the Nazi regime's victims—Jews in particular—but the writer adopted Nazi terminology to describe the civilians killed—they "fell," equating the death of a soldier at the front to that of a woman or child in the rear. This was Goebbels's doctrine of total war.[51]

Colloquially, many Germans have continued to use the former Nazi term, Heroes' Memorial Day, to refer to the People's Day of Mourning. The two names express, of course, entirely different concepts of the day's significance. There was very little criticism within German society about the messages conveyed by the new memorial day. In November 1955, in Wiesbaden, the writer and pastor Albrecht Goes offered his opinion:

> The People's Day of Mourning, ladies and gentlemen, will be a repellant display of self-commiseration (*Selbstbemitleidung*); of indescribable hypocrisy. If we do not grieve on [this day] for the horrible injustice done to the Jewish people; if we wish to cite the monument recently built in Tobruk [in Libya, in memory of the German soldiers killed in the North African campaign], but remain silent about the obelisk of Bergen-Belsen; if we seek to remember only provisionally the sorrow of Theresienstadt, Auschwitz, and Majdanek . . . if we do not wish to see honestly that even before that black day in June 1922, before the day Walter Rathenau was assassinated, that even then the antisemitism of [the historian Heinrich von] Treitschke and [preacher Adolf] Stoecker [one of the first political antisemites in Germany, at the end of the nineteenth century] had, despite all the "rule of law," generated the root of all evil among us.

Goes's exceptional plea for introspection on the People's Day of Mourning was also severe in relation to the postwar guilt discourse, which focused on political issues. It referred to the Germans' social and cultural guilt—pervasive German antisemitism—which ran deeper than political guilt. Goes, after all, tied the murder of Rathenau, the German-Jewish foreign minister in the Weimar government, and the extermination of Jews in the Third Reich's death camps to the rise of modern antisemitism in Germany.[52]

Goes was before his time. Only in the 1960s did other messages slowly start seeping into People's Day of Mourning ceremonies. This change occurred as the Jewish Holocaust narrative penetrated the Federal Republic's political culture, beginning in the late 1950s and intensifying in the early 1960s. The diffusion of the Jewish narrative into the German discourse also brought about a certain change in the message of the People's Day of Mourning. The reference to Jewish victims became much more salient than it had been in the 1950s, making the character of the day more universal. In his speech at the memorial's day's central ceremony, before the Bundestag in Bonn in 1967, the Volksbund's president, Walter Trepte, reminded his audience:

> When we speak on the People's Day of Mourning about the dead of the world wars, we must not just consider the Germans who died. . . . At this hour, we must not forget those who were sentenced to sacrifice their lives in all ways in these wars. All belong to our sorrowful memory. Including the 6 million Jews, whose brutal extermination lies on our souls like a nightmare.[53]

While Trepte did not go as far as Goes, the inclusion in his People's Day of Mourning speech of all Jews who were murdered in the Holocaust (rather than only German Jews), as well as other victims, is indicative of a transformation of the message the memorial day had borne since the mid-1960s. It went far beyond the sentiments President Heuss expressed in 1952, not to mention the general character the day took in local German communities.

From the beginning of the 1960s onward, as the German media and public increasingly addressed the Holocaust,[54] a new element entered the Federal Republic's culture of memory—the Jewish narrative of the Holocaust. It was not official, but it was hugely influential. On occasion, the conventional wisdom about the Nazi past sounded more like the Jewish narrative than the reconciliation narrative.

This process could also be discerned in some of the speeches at the annual central observance of the People's Day of Mourning, conducted since the mid-1960s at a plenary session of the Bundestag. In 1974, the Jewish sociologist and political scientist Alfred Grosser was invited to give the keynote speech in the Bundestag. Grosser, who as a child had been compelled to flee from Germany to France, was nevertheless known for his pro-German stance and chose to sound a conciliatory note toward the Germans on this occasion. Nevertheless, he also raised the question of political responsibility (not only in the past, but also at the time), and offered a historical contextualization of the memorial day. He declared that the Germans had sought for many long years, and much more than in other European countries, to limit the scope of their shared responsibility for events of the war. He referred to the lack of political involvement by the Germans during the 1930s, and then accused German Jews of having behaved much like their German fellow citizens. German Jews, he alleged, had kept themselves at arm's length when Eastern European Jews were persecuted by the Nazis.[55] This was hardly a real challenge to the Germans; when Grosser put the German Jews on the same moral plane as the entire German people, he encouraged German self-pity and divestment of responsibility for the Holocaust.[56]

Alfred Grosser was not the only speaker at these central ceremonies to take up issues of guilt and responsibility in the late 1970s. The Social Democratic minister Carlo Schmid, who gave the keynote central speech in 1978, also referred to the question of German guilt:

> We, the older ones, should have kept a better eye on our country during those decisive years. We failed to do that, we failed precisely as patriots, since civic sense and civic courage and the love for our fatherland should have summoned us to plan, while one could still resist the incipience (of Nazism), to defend peace, freedom, and human rights. We cannot say that we could have not recognized what was to come![57]

In addition, from the 1980s onward, far more than before the 1970s, one could hear in the speeches in the central ceremonies the German yearning for peace and the country's commitment to protect human rights and human dignity. In 1981, the Social Democratic vice president of the Bundestag, Annemarie Renger, dedicated most of her speech to the German commitment to peace:

> Our people commits itself to peace, aware that only peace gives us the chance to live in freedom and human dignity. The public's desire for peace determines our country's policies, but hardly for the first time. Our people have ceremoniously sworn in their Basic Law that they will serve the peace in the world and that no war will come out of or begin on our territory.[58]

In the 1980s, the Jewish narrative began to emerge as a powerful force in the way Nazi victims, Jews in particular, were represented in monuments. A large number of memorial plaques and monuments were erected throughout the Federal Republic as a result of local initiatives.[59] At the same time, the public, influenced largely by the 1968 generation, began to espouse certain egalitarian principles, evincing sympathy for social and ethnic groups that were persecuted by the Nazis and were still denied official recognition as victims of Nazism, such as the Sinti and Roma and homosexuals[60] (an atmosphere that has, regrettably, faded noticeably since the beginning of the 1990s). Paradoxically, some of the public support for such initiatives was fueled by a certain resentment against the ever-more pervasive presence of the Holocaust and the Jewish victim in German daily life and culture.[61] It was only at this time that some groups of the Nazi's victims, previously unrecognized as such by the authorities or the public at large, finally received official acknowledgment that they had been persecuted. As early as 1978, Carlo Schmid referred explicitly to the Gypsies as well as the Jews as victims of Nazism.[62] The speech of the Federal Republic's president, Richard von Weiszäcker, at the plenary session of the Bundestag on May 8, 1985, marking the fortieth anniversary of the end of the Second World War was symptomatic of this change. A couple of months later, Hans-Jochen Vogel was already following Weiszäcker's example, explicitly naming a long list of all groups of Nazi victims.

It is difficult, however, to assess the extent to which the contents of these speeches actually reflect contemporary German public opinion about the Nazi past. Conservative speakers, such as the moderate chancellor Dr. Helmut Kohl or the much less moderate Dr. Alfred Dregger, the leader of the right wing in the Christian Democratic parliamentary faction, continued apologetically to make the same arguments as in the past. In 1983 Kohl continued the 1950s tradition of omitting any expression of criticism or reference to questions of guilt or responsibility: "But today our subject is neither to worship heroes, nor are we called on to judge weakness and failure."[63] Dregger, a former Wehrmacht officer, proclaimed on the People's Day of Mourning in 1986 that German soldiers should not be portrayed as murderers. They, too, were victims, no different from the people killed in the extermination program, members of the anti-Nazi underground, and the German civilians incinerated in the Allied bombings. The soldiers were the victims of the political leadership that started the war, he said.[64]

In recent years, there have been grassroots as well as official initiatives in the realm of the landscape of memory that express wide German recognition of the Jewish narrative of the Holocaust. One project that seems to contradict the spirit of the people's memorial day is the thousands of "stumbling blocks" (*Stolpersteine*), a project of the artist Gunter Demnig that began in Cologne and spread to other German cities. These are brass plaques on city sidewalks, engraved with the names of mostly German

Figure 19. Gunter Demnig's "Stumbling Blocks" in Freiberg

Jews murdered in the Holocaust and the inscription "In 1933, ________ lived [or, sometimes, taught] here." The plaques are generally installed close to the doorways of what were the homes of these victims of Nazism. German citizens who wish to memorialize their Jewish neighbors order and pay for the installation. It is thus a personal, citizen-driven rather than institutional initiative.

In contrast, an official project began in 1988, organized by a circle of people around the journalist Lea Rosh. The plan was for the construction of a monumental Memorial to the Murdered Jews of Europe (*Denkmal für die ermordeten Juden Europas* or *Holocaust-Mahnmal*) in the center of Berlin. The process took years until the issue was taken up by the Bundestag, which passed a resolution in June 1999 to erect the memorial. Designed by the architect Peter Eisenman, the monument was erected near the Brandenburg Gate and the Reichstag building in central Berlin and inaugurated in May 2005. This official initiative demonstrates that the Berlin republic regards the Holocaust as a central event in modern German history, and as an essential warning signal for the future of German democracy.

The Jewish narrative's penetration of the German culture of memory came to a climax with the declaration by Germany's president, Roman Herzog, on January 19, 1996, of the institution of a memorial day for victims of the Nazis. The day was set for January 27, the anniversary of Auschwitz's liberation by the Red Army in 1945. The choice of date emphasized the Jews' centrality.[65]

Apparently, this constituted the German establishment's public recognition that the concept of memory that had been at the center of the People's Day of Mourning—which regarded as victims of the war and dictatorship all the dead, civilians and slaughtered Jews together with the Wehrmacht and Waffen SS troops who had died in battle—had reached its end. Yet the People's Day of Mourning was not canceled, nor did its basic concept change. Germany continues to observe it, and to use it as an expression of the reconciliation narrative.

A speech given on the People's Day of Mourning in 2006 precisely reflects the central concept of this memorial day. The speaker in question was Ralf Feldmann, a family court judge in the city of Bochum, who spoke at a VVN ceremony in his city. As noted, the VVN was a formerly pro-Soviet organization that had for years opposed the People's Day of Mourning and its message, but in recent years, some of its members seem to have made their peace with the dominant reconciliation narrative. Feldmann, who referred explicitly to the suffering of all groups of victims of the Nazis, saw fit on this day to cite other victims as well. In his speech, he quoted a letter from a Wehrmacht soldier serving in eastern Poland to his family in the summer of 1940. The letter contains blatant antisemitic language and expresses enthusiastic support for and absolute obedience to the Führer and his orders. Feldmann stated that thousands of such letters were written. Then he said: "On the People's Day of Mourning we recall all the human beings who became victims because they took part in murder, or because they allowed murderers to commit their crimes."[66]

5

The Bombing of Germany's Cities and German Memory Politics, 1945–1989

The Bombing of German Cities during World War II

The idea of using carpet bombing as a war strategy first appeared in the feverish brains of the Italian military theoretician Giulio Douhet and his British contemporary Sir Hugh Trenchard in response to the experience of World War I trench warfare. Such static battles of attrition, which killed hundreds of thousands of soldiers, were to be avoided at all costs. The total nature of World War I, characterized by general mobilization of the entire civilian population for the campaign, contributed to a perception that the civilian population was a legitimate target of attack. These writers proposed that bombing the enemy and its population from the air was a strategic offensive means of quickly deciding an engagement. They maintained that the damage such bombing would cause, in addition to the disruption in the distribution of food, would lead the population to force its political leadership to surrender. This, these theoreticians believed, would prevent a long war of attrition and mutual slaughter reminiscent of World War I.[1] But the first country to use the strategy of bombing civilian targets was Germany during World War II. The German air force, the Luftwaffe, began attacking cities across Europe at the war's inception—in Poland (Warsaw), Holland (Rotterdam), France, Yugoslavia, Greece, and especially Britain. Some 40,000 British subjects were killed in the Battle of Britain, the Luftwaffe offensive that lasted from the summer of 1940 to the summer of 1941. Hitler's goal was to destroy the RAF and facilitate a German sea and airborne invasion of the British Isles in what was called the Sea Lion operation.[2]

In 1940, after the fall of France and the British defeat at Dunkirk, the United Kingdom was unable to launch a ground campaign against the Nazis. Bombing German railways and oil targets was the only strategic offensive response it had to the attacks on its own cities.[3] But the navigation systems installed in RAF aircraft were quite primitive, so it was a major challenge for pilots to reach their targets. And even when this was accomplished, their bombings were often inaccurate due to other technological deficiencies. This failure to consistently hit selected targets impelled the bomber command to advocate a strategy of area bombing,[4] based on their experience from German air attacks, with the goal of destroying civilian property and morale, and so Germany's war resilience. The strategy was put into practice in 1942, but the first sorties were highly ineffective. Technical difficulties required British bombers to attack only under the cover of night. However, the force and destructive capability of the bombing raids steadily increased, as did the accuracy of the hits.

They bombed manifestly civilian sites. From the point of view of international law, this strategy was highly problematic. While the Hague Convention of 1907, promulgated to limit civilian casualties during armed hostilities, did not anticipate the bombing of civilian targets from the air, it forbade targeting the civilians of an enemy nation during wartime. The British bomber command, under Air Marshall Sir Arthur Harris, hoped to vanquish Germany by destroying German cities and taking the lives of many workers, thus disrupting civilian life in order to sap the German people's morale. They hoped that the German public would realize that they were being bombed because of Nazi aggression, and that they would rise up and topple the Hitler regime within a few months. Churchill, however, did not accept this forecast and regarded the strategy as an experiment "well worth trying so long as other measures are not excluded." Nevertheless, he favored its extensive use.[5] The British prime minister reasoned that the bombings were only one element in the campaign, and could not be a surrogate for the use of ground forces.[6] Another reason he supported the bombings was that he had no other way of opening a second front, as Stalin demanded. From June 22, 1941, the Soviet Union had borne the principal burden in the bloody fight against the Axis. Yet British flight crews sustained heavy losses, so by 1942 and early 1943, at least some prominent members of the British political and military elites were ready to abandon it.

In the end, this strategy incited no civil insurrection, but Germany's war machine was indeed impeded, even if production in many sectors, including those of many war industries, continued until very late in the war. Germany had to rebuild transportation arteries and manufacturing facilities vital to its war effort. The systematic bombing also forced German air wings and anti-aircraft batteries into defensive deployment and prevented their transfer to the front. The Allies were thus in a better position to invade Germany.[7] The British, later joined by the Americans, used a mix of both conventional and fire bombs. The latter set off firestorms that destroyed and killed on a large scale. Fatalities and destruction increased: in the summer of 1943, about 35,000 of Hamburg's inhabitants were killed in these attacks.

The Americans' technological superiority enabled them to conduct sorties during daylight and to focus on factories, roads, and train lines. Nevertheless, they also pursued carpet bombing operations, among them the bombardment of Dresden in February 1945.[8] The Allies further intensified the air war after D-Day in June 1944, focusing on Germany's interior. Historian Richard Overy concluded that the Allies achieved their goal of sapping Germany's resolve and accelerating its surrender,[9] though the U.S. and the British strategic bombing surveys conducted in the immediate aftermath of the war were more equivocal.[10] Nevertheless, both surveys regarded the bombing policy as having made a central contribution to the defeat of Nazi Germany.[11] The bombings destroyed most of the country's cities and killed approximately 400,000 German civilians.[12]

The Allied decision to bomb civilian targets as a means of turning the war in its favor was without a doubt problematic both morally and in the context of international law. However, it originated in a reality in which the British leadership's room for maneuver in the face of Nazi Germany was quite limited. In June 1941, Germany instigated a war of annihilation against the Soviet Union. During Operation Barbarossa, German occupying forces routinely murdered civilians in the territories it conquered from the Soviets, in complete disregard for international law. After cracking the Enigma code, the British were well aware of the unprecedented brutality with which the Nazis were conducting the war. They knew that Germany was committing crimes against the civilian populations of all the lands its forces occupied. At the same time, Britain did not, until the invasion of June 1944, have the capacity to defeat Nazi forces on the ground. Only exceptional measures could bring the war and the killing to a timely end, and so such measures were used both before and after the ground invasion (including by the Americans) in order to end the mass murders being committed by Germany as soon as possible.

Sir Arthur Harris hoped that the bombings would incite the German people to rise up against the Nazi regime. Yet no one knew at that time if this goal was achievable. In any case, the "experimental" strategy cost the lives of too many pilots and crewmen. This, and not just moral issues, was the background to the opposition to Harris's strategy within the Royal Air Force. It was also true that even while the war was in progress, some Britons—mostly, but not limited to, pacifists—opposed carpet bombing for a variety of reasons. However, when the philosopher Anthony Clifford Grayling today portrays some members of this opposition, such as the pacifist Vera Brittain—who had opposed the very idea of fighting against Hitler and Nazism[13]—as "people for whom it mattered that the war should be not only a justified one, but a justly fought one,"[14] he strays far from accuracy. Brittain and others like her condemned, a priori, not only the Allied bombing policy but in fact any armed struggle against Nazism. Such a position offered no reasonable alternative strategy for breaking Nazi tyranny and putting an end to Nazi bloodshed and mass murder.

Remembering the Firebombing of Dresden

Dresden, in what became East Germany, came to symbolize Germany's devastated cities. Exemplifying the destruction of German culture and the suffering of its civilians, it acquired this status only as a result of the Cold War.

In January 1946, as the anniversary of the bombing campaign approached, Dresden's city council resolved to hold memorial ceremonies. With regard to the character of these observances, the council turned to Major Broder of the Propaganda Department of the Soviet military administration in the city. He decreed: "Everything should be done to prevent February 13 from being a day of mourning (*Trauertag*). If it is granted an incorrect meaning, it will express movements opposed to the Allies. This should be prevented at all costs." Broder announced that the subject of the political rallies to be held on the anniversary would come up for discussion at the end of the month.[15]

On February 13, the local newspaper, *Sächsische Volkszeitung,* printed an article by Mayor Walter Weidauer:

> Catastrophes that could have been prevented are particularly cruel. Nevertheless, it is impossible to compare any event in our city's history to the night between the 13th and 14th of February, 1945. It was possible to prevent the deliberate destruction of Dresden, which was caused by the fascist criminals when there was not the slightest chance that Germany would win. Everyone knew that defeat was certain. Enduring the war, which everyone anticipated would end in disaster—this was the most worthless thing in all this worthless war. There is no need to prove other shameful acts by these criminals in Nuremberg. The destruction of Dresden is sufficient to convict those bandits and sentence them to the most severe punishment. Today we remember the dead in pain and sorrow. Our pain is double, because their deaths are meaningless and because—and we will say this openly—the blame for this war lies in the German people's political weakness. We could have prevented it. We could have done that, had we followed the example of the hundreds of thousands who knew that agony and death would be their fate, who passed through the prisons and the concentration camps, because they actively fought against Hitler and his war. For precisely that reason we must build a new, free Germany.[16]

From Weidauer's perspective, the Nazis who began the war and refused to halt it, even when their defeat was inescapable, bore the primary blame for the horrors of Dresden. Also guilty were the German people, who did not prevent the war. Yet Weidauer did not refer at all to the Allies, whose bombers were the direct cause of the city's wreckage. The statement by the city council, which appeared in the newspaper that same day, also addressed the guilt of the Nazi criminals who launched the war and left destruction in their wake. The forces that actually destroyed Dresden went unmentioned here, too. "The ruins scattered throughout the city testify to the guilt of German imperialism," the city council declared. The entire city demanded, in the name of those who died in the bombing, the severest punishment for the war criminals in Nuremberg.[17]

That same day, official speakers addressed twenty-nine convocations in the city. Max Liebermann, of the city's information service, reported to Major Broder that the speakers implicitly blamed the Western Allies for the bombing of Dresden. This testified to the desire to channel resentment against the United States and Britain, so as to shore up the Soviet Union's standing with the city's inhabitants: "The audience applauded when they mentioned that it was not the Red Army that had bombed civilian populations in the cities and villages." According to another report by Liebermann, Weidauer told one of the gatherings that

> during his visit to Dresden, Marshal Zhukov [a Soviet war hero] gave expression to the fact that the Soviet Union was not hostile to nor did it seek revenge against the German people, and that it would do all that was in its ability to ensure the future of the new Germany.[18]

The audience applauded wildly. Weidauer may have been hinting to his listeners that there were, in fact, other forces that were hostile and sought revenge. Hermann Matern, later a Cold War hardliner, also indicated this in a speech on the political significance of February 13. He reminded his audience that it was the Nazis who had dictated the war's combat tactics when they bombed Coventry, even though it was a civilian target without military value. Yet the Red Army, he dubiously maintained, did not attack civilians.

In 1946, DEFA, the official film studio in the Soviet zone and later in the GDR, produced a documentary film called *Dresden,* which included reenactments. After presenting the magnificence of the "Florence on the Elbe," a scripted segment traced the Nazi rise to power. It showed a prisoner in his cell. A voiceover addressed the issue of guilt that was debated after 1945: "In this country, everything has become a lie. . . . Germany no longer has a conscience! And for that reason, this Germany will go under. There is no conscience and there are no decent people! . . . People remain silent, so the stones will speak!" After this, the film depicts the destruction wreaked by the firebombing of Dresden, without identifying who the bombers were. The aerial attack is presented almost as a heavenly punishment for Germans' loss of conscience and human decency.[19]

A similar tone, although with a very clear political context, characterizes the film *Dresden Warns and Reminds,* produced by DEFA in 1951, after the Korean War began and the Cold War escalated. The film shows who bombed the city, stressing that Dresden contained no military targets and that the air attacks had no strategic value. Nevertheless, it links the bombardment to the issue of German guilt: "Most of Dresden's inhabitants believed Hitler and his air marshal, Hermann Goering." Against the background of a huge rally in the city at which Goering presided, apparently in the 1930s, the narrator says:

> Tens of thousands of the city's inhabitants thronged and joined the march willingly, or watched it enthusiastically. . . . At the time, [Communist Party leader] Ernst Thälmann alerted and warned the German people futilely. Tens of thousands in Dresden and millions throughout Germany followed the destroyers of the nation, instead of listening to Ernst Thälmann. . . . In 1939, Poland was attacked. A sixth of its population was destroyed. In Auschwitz, Treblinka, and the Warsaw Ghetto, monuments have been erected to Germany's turpitude, which cannot be expunged.[20]

Here, too, the bombing is not detached from the war crimes that Nazi Germany committed against the Slavs and the Jews, in which the nation's people were accomplices. However, the Cold War had changed the nature of the accusation. No longer was the crime a loss of conscience and inhumanity, as it had been during the democratic antifascist period that preceded the sharpening of the Cold War. Now the Germans were guilty of turning their backs on the Communist Party.

The Communist press inside and outside the Soviet zone of occupation began to cover the Dresden anniversary only since 1949. As tension between East and West grew, the Communist narrative of World War II changed.

In June 1945, the Central Committee of the Communist Party of Germany was still declaring: "Justice, freedom, and progress have been the priorities for the United Nations, led by the Soviet Union, Britain, and the United States. The Red Army and the forces of its Allies have saved humanity from Hitler's terrible barbarity."[21] But the story of the common struggle against Nazism quickly fell out of favor. In its place came the story of the Soviet Union's lone struggle against Nazism. In this narrative, the English-speaking Allies were implicated in cooperating with the Nazi state in its early stages.[22] The Communist press throughout the world was quick to trumpet these changes. Even in Mandatory Palestine, *Ahdut* (Unity), the paper published by the Communist Union of Palestine (the so-called Hebrew Communists), issued a call to the country's workers on May Day 1947: "The black forces of the Anglo-American capitalists are already whetting their swords and stoking the fire for razing the new world conflagration, for the crematoria of Majdanek and for the annihilation of Auschwitz." That year, even Albert Norden, a central figure in the Socialist Unity Party's propaganda arm, had not yet spoken so bluntly against the Western Allies. The articles he published at the time examined the money and political connections between what he averred were large American monopolistic concerns, such as Standard Oil and DuPont, and the Nazi Party. Some of these articles were later collected in his book *Lessons of Germany History,* published in 1947.[23]

In February 1948, *Neues Deutschland,* the SED newspaper, printed an extensive report from Moscow, according to which the Western Allies had encouraged Hitler.[24] In September 1948, *Neue Welt,* another SED newspaper, published an article in which Norden leveled harsh, unprecedented accusations against the Western Allies. He claimed that Churchill, in a secret memorandum of 1942, had called for a pan-European front against "Soviet barbarism." Norden also said that President Harry S. Truman, while serving in the Senate, had maintained that if Germany were to overwhelm the Soviet Union, the United States should reinforce the Soviets. But if the Soviets had the upper hand, Truman said, according to Norden, Germany should be supported, so that both countries would be weakened. Norden also asserted that the foreign policies of the Western Allies from 1918 onward had sought to sacrifice German youth on the altar of their monied interests:

> As we read the memorial plaques for the fallen soldiers in German churches; when we walk among the agony-stricken families of our nation, we are aware that nine-tenths of our youth who died in World War II lie on Soviet land. German youth was destroyed there, where the great Anglo-Saxon capitalists wanted them to be destroyed. The Wehrmacht marshals were only the implementers, consciously or unconsciously, of a policy conceived outside the borders of Germany.[25]

This was a huge change from the official line taken before the Cold War. Now the Western Allies, egged on by their rich capitalists, rather than Hitler and his generals, were to blame for the slaughter of Germany's youth on the killing fields. This terminology and attitude were reminiscent of Goebbels's propaganda.

The depiction of the bombing of Dresden changed accordingly. In 1949, on the fourth anniversary of the attack, *Neues Deutschland* devoted half of its Sunday supplement to the subject—a first. Alongside the testimony from inhabitants of the city and photographs of piles of bodies and ruins, it ran an article written by Mayor Weidauer. This time he took a position diametrically opposed to the article he had written only three years earlier, on the first anniversary of the bombing, for *Sächsische Volkszeitung*. He now accused the United States and Britain of bombing Dresden even though there was no military reason to do so. Although he repeated the ideas he voiced in his speech there on the first anniversary, this time he denounced the bombing as a crime. Instead of the Nazis, he blamed the Western Allies:

> True, it was Hitler's fascists who instituted and even improved the policy of barbarian warfare. But, unlike the Anglo-Saxon air forces, who in bombing Dresden adopted the Nazi example, the Soviet army is innocent of any barbarian desire to retaliate and of any thought of paying back Germany's population.

Of course, this propagandistic speech was far from the truth. In fact, Soviet aircraft were used mainly for combat and did not participate in carpet bombing. But Stalin and the Soviet Union had no reservations whatsoever against using such a strategy. Weidauer lumped together those responsible for the previous war—the Nazis—with "criminal warmongers in the Anglo-Saxon countries, who seek to plunge the world into a new war."[26]

Before 1950, the Dresden anniversary was commemorated only on the local level. But as the fifth commemoration approached, the SED Politburo decided to use the date for a broad public campaign against the "Anglo-American warmongers." It decided that the campaign would be conducted throughout Saxony, and that the City Council would invite representatives of European cities, including some in West Germany, to the ceremony.[27] In January 1950, the SED leadership in Saxony began planning the ceremony. It wanted Gerhard Eisler, who headed the East German Information Office, to be the keynote speaker. Responding to the invitation, he reiterated the previous official position, indicating that he had not yet been updated about the change: "It should not be forgotten that the Hitler regime nevertheless bears the principal blame for Dresden's destruction. It began the war, and the fact that it destroyed other countries even intensifies its guilt."[28]

The National Front of Democratic Germany (*Nationale Front des demokratischen Deutschland*)[29] issued on the occasion an information sheet containing photographs of the ruined city, the bodies of the dead, and the reconstruction of the city by the Communist government. The photographs were accompanied by a lengthy text about the Germans' suffering. It became the "constitutive formulation" of the East German propaganda machine:

> When Dresden fell victim to Anglo-American weapons of annihilation (*Vernichtung*), the war had already been decided. Why, then, did it have to die? Dresden became a pile of rubble because the American imperialists knew . . . that the city would end up in the Soviet zone of occupation. Dresden was thus a victim of anti-Soviet incitement.[30]

For the ceremony, the city's important buildings were emblazoned with slogans condemning the Western Allies and praising the Soviet Union: "We hate the warmongering Americans, the murderers of Dresden"; "American bombs killed, the Soviet Union did not bomb defenseless women and children"; "Here American bombs destroyed a cultural landmark [*Kulturstätte*]."[31] Nevertheless, the ceremony's organizers were aware of the problematic link between their propaganda and Nazi propaganda against the Allies. In consequence, they decided that they should look to the future, to the city's youth, rather than to the past. It was necessary to talk to the clergy, "so that they would not just wring tears out of their congregations." The aim was that they should speak also about the necessary steps to preserve peace.[32]

The mass ceremony was held on February 13, 1950, the anniversary of the bombing. Eisler adopted the new propaganda line in his speech. Early on in the war, he declared, the English and Americans had decided to bomb the area that was expected to fall to the Red Army, in order to prevent its liberation and reconstruction.[33]

The SED's new nationalist line also incorporated Goebbels's claim that the Allied air offensive consisted of "terror attacks (*Terrorangriffe*)." Another Goebbels argument they adopted was that the Western Allies were barbarians and destroyers of culture.[34] The Communist regime reinforced German resentment against the democratic Allies and the feeling of victimization that the bombing and the Nazis had nurtured. Its purpose was to mobilize East and West German public opinion against the rearmament of the Federal Republic by the Western powers. It removed the story of Dresden from the context of the just and heroic battle against Nazi Germany (of the pre–Cold War period) and placed it within that of the Cold War, transforming the Western Allies from the Soviet Union's partners in the fight against fascism into criminal enemies of the USSR and the German people. This change reinforced central elements in the Nazi narrative of the war, according to which a conspiracy by the Anglo-Saxon plutocracy (which, during the Third Reich, was taken to be composed of Jews) was no less instrumental than Hitler in the war's outbreak.[35] This challenged the Allied narrative, which held that the forces of freedom and justice had fought to root out Nazi evil. The Nazi narrative, it should be noted, did more than accuse Britain of the bombing—it also assailed Britain for starting World War II.[36]

From 1950 onward, a mass peace rally was held in Dresden annually in commemoration of the bombing. It generally convened in Karl Marx Square in the city center. The Communist press reported that more than 100,000 people took part in the rallies of 1950 and 1953. In 1951, when East Germany's prime minister, Otto Grotewohl, took part, more than 200,000 attended. (There is no way today to assess the reliability of these figures, but contemporary newsreels depict mass rallies.)[37] The fact that many Germans from Dresden and elsewhere have continued, even after German reunification, to take part in the ceremonies held on the anniversary of the bombing may be a sign that the mass participation during the Communist period was more than a product of totalitarian coercion. Instead, it may well have expressed the sentiments of Dresden's inhabitants, and in fact of Germans as a whole.

The politburo decided to elevate the 1952 anniversary to a national event. The decision by the SED secretariat stated:

> Everyone must be persuaded that the same imperialist mass murderers who ordered the destruction of the cultural city of Dresden, as an open expression of their cultural barbarity, are back cooking up a third world war, in order to bring even greater destruction upon humankind.[38]

In December 1954, the secretariat of the SED's central committee organized dozens of ceremonies for the following year's anniversary, among them one recalling "the American Air Force terror attack on Dresden."[39] In January 1955, the National Assembly of the German Democratic National Front (*Nationalrat der Nationalen Front des demokratischen Deutschland*, an allegedly democratic body uniting all political parties and mass organizations represented in the GDR parliament) issued political guidelines for the mass media in Dresden for the tenth anniversary of the bombing.

It stated that "the destruction of Dresden is a link in a chain of horrible crimes against humanity. They began in 1939, when militarist and imperialist Germany attacked Poland and destroyed Warsaw."

The authors of the document placed the Americans and Nazis on the same moral plane. Once the eastern front had collapsed, they wrote, there was no reason to bomb the city. The attack on it was equivalent to the SS's burnt ground tactics after the Red Army victory, aimed at making life in the liberated lands intolerable. This argument, which was repeated regarding other German cities (which were bombed on other dates and for different reasons), falsely portrays the collapse of the eastern front as if the armed forces of Nazi Germany had already surrendered and capitulated, and as if fighting had ceased. In fact, in many places in Germany itself (such as the capital, Berlin) and in Europe, German soldiers fought fiercely against Allied forces until the bitter end, and by doing so caused many casualties to the Allied troops. Commemorating the destruction of Dresden and other German cities and dwelling on the suffering of their populations were meant to mobilize the cities' inhabitants against the danger that the horrors of war would begin again. According to this Communist analysis, the risk of war had increased after the Bundestag in Bonn ratified the Paris agreements, bringing West Germany into NATO. Bonn's action was tantamount, according to the media guidelines, "to rearming the murderers of Warsaw and Coventry, Stalingrad and Rotterdam, Lidice and Oradour, in alliance with the murderers of Dresden and Hamburg, Berlin and Mannheim, Hiroshima and Pyongyang." This "moral equation" argued that there was no distinction between American and Nazi war conduct—both were equally criminal. And West Germany was the heir of the Third Reich.[40]

On the tenth anniversary, according to the Communist press, a quarter of a million of Dresden's inhabitants gathered for a rally against a new war. Mayor Weidauer rehearsed the main points handed down by the National Front's National Council: the Allied bombing was a war crime. Chancellor Adenauer should not enter into an alliance with "the hangmen of Dresden."[41]

Similar declarations were made at other ceremonies. In the guidelines for the one in 1955 at the site of the former Sachsenhausen concentration camp, the Anti-Fascist Underground Fighters' Committee ordered the use of the phrase: "The SS killers from Sachsenhausen and the American aerial gangsters [*Luftgangster*], the murderers from Dresden and Berlin hand in hand."[42]

DEFA produced another film entitled *Dresden Reminds Germany.* In this movie, the Cold War's winds blow through the country. The circumstances of Hitler's rise to power and popular support for his regime are not alluded to. It opens with a depiction of the city's beauty and its treasures. Afterward, the narrator describes Dresden as full of refugees on the eve of its defeat and of the bombing. On February 13, 1945, there are air raid sirens and the reverberations of bombs. A mother calls, "Dieter!" A child cries, "Mommy!" Suddenly there is a loud explosion and a terrifying shriek from the mother. "With no military justification at all, the Anglo-Americans murdered, on the night between February 13 and 14, 1945, the cultural city of Dresden. The Anglo-American attack was directed in full force against residential neighborhoods and cultural buildings." Against harsh photographs of the bodies of the dead and the burning of corpses, the narrator intones dramatically: "Women and men, babies and old people were cut through, torn to shreds, burned."

"Mothers and children were trapped, torn to shreds, and slaughtered!" the narrator shouts, and, now as the film shows the ruined city, with an American flag flying in the background, she adds: "Uncountable numbers of people, who like us loved life, were brutally murdered. The attack on the city was a trial run for new American bombs before the war ended. The blood of these dead is the gold of the American warmongers. Such was Dresden in 1945, and such is Korea today, and so it will be—according to the plans of the American warmongers—Germany tomorrow. The West German press and radio are preparing people, saying that the time is ripe for a new war in which they will use atomic bombs."

The next image is an issue of the Berlin newspaper *Der Tagesspiegel* from early December 1950, its main headline declaring that "President Truman Threatens the Use of the Atomic Bomb." A photograph of General Eisenhower appears, and then fades and is replaced by a fabricated photograph of the American general in a Nazi uniform.[43] Such blunt comparisons of the Americans to Nazis would disappear from Communist propaganda in the future, but the condemnation of the American bombing would not change fundamentally until the end of the GDR.

The tenth anniversary observance did become a national event in East Germany, but as the years went by its scope diminished. February 13, 1956, was marked only by a short item on the front page of *Neues Deutschland*, while in 1957 it was not noted at all in the SED mouthpiece. The change can apparently be attributed to the reduction of tension between East and West, initiated by Soviet Communist Party chief Nikita Khrushchev and Prime Minister Nikolai Bulganin as they attempted to improve relations with West Germany, and it received a favorable response from Adenauer.

A softening of tone is evident in another DEFA film, released on the Dresden bombing's twentieth anniversary in 1965, *Dresden—Memory and Warning*.[44] But for as long as it existed, East Germany viewed the bombings of German cities as criminal acts.[45] *Meyer's New Lexicon* (*Meyers neues Lexikon*), published in 1964, states:

> The Soviet air force attacked ground targets with determination and broke the backbone of the fascist air force . . . while the British and American attacks on Germany, with the exception of a handful of attacks against important targets . . . were directed against homes and cultural sites. The leveling of Dresden on February 13, 1945, is characteristic of these barbarian and useless attacks.[46]

The destruction in Dresden also found artistic-cultural expression. Max Zimmering, a writer who lived in the city and was a member of the Socialist Unity Party, published a novel in 1954, *Phosphor und Flieder* (Phosphorus and Lilac), about the bombing and the reconstruction that followed. The ruling party endorsed the work. By 1959 it had sold 65,000 copies.

The novel's protagonists are Dresdeners who do not support the Nazis. The liberal Professor Bregius and his wife, Anna, have lost their three sons in the war. Another character, Reichhold, a member of the Communist underground, endures the attack in his prison cell, which he shares with the Social Democrat Wennemann. During the bombing, the two discuss the reasons behind it:

> "Now of all times, when the war is already over for all practical purposes . . ." Wennemann said.
> "Maybe this bombing isn't even directed at Hitler," Reichold said.
> "Then against whom?"
> "The Russians."
> "The Russians, you say? How do you know that these aren't Russian bombers?"

> "So far, the Russians haven't initiated a single major attack on our city. Why would they do so now?"
> "But why do the Americans need to direct their bombs at the Russians?"
> "I'm not surprised," Reichold replied. "Do you really believe that Churchill and his American brothers are happy to see the Red Army deep in Germany?"[47]

Zimmering's other characters mouth the SED's official Cold War position.

Weidauer himself published a book in 1965, *Inferno Dresden* (The Dresden Inferno), a detailed historical study that sums up the official East German position on "the criminal bombing of the city." According to Weidauer, the Allies wanted to drop the first atom bomb on Dresden. But the bomb's development was completed only after Germany surrendered, so it was targeted on Hiroshima. Weidauer tied the bombardment of his city to "the plans of a group of imperialists" in Britain (led by Churchill), in the United States, and in Germany to make a separate peace between the Western powers and Nazi Germany, and then to conduct an anticommunist war against the USSR. According to Weidauer, Dresden was attacked to demonstrate the West's destructive powers, in order to weaken the Soviets.[48] The aerial assault was intentionally directed at civilian targets. Military installations and arms factories in the area were not hit at all. The historian Olaf Groehler, who during the Communist period studied the bombings, portrayed them in his books as massacres and "terror attacks."[49]

With the outbreak of the Vietnam War, the baldly propagandistic anti-American tone returned, along with the equating of the Americans with the Nazis: "What the American aggressors are now committing is shockingly similar to what happened not long ago under Hitler's [rule] over Europe."[50]

A special article published on the twentieth anniversary of the Dresden bombing in the *Freie Presse* stated: "Today, on almost the same day twenty years later, American bombers are wreaking death and destruction on the peaceful women and children of the Democratic Republic of Vietnam, destroying hospitals and schools. Whether twenty years ago, with the destruction of Dresden, or with the bombing of Vietnam or the planned nuclear annihilation of Germany, it is always the same forces who bear responsibility for the crimes. These are the imperialists. They are the deadly enemy of the nations."[51] Similar sentiments were expressed at a ceremony conducted in Dresden in February 1970 by the chairman of the council of ministers (prime minister) of East Germany, Willi Stoph.[52]

This depiction of an Anglo-Saxon imperialist plot was reminiscent of how the war was pictured by the Nazis in antisemitic terms. The Nazis spoke of an anti-German conspiracy of Western Jewish financiers. Many inhabitants of the German Democratic Republic, educated during the Third Reich, might have interpreted the East German line this way.[53]

The East German version of the reconciliation narrative was that the casualties of the Allied bombing of Dresden were comparable to the people injured and killed by fascism in the concentration camps and elsewhere in Europe. This thinking took shape in the design of the central axis in Heidefriedhof Cemetery in Dresden. The site contained a mass grave holding the ashes of some 20,000 persons killed in the bombings. (To prevent plagues from breaking out, their bodies were burned in the city center.) An official memorial site was erected along the axis, where two avenues converged: the Avenue of the Bombing Victims and the Avenue of the Victims of Fascism, constructed in 1951 as a continuation of the former avenue, dedicated to the victims of fascism. Prominent antifascists were interred along the Avenue of the Victims of Fascism. The architectonic integration of the space assigned to this group and to the victims of Allied bombardment expressed the view that both were victims of fascism and war. In 1963, a square was built in the middle of the avenue; a large stand for torches was installed at its center. Around the square's edge stood fourteen sandstone blocks of equal size. Seven were inscribed with the names of seven concentration camps: Auschwitz, Bergen-Belsen, Buchenwald, Dachau, Ravensbrück, Sachsenhausen, and Theresienstadt. The other seven bore the names of cities and towns destroyed in the war, six of them by German forces: Coventry, Leningrad, Lidice, Oradour sur Glane, Rotterdam, and Warsaw. The seventh was Dresden. The stones' uniform dimensions imply an equivalency: Dresden is like Auschwitz. Since the early 1950s, officials of state institutions have laid wreaths at the site.

Dresden's standing as a site of victimization was also cultivated by affixing plaques to public buildings that had been damaged in the bombing and were rebuilt in the early 1950s. Each plaque stated that the building had been destroyed in "the Anglo-American terror bombing." In Ham-

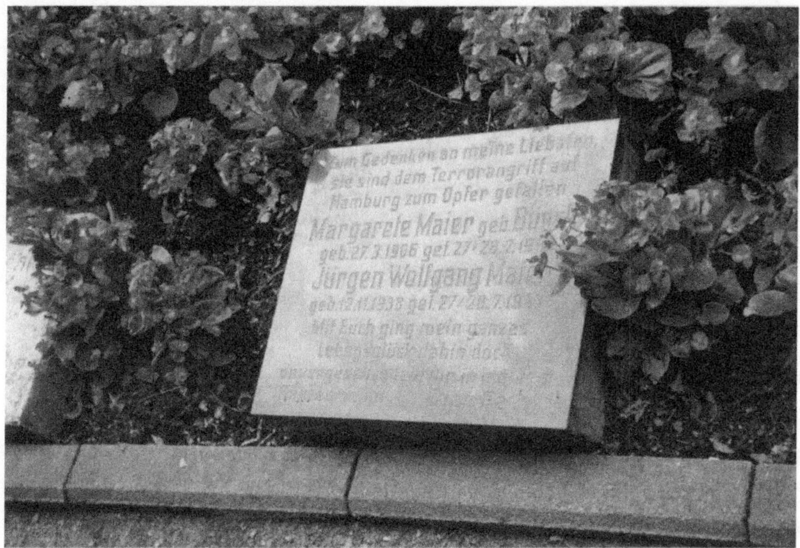

Figure 20. A family memorial plaque in the section of the Ohlsdorf Cemetery, Hamburg, where the dead from the bombings of the summer of 1943 are interred, with the inscription "terror attack"

burg, plaques bearing the city seal and the date of reconstruction were also placed on homes, but with no judgmental statement about the circumstances that caused the damage. The phrase "terror attack" (referring to the bombing) appeared in Hamburg only on a few private plaques installed by the families of the dead on the edge of the section of mass graves in Ohlsdorf Cemetery, where the ashes of the victims of the bombing of July 1943 were interred.[54] About ten percent of these private plaques bore, under the name of the departed, the word "*gefallen*"—"fell," the word used to refer to a soldier killed in battle. The inscription reflected the Nazi view of a "Nation in Arms," according to which the civilians killed in the war, like the soldiers who lost their lives at the front, died for their country. It also appeared prominently in Frankfurt's main cemetery and in cemeteries in other German cities, on many of the gravestones of victims of the bombings. The official forms of commemoration and mourning shaped by the Communist leadership, and the private forms employed by some families, were influenced by the Nazi gloss on the events.

The SED leadership decided not to rebuild the Church of Our Lady (*Frauenkirche*) in central Dresden, which had been demolished in the wake of the bombings (it was not directly hit). The ruins were used as a backdrop for mass party rallies. A bronze plaque was installed there with the inscription:

> The Church of our Lady of Dresden was destroyed in February 1945 by Anglo-American bombers. It was built by George Böhr, 1726–1743. Its ruins preserve the memory of the tens of thousands who died, and call on the living to struggle against the imperialist barbarism and for peace and the wellbeing of humanity.[55]

Ostensibly, it was a monument to peace. In fact, it was a memorial to Germans killed by the criminal war conduct of the Western imperialist Allies. The Third Reich terminology was preserved, even though its geopolitical context had changed.

In 1990, after Germany's reunification, a local citizen's initiative (*Bürgerinitiative zum Wiederaufbau der Frauenkirche*) called for the reconstruction of the Church of our Lady. Their initiative developed into a society that campaigned for reconstruction of the church and led to the establishment of similar organizations in the United States and in Britain (the Dresden Trust). These bodies collected contributions in Germany and worldwide for this expensive project, raising funds from some half million donors. The church was rebuilt and officially dedicated at the end of the summer of 2005.

A spirit of reconciliation pervaded the ceremonies and events surrounding the restoration project, conducted in the city with the participation of British representatives, as on the fifty-fifth anniversary of the bombing in 2000. On that occasion, the British Dresden Trust presented the church with a new tower cross. The cross was the work of the silversmith Alan Smith, whose father participated as a pilot in the bombing in which the church and its original tower cross were destroyed. This juxtaposition was considered highly meaningful. The bishop of Saxony, Volker Kress, said that "the cross of Jesus in the middle teaches us to forgive transgression suffered in the knowledge of our own transgressions committed. That is the secret of reconciliation. . . . Your gift grants us the experience of this secret." His words are, of course, reminiscent of the Lord's Prayer: "And forgive us our trespasses, as we forgive them that trespass against us," placing in a gesture of Christian reconciliation both of the former enemies on the same level.

Remembering the Bombing of Other Cities in East Germany

Beginning in the early 1950s, the Communist press in both Germanys published harsh denunciations of "the criminal war conduct of the Western Allies." The accusation was not restricted to Dresden. It included other German cities, among them Berlin, Chemnitz (Karl-Marx-Stadt), Potsdam, and Hamburg. Berlin was an Allied target from the beginning of the war; the next two cities were bombed at the end of the war, around the same time as the attack on Dresden. During the Cold War, official memorial ceremonies were conducted on the anniversaries of the bombings of East German cities. They interwove the suffering of the past with support for the SED's policies and adamant opposition to the West and the Bonn government. The local press printed the same sort of items that appeared in Dresden's and the national media: survivor testimonies, verbal and graphic depictions of the ruins, and wide-ranging political commentary that channeled nationalist sentiments, feelings of torment, and bitterness against the West ("A great danger threatens the Wundland family, our Berlin, and the entire German *Heimat*").[56] The East German press of the Cold War period primarily portrayed women and children as victims. When they wrote of men, they were antifascist activists, never members of the Nazi Party or representatives of the government or its agencies or soldiers.

Potsdam was bombed on April 14, 1945. On the tenth anniversary, *Märkische Volksstimme* published a close-up photograph: the innocent gazes of four babies in a crib, their thumbs in their mouths. The caption was "Bombs on them?"[57]

On more than one occasion, the official East German press published false figures of the numbers killed in the bombings, to make them appear more deadly and thus to deepen hatred of the West. On February 3, 1955, *Neues Deutschland,* the Communist regime's mouthpiece, told its readers: "Ten years ago today, 60,000 of Berlin's inhabitants were murdered. On that February 3, on Saturday night, Anglo-American aircraft carpet-bombed densely populated neighborhoods in our city."[58] In fact, 2,514 people were killed.[59] The exaggerated number can be attributed to the campaign against the Paris accords which, in 1955, ratified West Germany's integration into NATO.

The Allies bombed Chemnitz on March 5, 1945. A total of 3,715 were killed and the city center suffered severe damage. The bombardment's first anniversary was not even noted in *Sächsische Zeitung-Chemnitzer Ausgabe,* the SED's local publication. As elsewhere, the Cold War changed this. On March 5, 1950, the fifth anniversary, the National Front, the municipality, and the Communist youth organization held a rally. The next day, a short piece appeared on the back page of the local newspaper about the political significance of remembering Chemnitz's destruction. The author, referring to the "Anglo-American murders of children and women," wondered if friendship could be reestablished after such a crime, and lamented that the Germans were influenced by the "candies" they were being given "to the point that that they don't consider that the day will come when the facts will bring a rude awakening, just as happened in March 1945. But then it will be too late."[60] A year later, half of the front page of *Volksstimme* was given over to an appeal from the local board of the National Front to the inhabitants of Chemnitz. Under a photograph of the ruined city, and on each side, were pictures symbolizing death. On the right was a photo of a body in uniform, bearing a swastika armband on his sleeve. The head had been burned, exposing the skull. There was also a photo of a skeleton against the background of the city. The article opened as follows: "Six years ago today, our native city, Chemnitz, endured the most horrifying moment of its 800 years of existence. For 45 minutes, aircraft of an Anglo-American aerial terror wing destroyed our city." According to the article, the bombing had no purpose, because Germany's fate had already been sealed. The Red Army was surging westward. Nevertheless, "the Anglo-American aerial gangsters, the imperialists in New York and Washington, did not succeed in turning Chemnitz into a 'dead city,' as they believed on March 6, 1945."[61]

Here, the bombing is not perceived as integral to the campaign against the Nazis, but rather as a criminal act of terror against the city's inhabitants. In 1951–1953, the city planned a monument to the victims of the attack, to be erected in the municipal cemetery. The monument was designed by the local sculptor Hans Dietrich in a socialist-realistic style; it was dedicated in 1960. It consists of a wall in the form of a triptych, with two pictures engraved in the stone. In front of the wall, before the triptych's central section, stands a statue of a woman holding a dead child

Figure 21. The monument to bombing victims in the Chemnitz cemetery

in her arms. In other words, the motif is that of the pietà—Mary holding the body of the crucified Jesus. The Communist local authorities of Karl-Marx-Stadt (Chemnitz, Karl Marx's city) used a manifestly Christian image, that of the Pietà, as a symbol of the innocent victims of Anglo-American barbarians who were killed in the bombings.

On the left panel is a representation of the bombing attack. Above this is an inscription from the poet Louis Fürnberg:[62] "Once again, the awful wounds the barbarian has inflicted on humanity will heal," terminology generally used with reference to the Nazis. The implication is obvious: the Allied bombings were just like Nazi barbarism itself. The engraving shows a warplane swooping down like a bird of prey on six figures. In the center is a man dressed in overalls, wearing a laborer's cap, recoiling from the pouncing plane, yet directing his gaze straight at it. To his right is a woman shielding her head with her hands, and below is a seated, mourning woman, one hand holding her head, the other resting on her leg. On the man's other side is a woman cradling her head in despair. A small boy and a young girl, seeking shelter, extend their arms toward her. The message is unmistakable: the Allies bombed innocent women and children, and also anti-Nazi workers.

Engraved on the top of the right panel is another quotation from Fürnberg: "And the first light of dawn will shine on the soil of a new land under the plow." Underneath it is the engraver's vision of the city's reconstruction after the war. Three doves, symbols of peace, fly over the scene. Under them are another six figures: a construction worker laying a brick, a fellow worker gripping a shovel, and a third raising a flag (the flag of East Germany, or a red flag). Beside them is a woman with a toddler on her shoulders and another child holding a hoop. All three raise their eyes to the flag and the future.

The official East German press appropriated the term "terror attack," widely used during the Nazi period. Here it connoted slaughters of civilians, because the Red Army had already won the war and the bombings were thus pointless. But the Communist press also utterly condemned the attack on Hamburg in 1943 by the British Royal Air Force, before the opening of the second front and under very different circumstances.

In 1952, the *Hamburger Volkszeitung*, a Communist newspaper, published an article severely critical of the monument to the 55,000 people killed in the air assaults on the city.[63] The monument was erected in Ohlsdorf Cemetery, at the initiative of the city senate. According to the writer, the aggression against the city's working-class neighborhoods in 1943 constituted mass murder. And it was committed against "the most progressive people in enslaved Germany," who had fought against Hitler's fascism. According to the newspaper, the targets—residential neighborhoods rather than arms factories like IG Farben and Krupp—were chosen deliberately

> with the goal of prolonging the war, and to later prepare, with the help of these factories, for the war against the Soviet Union . . . while the Soviet Union, which conducted a just struggle of self-defense, did not during the war bomb a single [German] city. It helped the German people get rid of the tyrannical fascist regime and establish, in part of its country, the German Democratic Republic.

The newspaper argued that the new monument said nothing about the "people who sentenced the children and women of Korea to death from bombings and plagues."[64]

By emphasizing the suffering of the Germans and equating the attacks with the crimes of the Nazis, the Communist leadership sought to stamp the Allies with Hitlerism. The "Anglo-Americans" were, in its view, modern barbarians who were demolishing Germany's glorious culture. The link between this propaganda and Goebbels's view of the bombings is clear. The Nazi war narrative had still not been expunged from people's hearts, so many Germans might have understood the Communist message to be that the Nazis' crimes had not been unique.

The Bombing of Dresden and Hamburg in the Federal Republic's Consciousness

HOW WEST GERMANY ADDRESSED THE ATTACK ON DRESDEN

Communist propaganda turned Dresden into a symbol of German suffering. It positioned the policies of the Allies and of Nazi Germany on the same moral plane. These themes slowly permeated the West German media as well.

The bombing of Dresden was widely recalled by East German publications from 1949 onward. In West Germany, however, references to it were spare until the late 1950s.

For example, in its coverage of the fifth anniversary of the bombing, the *Wirtschaftzeitung* was sharply critical of the Soviet occupation regime (consistent with their view and that of the West German government that the GDR did not exist) for its macabre use of Dresden's destruction to make propaganda points against West Germany and the United States. "Propaganda will not save Dresden," the article's headline declared. The writer asserted that the Soviets had done nothing to rehabilitate the city. No such attempt to fool people could obscure the fact that Dresden was one of the most neglected of German cities.[65]

West German reports on the number of civilians killed in the city were highly exaggerated,[66] and it was not just the extreme right that was guilty of this.[67] Even *Neue Zeitung*, the newspaper founded by the American military administration, did so. In an article in February 1953, the newspaper reported the U.S. State Department's claim that the bombing raid had been carried out at the request of the Soviets, in order to prevent German reinforcements from moving via Dresden to join the fight against the forces led by the Soviet Marshal Ivan Konjew. Yet this article, the purpose of which was to refute the Communist claims about the circumstances surrounding the bombing, accepted without question the inflated estimate of a quarter million people killed in the attack. Even East German media reported 35,000 deaths.[68] In a publication issued by the Dresden municipality in 1994, a local historian, Friedrich Reichert, placed the number of dead at approximately 25,000. He based his figure on municipal data on the number of bodies recovered between the bombing and 1957.[69]

West German public interest in the bombing grew steadily. In 1953, Axel Rodenberger published his book *The Death of Dresden*, which had its origin in a report in a family magazine. Later editions appeared in 1958 and 1960.[70] On the tenth anniversary, many West German newspapers published articles on the subject, just as the Communist press did, indicating that the anniversary had become part of the West German calendar as well. These included selections published in the *Frankfurter Allgemeine Zeitung* from the diary of a Dresden woman who described the bombing and the destruction and torment it caused.[71]

Ceremonies marking the anniversary were held in West Germany as well. Since 1952, the organization of Dresdeners in West Germany has conducted such a ceremony each year in Frankfurt. On the tenth anniversary, high officials such as Vice Chancellor Franz Blücher participated. He spoke about the demand for reunification of the German people and regretted that the spiritual and cultural ties between East and West Germany had not found appropriate expression. Blücher stressed the central role Dresden had played historically in disseminating German culture to the East. The event concluded with the debut screening of the film *Dresden—The City That Vanished,* which described its magnificence before it was bombed.[72]

The mainstay of West German ceremonies marking the bombing was the motif of the destruction of German culture. This can be traced both to the Nazi press as well as the postwar Communist press. Detaching the event from its context—first and foremost from the Nazis' responsibility for starting the war—enabled West Germans to imbue it with anti-Western connotations, just as East Germany did, although free of Communist overtones however contaminated with wartime Nazi propaganda.

The local West German press went even further. In Kassel, a city also severely damaged by Allied air raids, a headline in the *Kasseler Post* proclaimed: "Dresden Was Worse Than Hiroshima . . . Ten Years Ago: One Of History's Greatest Acts of Annihilation."[73] The article, which asserted that the Soviets and the Western Allies accused each other of responsibility for the bombings, was obviously influenced by the Communist claims that tied the attack to the atom bomb, although these were stripped of their political content.

Interest in the subject grew in the wake of the 1964 German translation of David Irving's book *The Destruction of Dresden,* which had appeared in Britain the previous year.[74] Irving argued that the Dresden air raid was not intended to hasten Germany's defeat, as the Allies had claimed. Instead, it was meant to demonstrate Allied air superiority to the Soviets, a proposition that bears some similarity to the Communist line on how the Cold War began. According to Irving, 130,000 people were killed in the attack, an estimate that was accepted as a proven fact. In 1966, however, the author backtracked, accepted the validity of the East German estimate, and rejected the comparison of Dresden's fate to that of Hiroshima.[75]

The arguments characteristic of the Communists and the extreme right extended beyond the local West German press. They were legitimized by the political culture and penetrated the national press of the Federal Republic. An article on Irving's book, published in 1964 in *Die*

Figure 22. Burning bodies at the Old Market, Dresden (Saxony State Library, Dresden)

Zeit, opened with these words: "Apparently, the greatest mass murder [*Massenmord*] in human history that occurred in a single day was not that of the inhabitants of Hiroshima, as everyone immediately assumes, but instead that of the inhabitants of Dresden."[76] Similarly, in 1965, on the bombing's twentieth anniversary, a long article appeared in the liberal newspaper *Die Deutsche Zeitung* under the headline "Why Was Dresden Doomed to Die?" According to the author, "the most terrible massacre did not take place at Hiroshima, nor at Nagasaki, but rather at Dresden." The article was accompanied by a table presenting the worst aerial attacks of World War II. Dresden headed the list, with 130,000 killed. Afterward came Tokyo (84,000), Hiroshima (71,000), Hamburg (43,000), and Nagasaki (36,000).

Alongside the article was a photograph of a pyre of bodies in central Dresden. To the best of my knowledge, this was the first photograph of its type to appear in the Federal Republic's press. The same photograph had appeared in Irving's book.[77] The choice of illustration indicates an unspoken element inherent in the issue of Dresden. Until this point in the Cold War era, the bodies in the photographs published in the West German press had been those of Jews. Such photographs had become the standard visual representation of Auschwitz—a site of the Nazis' industrialized extermination of human beings—as an atrocity unique in human history.[78]

The ostensibly identical image from Dresden, presenting piles of bodies of German men, women, and children killed by the Allies, was provocative because, by using an icon indelibly associated with the Holocaust, it connoted that the British and Americans committed Auschwitz-like atrocities against innocent civilians. The purpose of publishing the photograph was thus to challenge the perception that had gradually permeated the German collective consciousness since 1945—that the Nazis' crimes went far beyond other instances of killing civilians in wartime—and to undercut the sense of collective responsibility for this unique horror that had grown in the minds of the German public beginning at the end of the 1950s.

On the twentieth anniversary, national newspapers again devoted long articles to the bombing, many of them stressing once more the destruction of German culture in the city. This theme has continued in some of these newspapers each decade thereafter, even following German reunification, as on the sixtieth anniversary of the air raid in 2005.

REMEMBERING THE BOMBING OF HAMBURG

Hamburg, in what would become West Germany, was the city hit worst by Allied bombings, with some 45,000 of its inhabitants killed. Before the Cold War in occupied Germany, even the Soviets evinced great caution when publicly addressing the aerial attacks on German cities. In the years immediately following the occupation, coverage of the subject in West Germany's local press contained not a single word of criticism of the Allies, with the subject also serving as an indirect means of underlining the enormity of the Nazis' crimes. In 1946, an article in the local SPD newspaper, the *Hamburger Echo*, on the third anniversary of the Hamburg bombing typified the official pronouncements at that time. The anonymous author wrote of his own experiences in July 1943. He related that, when he spoke to the refugees who fled the city because of the bombing, "everyone agreed with my opinion that it [the bombings] had to put an end to the war. This horrible aerial attack would liberate us from the Nazi regime. None of us could conceive that, unfortunately, this hoped-for event was still far away."

The author then wrote that the wave of refugees led to similar sentiments throughout Germany and that even then

> one spoke openly of the fact that a leadership that was unable to defend the populace from such incidents [the bombings] must resign, or at least give up this lost war. But the Nazi rulers never thought of taking such a step. They let the people bleed for more than two [more] years of senseless war. This in and of itself is sufficient to reveal the gravity of the National-Socialist crime, when we recall the terrible aerial attack on Hamburg.[79]

A comparison of this testimony with the reports of the SD (the security service) on the German public's response to the bombings shows that the author, if accurately representing local sentiment, was making a far-reaching claim about the population's dissent from the Nazi regime as a result of the bombing. Until that point, such a statement would have been rare among the general population, made only by opponents of the regime or its Jewish victims, such as Gerd Bucerius, the Communist mother of the famous singer Wolf Biermann. Her Jewish husband was murdered in a concentration camp. In 1943, she welcomed the British bombs on her city, seeing them as a sign of the impending collapse of the Nazi regime: "It's just not very practical that they dropped the bombs on us."[80] Henny Brenner, a young woman who was one of the last Jews left in Dresden, reacted in February 1945 to the bombing of her city in a similar way. She and her family were slated to be transported to a concentration camp (apparently Theresienstadt) two days after the attack. After learning the date of their impending deportation, her father told the family "half seriously, half joking: the only thing that can save us is a major attack on Dresden." Brenner emphasized: "For us, as macabre as it may sound, the attack was a rescue. That's how we viewed it."[81] The bombing indeed saved the city's last Jews from certain death, as Victor Klemperer reported in his diary. They ripped off their yellow Stars of David and mingled with the masses of refugees who fled westward from the city.[82]

Ordinary Germans generally expressed no rejoicing in reaction to the Allied carpet bombing. Only after the Nazi regime's defeat did they make an apologetic distinction, as did the *Hamburger Echo,* between the Nazis and the German public "which opposed Hitler's policies." The SD's reports of dissent during the war did not testify to a hope that the war would end. People in the bombed areas protested the helplessness of Germany's air defense and its air commander, Marshal Hermann Goering. They called for reprisals against England, which they believed would put an end to attacks on the German rear.[83] These reactions did not change fundamentally after the bombing of Hamburg, even though the very sharp tenor of the public response (for example, the demand to fire Goering) alarmed the SD and the Nazi leadership. Nevertheless, the authors of one of the reports stated: "The majority believes that Germany will still win the war."[84] In his book *My Brother, For Example,* Uwe Timm quoted a letter from his brother, Karl Heinz, a soldier in the Waffen-SS, sent from the Russian front back to his family in August 1943, after the attack on Hamburg: "Each day they announce the English aerial bombing . . . it goes beyond war. It's the murder of women and children. It's inhuman."[85] The double standard of these words, coming from a Waffen-SS soldier who was involved on a daily basis with Germany's murderous policies against civilians on the eastern front, is clear.

A parody of the hymn "Come Lord Jesus" (*Komm Herr Jesu*), sung in Koblenz in 1943, expressed the German public's sentiments at the time:

We await a day of revenge and repayment
When England will also taste these kinds of agonies
God, we beseech you, help Meyer
So that he won't come out a sucker in this great distress
Imbue him with the right spirit
So that he'll be called Goering—as he used to be.[86]

Like the Communist press before the Cold War, in 1947 the *Hamburger Echo* blamed the Nazis for the bombing, not Britain.[87] In the early years of the Federal Republic, established against the background of the Cold War, the subject of the bombings by the Western Allies became more sensitive, because Communist propaganda turned the subject into political capital that it used to assail the democratic bloc. Even though inveighing against "Anglo-American war crimes" first focused on Dresden, each year other cities were added, including some in the Federal Republic. Nevertheless, West Germany did not permit itself to propagandize against its Allies. On the anniversary of the Hamburg bombing, noncommunist publications in West Germany and speakers at the city's memorial ceremonies employed a tone of moderation and conciliation against those who caused the destruction. Often, the bombers were not identified at all. What was published most likely did not represent what most of the German public thought. The public no doubt continued to accept the Nazi view of the Allied aerial bombing. *Hamburger Abendblatt* reported the events at the bombing's eighth anniversary under the headline, "To Forgive But Not to Forget." The headline summed up the words of one of the speakers, the priest J. S. Waldmann: "We have not come here to accuse our nation or other nations. We must forgive, but we must not forget, lest we be swept into an even greater catastrophe."[88]

These words of reconciliation, which expressed the city's official policy about the past, were diametrically opposed to speeches at events organized by the Communist Party in Hamburg the year before. On these occasions, the bombing of Hamburg was linked to the Korean War and the pro-Soviet forces' struggle for peace and against nuclear armament. The slogan was: "No more Hiroshimas, no more bombings of Hamburg" (*Nie wieder Hiroshima—nie wieder Bomben auf Hamburg*).[89] At the ceremony conducted by the pro-Soviet Council of Fighters for Peace in Ohlsdorf Cemetery, Pastor Othmar Müllner of Lauenburg declared:

> Thirty-seven thousand inhabitants of Hamburg, women and men, old people and innocent children, lie in mass graves. They died horrible deaths, because of a few who wanted to mint a stream of gold coins from their blood and suffering in the war. The tears for the dead have not yet dried, but these warmongers are again prepared to lead human beings into the killing fields in the name of their god—money.[90]

Although Müllner's position is militantly pacifistic, he uses arguments and images with an antisemitic tinge, familiar from Nazi war propaganda. These presented Jewish financial interests as standing behind the Allied war goals and the Allied conduct of war.

This phenomenon was not restricted to pro-Soviet groups and the peace movement that functioned in West Germany under Soviet sponsorship. Other groups also made use of such messages and images. It may have been that, being the product of their times, they were not aware of the antisemitic nature of such images. It is more reasonable, however, to presume that they believed that the German public, which had been brought up on these materials, would be receptive to such tropes. Most Germans did not see the Allies' war against Nazism as a just war against an abominable, bloody regime. The Communist camp and peace move-

Figure 23. Marcks's monument to the victims of the bombing of Hamburg

ment it sponsored thus contributed to making elements of the Nazi view of the war and of its antisemitic images into an integral part of the German consciousness of the Cold War era.

The pacifists of various types (pro-Soviet or neutral), whose main concern in this period was the threat of nuclear war, drew equivalencies between the use of nuclear weapons and the Holocaust. Andrew Oppenheimer wrote that they "discussed the genocide of European Jewry in broad, universalizing terms that obscured the specifics of Jewish victimization and created room for West Germans to assert their own sense of suffering."[91] The German Peace Society, which was not a pro-Soviet organization, declared that "Hiroshima is more than a gas chamber, it is hell."[92]

In 1947, the Hamburg senate asked the sculptor Gerhard Marcks to propose a model for a monument to those killed in the bombing. Mayor Max Brauer suggested that it be placed at the ruins of St. Nicholas church in the city center, which had not been reconstructed. In the end, as with the decision on Hamburg's monument to the victims of Nazism, designed by Ruscheweyh (see chapter 4), the choice was to place it in Ohlsdorf

Cemetery, not downtown. The senate allotted DM 345,000 for the project, stirring public criticism for spending what was considered an exceptional sum for a monument in postwar Germany.[93]

At the dedication ceremony in August 1952, Brauer said:

> Why were they all condemned to die? We, the survivors, must not evade this question, because the victims themselves ask it of those responsible for World War II. But they ask us, too. And they warn us not to leave in the hands of demons the decision on the issue of life and death, luck and peace, growth or decline. We ourselves must decide. . . . The destruction of their lives was a terrible accusation for us. These 55,000 [people] were not killed by a natural disaster. It was not the blind law of nature. They, like the serene citizens of Guernica, Rotterdam, and Coventry, died at the hand of man, just as all wars are made by man. Because our nation lost its freedom, and allowed an inhuman, tyrannical regime to lead it to slaughter. A rainfall of bombs and fire poured down on foreign cities. Afterward the flames rose in our cities as well.

In keeping with the Allies' position, Brauer here emphasized the connection between the cause—the guilt and responsibility of the German people for the ascendance of Nazism and for its subsequent crimes—and the effect, the bombardment of Hamburg. He continued:

> This mass grave is a warning sign for us: this is the danger! And know that from the time a man gives up freedom and law, he marches on his way to his obliteration! So the dead warn us: do not permit any new tyrant to rule you! Seek peace and understanding among nations! Consider that any future war will be a total war. The number of casualties will be innumerably greater than the number of those whose graves we face today. The preservation of peace is the best guarantee for ensuring freedom and democracy for all peoples and in all countries of the world. We must recommit ourselves to that.
>
> To our youth I call: find the courage to understand correctly the deaths of your fathers and mothers, of your brothers and sisters! Their deaths were not the verdict of fate. They placed themselves in the hands of violent criminals, so violence befell our families and our serene cities. Because in a free nation, each mortal is responsible for this "why."[94]

These logical sentiments, in the same spirit as those expressed at Dresden's memorial ceremonies before 1949, may explain the choice of Marcks's monument. The work presents a panorama from Greek mythology: a boat of dead souls steered by Charon on the River Styx in hell.

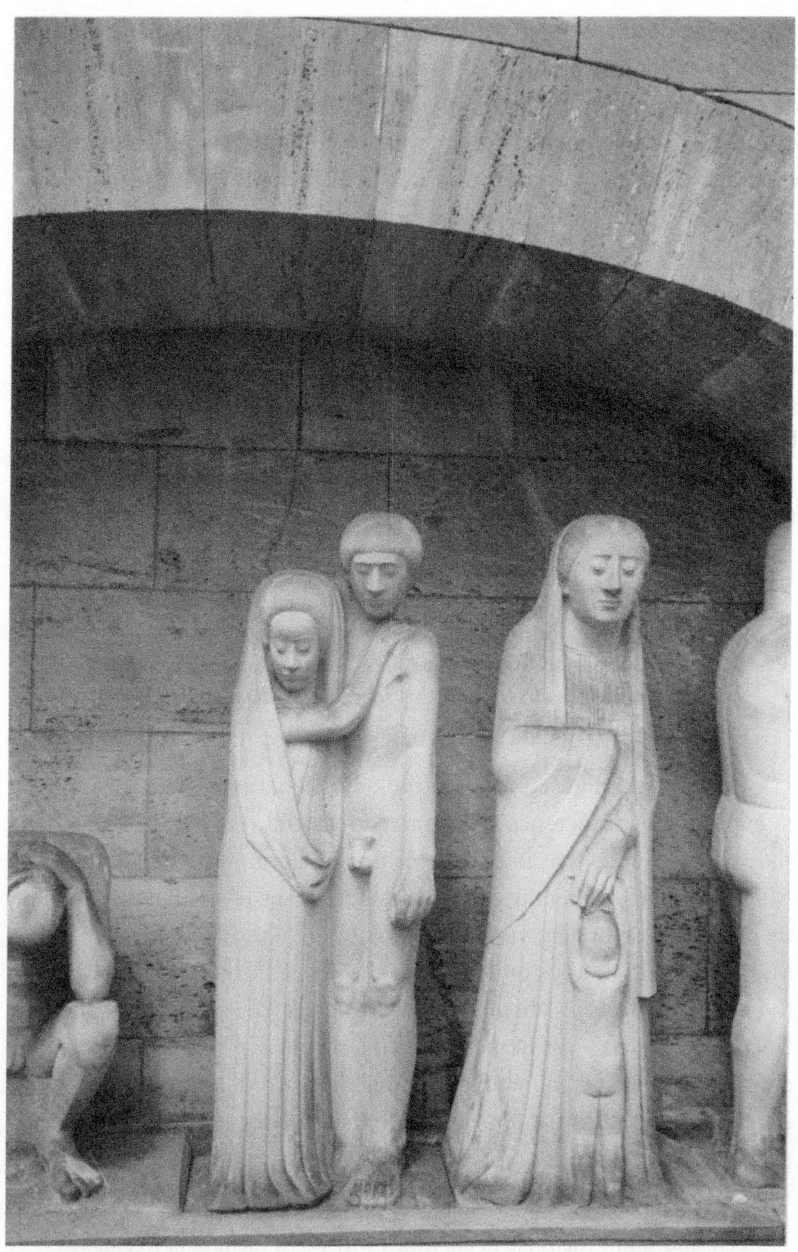

Figure 24. Figures from Marcks's monument in Hamburg

Among the dead are a man with a bent back, sitting with his hands clutching his head, an expression of despair and sadness (the subject of the defeated hero preoccupied many twentieth-century German artists). Also in the boat is a young couple, the woman laying her hand on the man's shoulder, their eyes cast down. The same gaze appears on the figure of a mother, who places a protecting hand on the head of a child who hides his face in her dress. The boat's prow is the profile of a nude man who directs his gaze toward the boat's destination. Only Charon looks, indifferently, at the monument's observer. His figure is devoid of any Christian component that might signify comfort. There is no cross, which symbolizes the victory of faith over death, nor a pietà figure, which symbolizes God's benevolence and mercy. The mythological sailor is unmoved by the tragic fate of his passengers. Marcks explained his choice of a pre-Christian motif:

> There was no place here for the Christian concept of death. It is impossible to see in the way they died anything conciliatory. Neither did the victims of the bombing die as martyrs to an idea. Instead, they all—men, women, and children—were torn to pieces in a destructive frenzy without an answer to the question "why?" that repeats itself on many of the crosses placed over their graves.[95]

By using the figure of the mythological boatman, the artist sought to express the indifference of organized mass murder.[96] His explanation showed, of course, that like many others in Germany, he compared the Allied bombing of Hamburg to the massacre of the Jews. That was not how the mayor, Max Brauer, viewed the bombing. Nor did Brauer know that Marcks had originally come up with the idea of Charon's boat in order to express his feelings about his Jewish friends who were forced to leave Germany in 1933.[97] But Brauer was not a member of the committee that chose the sculpture, and we may assume that he did not delve deeply into the monument's form and meaning. In its reasons for choosing Marcks's proposal, the committee wrote that it

> awakens hope of a human monument of artistic meaning that is sincere and comprehensible to all, which will aid in the task of freeing the memory of the victims of the bitter bombing, without expunging its harsh and profound pain. Since it asks what the meaning of these events is and addresses the question in an artistic way, the sculpture is also meant for the living.[98]

The committee's members seem to have perceived Marcks's sculpture as mitigating resentment. This fit in with Brauer's insistence that the memorial place the bombing in the political context of the issue of German guilt, and that it be unambiguously devoid of any wallowing in the feelings of self-pity and victimization that were promoted by the memorial ceremonies for the bombing victims held in both East and West Germany.

Brauer also took this position in his speech on the first People's Day of Mourning, observed in Germany in November 1952. Not only did he address the issue of responsibility and guilt; he referred explicitly to the Nazis' victims, in particular to the Jews of Hamburg and of Europe as a whole who were murdered by the Nazis. Yet this motif vanished from his speech on the People's Day of Mourning in 1958 (see chapter 4).

As with newspapers in other cities bombed by the Allies, the local Hamburg press has published a month-long series of articles, with testimonies, reports, and photographs, for anniversary commemorations of the bombing, beginning with the tenth anniversary in July 1953 and continuing every ten years thereafter. Both the national German and the local Hamburg press have tended to remove the bombings from the context of the war, stressing instead the suffering of German civilians and going to extremes in describing the intensity of the attack. In 1953, for example, the *Hamburger Abendblatt* claimed that the bombing of the city had been more severe than the atomic bomb attacks on Hiroshima and Nagasaki.[99]

In his book on Dresden, David Irving criticized the RAF's Sir Arthur Harris for "having taken less of an interest in international law than in winning the war."[100] When the book was translated into German, it contributed to legitimizing accusations against Allied war conduct in West Germany. Harris had already been harshly condemned in Britain, but he was not treated this way in the German press until the mid-1960s.[101] Before this, only Communists and those in the far right made such charges. The book was followed by Rolf Hochhuth's drama *Soldiers* in 1967, according to which the attacks on German cities, Hamburg in particular, were violations of the Hague and Geneva conventions. In this view, Churchill's military policies were war crimes.[102]

In the 1970s, newspaper articles increasingly included comparisons, usually by implication, between the bombing of Hamburg and the extermination of the Jews. Hamburg's newspapers applied the term "extermination" (*Vernichtung*) to the aerial bombardment of the city. In 1973, an article in the *Hamburger Abendblatt* stated: "'The Gomorrah Operation' [the RAF's code name for the mission] . . . was supposed to wipe Hamburg off the earth, just like what happened to Carthage."[103] And on the bombing's fiftieth anniversary, the same newspaper published a photograph of an original British document, from the bomber command in May 1943, which ordered "the total destruction of this city." The German caption under the photograph read: "The atrocity document: bureaucratic, business-like planning, over four pages, of how to destroy Hamburg," terminology reminiscent of that used to refer to the extermination of the Jews.[104]

But the public discourse on the bombings appropriated terms from the Holocaust not only to equate them implicitly. At times, the accusation was explicit: the bombing of cities is mass slaughter, a war crime, for which there is also a criminal. In general these accusations were aimed at Harris, though sometimes at Churchill. "The commander of the fleet of bombers that destroyed Hamburg . . . was Sir Arthur Travis Harris, nicknamed 'Bomber Harris.' Today he is 81 years old and lives in Goring-on-Thames in England. Is he guilty of the deaths of more than 40,000 inhabitants of Hamburg?" the *Hamburger Abendblatt* asked.[105] The newspaper's readers were quick to respond. One of them explicitly accused the Allies of war crimes, referring to a notorious incident from the American experience in the Vietnam War:

> When we read these reports and think of how Lieutenant [William] Calley was sentenced to a long prison term [twenty years] for having shot villagers in My Lai, when he did not know whether they were foe or friend, one must ask in astonishment what happened to the indictments and trials against those responsible for turning Germany's cities into ruins during World War II, while murdering hundreds of thousands of women and children? Are these not war crimes?[106]

The view of "Bomber Harris" as the man who embodied the destruction of Hamburg and the death of its inhabitants increased in 1983, on the fortieth anniversary of the bombing. Harris, not the British cabinet, was portrayed in the German local and national press as the enemy. The bombing was depicted as his personal revenge, completely disregarding the historical context of the war against the Nazis, at a time when the

British were unable to open a ground front against Germany but needed to respond to German aggression. The following headline appeared in the *Hamburger Abendblatt*: "Sir Arthur Harris's Murderous Consideration."[107] Harris was also cited in the speech of the city's mayor, Claus von Dohnanyi, at the city's central ceremony: "On the night between July 24 and 25, 1943, 800 aircraft from the bomber wing of Air Marshall Arthur Harris flew to Hamburg and dropped a carpet of bombs on densely populated areas in the city center and in the neighborhoods of Altona, Eimsbüttel, and Hoheluft."

The format of Dresden's memorial days, which crystallized in the 1950s in East Germany, was thus gradually adopted in Hamburg during the Cold War. However, public participation in Hamburg's ceremonies was much more limited. As in Dresden, formal language was used to stress and warn: "No more war!" (*Nie wieder Krieg!*). Like the Communist orators, Dohnanyi emphasized that the Germans had learned a lesson from the aerial attacks of the past that could be applied to the later nuclear conflict, which threatened to destroy humanity. This could be interpreted as an implicit claim of German moral superiority—a sinner who had atoned for her sins. Germany now sought to teach that lesson to all, to advocate reconciliation and peace among nations and to educate humankind in this sublime ideal. Nevertheless, these implied accusations against Britain never reached the venomous anti-Western level of the SED's rhetoric in Dresden.

Large ceremonies were conducted each decade. All the German media covered the fortieth anniversary of the attack on Hamburg, in July 1983. The local event thus took on national dimensions. At the observance, the ARD, West German television's Channel 1, broadcast—to a record-breaking audience—Hans Brecht's documentary *Operation Gomorrah*. This film was the first to bring authentic color footage of the aerial attack, the ruin it caused, and its horrors (including color photographs of dead bodies) into West German homes.

There is no polling from the 1950s and 1960s about the public's positions on the bombing of German cities, so there is no way to quantify the major trends in public discourse. Public opinion in the West, and the Allied military administrations, blamed the German people for the crimes of Nazism. The Germans, in turn, resisted and rejected this collective indictment. In 1951, close to half the public agreed that "the Allies bear responsibility for the war, or at least both sides do." This position was more prevalent among men. Such attitudes changed slowly during the 1950s and in subsequent decades.[108] A poll from 1992 shows that 45 percent of Germans rejected collective guilt for the murder of the Jews with regard to Germans' political support for Nazism and the failure to topple Hitler's regime.[109] Apparently, in that year most Germans accepted the criminal guilt of those Germans who had been directly involved in the crimes of the Nazis. Opinion surveys from 1953 demonstrate, however, that most Germans, at that time, denied such criminal responsibility. A majority—55 percent—believed in 1953 that such accusations could not be leveled at German soldiers who served in the occupied lands during the war. A year previously, most of the German public maintained that the surviving Nazi leadership and Wehrmacht officers tried for war crimes by the Allies in Nuremberg—Karl Dönitz, Rudolf Hess, Baldur von Schirach, Albert Speer, and Albert Kesselring—were imprisoned unjustly.[110]

At the beginning of the 1950s, Theodor Adorno and his colleagues theorized that the German public held a relativized view of the Nazis' crimes. In other words, they equated them with those of their opponents (by claiming, for example, that the bombing of German cities was the moral equivalent of the extermination of the Jews).[111] In his 1959 lecture "What Does Coming to Terms with the Past Mean?" Adorno addressed the equivalence that German discourse had produced since 1945: "Irrational too is the widespread 'settling of accounts' (*Aufrechnungen*) about guilt, as if Dresden made up for Auschwitz. There is already something inhuman in making such calculations, or in the haste to dispense with self-reflection through counter-accusations."[112]

Preoccupation with the Dresden bombing, which began as an element in totalitarian East Germany's memorial and propaganda policies, seeped into West Germany's political culture, stripped of its Communist connotations. There it became an important symbol of the Germans' suffering. Even though we know today that more people were killed in Hamburg in the bombing of July 1943 than in Dresden, it is the latter that has become fixed in German memory as a symbol of how the people suffered at the hands of the Allies. It is no coincidence that as public discourse on the Holocaust grew in West Germany, beginning in the mid-1950s, so too did the German preoccupation with Dresden. It is thus impossible to detach

West Germany's view of Dresden as "an event of mass murder without historical precedent" from the context of the murder of the Jews.

Communist propaganda compared Dresden, Hamburg, Berlin, and Mannheim, the German cities bombed by the Allies, to Warsaw, Coventry, Stalingrad, Rotterdam, Lidice, and Oradour—symbols of the criminal conduct of Hitler's armies—but also to Auschwitz, a unique, unprecedented event in human history. Some groups in West Germany joined this chorus. In doing so, Germans in both East and West sought to elevate the German tragedy and blur the Jewish one.

6

Flight and Expulsion in German Political Culture and Memory since 1945

The flight and expulsion of millions of Germans from the eastern German territories in the wake of World War II played a similar role in the official memory and politics of the Federal Republic to that of the Allied bombing of German cities in East Germany. Although the topic lost some of its notoriety during the period of the coalition between the Social Democrats and the Liberals (1969–1982), it remained firmly on the public agenda, and Christian Democratic (CDU) and Christian Social Union (CSU) politicians continued to speak of it publicly. With the CDU's return to government in 1982 under the leadership of Chancellor Helmut Kohl, some of the former preoccupation with the expulsion returned to the fore. This lasted until German reunification in 1990.

In contrast, the German Communists, after a brief period of ambivalence, consolidated their position on the flight and expulsion. They supported it as a just punishment inflicted on Germany for its crimes against its eastern neighbors. Yet, given German bitterness over the active role played by the Soviet Union and its future Communist allies (mainly Poland and Czechoslovakia) in the implementation of the expulsion, this position had potentially explosive political implications in the GDR. Therefore, the Communist state enforced an absolute taboo against any public discussion of the suffering endured by German refugees, who were said to have been "resettled" rather than expelled. It was permissible to refer to "resettlement," but the taboo applied all the more so to crimes, such as rape and murder, committed against German refugees by Red Army soldiers or by citizens of East Germany's future socialist sister countries.

The GDR's leadership was also quick—too quick—to tout its success in solving the problems of resettlement.[1]

Whatever the similarities, West Germany's use of the flight and expulsion in its propaganda against the Soviet bloc during the Cold War was much more restrained than Communist propaganda's venomous use of the Allied bombardments in its campaign against the United States and Britain. East German public commemoration of the Allied bombings stressed the dead. Memorials to these victims were erected in all major cities in the GDR. In the Federal Republic, the Germans killed during the flight and expulsion were also commemorated in hundreds of local monuments, but they played a relatively small part in the public mind in comparison with other aspects of the expulsion. While this book focuses on the memory of the war dead, it also necessarily addresses the issue of the expulsion. Comprehending the importance of the memory of expulsion in the Federal Republic is crucial for understanding developments during the late 1990s and the beginning of the new millennium.

The public viewed the flight and expulsion as an illegitimate and collective punishment, even a crime, and also supported the Federal Republic's official demand that the Potsdam agreement be revised to restore Germany's borders to those of the German Reich in 1937. (Since West Germany regarded itself as the sole legitimate German state and therefore did not recognize East Germany until 1969, it behaved as if it had a border with Poland.) A corollary of this demand was the refugees' and expellees' right to a homeland (*Recht auf die Heimat*) in their former habitations, which meant at the very least their right to return to their homes in central and eastern European countries. Implicitly, West Germans also made a claim for collective rights for the returnees in the central and eastern European countries that ruled their former areas of residence. They portrayed the experience and memory of the Germans from the Reich's eastern provinces as an integral part of German national experience in the final months and early aftermath of World War II.

Just as the Communists kept silent about the Soviet Union's support for carpet bombing of Germany, so the Federal Republic glossed over the Western Allies' support at the Potsdam conference for the expulsions from the German East. It placed the blame for the suffering and misery that the German refugees and expellees endured in their westward treks on the rival superpower, the USSR and its satellite states, in particular Poland and

Czechoslovakia.[2] The expulsion and border issues, rather than the Hallstein doctrine (the West German policy of not recognizing any state that had recognized the GDR),[3] were the main reason why West Germany had no diplomatic relations with Eastern bloc countries until the late 1960s. Of course, blaming the Soviets, Poles, and Czechs for inflicting injustice on German civilians fit in perfectly with West Germany's anticommunist position during the Cold War.

In that period, the expulsion was a highly politicized topic, touching the core issues disputed by the two Germanys: West Germany's claim to be the sole representative of the German people, Germany's future eastern border, the fate of the former German territories, and the rights (including property rights) and status of the Germans who had been forced out or who fled those territories.

The Allies, the Expulsion, and the Expellees during the Military Occupation of Germany, 1945–1949

At the Potsdam conference in the summer of 1945, the United States and Britain acceded to the Soviet demand that Poland's western border be drawn along the Oder and Neisse Rivers. The Potsdam agreement that emerged from the summit stated that the fate of the former German territory to the west of the Oder-Neisse line that had been handed over to the Polish administration would be determined by a future peace agreement between Germany and Poland. As the historian Pertti Ahonen has written, there was a disparity between the agreement's wording and Allied intentions: "Technically, the wording left open the possibility of subsequent boundary changes. . . . In reality, however, all three signatories expected the de facto border agreements to become permanent."[4] In any case, the decision to uproot millions of Germans from their homes and resettle them in occupied Germany was viewed by the Allies as final and irrevocable.

The Allied military governments in Germany sought to quickly integrate and assimilate the refugees and expellees into German society in their places of resettlement. This included supplying them with housing and jobs. In the early postwar years, the Allies and German authorities were very concerned that this population might be radicalized if it faced unemployment and deprivation.[5]

The Allies sought to preclude the entrenchment of the refugees as a unique group. With this goal in mind, in August 1946 the American military governor in Germany, General Lucius D. Clay, ordered the dissolution of all refugee and expellee organizations. Clay explained that this measure was necessary to expedite the assimilation of the refugees and expellees into German society. The military government sought to prevent the proliferation of small, particularistic political parties that were liable to become nuclei of political foment. The corollary of the policy was that refugees and expellees could and should find political homes in the existing political parties—a sentiment those parties shared.[6]

Later, however, the Americans allowed the establishment of particularist refugee and expellee organizations on a local level. The Cold War without a doubt encouraged this change of heart, since such groups were useful tools for goading the Soviet Union and its Polish and Czechoslovakian clients.[7]

As the Cold War intensified in 1946, the United States issued a number of public declarations that referred to the wording of the Potsdam agreement regarding Germany's eastern borders. This was interpreted, among certain expellee groups and in the Eastern bloc, as American advocacy of a revision of the German-Polish boundary. The first of these declarations was U.S. Secretary of State James F. Byrne's "Speech of Hope," delivered in Stuttgart in September 1946; his successor, George Marshall, took the same position at meetings held for foreign ministers in Moscow and London. Poland interpreted these statements as a threat to its western territories.[8] For expellee circles, however, such encouraging statements induced them to support the United States, even though America bore the same responsibility as the Soviet Union for the wording of Article VII of the Potsdam agreement and for the determination of the Polish-German border, as well as for the mandate for the transfer of German populations in Article XIII. On February 21, 1947, Alfred Noske, an expellee and a representative of the Bavarian Landtag (parliament) in the Economic Reconstruction Association (WAV), said at a gathering of refugees from all over Bavaria: "We are grateful for what the U.S. foreign minister said on September 6, 1946. We have carefully noted his words and will never forget them."[9] During the same period, far more sweeping rumors and leaflets circulated among expellees. The intelligence division of OMGUS in Bavaria received a pamphlet, allegedly mailed from the United States to

Silesians and Sudeten expellees, telling them that America would liberate the former German territories from Polish and Czech rule and return the expellees to their former homelands.[10]

The United States, for its part, viewed the expellees as solidly anti-communist and firm allies in the Cold War. Having been granted full civil rights in the western zones of occupation in 1947,[11] most refugees and expellees were courted by all the existing German parties, since they were considered a decisive block of voters in any election campaign. Despite this, no expellees' party was established until January 1950, since any new political party still required the sanction of the Allies. In this period, then, they tended to view the United States as the only force that could help them return to their ancestral lands in Eastern Europe.[12]

Nevertheless, with the exception of a few small parties that displayed no interest in the refugees or were even hostile to them (for example, the local Bavarian Party and the Danish Party in Schleswig-Holstein),[13] most West German political parties advocated the interests of the refugees. The fact that even the West German Communist party (KPD) fell in line on this issue, at least until the escalation in the Cold War that followed the outbreak of the Korean War, highlights how much of a consensus prevailed in the country. In some areas the Communists even succeeded in enlisting expellees in their cause.[14]

The Positions of German Communists on Expulsion, Expellees, and Germany's Future Borders

German Communists, including the Socialist Union Party (SED), which would become the ruling party in East Germany, did not formulate its position on the expellees and Germany's permanent borders until 1948.[15] Their challenge was to balance two strongly competing interests. An OMGUS report on a stormy KPD meeting for refugees and expellees from Czechoslovakia and Silesia (Poland) in the Bavarian county of Altötting on July 28, 1946, vividly portrays the German Communists striving to reconcile their commitment to the Soviet (and Western Allied) policy on expulsion and its consequent German border changes with the perception and wishes of the expellees themselves and the broader German public.

In Bavaria, where in 1947 the expellees numbered 1.7 million, about 25 percent of the state's population, the KPD—despite being aware of the anticommunist sentiments held by many of these refugees—sought to portray itself as the only party in the state truly concerned with their plight. According to the OMGUS report of the Altötting meeting, "the [anonymous] speaker touched [a] tender spot of the attandents [*sic*]: the historical and political rights of the Poles and Czechs to the territories the Germans were forced to leave." The people in the audience reacted passionately. Stressing that they were not willing to give up their hopes of returning to their lost lands, they maintained that Germany could not exist without its eastern provinces.[16] This latter claim had wide credence, and not just in the expellee community. It is a manifestation of the Nazi concept of *Lebensraum*.[17] "The Communist speaker tried to appease the audience by telling them to endeavor to better their condition within the limits of present possibilities," the report states. Then, trying to induce them to support the KPD, "he insinuated, at the end of the meeting, that it might be possible for them to return to their home countries, if all of Europe were to become Communist."[18] This was, of course, an empty promise.

On February 16, 1947, the Communist Party in Bavaria convened a refugee conference in Munich. In his greetings, Fritz Sperling, the chairman of the party's Munich branch, reiterated the KPD's official position on the Potsdam agreement and the expulsion of the Germans from the eastern German territories: it was a fait accompli. "We must accept that our German *Heimat* will be smaller than before, but the restoration of unity in this new smaller *Heimat* is the most important prerequisite for democracy, peace and progress."[19] A noncommunist representative of the Bavarian Commissar for Refugees protested the cruel evacuation methods employed by the Poles against the German expellees, which had resulted in the death of many deportees. In response, Sperling called on the audience to stick to facts and to consider that 4 million Polish citizens had been murdered by the Third Reich. True, the Poles had inflicted evil on the expellees, as the refugees claimed, but it was the far greater evil of the Nazis that created Polish rage against the Germans and impelled them to expel the Germans.[20]

One of the key speakers at this conference was Alfred Hadek, a Communist expellee from Sudetenland. Hadek was also a member of the Chief Committee for the Refugees (*Hauptausschuss für die Flüchtlingsfragen*), a state-financed body formed in Bavaria consisting of expellee representatives from the different political parties. Hadek presented a comprehensive program for solution of the refugees' problems in Bavaria. It consisted of land reform (tellingly, Hadek refrained from connecting his proposal to the land reform conducted in 1946 in the Soviet occupation zone), housing for all refugees, equalization of the burdens (*Lastenausgleich*)—meaning easing the fiscal burden on those harmed by the war—and creating jobs for this group. The purpose was to facilitate the refugees' assimilation into the local West German population. To achieve this goal, he advocated state investment in local industries and presented the necessary legislative proposals that the Bavarian parliament would have to pass to implement his program.[21]

At the beginning of his speech, Hadek referred to the reasons for the evacuation (*Aussiedlung*) of the Germans from the eastern territories. (The Communists did not use the term "expulsion." As early as 1945 they referred to the expellees in the Soviet occupation zone, later the GDR, as "resettlees"—*Umsiedler.*) "These measures," he said, "are the consequence of the criminal Nazi war. The consequences of a repeated historical phenomenon in which German minorities [in other countries] allow themselves to be abused for the sake of German imperialism. These measures are a consequence of the rise of the national consciousness of all the peoples who were the victims of Hitler's explicit extermination policy."[22]

In other words, Hadek portrayed the expulsion as a punishment meted out to the Germans of the east as a punishment for their collaboration with Hitler. Similar positions were taken by KPD members in other parts of Germany as well.[23] However, the German populace, and the expellees in particular, do not seem to have been particularly persuaded by these arguments.

The SED leadership was much less resolute than its Bavarian comrades. They stated publicly that they were unenthusiastic about the Oder-Neisse line, but that there was nothing they could do to change the Allied decision. For example, Wilhelm Pieck said in a speech in Munich in March 1947:

> Our position is that we are not for this border settlement in the east. We have not been asked but it was the decision of the four great powers.... The resettlement of the population shows that this measure must not be considered as a provisional one, but as a fait accompli. We want a revision of this border, but we are against the chauvinistic and nationalistic powers making use of this border issue and causing still greater damage by so doing.[24]

Leaders of both parties made public pronouncements in 1947 to the effect that there was still hope for a revision of Germany's eastern boundary, at least with regard to the territory to the east of the Oder and Neisse Rivers that had been handed over to Polish administration in the Potsdam agreement.[25] Only in 1948 did the SED endorse the Soviet position. In June 1950, East Germany recognized the Oder-Neisse line as the permanent German-Polish border, in the Görlitz agreement it signed with Poland (in accordance with the Potsdam agreement of the summer of 1945).[26]

But the West German Communist Party lagged behind its sister party in the GDR. The KPD was desperately trying to gain political support from the expellees, and sought to overcome their resentment by deemphasizing its Communist profile and ideology. Yet Linus Kather, a prominent expellee leader, had written in October 1946 that the expellees rejected the KPD "not because they rejected its ideology, but because of the Red Army's atrocities and the KPD's identification with the Russians."[27] According to a report composed by the American military government, the KPD was not mentioned on the posters that advertised the abovementioned refugee conference in Bavaria.[28] Another strategy employed by the party to circumvent the expellee resentment was to use ostensibly independent expellee activists as vote-getters for the KPD. For example, in 1949–1950, the Bavarian branch of the party employed Egon Hermann, an expellee from Czechoslovakia, who relatively shortly after his arrival to Germany became a leader of the refugee and expellee camp in Dachau. In September 1948 Hermann played a key role in organizing a hunger strike there, demanding improvements in their living conditions and employment.[29] During the election campaign for the first Bundestag in the summer of 1949, Hermann had spoken before a number of expellee gatherings in Bavaria.[30] At an assembly convened in Kulmbach in July 31, 1949, he presented himself as an expellee who had no party affiliation, and had nothing to do with the Communists. He told his audience about his personal experience in Prague after the collapse of the Third Reich, recounting the agony of Germans who had been humiliated, beaten, and murdered by Czechs. His speech was rife with anti-Czech sentiments, but he made no mention of the Soviets. Herrmann presented a very original argument for why Germans should support the Communists at the polls. He claimed that the events in France and Italy had shown that American bankers' fears of strengthening Communists would lead them to pour dollars and support into Germany, which would quickly reduce unemployment.[31]

In March 1950, Hermann did further service for the KPD by convening a rally at the Krone circus in Munich under the banner of the Union for the Struggle of Bombed-Out Refugees and War Victims (*Kampfbund der Flüchtlingen, Ausgebombten und Kriegsopfer*). The announcement demanded an end to "neo-fascism and the danger of war," typical contemporary Communist slogans. He called for liquidating war criminals while they were still plotting their crimes. And he called on Germans to disobey the Russians and Americans should they seek to arm the Germans to mobilize them for a future war.[32]

Eastern and Western Policies for the Absorption and Integration of Refugees and Expellees

East Germany absorbed about one third of the expellees—4.3 million people, according to the official figures, about 24 percent of its population.[33] As we have seen, the Communists used the term "resettlee" (*Umsiedler*) for expellees and presented the expulsion as the inevitable consequence of the Nazi policy of annihilation of Eastern European countries and their peoples. The expulsion, they argued, was irreversible, so they adopted the Allied policy of assimilating the refugees and expellees into the local population. Similarly, they adhered to the Allied policy that forbade the founding of any refugee or expellee organization, and all the more so political parties.

As a consequence, no expellee organizations or parties functioned in the East German state throughout its existence, no museums were build to preserve the expellees' unique traditions, and no monuments were erected to commemorate their suffering. The Communist dictatorship was suspicious of all preoccupation with this topic, and termed the West German revisionist position "revanchism," a wish to reconquer former German territories.[34]

During the initial years following the war, the Soviet military administration and later the East German government invested enormous financial resources and organizational efforts to facilitate the integration of the "resettlees," and to find solutions to their unique problems. As part of its egalitarian vision for reconstructing society, the Communist regime aspired to grant the resettlees parity with the rest of the GDR's population, rather than to compensate them for their lost possessions, thereby exacerbating inequality.[35] Before West Germany implemented, in 1952, its law regarding the *Lastenausgleich*—shared war burden—these measures exceeded the resources that were allocated for accelerating the absorption of the refugees and expellees in West Germany.[36] As early as 1946, the Soviet military administration (SMAD) ordered the provision of immediate aid to the refugees and expellees, and to grant those who could not support themselves a one-time immediate stipend of 300 marks.[37] The Communist authorities regarded the resettlees as part of the rural proletariat, so they were given preference in the distribution of farms under the Communist land reform program.[38]

At the same time, SMAD and the Communist authorities made great efforts to provide housing for the resettlees. By 1948, most of the refugee camps and temporary residences were no longer in use—meaning that the administrators of the Soviet zone found the refugees permanent dwellings much earlier than did those in the western zones.[39] In 1950 the GDR issued a law benefiting the resettlees (*Umsiedlergesetz*), granting interest-free loans of 1,000 marks per family for the purchase of furniture, work tools, and other equipment. The same law mandated scholarships and apprenticeships for young resettlees.[40] Yet, while the authorities had good intentions, their desire to help kept running up against the GDR's chronic shortages of revenues and commodities.[41]

In 1952–53 the GDR terminated its integrative social policy for the resettlees, and resources were redirected toward the collectivization of East German agriculture.[42] In the late 1940s, all state agencies that oversaw the absorption of resettlees were dismantled. Nevertheless, the GDR's economic and social development during the 1950s opened up avenues for the integration of resettlees.[43]

The Federal Republic absorbed many more expellees than did the GDR. On April 1, 1950, there were 7.74 million refugees in West Germany, or 16.2 percent of its population. Since the nation's founding in 1949, all West German federal and state governments have advocated and assisted in refugee rehabilitation and integration.[44] In 1949, West Germany established a special ministry for refugee and expellee affairs, charged with looking after both the refugee's material well-being and with providing for their presumed special cultural needs. The ministry functioned until

1969, long after the beneficiaries of its programs had been fully integrated in West Germany. Notably, the West Germans have always called the refugees "expellees"—*Vertriebener* or *Heimatvertriebene*—terms that imply that these Germans were unjustly and unlawfully uprooted from their native soil in Eastern Europe.[45] The Federal Republic's integration policies reflected this view. East Germany, in keeping with the policy advocated by the Allies, sought to assimilate the refugees into its society. West Germany, in contrast, worked to preserve the distinct ethnic identities and cultures of each expellee group. In part, this was motivated by a *völkisch* outlook that valued the dialects and unique customs of different German subcultures,[46] but it also served West German foreign policy revisionism. By fostering expellee identity, the West Germany leadership fed refugee hopes of eventually returning to their ancestral homes, thereby maintaining its claim to these territories. Since, as time went by, the prospect that these lands would be restored became ever more remote, the policy was inherently contradictory and caused considerable tension.[47] Refugees' integration into West German society led inevitably to intermarriage—which reached a rate of 75 percent—thus harming the very preservation of the distinct ethnic identity that the government hoped to keep intact.[48]

In 1952, the federal government instituted a policy aimed at equalizing the war burden, known as the "*Lastenausgleich*." This policy focused more on relieving the economic distress of the expellees than on compensating them for their losses. The economic surge of the 1950s also helped wipe out the refugees' economic disadvantage, and by the 1960s it was clear that, in spite of the difficulties involved, West Germany had successfully absorbed and integrated this population.[49]

Expellee Organizations and Political Parties in West Germany

In the late 1940s, refugees and expellees in West Germany began to found homeland societies (*Landsmanschaften*), which sought to unite all former residents of a specific native territory. In 1949 the homeland societies founded a loose coordinating body, the United East German Homeland Societies (*Vereinigte Ostdeutsche Landsmanschaften*—VOL), shortly thereafter renamed the Association of Homeland Societies (*Verband der Landsmanschaften*—VdL).

Another expellee organization was founded that same year, the Central Association of Expelled Germans (*Zentralverband vertriebener Deutschen,* ZvD); it later changed its name to the Alliance of Expelled Germans (*Bund der vertriebenen Deutschen,* BvD). Its president was a member of the Christian Democrat party (until 1954), Linus Kather.[50] It sought to unite all expellees and was built according to the regional basis of the Federal Republic rather than the lands of origin, as were the homeland societies and their umbrella organization.[51] The government pressured the two nationwide organizations to unite into a single representative body, but because of internal political rivalries, a merger was accomplished only in 1959.[52]

In West Germany, the entire political leadership, from the ruling Christian Democrats to the Social Democratic opposition, embraced the refugee and expellee organizations as well as their revisionist agenda, especially when they could benefit in the elections from declaring their support. The federal government subsidized the expellee organizations generously from the start.[53] Its financial support gave the state the power to intervene in their internal politics and enabled it to pressure the organizations to toe the line on official state policy. The state's interest was to head off any provocations by the expellee groups that might damage relations with the Western powers, and to prevent the expellees from sullying West Germany's hard-won image as a democracy among skeptics in the United States and Western Europe, for whom the memory of Nazi persecution and atrocities was still very much alive.[54] The story of a special national memorial day, Homeland Day (*Tag der Heimat*), instituted to mark the expulsions from the east, illustrates the complex relations between the state and the expellee organizations. It was first observed in 1950, at the initiative of the homeland societies and the two national expellee organizations. The ceremonies were funded by the government, as were the lion's share of the organizations' other activities. National political leaders participated in the ceremonies then and in the years that followed, and through the late 1960s, seeking the good will of expellee voters, they used the ceremonies as a platform for advocating the restitution of former German lands. However, as long as the Cold War lasted, it was not made into an official national observance out of fear that this would harm West Germany's image abroad. Homeland Day was originally observed at the beginning of August on the anniversary of the Potsdam agreement. In 1955, however, that date fell during Chancellor Konrad Adenauer's historic official visit to Moscow; fearing repercussions, the government pressured the expellee organizations to move the day to the second Sunday in September.[55]

Initially, the homeland societies and the other organizations sought not only to help the refugees cope with the social and material difficulties of integration into West Germany and to help them preserve their cultural heritage, but also to work for manifestly political goals. These goals, which were part of the West German consensus until the late 1960s, included a demand for a major revision of the Potsdam agreement that would not only allow the expellees to return to their homes in Eastern Europe, but also reinstate German sovereignty in its former Eastern European territories by reestablishing the borders of the German Reich as they were in 1937. Sudeten German activists also demanded the inclusion of their homeland—which had been part of Czechoslovakia in 1937, prior to the Munich agreement—within Germany's future borders. All these activists viewed themselves as the vanguard of the German nation as a whole.[56]

During the Cold War the expellee organizations functioned as extra-parliamentary pressure groups. Each *Landsmanschaft* invited federal, state, and local government representatives to their annual Homeland Day ceremonies and to other activities. At all these events, the expulsion was declared to be "the greatest collective crime in human history," of the same gravity as the Holocaust.[57] Speakers asserted the expellees' right to a homeland (*das Recht auf die Hiemat*)—that is, a return to their places of birth, from which they had fled or been expelled—and their right to self-determination in those lands. Taken together, the demands meant the annexation of these territories to Germany.[58]

Expellees could be found in every West German political party until the SPD-Liberal coalition signed treaties with the Soviet Union and Poland in 1970 as part of Chancellor Willy Brandt's new Eastern policy (*Ostpolitik*), thus estranging expellee groups from these parties. The Sudeten Germans' homeland society, for example, encompassed most of the political tendencies that had prevailed among these people before their expulsion. However, most Sudeten Germans had supported the Nazis in the late 1930s, and this political preference could be seen in organizations established in West Germany after the war. Sudeten political organizations included the Witiko-Bund, a right-wing group that contained former

Nazis and members of the German Sudeten party of Konrad Henlein, who had coordinated his moves with Hitler in the 1930s;[59] the Ackermann Gemeinde (Community) of the Sudeten Social Christian Party; and the social democratic Seliger Community.

The Seliger Community was founded in 1946 by expellees who had belonged to the German Social Democratic Workers Party in Czechoslovakia. Their leader was Wenzel Jaksch. He fled Czechoslovakia in 1939 and that country's government-in-exile in London. President Eduard Beneš's plans to expel the Sudeten Germans after the war estranged Jaksch from the government-in-exile. In 1948 he settled in West Germany and worked in the Sudeten German homeland society together with the Witikons and former Nazis, despite their disagreements and past rivalries. He served as president of the umbrella organization of expellee organizations from 1964 to his death in 1966.[60] Jaksch fiercely objected to the concessions that later were part of Brandt's *Ostpolitik* and attempted to deter any rapprochement between the federal republic and its eastern neighbors.[61]

In 1950, a group of expellees of *völkish* background founded a political party called the Bloc of Expellees and Disenfranchised (BHE). The new party scored an impressive electoral success in the 1953 elections in those states with a high proportion of refugees and expellees: 11.6 percent of the vote in Schleswig-Holstein, 10.8 percent in Lower Saxony, and 8.2 percent in Bavaria. Historian Ian Connor viewed these BHE tallies as indicating a rupture between the newcomers and the native local populations. The established parties had not found a way to give the expellees a sense of belonging and partnership, he maintained. Connor also argued that the BHE's electoral success showed that much more remained to be done before the refugees and expellees would be politically and economically integrated into the Federal Republic.[62] However, as Waldemar Kraft, one of the party founders, admitted, the results actually disappointed the BHE's leadership.[63] Given that far greater proportions of refugees and expellees lived in these states (35 percent in Schleswig-Holstein, 26.8 percent in Lower Saxony, and 20.9 percent in Bavaria) than had voted for the BHE, the results actually show how rapidly large parts of this population had been integrated or at least did not feel like supporting such a particularist party.

In fact, the BHE disappeared from the West German political map a few years later. In the national elections of 1957 the party failed to receive the minimum of 5 percent required for Bundestag representation. At the beginning of the 1960s it ran a joint slate of candidates with the nationalist German Party (DP), but still failed to pass the bar for representation. From the start, then, the BHE had been supported only by a segment of the expellees and refugees, and once the economic boom had brought about their material rehabilitation and successful integration into West German society, even its erstwhile supporters switched to other parties. Furthermore, the expellees, like most Germans, increasingly accepted that Germany had lost its eastern territories forever and that the hope that they would be returned some day was an illusion.[64] The expellee organizations' relentless apprehension was that any improvement in relations with the countries of Eastern Europe was liable to come at the expense of West Germany's commitment to the German territories in the east.[65]

West Germany's Revisionist Rhetoric and Policy on Germany's Eastern Borders, 1949–1966

The Federal Republic's leaders advocated territorial restitution and repatriation until the end of the 1960s. Only with the signing of the Treaty of Warsaw in 1970 did West Germany drop its refusal to recognize the eastern German border imposed by the Allies in the Potsdam agreement.[66] Until then, official rhetoric proclaimed that the German state's 1937 borders were the only ones with legal force. For example, in 1951 Chancellor Adenauer declared that Germany in its 1937 borders had not ceased to exist.[67] The expulsion was portrayed as an illegal measure in violation of international law. While deploring the expulsion of the Sudeten Germans, the Federal Republic raised no territorial demands for the Sudetenland, because it had not been part of the German state in 1937. Nevertheless, up until 1964 Germany avoided making any official statement on this issue, or about the Munich pact of 1938. As late as August 1967, Chancellor Kurt Georg Kiesinger stated in a letter to Hans-Christoph Seebohm, the head of the Sudeten expellee organization, that the Munich pact was invalid *ex nunc*—that is, from the present forward, but not in the past.[68]

Because of this border dispute and the Hallstein doctrine, West Germany did not establish diplomatic relations with the Communist regimes of Eastern Europe until the late 1960s. The federal government's revisionist rhetoric appealed to important sectors in its population. A great majority of West Germans (80 percent) rejected, in March 1951, the Oder-Neisse line that the Potsdam agreement had established as the German-Polish border. An only slightly smaller but still considerable majority (66 percent in 1953) believed that one day the eastern territories would again be German. This majority probably took the government's word on this issue at face value.[69] However, a similarly large majority (82 percent)—even among the refugees and expellees (81 percent)—thought that not all means should be employed to regain the eastern territories.[70]

Publicly, until the late 1960s, all West German parties except the Communists refused to accept the Oder-Neisse line as a permanent border and demanded a revision of the Potsdam agreement that would restore to Germany its former territories to the east of that line. Adenauer shrewdly made use of revisionist rhetoric, speaking of the expellees' future return to their homelands in order to appease both the expellees and conservative and nationalist voters, in the hope of bringing them into his political camp.[71] The chancellor was careful, however, to qualify such declarations so as not to alarm the Western Allies or to aggravate public opinion in the West and in Communist Eastern Europe. After an incident in which he made a comment that sounded too blatant to foreign ears, he was even more diligent about balancing his pronouncements with conciliatory language. Although Adenauer welcomed expellee support, he was generally careful to avoid backing the extremist positions of some expellee groups, which deviated radically from the wording of the Potsdam agreement and American policy. In his first speech to the Bundestag in Bonn as chancellor, in September 1949, Adenauer referred to the issue of the eastern territories. He pointedly refrained from addressing the issue of the Sudeten Germans, ignoring a Deutsche Reichspartei member, Dr. Franz Richter, who shouted, "Please don't forget the Sudetenland, Mr. Chancellor."[72] At one of the Federal Republic's first cabinet meetings, in September 1949, Minister of Transport and Mails Hans-Christoph Seebohm queried the legality of the border with Czechoslovakia and maintained that Egerland, one of the Sudeten districts, should be annexed to Bavaria. This possibility, he claimed, had already been discussed in talks between President Beneš and the U.S. government. Adenauer reprimanded him for always thinking only about the expellees rather than about the implications that demands of this sort would have outside Germany.[73]

In a speech in Berlin on October 6, 1951, Chancellor Adenauer asserted: "Allow me to state with absolute clarity: the territory beyond the

Oder-Neisse [line] belongs to us, the Germans." Historians today agree that Adenauer's statement was a deliberate provocation rather than an actual demand representing his political credo. The chancellor's purpose was to frustrate a proposal made in September 1951 by East Germany's parliament and its prime minister that Germany be united and declared neutral.[74] Nevertheless, as attuned to public opinion polls as he was,[75] Adenauer must certainly have had his domestic electorate in mind, and not just the GDR and Soviet Union, when he made this statement.[76]

Adenauer voiced such sentiments time and again. In a speech to the fourth Congress of Silesian Expellees in July 1953—during an election campaign—he said that he had been won over by the expellees' abiding devotion to their native soil and that he was profoundly certain that their right to their land was inalienable: "If you [the Silesian expellees] never cede our German Silesia, one day you will return to your homeland."[77]

Six weeks later, on September 7, 1953, a day after Adenauer won a huge electoral victory, his government issued a clarification stating that the Federal Republic was committed to the peaceful reunification of Germany. A day later, Adenauer granted an interview to the Associated Press in which he issued a call to place the German territories beyond the Oder and Neisse Rivers under a German-Polish condominium, or under the control of the United Nations.[78] Although this creative position was highly irritating to the Soviets and Poles governments and did not exactly comply with the U.S. position that the Oder-Neisse line was a permanent German border, it nevertheless deviated from his hard-line domestic rhetoric.[79]

In another speech Adenauer gave two years later, on the tenth anniversary of the expulsion of the Germans from the east, he again stressed that these territories had been German for generations and that they had not been forgotten. In the speech, broadcast on the U.S. radio station (RIAS) in Berlin, he also asserted that the position of the Federal Republic was that human rights include the right to one's homeland.[80] (The expellees' organizations repeatedly asserted their right to a homeland, although this right was not recognized by international law.) However, in an intimate conversation in 1957, Adenauer confirmed that he believed that the postwar settlements could not be revised. He repeated this view at other times and places.[81]

Nevertheless, during the chancellorships of Adenauer and Ludwig Erhard, the federal cabinets included some ministers who were members of either expellee organizations or expellee political parties and who took positions far more radical and nationalist on this issue than did their chancellors and cabinet colleagues.

The Cabinet's Hardliners: Oberländer and Seebohm

In 1953 Chancellor Adenauer brought the BHE into his active coalition and cabinet. Its most prominent leader was Theodor Oberländer, who had been an active Nazi from the time of the Hitler's aborted beer hall putsch in Munich in 1923. Adenauer named Oberländer to be the minister for expellee, refugee, and war victim affairs. In 1955 the party split, and in 1956 Oberländer and the BHE's other cabinet minister, Waldemar Kraft, joined Adenauer's Christian Democrats.

From the time he was appointed, Oberländer was the target of public criticism for his practice of appointing other former Nazis to posts in his ministry. He also proposed reviving the Third Reich's mandatory labor service for young people.[82] Furthermore, his speeches about the expulsion and the border question were full of terminology used by the Nazis.[83] In 1954 he gave a radio address in Bavaria on the national mission of the expellees in the east, saying that "the eastern borders [of Bavaria, along which lies] a frontier area, should be strengthened to create a solution for the problem of the Sudeten Germans as a general European solution in the sense of the Munich agreement." Although this implied moving the German border to the east, Adenauer did not rebuke him for saying it.[84] On the other hand, Oberländer complied with Adenauer's policy, not only regarding West Germany's integration into the democratic West. He took on Linus Kather and the radicals in his own party on various issues; for example, on some occasions he advocated a lower profile of expellee protest actions. One such case was a demonstration in 1955 planed by the expellees to mark the tenth anniversary of the Potsdam agreement, which fell during Adenauer's important visit to Moscow.[85]

In 1959, a Communist newspaper revealed that Oberländer had participated in the murder of Jews in Lvov in the summer of 1941.[86] While Adenauer defended Oberländer at first, the scandal escalated, and Adenauer finally accepted Oberländer's resignation after East Germany tried and convicted him *in absentia*.[87]

Hans-Christoph Seebohm enjoyed a career in the federal cabinet much longer than Oberländer's. In fact, Seebohm served longer as a minister than any other expellee politician—seventeen years. He began as Germany's transport and posts minister, a portfolio he held from 1949 to 1966 under Adenauer and Erhard. During his long career, Seebohm's frequent radical nationalist pronouncements about the expulsion, the expellees, border issues, and other highly sensitive German topics often turned into international scandals.

Seebohm began his political career in the nationalist DP and switched to the Christian Democrats in the early 1960s. From 1959 onward, along with his cabinet posts, he also served as the head (*Sprecher*) of the Sudeten German homeland society (*Landsmanschaft*).[88] Seebohm repeatedly declared that the Sudeten region was German territory, and that the Germans had never ceded this part of their homeland. His rhetoric roused the ire of the Allied high commissioners in Germany, foreign governments, international public opinion in East and West alike, and Germany's political opposition.[89]

From the inception of the Federal Republic, he repeatedly declared, in a variety of public forums, that Germany should not even recognize its 1937 borders, the lines the Federal Republic said it would demand in future peace agreements with its neighbors. "Have we forgotten that the 1937 borders in the east are the borders of the Versailles Treaty?" Seebohm declared at an assembly of his DP in Gosslar in 1951. "Have we ever recognized these borders at any time in our history? No, we have always, as long as we have been conscious of our Germanness (*deutschbewußt*), we would never have done so."[90] He claimed that the Versailles Treaty created the nationalities problem in 1919 and that the failure of the League of Nations in Geneva to guarantee the rights of national minorities had created the conditions that led to World War II.[91]

Like other leaders of the Sudeten German homeland society, Seebohm repeatedly maintained that the Munich agreement of 1938 was a justified revision of the Versailles and St. Germain treaties, which had denied self-determination to the Sudeten Germans as well as to other minorities in Eastern Europe. This agreement received international recognition, he claimed, and emphasized that the support of the Sudeten Germans for the annexation of the Sudetenland to Nazi Germany had nothing to do with support for Nazism or with support for the dismemberment of Czechoslovakia in 1939.[92]

In 1964, he declared that the Munich agreement of 1938 was still valid and that "the determination of Germany's eastern border with Czechoslovakia can be accomplished only under the auspices of a All-German regime."[93] Nevertheless, he always tried to mitigate the political implications of such statements by saying that the demand for the return of the Sudetenland was not tantamount to a demand for border revisions.[94] In line with Adenauer's 1953 proposal that former German areas east of the Oder-Neisse line be administered by the United Nations or some other international body, Seebohm proposed a similar arrangement for Bohemia, Moravia, and Silesia (the districts comprising the Czech lands in Czechoslovakia) in the framework of a future free and united Europe. In spite of his declared commitment to the Czech right of self-determination and his famous apology of 1963 to the Czech people for the crimes during the German occupation, Seebohm always prevaricated about the fact that he actually did not acknowledge the right of the Czech people to a nation-state.[95] For example, in 1951 he claimed that central Europe's problems could not be solved by establishing nation-states, as the powers sought to do in 1919. Since the peoples of central Europe lived in overlapping territories that could not be separated, the only way to resolve all problems was to place human rights, and above all the right to a homeland, above the interests of nation-states, in the framework of a new, supra-national European order. The new order would be based on peoples rather than on nation-states. Like the United Nations, which was founded on the principle of the rights of the individual, so should the new Europe (after the liberation of the countries of Eastern Europe from the Soviet yoke) be based not on national sovereignty but rather on the civil rights of the citizens of Europe. One fundamental human right was the right of every European to a homeland (*Heimat*). The expellees would thus be returned to central Europe and would live there, while the Slavic nation-states would be dismantled.[96] These arguments combined *völkisch* elements from the past with the discourse of universal human rights that developed in Germany under Allied inspiration after 1945.[97] Seebohm in fact did not accept the right of the region's Slavic nations to self-determination and national states. Most likely he believed, like the sociologist and ideologue of the Sudeten Germans, Egon Lemberg, that the Slavs, due to their racial characteristics, were incapable of maintaining a proper nation-state.[98]

The experience of the years following 1919, when Slavic nation-states oppressed national minorities and sought to force them to assimilate into the Slavic milieu, served as further evidence that these countries had no right to exist. (Obviously, it never occurred to him that the same argument could be used to obviate the case for a German nation-state, given Germany's oppression of minorities from the nineteenth century onward, not to mention during World War II.) However, Seebohm equivocated when it came to the question of the German nation-state's relationship to the German populations in central and Eastern Europe that would live under his proposed super-national sovereignty. His statements contradicted the Bonn government's position that the Munich pact no longer had the force of international law (*Völkerrecht*), and therefore Germany had no territorial claims against Czechoslovakia.[99]

In 1951, Seebohm declared that all national symbols under which Germans had fought should be respected. As one might expect, the public understood this as a call to honor Nazi symbols. Seebohm rejected this interpretation, claiming, as he frequently would in the face of similar scandals surrounding his pronouncements, that young, sensationalist journalists had taken his words out of context.[100] In 1952, Seebohm asserted that the expellees had difficulty understanding Germany's reparation payments to Israel. He excused his signature on the agreement by stating that Germany should recognize that Israel had taken in some half a million Jews who had suffered injustices under the Third Reich. Implying an equivalence between the murder of Jews and the expulsion of Germans, he then added: "We must ask whether the Allies did not assume similar guilt in expelling 15 million Germans from the territories in the east, and whether they should not act as we act toward Israel, in order to preserve their moral standing among Germans."[101]

Like other expellee politicians, Seebohm also took special interest in the issue of South Tyrol, a German-speaking region in northern Italy. This seemed to be an attempt to apply a pan-German policy of the *völkisch* sort to German minorities. Chancellor Adenauer and Foreign Minister Heinrich von Brentano opposed the interventionist position of Seebohm and his colleagues.[102] In 1960, after the establishment of the South Tyrolean Liberation Organization and the beginning of its terror campaign, Seebohm saw fit to create an international scandal by claiming that "our [German] brothers in South Tyrol are so oppressed." The Italian press referred to this as "the recent reinforcement of a pan-German orientation in Germany."[103] Two years previously, Wenzel Jaksch, a member of the West German SPD's executive committee and of the Bundestag, as well as a leading member of both the Sudeten Organization and the Union of Expellees, went with another member of the Bundestag to South Tyrol to investigate the Italian government's treatment of the local German population. The trip was spurred by the conviction of a group of young local Germans for the murder of an Italian customs official. The region's German population viewed the case not as murder but rather, at most, as manslaughter. Upon his return, Jaksch declared, in Austria, that "a police state reigns in South Tyrol." Then, in Bonn, he warned against the radicalization of the German youth of South Tyrol because they were "losing their faith in justice." He claimed that the Germans of South Tyrol were disappointed by the Federal Republic's indifference to them. In his words, "The recent bombings by nationalists in South Tyrol was just an attempt to attract Europe's attention to their cause." Jaksch sought to encourage the German government to take an active role in the dispute in Italy, in support of the German minority in South Tyrol.[104]

Seebohm's rhetoric angered governments and public opinion both in the West and in Eastern Europe,[105] and he was lambasted by the German media and political opposition.[106] Despite calls for his dismissal, Adenauer, while harshly critical of Seebohm in internal forums, took no such action.[107] On occasion, the chancellor even made excuses for Seebohm's pronouncements.[108] Chancellor Erhard also refrained from firing Seebohm in 1964 after the latter proclaimed the validity of the Munich Pact of 1938. In response to American journalists' astonishment at his failure to act, despite the frequent international brouhahas the minister was causing, Erhard said that Seebohm represented 10 million refugees and expellees in the Federal Republic.[109] Yet most of these people did not vote for Seebohm, nor did they see him and other expellee politicians and organizations as their political representatives.

Seebohm's lengthy service in the West German cabinet granted legitimacy to his declarations. His extremist positions gave Eastern Europeans and the rest of the world the impression that the Federal Republic was trying to play both sides of the game. On the one hand, Chancellors Adenauer and Erhard themselves voiced relatively moderate revisionist positions that repudiated the use of violence, but on the other, they supported and cultivated expellee ministers who promoted a radical revisionist agenda and who for all intents and purposes rejected the right of the Slavic nation-state to exist.[110] When Chancellors Adenauer and Erhard refrained from firing Seebohm even when he no longer had many voters behind him, they gave the impression that they actually wanted a man with such provocative positions in the cabinet, as part of their Eastern policy during the Cold War. They may have seen him as a means of exerting pressure in negotiations with the Soviet Union and the countries of Eastern Europe—not to mention as a counterweight to American pressure on Germany to compromise on its eastern borders.

With his problematic views, Seebohm was a mouthpiece for circles that extended beyond the expellee community. Germany's hyper-nationalist camp depended, however, on the government's willingness to provide financial support for its power centers. Adenauer feared the potential radicalism of this group and preferred to use money and sympathy to keep them close and thus make it difficult for them to act contrary to the principles of his new German state.[111] Most West German political leaders, whether cabinet ministers or backbenchers, preferred over many long years not to confront their constituents with the unrealism of the revisionist rhetoric that they themselves used, and in which most of the West German population believed until the end of the 1960s. In backroom conversations, however, these same political figures acknowledged that the official position was ineffectual and had no chance of achieving its goals.[112] It was the rare politician who dared state publicly what many of them said behind closed doors, and those rare ones generally paid a political price for doing so.[113]

In other words, Germany held fast to an anachronistic foreign policy that did not answer its needs, and which produced distrust and concern among its neighbors. The entire political system acted with excessive caution, synchronizing its policy toward the east with the public mood. Only when the public's position changed did the leadership of the liberal and left wings of the political spectrum dare, under the leadership of Willy Brandt, first in his capacity as West Germany's foreign minister and later as chancellor, to utterly revise its stance on the territories in the east and on its neighboring countries. Intellectuals such as the historian Golo Mann[114] and the liberal-left media were the only Germans bold enough to doubt, as early as the late 1950s, the political wisdom of revisionist policy. In doing so, they commenced a guarded public discourse which the Protestant Church joined in 1965. This discourse was a step ahead of the politicians, contributing to a change in the public atmosphere that made policy changes possible.[115]

The Gradual Change in Public Opinion

Beginning in the 1960s, public support for conventional revisionism and nationalist rhetoric about Germany's eastern borders and the expulsion began to decline sharply. Yet, despite this steadily diminishing public support for the revisionist agenda, no politician, whether from the Christian Democratic-led coalition or the Social Democratic opposition, revised his nationalist rhetoric regarding Germany's former eastern territories. In 1961, a group of eight prominent and prestigious West German scientists (among them Werner Heisenberg, Ludwig Raiser, Klaus von Bismarck, and Carl-Friedrich von Weizsäcker), all affiliated with the Protestant Church (EKD), resolved to encourage public debate on this issue. They published, in the weekly *Die Zeit,* a statement that came to be called "The Memorandum of the Eight": "We say nothing new . . . [in saying that] that we must concede the claim to sovereignty over the territories beyond the Oder-Neisse line. We have grounds for believing that responsible political circles in all parties share this judgment, but avoid stating it publicly because of internal political considerations. An atmosphere that makes it impossible for the political leadership to tell the people the truth is poisonous."[116] Their call set off a passionate debate in the German media. They were reproached by, among others, the Social Democratic politician Herbert Wehner, who accused them of weakening Germany's position against the Soviets.[117] The political scientist Wilhelm Hennis, appearing on *Panorama,* a television newsmagazine, acknowledged the argument that the claim to the eastern territories might be a bargaining chip in future peace negotiations.[118] The historian Pertti Ahonen questioned in a 2003 book whether such diplomatic considerations really played the leading role in German policy making.[119] A public opinion survey conducted in March 1962, during and shortly after this public debate, showed that, for the first time since the founding of the Federal Republic, a plurality of Germans (45 percent) thought that the eastern territories were lost for Germany.

Nevertheless, the public debate and the change in public opinion failed to induce the Social Democratic opposition to change its positions. In 1963, the SPD's three leaders, Erich Ollenhauer, Herbert Wehner, and Willy Brandt, signed a greeting to a gathering of Silesian expellees in Cologne which stated in part:

> Breslau, Oppeln, Gleiwitz, Hirschberg, Glogau, Grünberg. These are not just names. They are living memories, rooted in the souls of generations, that pound incessantly on our conscience. Giving up [the German territories in the east] is betrayal [*Verzicht ist Verrat*], who wishes to dispute that? The Social Democratic Party's one hundred years means, more than anything else, one hundred years of struggle for the right of self-determination of peoples. It is impossible to sell the right to a homeland for a mess of pottage. One must never play at the expense and behind the backs of those who were expelled or who fled from their homeland.[120]

The gradual change in German public opinion on Germany's eastern border brought with it a bold political statement by Adenauer, which he made abroad in November 1964 after leaving the chancellorship. In an interview with the Israeli newspaper *Ha'aretz*, Adenauer claimed that he had never demanded a return to the 1937 borders—even though this had been explicit in the platforms of both his party and the SPD.[121] He implied that the claim had been made only to establish a bargaining position. Expellee organizations reacted angrily, but Adenauer gracefully finessed their remonstrations.[122]

Adenauer's successor, Ludwig Erhard, followed his predecessor's line of public commitment for the cause of the expellees balanced by compliance with the policy of the Western powers.[123] Before the 1960s, both the government and the opposition avoided any explicit statement that the Munich agreement of 1938, which countenanced the annexation of the Sudetenland by Germany, was null and void.[124] The Erhard government's statement in 1964 that it would be satisfied with a return to the 1937 borders, and that it had no territorial demands against Czechoslovakia, incensed the expellee organizations, especially that of the Sudeten Germans. Seebohm, who, it will be recalled, was both a cabinet minister and the spokesman for the Sudeten organization, claimed that the cession of the Sudetenland to Germany under the terms of the Munich treaty was and remained legally binding. The BdV maintained this position until the 1970s.[125]

In 1965 the Protestant Church issued a statement calling for reconciliation with the countries and peoples to Germany's east, to be accomplished by recognizing the Oder-Neisse line. It stressed the political and moral culpability of the German people toward its Slavic neighbors, asserting that "one cannot disconnect the injustices inflicted on the Germans from the context created by the political and moral iniquity into which the German people let it be led by the Nazis."[126] The statement provoked the outrage of the BdV, but in the long run it seems to have contributed to the dramatic change in German public opinion between 1964 and 1967. In September 1964, only 22 percent of West Germans said that they could live with the Oder-Neisse line, while a majority (59 percent) rejected this border. Three years later, the tide had turned: 47 percent said they could live with the existing German-Polish border, while 34 percent continued to reject it.[127] The trend was especially noted among the educated.[128] Even the SPD's Willy Brandt continued to voice, if not explicitly revisionist opinions, at least ambivalent and sometimes ambiguous (if not embarrassing) positions on Eastern European issues until as late as 1967.[129] Only then, when he assumed the post of foreign minister in the "grand coalition," did he begin to indicate that he and his party were ready to discard traditional West German *Ostpolitik*.[130]

Brandt's "opening to the east" initiative had its inception during the grand coalition government but reached its peak only in 1970, after Brandt became chancellor. His *Ostpolitik* and the elimination of the Ministry for Expellee Affairs in 1969, were indications that both the political establishment and the public at large were retreating from the commitment to the expellee organizations' agenda.[131] Brandt's new *Ostpolitik* led to treaties with the Communist regimes of East Germany and Eastern Europe (*Ostverträge*), and to the opening of a new chapter in the German relationships with these nations.[132] This dramatic change in West German foreign policy reflected a widespread feeling at the time that the revisionist agenda had been an obstacle to reducing inter-bloc tensions in Europe and to improving relations with the Communist world.

Brandt's *Ostpolitik* was a blow to all hardliners, including expellee politicians and lobbyists. Nevertheless, in spite of their estrangement from the Social Democratic-Liberal government and its cuts in their financial subsidies,[133] the expellee cause continued to be championed by the main opposition faction, the CDU/CSU, and not only by the extreme right, which had always supported a nationalist agenda. A number of SPD expellee politicians left their party because of its new foreign policy, and these crossed the aisle to the CDU. The best known of these was Herbert Hupka, the chairman of the Silesian homeland society and an SPD parliamentarian who defected in 1972.[134] The Christian Democrats stuck to their traditional positions and condemned the new *Ostpolitik* as a shameful and harmful concession to Communist dictators. It is true that a gradual change on Eastern European issues also occurred within certain circles of the CDU, and these called for their party to support the government's new foreign policy.[135] But even then, in a period during which their influence and their political influence seemed to decline, the expellee's narrative of suffering remained legitimate and respectable in the West German political culture. Their activists were still able to influence the national agenda, even when the West German public and most of its political establishment rejected their goals.

Historians agree that the conservative turn in West Germany, which began with the CDU/CSU's return to power in 1982 under the leadership of Helmut Kohl, did not bring with it a real change in the *Ostpolitik* pursued by the previous SPD administrations.[136] The expellee lobby did not regain its former influence on West German foreign policy. Michael Schwartz claims that Kohl was "Adenauer's grandson," giving lip service to the expellees but in fact progressing further along the course laid out by Brandt and his Liberal coalition partners, who were now Kohl's partners.[137] In 1985 Kohl refused to participate in a rally of the Silesian home society unless the organization changed the rally's slogan, "Silesia Remains Ours!" (*Schlesien bleibt unser!*). Silesia was annexed by Poland under the Potsdam agreement, but the expellee press termed this treaty—which legitimized the expulsion of the Germans from the eastern territories—as a crime and the expulsion as a genocide.[138] Kohl did not think that the German East was worth risking the flourishing relationship West Germany had cultivated with Poland and the other Eastern European countries since the 1970s. However, he revived Adenauer's strategy of using ambiguous revisionist terminology and pouring money into the expellee organizations. Under Kohl, the German government increased its support for the expellee organizations from DM 3 million to DM 45 million.[139] He thus gave them the impression that their cause was not lost. Furthermore, they continued to hear statements from top CDU and CSU figures about Germany's commitment to the expellees and to the former German territories.[140] Kohl maintained this rhetoric almost until the very last moment, when, in 1990, he went to Moscow to sign the Two Plus Four treaty. According to its terms, Germany formally accepted the principles of the Potsdam agreement, including the established border with Poland, and renounced its previous territorial demands.[141] Yet, even after offering an unambiguous explanation for his acceptance of the Two Plus Four treaty, he suggested that "his government reacted to external pressure and possibly even acted contrary to the chancellor's personal preferences."[142]

Expellee activists and historians who sympathize with their positions have regarded Kohl's statement about having been forced to sign the treaty as simple hypocrisy, just another manifestation of the dishonesty of West Germany's governments, and the Christian Democrats in particular, toward the expellees and the German claim to its eastern territories. Yet Kohl made no public gesture like Brandt's twenty years earlier, when he knelt at the Warsaw Ghetto monument before signing a treaty with the Poles. Nor did he issue a statement addressing the moral and legal claims of the country's previous revisionist policy and historically contextualizing the expulsion and the loss of the territories, as Jacob Kaiser, the minister of All-German affairs, had done in 1955. Kaiser had the courage and integrity to declare publicly, before a congress of expellee organizations in Berlin marking the tenth anniversary of the Potsdam treaty: "I may say it and also I must say it: neither do we forget that Yalta and Potsdam, with all the harm they brought on us, were a result of Hitler's war, with its genocides and murders."[143] Rather, Kohl's rhetoric contributed to the preservation of German resentment against Potsdam.

In short, to paraphrase and at the same time contradict the title of Manfred Kittel's polemical 2007 book, *The Expulsion of Expelless?*[144] the expulsion was not expelled from Germany's public agenda until German reunification in 1990. However, collective memory certainly does not exist solely in political discourse, and it cannot be judged only by its presence on the public agenda. Outside the political realm, the expulsion was commemorated in West Germany's culture and landscape.

Memory Politics

Manfred Kittel laments that by the 1960s, the memory of the German East was restricted mostly to the "ghettos" of the homeland societies, isolated from the rest of West German society.[145] It is only natural that the homeland societies, more than other groups, would be concerned with preserving this memory, especially when they received generous government subsidies precisely for the purpose of fostering their heritage and fortifying the memory of the homelands from which they had been expelled. During the Federal Republic's first two decades, this policy of memory served a political purpose for West German foreign policy. It underlined and symbolized the fact that behind West Germany's revisionist demands stood refugees and expellees, and that they were prepared to return to their places of origin forthwith.

What was the nature of the homeland societies' occupation with the German East, and why did German society in the end move away from the particular memory of the German East that had been fostered there? The organizations took an extremely hard line on the goals of West Germany's *Ostpolitik* and its rapprochement with its Eastern European neighbors.[146] For years, the homeland societies had advocated revisionism, using nationalist arguments reminiscent of Nazi propaganda. At the same time, in accordance with the *Zeitgeist,* they buttressed their claims by citing human rights and international law. The Potsdam agreement, which established Europe's postwar borders, violated these principles, they claimed. They portrayed the expulsion as the most terrible crime in history, and depicted the expellees as innocent victims. Up until the early 1960s such positions were very popular with the German public; from that time onward, however, they gradually lost their appeal, not only among native West Germans but even among most expellees. In fact, most expellees never joined homeland societies or any other expellee organization, distanced themselves from the organizations' political positions, and sought reconciliation and peace with the countries of Eastern Europe. Nevertheless, the West German state fostered and subsidized not only the expellees' political organizations but also the establishment of cultural organizations, monuments, museums, and research institutes to preserve the unique cultures and heritage of the Silesians, Pomeranians, East Prussians, Sudeten Germans, and other expellee groups.[147]

At the beginning of the 1950s, the federal Ministry of Expellees, Refugees, and War Victims, headed by Hans Lukaschek, commenced a major oral history project on the expulsion of Germans from Eastern Europe and the southeast. The material was published in five volumes. At that time, more than a few of the activists in the expellee organizations, as well as the academic researchers involved in the project, were sworn Nazis who had had careers in the Third Reich and who had worked energetically during the war to expel Jews from the east.[148] Some of them did not think the principles of Nazism were a dead letter. The project's head was a historian, Theodor Schieder, who had been acquainted with Oberländer during the Third Reich. During that time, Schieder had recommended to the Nazi regime that it expel the Jews from Poland.[149] Another historian involved in the project, Friedrich Valjavec, had served in the SS and participated in 1941 in the slaughter of the Jews of Chernowitz by his unit, the *Einsatzgruppe* D.[150] The project was aimed at supporting Germany's territorial and material demands against its Eastern European neighbors in a future peace treaty. In recent years, historians have analyzed the dubious ways in which the oral testimonies were collected and have revealed serious political and methodological bias.[151] In his introduction to the work, Schieder says that Germans fled their homes not only because of the war that raged in the eastern territories, but also because of

> the enemy who, the experience of the autumn of 1944 in East Prussia and before that in the Baltic lands has proved, did not take the civilian population into account at all, but rather was urged to avenge and despoil the German population. It brutally ravaged, sowed chaos, raped women, shot civilians for fun, imprisoned thousands in temporary camps, and dragged them eastward.[152]

Schieder's portrayal of the expulsion and flight from the eastern territories bears a certain resemblance to Nazi narratives of innocent Germans suffering from victimization by Russians and other Slavic peoples. But, at the time, this was not only his personal position and not only that of the expellee organizations. It was the official position of the Federal Republic. Even his unpublished concluding volume, which presented the expulsion of the Germans as a product of the development of the idea of the nation-

Figure 25. A memorial for the millions of victims of expulsion and especially for the children. Pforzheim.

state and these states' nationalistic policies of homogenizing their populations, disregard the uniqueness of Nazi annihilation policy.[153]

The historians Manfred Kittel and Andreas Kossert deplored Willy Brandt's decision in 1969, as foreign minister, not to republish the series. Brandt was concerned that it might create misunderstandings abroad as he made the first steps toward his new *Ostpolitik*. However, the books, originally published by the federal Ministry for Refugees and Expellees between 1954 and 1961, have since been republished in paperback twice, in 1984 and in 2004, by a commercial publisher (DTV).[154]

Until the 1980s, the expulsion had much more of a presence in West Germany's memorialization landscape than the Holocaust. Hundreds of monuments to the expellees had been erected throughout the country in the 1950s, some of them with subsidies from the state. The BdV web site lists 1,400 such monuments,[155] and municipalities throughout West Germany have named streets, public buildings, and even highway service areas after German areas in the east. The city of Wolfsburg, for example, has a Sudeten Street and a Sudeten Road (*Sudetenweg*), a Silesians Road (*Schlesierweg*), an East Prussia Street and an East Prussia Road (*Ostpreussen Weg*), a Pomerania Street (*Pommern Strasse*) and a Pomerania Road. Similar names can also be found in other West German cities, including Wiesbaden, Ulm, Regensburg, Paderborn, Osnabrück, Munich, Bremen, Bonn, and Berlin.

Likewise, the Federal Republic issued stamps to mark the tenth (1955), twentieth (1965), and fiftieth (1995) anniversaries of the expulsion.[156] Up until the 1970s, the weather reports in the German media included territories and names from the eastern territories that were no longer part of Germany.[157] While the policy changed under the Social Democratic-Liberal coalition, this landscape of memory was not erased. To this day, if you enter the web site of the German train system (www.bahn.de) and type in "Breslau" (the German name for the Polish city of Wrocław), the system will accept your query. This may seem trivial, but it reflects the fact that for many Germans, Wrocław in Poland remains to this day the German city of Breslau.

The expulsion received artistic expression in German literature. Despite Andreas Kossert's claim that the subject had been politically taboo since the establishment of the Federal Republic, his survey of literary

Figure 26. German stamps issued in 1995 marking the fiftieth anniversary of the expulsion (right) and the end of World War II

manifestations of the subject from 1945 onward shows that such works began appearing in the 1950s. These included major works by West Germany's most important writers, such as Günter Grass, Wolfgang Koeppen, Arno Schmidt, Sigfried Lenz, and Peter Härtling. Furthermore, these works were translated into many foreign languages.[158] In fact, it seems that the subject received much more literary attention than the bombing of German cities, the subject that W. G. Sebald lamented (see chapter 7). Moreover, Kossert's survey shows that even East German novelists and playwrights took up the issue. While some of these simply served as mouthpieces for the official Communist position on the expulsion, some of East Germany's most important writers, such as Heiner Müller and Christa Wolf, served as dissident voices, writing of the pain of the expulsion and of the cold welcome the refugees received when they arrived in Germany proper.[159]

While interest in the former German territories has declined considerably in the political left and center since the 1970s, the expulsion and even the "perspective of its victims," by which Kittel means public legitimization of equating the expulsion with the Holocaust,[160] have hardly disappeared from West Germany even in these years. For example, at the height of the Social Democratic-Liberal coalition, a revisionist history book, *Nemesis at Potsdam*, by the American historian and jurist Alfred M. de Zayas, was translated into German immediately after its appearance in English in 1977. The book was issued by a reputable publisher and became a bestseller in Germany, appearing in a paperback edition as well. In the three decades since, fourteen new editions have been issued in Germany, as opposed to only six in the United States.[161]

After the broadcast of the American television miniseries *Holocaust* in Germany in 1979, Dr. Walter Becher, a member of the Bundestag and head of the German-Sudeten Homeland society, called on the German government and media to prepare a similar program on the expulsion of 14 million Germans, during which 2.5 million people were murdered. The Bavarian branch of the same organization seconded his call for the purchase of photographic documentation that could be used to counter the American program.[162] The presence of the journalist Franz Schönhuber,[163] later the leader of the extreme right Republican Party, most likely aided the 1981 production of the Bavarian broadcast authority's three-part documentary, *Flight and Expulsion* (*Flucht und Vertreibung*).[164] The historian Peter Fritsche stated explicitly what Kittel only implied—that this nationally televised program was a response to the American production.[165] Like de Zayas's book, it was based on the familiar narrative promoted by the expellee organizations, recounting the injustices committed against the German people, beginning with Versailles and ending with Potsdam. These treaties, the program asserted, violated the principles advocated by President Woodrow Wilson during World War I and the leaders of the Allied countries in World War II.

The segments were broadcast in prime time on West Germany's Channel 1 (ARD) in late January and the beginning of February 1981. Between 6 and 10 million Germans watched the series, 26 percent of the viewing audience.[166] Kittel complained of the harsh criticism the series received from the SPD and the liberal press, as if the broadcast of *Holocaust* two years previously had not evoked much fiercer criticism from the left.[167]

In the 1980s, historical research on the expulsion and later integration of the expellees began to appear, in both East and West Germany. In West

Germany, this was the second wave of publications following Schieder's project, but this time it was academic research, not a project sponsored by the state for political purposes.

The expulsion, in all its aspects, was thus never off the public agenda in Germany, nor was it silenced. This was true even when the West German public and the Social Democratic and Liberal political leadership, beginning in the late 1960s, reached a clear awareness that Germany should prefer reconciliation and peace with the countries of the Eastern bloc over a commitment to the German East and to the political agenda of a small group of functionaries of the expellee organizations and nationalists. Germans apparently changed their position out of considerations of *realpolitik,* not because they were now persuaded that Germans had been expelled for their complicity in Nazi crimes and for cooperating with Hitler and his attempt to destroy the Slavic nation-states. In this sense, the expellee organizations' interpretation of the expulsion's motives and context was not defeated in the battle over German collective memory in the 1970s through the 1990s. This may well be why it surfaced again after the end of the Cold War and the reunification of Germany.

7

The Resurgence of the German Sense of Victimization since Reunification

The reunification of Germany accompanied the end of the Cold War. Observers might have expected that the creation of a united German state would end the use of the Nazi past to stoke ideological rivalry between the two Germanys. The eternal flame of Germans' self-image as victims might finally have flickered out. After all, it had become much fainter after the Jewish Holocaust narrative entered German discourse in the late 1950s. The detente in East-West relations and East German–West German relations in the 1970s further dimmed it.

Yet the German public's preoccupation with its own suffering during and after World War II enjoyed a renaissance after reunification. The way the victors and occupiers treated German POWs and civilians, the bombing of German cities, and the expulsion of Germans from the east once again became critical issues. The discourse that grew up around these subjects integrated certain characteristics the Nazis had used to depict Allied war conduct. In some ways, the atmosphere created by the discourse was reminiscent of that in the young Federal Republic in the 1950s, even though the political setting and context has totally changed since then.

The German political culture's increased preoccupation with national suffering has been bound up with a growing inclination to view the entire German people during World War II and its aftermath as innocent victims of historical circumstances. In fact, the process began before reunification. After all, both German states' official culture of memory and commemoration during the Cold War, sometimes more implicitly and sometimes less implicitly, declared that the German people were not responsible for

World War II. Embedded in this culture was a distinction between "evil Nazis" and the rest of the German people, who were seen as having been seduced into supporting Hitler. The great agonies the German people suffered during the second part of the war and at its end seemed to be a justification for seeing themselves as victims of Hitler and the war.

Nevertheless, by the end of the 1960s, those who held this position found themselves on the defensive. The Jewish Holocaust narrative made its mark on German public discourse, challenging the official line and forcing it to change. The Jewish victims and the crimes committed against them moved into a higher place on the Federal Republic's political agenda than ever before. However, the change produced a reaction, primarily in conservative circles. Germans on the right felt that accusing the country's elites and institutions of committing or ignoring crimes called into question not only the official culture of memory, but also delegitimized German nationalism and impaired the Germans' self-image. The right was also concerned by the erosion of military spirit and the decline of the cult of the fallen soldier. With such a set of values, they feared, the new democratic Germany could not play a central role on the global stage, as its size and economic strength demanded and deserved.

By the late 1970s, some conservative voices were calling for "a return to the nation," setting off a public debate of major proportions on the question of German nationality and identity. The end of the Social Democratic-Liberal period and the election of Helmut Kohl as the Federal Republic's chancellor in 1982 was an important milestone in this process. Nationalist tendencies grew stronger in West Germany, and not just among conservatives—the same happened on the radical left. Inspired by East German propaganda, some on the far left accepted without question the nationalist position that the bombing of German cities had been an American attempt to undercut the population's German identity.[1]

Kohl's ambiguous attitude, coming from a man trained as a historian and who displayed, as a statesman, a well-developed historical consciousness, lies beyond the scope of this discussion. It is sufficient to note the fact that, at the beginning of his long tenure, he sought to conduct a more conciliatory policy of memory regarding the Nazi past, and to contribute to solidifying a German identity free of Auschwitz's shadow. Kohl had pushed for the establishment of a new museum in Bonn dedicated solely to German history after 1945 and meant to present the past from a national point of view.[2] His goals also found expression in the "historians' polemic" that broke out in the summer of 1986 over the question of the Holocaust's uniqueness.[3] A blunt expression of the chancellor's position could be seen during President Ronald Reagan's visit to Germany in 1985. Kohl hosted Reagan at a ceremony in the Bitburg military cemetery, where SS soldiers are among those interred. Kohl and Reagan pictured the ceremony as a gesture of reconciliation between the two nations. It was also intended as a symbol of making peace between soldiers of the SS, who were depicted by both politicians as ordinary soldiers and victims of the war, and their American enemies. In his speech in Bitburg, Reagan asserted that the SS soldiers were indeed victims. World War II was portrayed as a war of the same type as World War I, rather than as a Nazi war of murderous extermination.

The ceremony elicited protests around the world, which in turn led to fierce reactions in Germany as well.[4] The conservative German historian Ernst Nolte lashed out at the Bitburg critics: "How would they have reacted had Chancellor Adenauer refused, in 1953, to visit the military cemetery in Arlington, on the grounds that some buried there had participated in the terror bombings [*Terrorangriffe*] against the civilian population?"[5] Nolte thus equated the bombardments with the war crimes committed by SS soldiers. He even used the Nazi term for the bombings, which the Communists had adopted during the Cold War.

In Nolte's view, German civilians, like SS soldiers, were the victims of a criminal policy. Therefore, Allied air crews who attacked German cities were on the same moral level as these Nazi murderers. Up until the 1960s, many Germans had concurred again with this blunt assessment.

Memory Politics and the Public Debate on National Suffering during the Long 1990s

When Germany was reunified, its conservative leadership wished to create a common culture of memory and commemoration. It incorporated previous attempts to rehabilitate the legitimacy of the Federal Republic's official culture of memory and memorialization, the prime example of which was the perception of victimization and suffering manifested on the People's Day of Mourning, with certain adaptations of this culture to the zeitgeist.

Figure 27a. The façade of the Neue Wache

After reunification, Chancellor Kohl sought to create for the newly united Germany a central national memorial site for the victims of the war and the tyrannical Nazi regime. Neue Wache, in central Berlin, was the perfect site for the chancellor and his supporters. It embodied a continuing tradition of memorialization, having served as a monument for Prussian and German soldiers who gave their lives for their nation. This tradition began in the wars of liberation against Napoleon at the beginning of the nineteenth century and continued through World War I. During the Third Reich, the site was central to Heroes' Memorial Day, Nazi Germany's official day of mourning. Hitler himself laid a wreath there each year. Under Communist rule, the site served as a memorial for the victims of fascism and militarism (as discussed in chapter 3).

The memory that the site's design was intended to perpetuate was akin to the prevailing views, as embodied in the Federal Republic by the People's Day of Mourning and in East Germany by the Memorial for the Victims of Fascism and Militarism, erected at the Neue Wache. During the Communist period, the remains of an anonymous prisoner from a concentration camp and of an unknown German soldier were interred there.

Figure 27b. Kollwitz's pietà

After reunification, the site was redesigned to include a plethora of Christian symbols of reconciliation. Kohl's staff installed a large replica of a small statue of a mother and her dead son, created by the Socialist sculptress Käthe Kollwitz, at the center of the structure. The sculpture was more than a gesture to East Germany's socialist heritage. The image, in fact, is a take on a Christian icon, the Pietà. As such, it symbolizes God's mercy and pity for all victims, including German soldiers—of all units, with no explicit distinction between the Wehrmacht and SS—and also to those who were involved in war crimes and crimes against humanity. In both Germanys, one refers to soldiers in general as victims of the Nazi dictatorship and of the war.

The chairman of the Central Council of German Jews at the time, Ignatz Bubis, protested to the chancellor that the plan for the site did not distinguish between murderers and their victims. An attempt was made to appease him—a bronze plaque was added to the façade, bearing an inscription including an unequivocal reference to the Jewish victims. Kohl's staff chose a passage from a speech given by the Federal Republic's president, Richard von Weiszäcker, to the Bundestag in 1985, on the fortieth anniversary of Nazi Germany's defeat. The speech referred explicitly to all the victims of the war and of Nazism.

The president cast his words in the accepted mold of honoring the dead on the People's Day of Mourning, but here he explicitly identified the dead—some of whom had never before received official and ceremonial recognition. The speech was heralded around the world as indication of Germany's willingness to face up to its Nazi past. Von Weiszäcker said:

> Today we remember with great sorrow all the dead of the war and of the rule of violence. We especially remember today the 6 million Jews who were murdered in the concentration camps. We recall all the nations that suffered during the war, and above all the innumerable civilians of the Soviet Union and Poland who lost their lives. As Germans, we remember with sorrow the people of our own country who lost their lives as soldiers, in aerial attacks on their homes, the imprisonment and expulsion [of Germans from Eastern Europe], the homosexuals who were put to death, the mentally ill who were killed, and the people who paid with their lives for [adhering to] their political or religious positions.

However, in adapting these lines for the plaque, the chancellor's staff cut and edited them to fit their own view of what was appropriate for the post-reunification era:

> We remember the nations that suffered in the war. We remember their civilians who were persecuted and who lost their lives. We remember those who fell in the world wars. We remember the innocents who were killed

> during the war and in its wake—at home, in imprisonment, and during deportation. We remember the millions of Jews murdered. We remember the Sinti and the Roma who were murdered. We remember all those who were killed because of their origin, because of their homosexuality, or because of their illnesses and handicaps. We remember all those murdered, whose right to life was taken from them. We remember the men and women who were persecuted because they opposed tyranny after 1945.

In von Weizsäcker's speech, the victims of the Germans are singled out first, headed by the Jews, and the Germans themselves mentioned only afterward. In the revision, all the dead and suffering are mixed together before specific mention of Nazi victims. Thus German victims are implicitly included both at the beginning and the end. The explicit reference to Soviet and Polish victims, which came second in the president's draft, was eliminated. Von Weiszäcker's unequivocal summons to his people to remember the peoples who suffered and died under German occupation (*die im Krieg gelitten haben*) was converted into a general statement citing the nations that suffered during the war (*die durch Krieg gelitten haben*).

The second category included those persecuted by the Nazis: the Jews, the Gypsies (Sinti and Roma), homosexuals, and those persecuted and mistreated for their faith or political views. At the end of the edited list came the victims of the war, Nazism, and the Communist dictatorship after 1945. In other words, the deadly Nazi dictatorship was equated with that of the Communists. While the latter indeed oppressed the East German population, the harm they did hardly compared to the terrors of popular Nazi rule, which was directed mostly toward political opponents, Jews, and foreigners. Nazi violence was thus cast as a specific instance of a larger phenomenon, rather than held up as a singular evil, as von Weiszäcker had done. The intent and context of the president's declaration were entirely distorted. The reworked formulation, inscribed on bronze plaques at the entrance to the Neue Wache, was a perfect example of coerced reconciliation between murder victims and their murderers, the latter portrayed as having acted under circumstances beyond their control.

NAZI CRIMES = COMMUNIST CRIMES?

After Germany's reunification, a debate began over the fate of those whom the Soviets imprisoned after 1945 at former Nazi concentration camps, most of them located in the Soviet occupation zone. The prisoners there were predominantly Nazi officials and fervid sympathizers who had refused to surrender even after Germany capitulated; the Soviets also incarcerated those thought to be anticommunist, including some anti-Nazis and even certain Jews. Many of the prisoners died, though these numbers were far smaller than those killed in the same camps during the Nazi period.[6] When memorial sites were established in the camps during the Cold War era, the victims of Communist rule were not commemorated. It was the public discussion of their fates in the wake of reunification that led to the establishment of memorial sites for these victims as well—for example, at Buchenwald and Sachsenhausen in former East Germany. This new concept of memory equated the suffering of the Germans under Communism to that of the Nazis' victims.

Conservative circles, with the moral support of former East German dissidents and nationalists, some of them from the extreme right, promoted a memory of the Communist dictatorship's terrors that repositioned the Nazi past in German consciousness. In January 2004, the Central Council of Jews in Germany, followed by other organizations of groups persecuted by the Nazis, announced that they were ceasing cooperation with the Saxon Foundation for Memorial Sites (*Stiftung Sächsische Gedenkstätten*). The reason: a law passed by the Saxon parliament in 2003 that equated the crimes of Nazism with the crimes of Stalinism and of the State Security Office (the Stasi) in East Germany. Those who supported the comparison argued that both the Nazi and German Communist dictatorships were totalitarian regimes and hence directly linked. Yet, since the mid-1960s, the political culture of West Germany had been focused on viewing the Nazi crimes as a singular and incomparable phenomenon. The equation of Nazi and Communist crimes, typical of the 1950s theory of totalitarianism, lost its currency in the West German public. The 2004 law may be seen indicating a revival of the view that had pervaded West Germany during the 1950s, at the height of the Cold War. On this rationale, they pressed for legislation to promote the memory of the opponents and victims of Communist tyranny. Such legislation would take funds designated for memorializing Nazi crimes and divert them to preserving the memory of Communist crimes. This weakened the standing of the organizations of Nazi victims in the Saxon Foundation, whose number dropped as the ranks of representatives of organizations representing the victims of Communism increased.[7] On June 17, 2004, the fifty-first anniversary of the rebellion against the Communist regime in East Germany, a group of parliamentarians led by Günter Nooke of the Christian Democrats, a former anticommunist dissident, submitted a bill in the Bundestag in Berlin in the name of their faction. It called for formulating a common culture of memory for the Federal Republic of Germany, which would honor the victims of both tyrannies—the Nazi and the Communist. While the preamble to the proposal stated that the Nazi regime had committed a unique crime in murdering millions of European Jews, it went on to claim that both despotisms violently and systematically persecuted and oppressed entire populations. This measure was part of the campaign by German conservatives to create a national memory liberated from the views of both the Jewish victims and the war's victors, which, the bill's supporters alleged, had been forced on the Germans by the Allies.

The federal bill was based on a law already passed by Saxony's parliament concerning the Saxon Foundation for Memorial Sites. At the margins of the Bundestag proposal were three subjects that had no direct connection to the victims, but were linked to the history of the tyrannical regimes and the war. These issues (the German expellees, those killed in the Allied bombings, and the promotion of German reunification, including the mass demonstrations in the GDR calling for an end to Communist dictatorship) were to be vigorously stressed in the national culture of memory. The measure proposed the establishment of a Center Against Expulsions and a central monument for those who died in the bombings. While it did not deny the Holocaust, the bill dealt a blow to its portrayal as a uniquely horrifying event. Instead, it addressed the Holocaust as just one of many awful events, on the same level as the crimes of the Communist regime. Yet the German Democratic Republic did not start a world war, nor did it engage in the systematic killing of millions of human beings. The use of ambiguous terminology, the vagueness of a common term in the German culture of memory, "Dictatorship" (in German, "violent regime"—*Gewaltherrschaft*), and the reference to the persecution of entire populations without specifying which populations—all were attempts to obscure the fact that Nazi Germany, unlike the East German Communist regime, not only oppressed and persecuted European peoples, but in fact physically exterminated them.

The historian Götz Aly criticized the comparison, arguing that it is easy enough to tell the difference between the two German tyrannies: "You can laugh about Communist East Germany. About the Third Reich—no."[8]

The proposal, which sought to budget equal resources for official commemoration of both dictatorships, infuriated Israelis and Americans as well as German politicians of the Red-Green coalition. Realizing the damage it was causing Germany around the world, the ruling coalition in the Bundestag did not bring the bill to a vote, instead referring it to committee.[9]

THE DISCUSSION OF THE EXPULSION OF THE GERMANS IN THE 1990S

The end of the Cold War produced a dramatic change in the geopolitical position of united Germany. West Germany had been a satellite state of the Western bloc and especially of the United States. Its greatest fear was direct conflict between the two camps, in which Germany would become, once again, a battleground. Now a European power and relieved of the Soviet threat, united Germany bordered on small Slavic nation-states that were economically, politically, and militarily weak. Previously it had coordinated its foreign policy with its NATO allies, the United States first among them. Now Helmut Kohl's Germany conducted an independent foreign policy, one that was sometimes at odds with its allies, including the United States.

In 1991, for example, Germany pushed for recognizing the independence of Slovenia and Croatia, contrary to the position taken by the United States, Britain, France, and other Western European countries, which feared that such recognition would lead to war—as indeed it did.[10] Germany's foreign policy expressed a broad domestic consensus within Germany—the SPD also supported it, if not by a very large majority—-that identified with Croatia and portrayed the Serbs as the villains in the story. The pro-Croatian and anti-Serbian policy of Germany, which Austria and Italy soon joined, impelled its critics to point to the historical continuity of Germany's geopolitical alliances, dating back to the Third Reich.

When war spread through Yugoslavia, ravaging civilian populations with expulsions and rape—all brought into private homes via television—

it shocked the Germans, and apparently also evoked memories of World War II. In 1992, for example, the Balkan wars spurred a debate within the Green Party (*die Grünen*) about intervention to put an end to the violence, but at that time the majority of the party was opposed, presuming that intervention would only escalate the fighting. Three years later, in 1995, after the massacre in Srebrenica, the party's leader, Joschka Fischer, succeeded in getting a majority in the party to support a German military operation to protect civilians. He justified the move as a lesson from the Holocaust.[11]

The Balkan conflict, and in particular the expulsions that typified it, revived the issue of the flight and expulsion of Germans from Eastern Europe at the end of World War II. This was the first time the issue returned to the public agenda after the signing of the Two Plus Four agreement, which ended German claims to its former territories and its demand for border rectification in Eastern Europe. The end of the Soviet threat, along with the withdrawal of its revisionist demands, led central circles in the German left to rethink their view of the expulsion of the Germans from the east. From the 1970s onward, the left had distanced itself from the expellee organizations and their militant positions. But once the Cold War had ended, many on the left believed that the time was ripe for a reexamination of the issue. No longer would such a reexamination endanger Germany's relations with its eastern neighbors. A German nationalist perspective thus replaced the more political perspective that had been dominant on the left from the 1960s through the end of the Cold War.

This change in atmosphere and in public opinion could be seen in the results of surveys conducted that year. A public opinion poll published by *Der Spiegel* in 1995 showed what repercussions these views had. It revealed that 36 percent of those polled agreed with the statement that the expulsion of Germans from the east was a crime against humanity, just like the murder of the Jews in the Holocaust.[12] This might indicate that a significant portion of the population held revisionist views about the Holocaust. It also shows a clear turn toward a nationalist view of the expulsion on the left. The first harbinger of this was Antje Vollmer, vice president of the Bundestag from the Green Party. In 1995, Vollmer became the first Green Party representative to attend the traditional gathering of the Sudeten homeland society (*Sudetendeutscher Tag*). In an interview she granted six years later, after an SPD-Green coalition came to power in 1998, she explained that "after the war in Bosnia, many on the political left were shocked that the issue of the expulsion was still a real one. Previously, silence had prevailed for many years." As far as she was concerned, it was merely a meeting with Sudeten Germans, "a sincere effort to recognize that the silence had been an error. Just the scale, 12 million, these were entire nations!" It may be surprising that Vollmer chose to meet a group that was generally considered the most hard-line of the expellee associations. But an examination of the political position she has taken subsequently on the expulsion, and in particular its historical interpretation, shows a great deal of convergence between her views and those of the Sudeten homeland society. Later in the interview, Vollmer asserted that, in the past, "the left viewed the expulsion as the price we paid for our crimes," and she regretted that the left had not taken any special interest in the expellees. "The result was political manipulation that made it into a right-wing issue," she maintained, "even though it was first and foremost a humanitarian matter."[13]

Vollmer continued to take this line in public appearances and in articles. In a speech in 1997 at Karl University in Prague, she offered her insights and interpretations of the expulsion of the Sudeten Germans to her Czech audience. Since the 1970s such positions had been the preserve of expellee groups, not the Green Party or others from the left. She argued that "just as it is clear to everyone that Hitler attacked Czechoslovakia and not the opposite, as the individual fates of the two peoples become intertwined, they nevertheless find that they are switching off in the roles of persecutors and victims." After stressing the fundamental, essential difference between the Germans and the Czechs during World War II, Vollmer quickly asserted the equivalence of the two peoples, both of whom had come out badly: "The idea of expulsion, of ethnic cleansing [a term that originated in the Yugoslavian conflict], there can be no doubt, is part of the totalitarian crime of the current century." In other words, not just Nazi racist murder but also expulsions were an expression of the nadir reached by the human race during the twentieth century. She continued:

> Even worse, and even more frightening: it is one of those horrible ideas that oppressed and oppressors can entirely share. All expulsions have their roots in the distorted idea that a nation, religion, or social class will be most fortunate only when it exists alone in a place. This delusionary idea has fed all totalitarian ideologies, in particular by creating the image

> of a monster enemy. The reason lies in nationalism, and in the lunacy that can always be expected to come out of it. In ethnic cleansing, nationalism bares its inhuman core. It begins when the construction of national identity does not succeed. Then the image of the adversary, the external enemy, serves to tell me who and what I really am.

Vollmer digressed to enlighten her Prague audience about why they or their parents had expelled the Germans from their land: "When the Czechs and the Slovaks expelled their German fellow-citizens from their land in 1945 and in 1946, they certainly did not do so because the Potsdam conference allowed it, or because President Beneš ordered it." Here Vollmer adopted the revisionist interpretation of the expulsion of the Germans as being a product of the struggle between Germans and Slavs in the Bohemian lands, with its clear *völkisch* flavor, as marketed by the expellee organizations during the Cold War.[14] According to this view, the expulsion of the Germans from the Sudetenland was in no way a reaction to Nazism and its destruction of the Czechoslovakian state. It was not connected to the fact that the German minority there largely supported the Nazis and actively assisted their destructive aims, nor to the crimes the Nazis committed during their occupation of the country. The expulsion was an expression of the hatred of Germans that was part of the Czech national heritage. This view tacitly nods toward the Sudeten German claim that Eduard Beneš had proposed the expulsion even before the war—a claim without basis in fact.[15] Vollmer went on:

> They apparently also did not do so out of a consciousness of collective guilt of all the Germans for the crimes of the Nazis. They did not even do so only out of revenge, retribution against the Germans for their own expulsion and the injustice that Czechoslovakia experienced at the hands of the Germans. They apparently did it largely out of fear and weakness. They did not feel themselves strong and confident enough to be able to live again with those Germans together in the same country.

Obviously, when a guest, a German in particular, makes such comments before a Czech audience, she is liable to seem insensitive and disrespectful of her hosts. That is especially the case when a small and weak binational state like Czechoslovakia had, at the end of World War II, good reasons not to feel secure with a minority that had supported and aided Nazi Germany in subjugating and bleeding their country. The expulsion took place before the division of Europe between the Soviets and the West was anticipated. Beneš and the other Czech leaders could not have foreseen at the time that the Cold War and the subsequent partition of Germany, as well as the conditions that the superpowers demanded (in the Two Plus Four treaty) for German reunification, would guarantee Czechoslovakia's territorial integrity and defend the country against German territorial demands. Czechoslovakia's subjection to the Soviets brought much evil on the country, as the events of 1968 demonstrated, but at least guaranteed its territorial integrity against Germany.

At the end of her remarks, the vice president of the Bundestag again expressed her remorse for the left's disregard of the expellees. She went so far as to say that the thesis of collective guilt was baseless and should be discarded. Furthermore, she took the opportunity to tell the Czechs that they should open a dialogue with the Sudeten homeland society.[16] Vollmer continued in this vein in the years to follow, both on the floor of the Bundestag and in print.[17]

The major lines of her views were adopted by central figures in the SPD when it regained power in 1998, led by Chancellor Gerhard Schröder, and became prevalent among left-wing intellectuals, including some German historians, in the years that followed.[18] Perhaps the protest against Germany's active involvement in the war in the former Yugoslavia that came from the left wings of the two coalition parties, Schröder's Social Democrats and Fischer's Greens, contributed to the official adoption of the new interpretation of the expulsion of the Germans. The new position on the expulsions had an unambiguous nationalist tone that rejected expulsion in any way, shape, or form. It carried forward the traditional consensual policy of the Federal Republic, which rejected the expulsion of the Germans from the east on legal and ethical grounds. It also drew a direct parallel between the German experience and the expulsion and murder in the collapsing Yugoslavian state. When the Bundeswehr took part in the NATO bombing of Serbia in May 1999, the coalition parties' left wings, together with other groups, erupted in protest. Not only did the bombings exact a heavy toll among Serbian civilians, the critics argued, but they were also relatively ineffectual in halting Serb expulsions of Albanians from Kosovo. Furthermore, the NATO bombings were extremely problematic from the point of view of international law.[19] The adoption of a revisionist policy of memory regarding the expulsions of Germans from Eastern Europe supported the SPD position. Schröder probably also sought to compensate for his loss of support from the left by reinforcing his position among right-wing voters. True, the policy did not demand the return of these lost territories, but it was clearly linked to the old nationalist and revisionist line taken by the young Federal Republic. In a fiery debate in his party in May 1999, Foreign Minister Joschka Fischer presented the Bundeswehr's involvement in the Kosovo conflict as the ultimate expression of "a modern and enlightened Europe against the Europe of the past, which was defined by nationalism and hatred of the humanist position and of European values."[20] Fischer, unlike Vollmer and SPD figures like Schröder, continued to advocate the left's traditional position that the expulsions were a product of Nazi Germany's crimes during World War II. But he nevertheless rejected expulsion, in principle, as a form of collective punishment, and as such also carried on West Germany's traditional position.

In the 1990s a new generation came into the leadership of the expellees' umbrella body, the BdV. In 1994, Fritz Wittmann, a CSU political figure from Bavaria, was named to head the organization, the first member of the younger generation to hold this post. Wittman had experienced the expulsion from the Sudetenland as a child. But his four-year tenure did not leave much of an impression on the expellee union. In 1998 he was replaced as president by Erika Steinbach.

Steinbach herself did not belong to that generation, nor was she the typical daughter of expellees. She was born in 1943 in Rumia, West Prussia, a town she made a point of calling by its German name, Rahmel, where her father was stationed as a German soldier. In 1945, she and her family fled westward to Germany.[21]

In a speech on the floor of the Bundestag, she related that her grandfather, who had been imprisoned in a concentration camp, had died as a result of the conditions in which he was held. Her organization's demands were framed in universal values, specifically the principle that people should not be driven from their homes. Such expulsions, Steinbach asserted, were forbidden by international law and were gross violations of fundamental human rights. Unlike some of her predecessors, Steinbach explicitly referred to the Holocaust as a unique crime and Nazi Germany as a criminal regime that opened the Pandora's box that led to the expulsion of Germans from the east. Yet she minimized the German people's political responsibility for the rise of the Nazis, the outbreak of war, and the atrocities that Germans committed at the service of their state during World War II. She proclaimed that the German people as a whole should not be held guilty for the deeds of the Nazis. In fact, she absolved the Germans of the Third Reich of collective wrongdoing and portrayed them as a persecuted collective, in the style that was common in the 1950s. When she spoke of the expellees, she referred only to defenseless women and children, never including members of the Nazi Party and soldiers. The only criminals active in the Third Reich were, in her version of events, members of the Gestapo and secret police. All others were innocent victims. Even Wehrmacht soldiers were victims, not criminals.

In a debate in the Bundestag in 1997 on an exhibition about Wehrmacht crimes, initiated by the Hamburg Institute of Social Research, she cited the example of a young 18-year-old soldier killed in 1944 and a 25-year-old officer killed in 1945. She regarded both as victims. Since they had not reached voting age in 1933, she argued that they bore no responsibility for Hitler's ascent to power. Such soldiers, Steinbach maintained, acted solely out of love for their homeland, not out of devotion to the Führer or blind obedience to authority.

In a speech she made in Hamburg in 1999, Steinbach stressed that, in the battles of the war's last months, Wehrmacht soldiers defended German refugees from the east from violence and rape, giving their lives for the sake of these civilians. She ignored the fact that these same soldiers had been involved in crimes against those persecuted by the Nazi regime and non-German inhabitants of Eastern Europe, and that their fealty was to Hitler. Their actions at the end of the war simply lengthened the bloodshed and allowed the Nazi regime to persist in its crimes.

Her major focus, however, was the "great crime"—the expulsion of the Germans from the east. "The crimes of Nazism cannot justify it, because one crime does not justify [another]," she claimed, adopting a formula frequently used by German politicians on such occasions.[22] She further contended that the expulsion of the Germans had been mapped out before the war. It was not the result of the behavior of the German minorities in Eastern Europe between the world wars, or of Hitler's policies regarding them before and during the war.[23]

In the decade since Steinbach assumed her post, she has, with a combination of charisma, talent, and good fortune, succeeded in taking advantage of the trends and events to reestablish the BdV as an important player in Germany's political culture and also made herself a familiar name throughout Eastern Europe. This resurgence has come after the organization lost influence in the 1990s and was unable to regain it even during the long years of the Kohl administration. On the eve of the 1998 elections, in which the veteran chancellor was defeated by Gerhard Schröder, Kohl acceded to the longstanding expellee demand to establish a monument to the expellees in Berlin. The demand was raised against the background of a long public debate over the establishment of a memorial to the Jews of Europe murdered by the Nazi regime.[24]

An important milestone in the process of rapprochement between the SPD-Green coalition that came to power in 1998 and the expellee organizations was the appearance of Interior Minister Otto Schily at the Berlin Cathedral on May 29, 1999, two weeks before the election for the European Parliament, during which he expressed sympathy for the organizations and their demands. Relations between these organizations and the SPD had been chilly since the 1970s. Expellee leaders were profoundly disappointed with the foreign policy shift led by Willy Brandt and with key figures in the party, such as Herbert Wehner, who had, they felt, betrayed them.[25]

Schily, a former member of the Bundestag and a central figure in the Green Party who crossed the aisle to the SPD, took a lead from his former party colleague, Vollmer, and announced his regret at the left's disregard for "the crimes of the expulsion, from the suffering of millions of expellees. They act that way, whether out of apathy, fear of being branded revanchist, or a mistaken belief that silence and repression would lead us more quickly to accommodation with our neighbors to the east. Such behavior was an expression of fear and timidity."[26] Later in his remarks, Schily said that the right had tried to present the expellees as victims of Czech and Polish expansion, but the truth should be stated clearly: the expellees were Hitler's last victims. This formulation of Schily's mitigates Germany's responsibility, since a large proportion of the Sudeten Germans enthusiastically supported Hitler and his expansionist policies, which destroyed the Czechoslovakian state. To portray the Sudeten expellees as victims of Hitler means to maintain that they were punished despite their innocence—that is, that they were innocent victims, just like the Jews. Following Schily's appearance, the government and the BdV strengthened their ties, and the state subsidy to the organization and its commemorative and aid activities was increased. In a Homeland Day greeting that he sent to the BdV in 1999, Schröder wrote that "every act of expulsion, no matter what its historical context" is "a crime against humanity." And he added that "the progress of the European Union and the integration of all of Europe will make current borders more permeable, and as a result it will be easier to maintain ties, make visits, and return to the old homeland (*Rückkehr in die alte Heimat*)." In other words, in this letter Schröder not only adopted—even if only for opportunistic reasons—the approach advocated by Vollmer and the expellee organizations. He also continued to raise hopes among the expellees that, even after the signing of the Two Plus Four agreement, a return to the old homeland might still be possible. This was diametrically opposed to the stand his own party had taken since the end of the 1960s.[27] A year later Schröder was invited to be guest of honor and to speak at the central Homeland Day (*Tag der Heimat*) ceremony. This time he explicitly traced a direct line from the Balkan wars of 1912–1913 to the murder and expulsion of the Armenians in eastern Anatolia, to Hitler's criminal policy of *Umvolkung* (a Nazi term for changing the ethnic nature of Eastern Europe by enforcing Germanization of the region), to the expulsion of Poles, Ukrainians, Finns, Hungarians, Russians, and Belorussians by Germany, to the expulsion of 12 million Germans after World War II, "an issue that has troubled us to this very day," and on to the huge waves of refugees created by conflicts in the Indian subcontinent, Palestine, and more recently Rwanda, Burundi, Congo, and Kosovo. All these events dripped with the blood of injustice, he said, and all concerned the ejection of people from their homes.[28]

Ulla Jelpke, a member of the Bundestag for the PDS (the successor party of the SED), said in 2002 that this was an attempt by the chancellor to fish for votes among the expellees.[29] While vote-getting was certainly a motive, it appears that Schröder had others. After all, in the first decade of the twenty-first century the number of expellee votes was much smaller than it had been in the 1960s. Schröder seems to have been directing his remarks at a much broader public. In 2003 the BdV granted an award to Interior Minister Schily for having paved the way for understanding between the SPD and the expellees. The evening's master of ceremonies, Guido Knopp, who headed the historical programming division of Germany's Channel 2 public television station (ZDF), said, "Today there is greater courage to speak of the Germans as victims." He compared the contemporary public mood with that of the period beginning in the 1960s. "Confrontation with the past," he said, "produced a political correctness that was, for the most part, cold-hearted. Germans as victims was a taboo."[30] Schröder also seems to have sensed this change and therefore adopted a position that had become common among the public. Of course, neither can we rule out that this in fact represented his personal opinion, and that his previous advocacy of the position that had thus far prevailed in his party had been instrumental, aimed at improving relations with Germany's eastern neighbors. It may be that once those relations were stable, Schröder and Schily chose to reveal their real feelings about the expulsion. The conversion of the left government's stance with that of the expellee organizations and the political right was expressed not only in the policy of memory, but also in its policy toward the Czech Republic. In 2002, before that country's entry into the European Union, Schily lent his support to the demand of the expellee organizations and of the German and Austrian right that the Czech government officially revoke President Beneš's expulsion order of 1945. This ran directly against previous understandings reached by the leaders of the three countries.[31]

NAZI CRIMINALS, WEHRMACHT SOLDIERS, AND GERMAN CIVILIANS AS VICTIMS

In 1995, Bernhard Schlink's novel *Der Vorleser* (*The Reader*) was published in Germany. The book, which had great impact both inside and outside the country, takes as its theme the change in Germany's spiritual climate. (The film version, a German-American coproduction from British director Stephen Daldry, appeared in 2008.) The transformation began after reunification, influenced by a number of prominent members of the generation of 1968 (including, for example, Schröder), who had in the past been prominent advocates of confronting the Nazi past.[32] *Der Vorleser* was the first example of what the social psychologist Harald Welzer recently claimed had become symptomatic of the autobiographical literature of the 1968 generation, the generation of the sons, with their two typical characteristics: an anti-authoritarian education coupled with a complete absence of paternal authority; and an enlightened attitude toward the Holocaust while ostensibly enforcing a taboo against any mention of how the Germans suffered. In this novel, the Nazi criminal is portrayed as a victim.[33] The same model could be seen in the popular German literature and cinema of their parents' generation, after the war.

The first part of the book takes place in 1958 and tells of an animal passion between the narrator, Michael Berg, a boy of about fifteen, and Hanna Schmitz, a woman some twenty-one years older. She initiates him into the secrets of sex; he reads novels aloud to her (seemingly in exchange). Some months later the woman suddenly disappears. The affair ends.

The book's second part takes place about seven years later. Michael Berg, now a law student, discovers his former lover, Hanna, among the defendants in a trial of female SS guards. These women had served on one of the death marches from Poland to Germany. One night they reached a largely abandoned village and locked hundreds of Jewish women prisoners in the local church. The building was hit by an Allied bomb and went up in flames. The guards did not allow the prisoners to flee, so they were burned alive. This was the most serious charge against them.

Instead of denying her guilt or relying on the lack of solid evidence, Hanna prefers to confess her culpability. She apparently does not comprehend how grave her actions were (or perhaps she does not want to comprehend). Her attempt to justify her deeds with the excuse "We didn't know what to do" is utterly undermined by the rest of her testimony:

> Then the screaming began and got worse and worse. If we had opened the doors and they had all come rushing out. . . . We could not just let them escape! We were responsible for them . . . I mean, we had guarded them the whole time, in the camp and on the march, that was the point, that we had to guard them and not let them escape. That's why we didn't know what to do. We also had no idea how many of the women would survive the next few days.[34]

Her testimony corroborates the description found in SS documents: "It indicated that the women guards had stayed behind to wait out the end of the fires, to prevent any of them from spreading and to prevent any attempts to escape under cover of the flames. It referred to the death of the prisoners."[35]

It also turns out that, while serving as a guard in a camp near Krakow, Hanna always took a young and frail prisoner under her wing and saw to it that she would not be sent to work. In the evenings this prisoner would read stories to Hanna. After a while, Hanna would send the girl to Auschwitz and choose another girl to read to her.[36]

Michael is terrified by Hanna's satanic character, as it is revealed to him during the trial. At the same time, he tries to understand her—but cannot. In contrast with the numbness that overcomes him with regard to the atrocities the trial reveals, and with regard to the victims of those acts, his passion for the Nazi criminal flares again. He tries to make a case for Hanna. She enlisted in the SS so that the factory where she worked would not discover she was illiterate. Michael grasps at this defense as if it could somehow lighten the burden of her guilt, and of the responsibility that Hanna took upon herself of her own free choice. Hanna's compulsion to conceal her ignorance, which reappears throughout the work, retrospectively explains anomalous aspects of her behavior during her affair with the young Michael. It is also what motivates her to incriminate herself even beyond her actual guilt. As a result, she is the only one of the guards to be sentenced to life in prison. Michael theorizes: "I could go to the judge and tell him that Hanna was illiterate. That she was not the main protagonist and guilty party the way the others made her out to be . . . That she was guilty, but not as guilty as it appeared."[37] Schlink thus depicts this brutal, murderous SS woman as a victim of circumstances. At the end of the novel, it turns out that Hanna has learned how to read and write in prison. She reads books written by Holocaust survivors and wishes to donate her savings to Jewish causes. The Nazi criminal has repented.

Schlink criticizes the self-righteousness of the rebellious younger generation of 1968. They charged their parents with infamy, whether they were active Nazis or simply did nothing to oppose the regime. This intergenerational confrontation is, he claims, a strident attempt by the young to overcome their own feelings of guilt for loving their parents. Schlink asserts: "The pain I went through because of my love for Hanna was, in a way, the fate of my generation, a German fate."[38] So the story is nothing but a metaphor for the Germans as victims of the Nazi era and its aftermath. "What should our second generation have done, what should it do with the knowledge of the horrors of the extermination of the Jews? We should not believe we can comprehend the incomprehensible."[39]

This can be understood as a rejection of the critical view of the Nazis that was at least the public face of the 1968 generation in German political culture, whose cohorts were seen as breaching the silence about the Nazi past.[40] The historian Omer Bartov wrote:

> Schlink contextualizes his tale within a framework of emotional numbness and sexual obsession, both of which are above or below morality, since the former is a blank and a void, and the latter is involuntary and uncontrollable. Thus numbness and obsession are a means to avoid responsibility and reject all ethical categories.[41]

And if patent Nazi criminals are depicted as victims, it is hardly surprising that, in united Germany, public preoccupation with the vulnerability and suffering of German soldiers and civilians during the Nazi period increased. It was not for nothing that the public discourse focused on the end of the war (the defeat of the Wehrmacht, and the despair of the citizenry), rather than its beginning, when enthusiastic crowds cheered the Führer's "brilliant" victories.

In recent years, the subject of the rape of German women at the end of the war by Red Army soldiers has attracted more and more public attention. The common wisdom in Germany is that a million women fell victim to this crime. However, there is a lack of data to scientifically support such an estimate.[42] The subject had been taboo in East Germany because it sullied the image of the Soviet liberators. Only after the fall of the Communist regime, at the beginning of the 1990s, could it be discussed publicly. The dizzying success of *A Woman in Berlin,* an anonymous diary reissued in 2003 and made into a film in 2008,[43] is evidence of escalating public interest in the suffering that the diarist symbolized when she wrote: "How degraded we are, deprived of all rights—prey, dirt."[44] Today's many Germans want to view those times through the eyes of fellow nationals who lived through them and were not anti-Nazis and even identified with at least some of the regime's policies during the war.

The book was first published in the United States and England in 1954. Its bright red and yellow cover displayed the image of a horrified woman, her eyes open painfully wide, her dress torn, covering her breast with her hand. Below her was an image of the Brandenburg Gate, with the caption: "April 1945 . . . A woman's night-by-night account of how the Russians ravaged a city and its women."

This is how the book was marketed in the United States at the height of the anticommunist witch hunts. The German writer Kurt W. Marek, a friend of the author, provided an introduction. He served as liaison between the author and the American publisher, and to this day it is not clear whether he had a hand in writing or rewriting the diary.[45]

In his introduction, Marek described the memoir as testimony from the "red apocalypse" that raged through Germany in 1945—the crimes and atrocities committed by the Red Army against German civilians. At that time, this scourge was perceived as an indication of what awaited the entire free world if the Communists were to overwhelm it. Marek clearly sought to portray the German people as victims of Communism. The Cold War atmosphere created a climate amenable to such a depiction of the Red Army, which smacked of German superiority and racism. He pictured the Russians as rapists and looters who abused the population of occupied East Germany.[46]

We know today that the author was the journalist Martha Hillers (1911–2001). While she was not a member of the Nazi Party, she wrote pamphlets for the Nazi Labor Front (DAF) and other works of propaganda.[47] The book describes what happened to her from April to June 1945, including her rape, on several occasions, by Red Army soldiers. In the end, she decides to offer herself to a Russian officer so that he would protect her from other soldiers and feed her during this period of severe food shortages.

The depiction of the German soldier as a victim had its roots in the country's literature and cinema of the 1950s. Writers and directors chose to create works set in periods conducive to depictions that allowed them to depict troops' hopelessness and misery. The stories were about soldiers routed in battle at the end of the war, hungry and exhausted, or about POWs languishing in prison camps after the war, at the mercy of harsh, pitiless captors, who are portrayed with all the stock stereotypes associated with Nazi concentration camp guards.[48]

These writers and directors leave out the same soldiers' elation at Germany's early successes on the eastern front, the war crimes they committed, and the boastful letters many of them sent to their parents. In 1995, the Hamburg Institute for Social Research sponsored an exhibition about the Wehrmacht's crimes during the war. It displayed the crimes Hitler's army committed against the Jews, against Red Army POWs, and against civilians.[49] Although the exhibition provoked an intense public debate in Germany and Austria,[50] a survey of the media, cinema, and popular literature about the German soldiers following the exhibition raises questions about whether it in any way tarnished the image of the German soldier in German popular culture. One indication that the spirit of the 1950s had returned was the remake, in 2001, of a popular film from the end of the 1950s, *As Far As My Feet Will Carry Me.*[51] Based on Joseph M. Bauer's 1955 novel, it was first filmed in 1959 in the form of a highly rated six-part television series, broadcast in 1959 on West Germany's Channel 1.[52] A saga of flight, it is based, according to the author, on the actual experiences of a German officer named Clemens Forell in the novel. (Bauer said that the real protagonist did not want his name revealed.) Forell is sentenced to twenty-five years in prison for war crimes committed during the "campaign the Germans carried out against partisans in the Soviet-occupied territories during the war," and is sent to a prison camp deep in Siberia. This is the only reference the film makes to his actions during the war. The proud officer cannot bear the humiliation and beatings he receives from the brutal Soviet guards, whom the film likens to stereotypical Nazi concentration camp guards. He decides to flee, against all odds. He treks through danger and adventures, nearly 9,000 miles, ending up in Iran. During his journey he reaches the city of Novo-Kazalinsk. Igor, an Armenian Jew and a member of the anti-Soviet underground, aids him. Igor sends him to two agents who help him over the Iranian border on his way to freedom. The second film version includes some details that did not appear in the book or in the television series.[53]

In the remake, Igor is a loner, not a member of an underground group. It is not clear what motivates him to help Forell. He provides the German with forged documents. After Forell leaves him, the KGB captures and tortures Igor, but Igor divulges nothing and dies from this treatment. Earlier, when Forell asks Igor why, as a Jew, he is helping a German officer and risking his life for him, Igor tells him that his brother was murdered in the Holocaust. "We didn't know they were murdering Jews," Forell says in his own defense. "Of course not," the Jew replies. "You would have acted against the murder of women and children. You would have shot your commanders first, but you didn't know. You didn't know anything about it. You only did your duty (*Ihr habt nur Ihre Pflict getan*)." Here, taken out of context, this exchange could be read as a Jew's sarcastic jab at a German soldier, but that is not the context in which it appears in the film. After all, if he had anything against the German officer, he would not have helped him escape the Soviet Union and his sentence for war crimes. Igor, who represents the Jewish victims, clears Forell (and, implicitly, all Wehrmacht soldiers) in the film. Even the victims know, in this version of events, that the German soldier is decent and observes the rules of war. It recalls the myth of the Wehrmacht's decency that was pervasive in the Federal Republic of the 1950s, when such portrayals of German soldiers were very common. The film ends with Forell's homecoming: on Christmas Eve 1952, he returns to his family in Germany.

There were similar depictions of the Wehrmacht soldier in Germany's popular press, even in German television broadcasts of a scholarly, documentary character in recent years. Since the late 1990s, a large number of these documentary films and popular works of literature have portrayed Wehrmacht soldiers as victims. For example, close to the sixtieth anniversary of the German Sixth Army's surrender to the Red Army at Stalingrad, the German print and electronic media addressed the event. Most of the programs focused on the suffering of the individual soldier, rather than on the political and general background to the battle of Stalingrad and its larger significance.

The popular daily tabloid *Bild Zeitung* published an eight-part series on a daily basis in November 2002. It presented passages from the last letters of soldiers who died in the battle of Stalingrad. The letters tell of their despair, agony, and longing for home. Quotes from the letters were used as headlines for each installment: "We live like animals in their lairs"; "Whoever gets out of here can thank God"; "Eighty-six degrees [Fahrenheit] below zero! The soldiers are collapsing completely"; "Eight of us share a loaf of bread a day." At the end of each segment, the newspaper urged on its readers to send in any other servicemen's letters and photographs from Stalingrad in their possession.[54] The series ignored the death, destruction, and suffering these same soldiers wreaked in the Russian city, and concentrated exclusively on the soldiers' agony. At the same time, additional passages from letters of the fallen soldiers at Stalingrad were read on the Deutschlandfunk radio station.

In January 2003, Germany's Channel 2 (ZDF) broadcast a three-part documentary prepared by a team headed by Guido Knopp, who was in charge of the channel's historical programming.[55] The name of the series was *Stalingrad: The Offensive, the Siege, the Downfall.* The first part was devoted to the historical circumstances that brought the Germans to Stalingrad. The next two programs were devoted largely to the suffering of the besieged German soldiers in the city. In conjunction with the series, a book was issued, filled with photographs and prominently displaying Knopp's name (as was accepted practice in Channel 2's history department).

From the mid-1990s onward, Knopp produced documentaries based on a wealth of photographic material. The programs included stills and contemporary film footage (mostly taken from Nazi newsreels) alongside historical reenactments accompanied by voiceovers and brief recollections from witnesses to the events. These were the testimonies of the "common man" rather than of high officers or declared Nazis. During this period, as private stations grabbed market share from public ones, such programs found large audiences, despite sharp criticism from historians.[56] Knopp's television series, like the *Bild Zeitung* series, focused on the passages of despair and agony in the letters written by German soldiers in Stalingrad. They were frozen, starving, and tortured by their longing for the families they would never see again. The series gave special attention to cases of cannibalism, while entirely ignoring the political circumstances of the Stalingrad campaign—an aggressive German invasion deep into Soviet territory. One of the witnesses described it as a personal rivalry between two tyrants, Hitler and Stalin, who sacrificed their soldiers' lives in a meaningless struggle for personal prestige. Somewhat narcissistically, the series focused on the torment of simple German soldiers, presented as victims, completely ignoring their crimes during Germany's war of total destruction against the Soviet Union. The program related the iron discipline brutally imposed on Red Army soldiers and offered testimony of the execution of Soviet soldiers who refused to return to the front—in contrast with German soldiers' humane treatment of the populations in the territories they occupied. A Wehrmacht officer related that he and his men gave chocolate to Russian children and told of a German soldier who refused to shoot at Russian civilians. "However," the narrator continues, "there were officers who gave criminal orders." Everything is backward—murder is depicted as exceptional rather than part of the Wehrmacht routine. And it all drips with sentimentality. Elderly Wehrmacht veterans, widows, children, and grandchildren tearfully recount how their loved ones suffered, "and there is not even a grave."

According to Yehudit Keilbach, who has studied German television's representation of history, the transmutation of German television documentaries about the Nazi regime results from changes in the nature of the medium. In the 1950s and 1960s, West German public television viewed itself as an agent of education and as a participant in the process of democratizing its society. As such, the documentaries on Nazism that it produced and screened were critical of German actions and grappled with the crimes of the past. Now, in the age of infotainment, ratings are all that interest producers.[57] Furthermore, the global trend of making television into a medium of entertainment has produced a genre of "histortainment." Producers, television journalists, and station executives do not want to alienate viewers, so today's documentaries present the Nazi years in a way compatible with the collective German memory, rather than with the critical approach practiced by historians. In these programs, the Germans appear principally as innocent victims, individuals without any control of or influence over historical circumstances. In this view, the German public was simply a pawn in a game played by Hitler and the Allies. Consequently, the German media is today inculcating the German masses with a historical consciousness made up of myths and subjective memories, which repress and expunge the historical reality of World War II: that the Nazi regime was popular with the German people and came to power at their behest. And, thanks to the cooperation of so many of them, it remained in power, conquered its neighbors, and destroyed lives until it fell.

THE AERIAL BOMBARDMENTS OF GERMANY

Much was published in the 1990s about the Allied bombings of German cities, and memorial days are still widely attended in the former East Germany. Other forms of commemoration continue as well. In 1995, a monument to those killed in the bombardment of March 5, 1945, was dedicated in the center of Chemnitz, the work of the artist Sylke Rehberg. Souvenir shops throughout Germany sell postcards with pictures of the country's ruined cities at the end of World War II; in Dresden, one card for sale shows burning pyres of the dead. All German newspapers addressed the attack on Dresden in great detail on the fiftieth and sixtieth anniversaries of the event.

German suffering stood at the center of an impressive ceremony held on February 12, 1995, the fiftieth anniversary of the Dresden firebombing. That same day there was a special prayer service in memory of the tens of thousands who died. Delegates of the Anglican and Russian Orthodox

Figure 28. Sylke Rehberg's monument in central Chemnitz

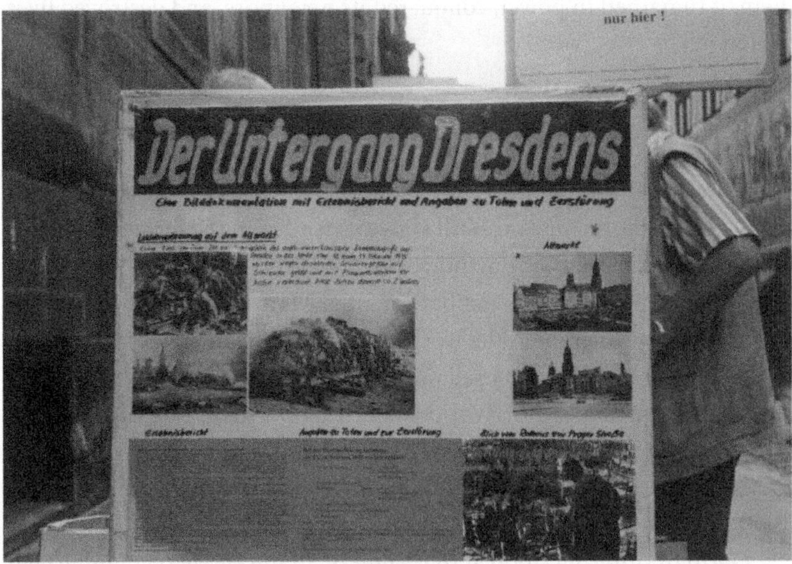

Figure 29. An advertisement about the Allied bombing at a postcard stand in Dresden

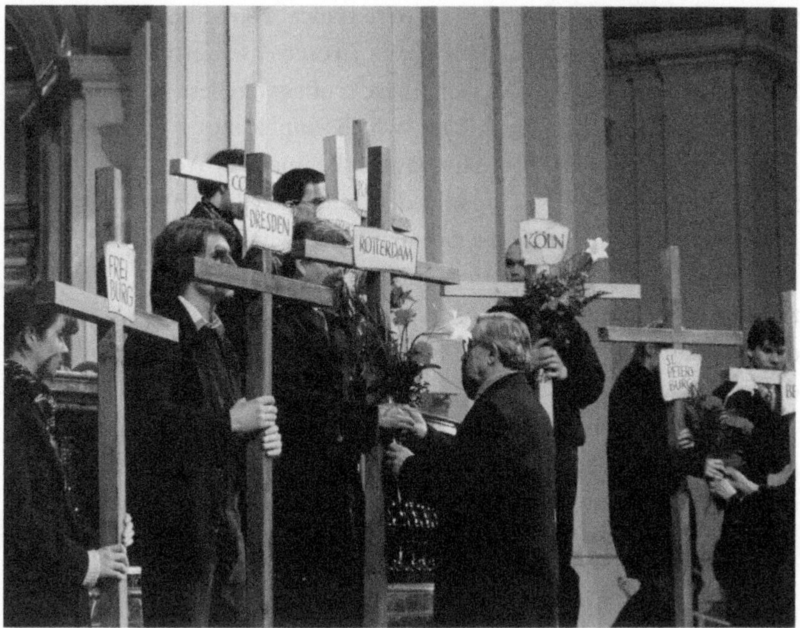

Figure 30. The procession of crosses in Dresden, 1995 (Press and Information Office of the Federal Republic of Germany)

churches participated in the service as representatives of the Christian peoples ravaged by the war and as an expression of Christian reconciliation between former enemies. Chancellor Helmut Kohl also participated. The event opened with a procession of clergymen, followed by nine cross-bearers, symbolizing the nine cities seriously damaged during the war. Most of them were German (Dresden, Leipzig, Freiburg, Hamburg, Berlin, and Cologne), but Rotterdam, St. Petersburg (Leningrad), and Coventry were also represented.

Other sites of Nazi atrocities, however, such as Lidice, Warsaw, and Oradour sur Glane, which along with the concentration and death camps had been commemorated in the GDR on such occasions, were not mentioned. The ceremony focused on the air war alone. While the SED had previously considered reconciliation with Poland and Czechoslovakia to be important, these nations were apparently held in less regard after German reunification, in contrast to Russia and the West. Thus the terrible Nazi bombardment of Warsaw in 1939 was omitted. On the other hand, the crimes of Oradour and Lidice were typical Nazi-like atrocities that land troops committed against civilians. In each case Germans murdered French or Czech victims. As such, these crimes were less suitable for the German concept of reconciliation, which emphasizes equity and reciprocity between two belligerent sides (as the image of World War I). The reconciliation gesture was organized around the Christian motifs of the passion and crucifixion of the German cities, which granted these cities and their inhabitants the status of innocent victims similar to Christ. At the same time, it seemed to signify atonement for the sins of the Germans during World War II, and for those of humanity as a whole, and by so doing reconcile the nations.

This phenomenon is tacitly, though not always consciously, a preoccupation with the issue of guilt. The Germans' passion is perceived as atoning for and purifying them of their transgressions, which in the Federal Republic's case was perceived as being primarily against the Jews, and in East Germany against the neighboring Slavic peoples and the peoples of the Soviet Union. This similar approach to the suffering of the Germans in the two ideologically opposed Germanys created a foundation for a common culture of memory, centered on a sense of victimhood and suffering whose three major symbols are Dresden, the expellees, and POWs.

In 1998, the public debate over the bombing of Germany had a resurgence, inspired by the writer W. G. Sebald.[58] The novels Sebald published in the 1990s addressed the Holocaust and its survivors in a manner exceptional among German writers, who were generally silent about the issue.[59] His empathy for his Jewish characters and the way he portrayed them can easily lead his readers to assume that Sebald himself was a Jew.

Thus it was noteworthy that, in a lecture he gave in the fall of 1997 in Zürich on "The Air War and Literature" (*Luftkrieg und Literatur*), Sebald argued that, with the exception of a small body of works,[60] postwar German literature had not addressed the Allied bombings of German cities. The bombardments, which were daily events beginning in 1942, killed some 400,000 Germans and wreaked terrible destruction throughout the country. They were, in Sebald's words, a

> unique act of annihilation (*einzigartige Vernichtungsaktion*) on a scale without historical precedent [that] entered the annals of the nation, as it set about rebuilding itself, only in the form of vague generalizations. It

> seems to have left scarcely a trace of pain behind in the collective consciousness, it has been largely obliterated from the retrospective understanding of those affected, and it never played any appreciable part in the discussion of the internal constitution of our country.[61]

Sebald's lecture opened a new age in Germany's confrontation with the bombing of its cities. First, this was no longer the extreme right or left ranting about "Allied crimes," but rather an ostensibly apolitical debate conducted by an enlightened liberal figure from the center of the political spectrum. It was a discussion of the bombardments' effect on the German soul. Yet when Sebald called Allied belligerence against Nazi Germany "a unique act of annihilation," he was using the kind of language heretofore used by enlightened Germans only with reference to the Holocaust (which was shunted to the sidelines in the debate Sebald engendered). This raises questions about the political implications of such a discussion for the view of World War II and the understanding of the nature of the struggle between Nazism and its enemies.

In using terminology drawn from the Holocaust, Sebald's claim that there was a taboo against mentioning German suffering, though offered in a muted, non-accusatory tone, recalled the cries widespread from the 1960s through the 1990s, primarily on the extreme right. By the end of the 1990s, however, the claim that such a taboo existed had entered the mainstream. In keeping with the spirit of the times, Sebald formulated his claims in a humanistic language and an emphasis on supremacy of the principles of international law, and not, as others previously did, in a hostile manner against old enemies with nationalist tones.

The German press by and large agreed with Sebald's claims. He addressed the problematic subject of the bombardments in a proper way, they maintained, so there was no reason to oppose him. Sebald explained the silence on this subject of most German writers after the war as self-censorship: "The darkest aspects of the final acts of destruction, as experienced by the great majority of the German population, remained under a kind of taboo, like a shameful family secret, a secret that perhaps could not even be privately acknowledged."[62] In fact, it was a hoary claim that Sebald was raising, however unassumingly. But unlike the extreme right, he did not describe the taboo as a product of political pressure on Germany. He stated that the reason for German silence about the bombings was the recognition that "a nation that murdered millions of human beings and enslaved them in camps until they died" should not expect any other treatment by the powers that defeated it. He went so far as to say that the view that the bombings were a justified punishment, if not divine retribution, was shared by many Germans, as the author Hans Erich Nossack claimed in his literary report on the air attack on Hamburg of 1943.[63]

Later in his lecture, Sebald took up the question of whether the bombardments had been necessary. He displayed understanding for how the British formulated their strategy of bombing German cities in the wake of the Battle of Britain, even though the strategy violated the laws of war and morality. However, he denounced the persistence of the RAF's Sir Arthur Harris in bombing civilian targets after it proved ineffectual and did not bring the war to an end. Sebald was not the first to assert that, even after Britain developed the ability to paralyze German manufacturing through precision strikes against war industries and transportation arteries, the British persisted in bombing civilian targets. Their only purpose was to take revenge on the Germans and boost British morale. In line with the trend already evident in a part of the German media, Sebald depicted Harris in demonic terms, as being solely responsible for the area bombing strategy,[64] and as a man who advocated bombing cities simply out of an infatuation with destruction for its own sake.[65] Sebald also offered vivid descriptions of the bodies of the dead taken from contemporary sources, and later included in a book (where the essay "The Air War and Literature" also appeared) a photograph of the corpses of civilians in a bombed German city, as was typical in German publications on the subject since the 1950s.

Sebald's lecture reverberated through the literary supplements of Germany's and Switzerland's leading newspapers. Joachim Güntner claimed correctly in the *Neue Zürcher Zeitung* that "Sebald entirely ignores the literature and poetry written in East Germany that dealt with the bombings of the cities" (though these were at the encouragement of the Communist regime).[66] Furthermore, Sebald seems not to have been acquainted with Max Zimmering's *Phosphorous and Lilac*,[67] nor with other German literary works that touched on the subject.[68] Second, Sebald's taboo thesis ignored the fact that the media in both German states had frequently taken up the subject of the bombings. Furthermore, he was oblivious to its constant presence in German discourse since 1945, and the common practice of comparing German suffering at the hands of the Allies to that of the Jews at the hands of the Nazis. Beyond Güntner's reservation, however, no one mentioned the considerable attention the German media had given the bombings.

Frank Schirrmacher,[69] editor of the cultural pages of the *Frankfurter Allgemeine Zeitung,* mentioned that German literature had also, for obvious reasons, avoided the subject of the Holocaust, and agreed that it had indeed ignored the bombings of the cities. He added that the expulsion of Germans from the east had likewise not been processed in German literature. The reason, he said, was that in the 1950s this was taken to be revanchist and was still suspect of being an attempt to evade the burden of guilt.[70] Volker Hage summed up his article in *Der Spiegel* in this way: "Perhaps postwar German literature really only begins at the end of the century, at the turn of the century." After all, Hans Jakob Christoffel von Grimmelshausen wrote *Simplicissimus,* the great German novel of the Thirty Years War, only twenty years after that conflict had ended.[71] In other words, only today, when the Holocaust and its horrors had dimmed in German consciousness, could the Germans accept seeing themselves as they really were—as victims. The Holocaust had obscured that.

Another commentator who participated in a later stage of the discussion—a novelist and playwright whose works Sebald ignored in presenting his thesis—was Dieter Forte. Born in 1935, Forte had experienced the bombing of his native city of Düsseldorf as a young boy. The terror of the attack left him with a profound trauma that he still bore with him, he wrote.[72] In his novel *The Boy with the Bloody Shoes,* published in 1995, part of a trilogy that chronicles the history of the Forte family, he depicts the Allied bombing of his city.[73]

The British historian Bill Niven stresses that the work obscures the causal connection between the war that Hitler initiated and the bombings committed by the Allies. Forte, he writes, portrays Düsseldorf's Oberbilk neighborhood, the setting of his story, "as a place where civilian Germans, Jews, and forced laborers are linked by acts of solidarity into a collective which is then ruthlessly bombed from the air." In the book, the neighborhood's populace is anti-Nazi, assists and supports the Jews and forced laborers, and hides them from their Nazi persecutors. In Forte's saga, his neighbors become, just like the Jews, the victims of barbarity, but of the Allied rather than the Nazi variety.[74]

Even though he disputed Sebald's thesis that the amnesia that Germans ostensibly exhibited had its source in guilt feelings, he found fault with Sebald's assertion that there was a taboo against discussing the issue. In Forte's view, the amnesia was the product of the terrible nature of the trauma. Those who experienced it repressed the memory, not because they felt guilty, but as a survival tactic, as with the survivors of a natural disaster.[75]

In response to the reservations and nationalist feedback he received regarding the thesis he presented in Zürich, Sebald took an unambiguous position in 1999, when he published an essay based on the lecture with an added third chapter. He wrote:

> The majority of Germans today know, or so at least it is to be hoped, that we actually provoked the annihilation of the cities in which we once lived. Scarcely anyone can now doubt that Air Marshal Göring would have wiped out London if his technical resources had allowed him to do so.[76]

Günter Grass, one of Germany's great novelists and a Nobel Prize laureate, sided with Sebald. In a speech he gave in Vilna in October 2000, in the framework of a Lithuanian-German-Polish dialogue on the future of collective memory, he stressed:

> Not a week goes by that we do not hear a warning against forgetfulness. After having reminded ourselves, as one might hope, fairly frequently about the huge and ungraspable number of Jews who were persecuted, deported, and murdered, we have, belatedly, reminded ourselves of the abandonment and murder of tens of thousands of Gypsies. Now, much too belatedly for many, we are compelled to recall the fate of hundreds of thousands of slave laborers who came from Poland, Lithuania, the Soviet Union, and many other countries who were placed on the production lines of the German war industry. It is as if crimes that can be defined as shameful, committed over only [a period of] twelve years, become weightier as they become more distant in time than do crimes that can, in general, be defined as reprehensible.
>
> At the same time, it is worthy of note and of concern that, so belatedly, and always with hesitation, we remember the suffering inflicted on the Germans during the war. The results of the war that was conducted without forethought and criminally, that is, the destruction of Germany's cities, the deaths of hundreds of thousands of civilians in bombardments and expulsions, and the suffering of the flight of 12 million East Germans

> [expelled from Eastern European territories] have only stood in the background. Even in postwar literature the memory of the many who died in the nights of bombings and mass flight have taken only a small place. One injustice has shunted aside another. We are forbidden to compare it, not to speak of setting off one [injustice] against another.[77]

Here Grass made the age-old and baseless argument that the Germans' suffering and the sacrifices they made during the war played only a limited role in Germany's collective memory.

In November 2002, the debate over the Allied bombings surged again. Jörg Friedrich, a journalist and autodidact of the 1968 generation, had already written several books and articles on the problematic way in which the Federal Republic coped with the Nazi past.[78] In the introduction to his book *The Cold Amnesty,* published in 1984, Friedrich surprisingly linked the death wreaked by the Allied bombings to the extermination of the Jews. He also wrote that, after the firebombing of Dresden, SS officer Karl Streibel and his men were brought to the city to help burn the bodies of the dead, Streibel having gained expertise in this task at death camps. Later in his book the author, having provided graphic descriptions of the bodies of those who died from carbon monoxide poisoning, claimed that this same agent used to kill Jews in the Treblinka gas chambers also caused most of the deaths in the bombings of German cities. Friedrich maintained, however, that those who ordered the bombings had not planned the gas poisoning, which was caused by the attack's subsequent firestorm.[79]

In his 2002 book, *The Fire: The Bombing of Germany, 1944–1945,* Friedrich revised his position.[80] In fact, a change in his writings had been evident since the early 1990s. His 1993 book *The Law of War* was a far cry from a rebellious, angry tract against forgetting the past. It was a revisionist attempt to argue that the Wehrmacht's criminal war of extermination, especially on Soviet territory and against the Jewish people, was not in fact the product of a racist and antisemitic doctrine, but the result of a total war and the need to deter local populations against rebellion.[81]

In *The Fire,* Friedrich pursued with greater vigor the trend Sebald had begun. He did not examine all of World War II's aerial bombardments according to a single set of moral criteria, as some of Friedrich's supporters claimed he did during the public debate in the German press that followed the book's appearance. The core of Friedrich's argument was this: the United Kingdom's bombings were not responses to German attacks on British cities during the Blitz, "whose damaged was limited." He contended that the British bombings were "a quantum leap," something of an entirely different nature. They constituted a strategy Britain had developed since World War I, aimed at winning the war from the air. After World War II broke out, the British developed and refined the integrated use of regular and fire bombs to produce huge conflagrations. These infernos were designed to destroy large numbers of homes and their inhabitants. The goal was to break the Germans' will and to incite them to rebel against and topple the Nazi regime. Friedrich argued, in short, that the killing potential of these bombings was equal to that of the atom bomb and much greater than that of German conventional bombs. The attack on Pforzheim in February 1945, he claimed, killed about a third of the people who were in the city at the time, whereas the atom bomb dropped on Nagasaki had slain a little more than ten percent of the population. His comparison recalls the commentary on the bombings in East Germany.[82]

Friedrich isolated the bombings from the reality of the war and depicted the Allies and the Nazis as operating on an identical moral plane. To reinforce his claims, he deliberately did not shy away from employing terms from the Nazi vocabulary of the Holocaust and the Holocaust discourse to characterize the roles and actions of the bombing command. He compared the British bureaucrats who developed incendiary techniques with the criminals of the Nazi *Schreibtischtäter* ("desk perpetrators") who killed thousands with a stroke of a pen. He compared the inhabitants of the bombed cities to the European Jews who were massacred by the Einsatzgruppen, the SS killing units that operated in the territories Germany conquered in the east, and later in the gas chambers. Bomb shelters where Germans suffocated from a lack of oxygen, burned away by the fire storm that raged outside and from the unbearable heat, became "crematoria"; the Allied bombing policy was an "extermination policy" (*Vernichtungspolitik*); those killed in the bombings were "exterminated people" (*Ausgerottete*). And if that were not enough, he labeled one of the Allied bomber wings an "*Einsatzgruppe*."[83]

In his implicit linking of the Allied bombings with the Holocaust, Friedrich entirely disregarded the fact that Germany's civilians had an advanced system of shelters. Anti-aircraft guns defended its skies, and its squadrons of interception planes caused heavy losses to the British and American bombers. About a quarter of the losses suffered by both these country's armed forces during World War II were incurred during the bombing operations against Germany.[84] These heavy casualties, as well as the questions of the operations' legality and morality, led to acrimonious debates in Britain while the war was still in progress.[85]

Like Nazi propagandists during World War II,[86] Friedrich stressed that major cultural assets were systematically destroyed, that German heritage was entirely obliterated. The bombing campaign was responsible for "the largest book burning of all time." He enumerated the libraries and archives that were damaged, hinting that the bombings did more damage to human culture than did the burning of books by the Nazis.[87] Friedrich questioned the efficacy of the bombing strategy. In his view, it achieved the precise opposite of what its authors intended—like the blitz against Britain's cities, it only served to unite the German nation behind the Nazi regime. The air campaign contributed nothing to the military effort to end the war quickly, he claimed, even though many historians have reached the opposite conclusion.[88] He also charged that the bombs horribly damaged the German people and urban landscape, forgetting to mention that they were a response to a war of expansion, annihilation, and destruction that Germany had started.

Friedrich chose an unusual medium in which to present the main points of his new book's message: a five-part series of articles, with little text and many colored photographs, in the popular tabloid *Bild Zeitung*, Europe's largest-circulation newspaper. The first part was laid out so that on either side of the headline were half-portraits of Hitler and Churchill, both fixing their gazes at some point in space. The caption under Hitler: "The dictator started the mass bombing war." Under Churchill was the statement that the British prime minister "responded with many bombings."[89] The presentation implied a moral parallel. It was hardly surprising, then, that many German and British critics took this as an accusation that Churchill had committed war crimes.[90] While Friedrich refrained from explicitly making such a claim in his book, it was certainly implicit in a press interview he granted: "Churchill was responsible for the extermination [*Vernichtung*] of half a million civilians, in order to break their morale. . . . Is that a war crime? Everyone has to decide for himself. I don't take a position."[91]

The book climbed to the top of the German best-seller lists at the beginning of 2003. Riding the wave of success, a year later Friedrich published an album of photographs containing pictures of the burnt and charred bodies and body parts of German civilians. He wallowed in these horrors, as he had in his first book, apparently to shock his readers and create an emotional identification with his assertions.[92]

The latter book aroused harsh criticism of Friedrich's thesis and insinuations. Nevertheless, it became another best seller, and the very fact that such a public debate took place legitimized some of his explicit claims, all the more so his implied intentions.[93] In the past, such arguments had been made only by extremists on the left and right. By the turn of the millennium they had migrated from the fringes to the center of German political culture and were used by individuals and also among the same German mainstream groups that in the past kept them at a distance.

The works of poet Durs Grünbein, born in Dresden in 1962, offer a fascinating example of the evolution of memories, some of them fictitious, of the Allied bombings and their crystallization through art into a cultural memory of the period. His poem cycle "Europe after the Last Rain" is dedicated to his city of birth.[94] Writing in the period after East Germany's collapse, he uses Dresden and the city's bombardment as a metaphor for all German cities. Grünbein weaves into these poems two myths about the firebombing. The first probably comes from the Third Reich, while the second has its origin in the Communist regime, as part of its anti-Western propaganda. The two myths are still very much alive for the inhabitants of Dresden.

In their version of events, on the morning of February 14, 1945, the day after the attack, low-flying American planes hunted down the survivors. This claim, recorded again and again in books about the event, was based on "eyewitnesses." But all historians who have investigated the matter have ruled that such a thing never happened. Many other eyewitnesses, among them diarist Victor Klemperer, testify that on the contrary, absolute silence prevailed. In one passage from his cycle, Grünbein seems to be referring to the animals of the Sarrasani Circus, who were hit in the bombings.[95]

> [A] horse who knew math, and a tiger named William Blake
> None of them were an ogre, compared to
> The smart guys, the pilots.
>
> Who, flying low, hunted down man and beast.
> Their art needed neither trapeze nor net
> Strung high above the manège.

The charred angels on the roofs
Stood terror-struck.[96]

This myth obviously seeks, probably unconsciously, to depict the Americans as brutal, evil enemies who obtain sadistic pleasure from killing—a characteristic otherwise attributed to the Nazis.

In the same cycle, Grünbein immortalizes another myth:

Alas, Hiroshima was only the second choice.
The premiere was supposed to be held (they say) in Dresden
The bomb, which today every school kid draws—
The giant mushroom, the world-renowned farewell gesture
The ancient opera skies;
How much more beautifully would the radiant puffball here flourish.[97]

Grünbein here referred to the contention first made by Holocaust denier David Irving in 1963 in an interview with a local Dresden newspaper, according to which the Americans had considered the city the first target for the atom bomb.[98] In 1965, Walter Weidauer, Dresden's mayor from 1946 to 1958, repeated the charge. He said that he had been told this by the German physicists Werner Heisenberg and Klaus Fuchs.[99]

The eighth poem in the cycle seems to deny the possibility of drawing any moral lesson from Dresden's fate. But, in literary scholar Amir Eshel's view, it symbolically combines different historical memories—those of the mass murder of the Jews expelled from German cities in the east, and those of the horrific destruction of these cities in the bombardments. Grünbein asks:

Was it worth it? That from entire cities
From which the trains rolled to extinction
Remain a desolation on the banks of the Lethe?[100]

In Eshel's view,

> Dresden, the mnemonic space of *Europe nach der letzten Regen* (the title of Grünbein's cycle), uncovers the simultaneity of different time layers, different memories, and thus both amalgamates and keeps apart the image of those who were burned alive in the cellars of the cities and that of those killed and burned in the camps. The evocation of the crimes committed by, among others, inhabitants of many German cities (or in their names) is boldly entangled with, yet not "balanced" or "neutralized" (*aufgehoben*) by the evocation of these cities' destruction.[101]

Eshel believes that Grünbein and other writers of his generation, "while working through their own private and collective histories, seem to be well aware of the memory of others and its meaning."

Unlike Eshel, I tend to doubt whether the poet, who places one suffering alongside another, really sees two entirely different fates here. Speaking of German and Jewish suffering in the same breath has its roots in the reason the SED regime said that the city was bombed, a claim to which Grünbein was exposed in Dresden from his childhood. The GDR authorities had reiterated it from the time the Cold War began: the Allied bombing of Dresden's inhabitants was one in a chain of crimes committed by the imperialists, no less awful than those of the Nazis, in particular the murder of the Jews.

"Was it worth it?" The question is provocative. Does the poet mean to ask whether the Nazis' crimes were not in some way offset by the bombing of Germany's cities? Did he mean to imply, in this utilitarian formulation, that the price of defeating the Nazis was so high that perhaps it was not worth paying? If that is the case, then it defies Martin Niemöller's unambiguous rejection of any utilitarian calculus. At the Treysa conference he declared that the Germans' anguish was not the result of their defeat, because "who among us would have wished for our victory?"

THE EXPULSION OF GERMANS FROM THE EAST—A TABOO?

Volker Hage's contribution to the discussion following Sebald's lecture was a call for art to address German suffering during the war. Günter Grass's *Im Krebsgang* (*Crabwalk*), published in February 2002,[102] was ostensibly a response to that call, or so Hage presented it in *Der Spiegel*.[103] Indeed, many German readers viewed the book as an epic portrayal of their suffering, the kind of book whose absence Sebald had lamented. Yet at the novel's center lies, in fact, a discussion of the implications of the silenced German suffering for the younger generation, years after the defeat of 1945. True, the background to the story is the tribulations of the thousands of German refugees who fled the Red Army from East Prussia on the ship the *Wilhelm Gustloff*, which was sunk by a Soviet submarine. This is only one element of the novel, yet the discussion of the book in Germany concerned nothing else. When it was published, the last living survivors of the disaster appeared on television talk shows. Many of them spoke about the change in the German public climate regarding their story. In his book, Grass himself contributed to the claim—controverted and baseless—that there had been a taboo:[104] "No one wanted to hear the story, not here in the West, and certainly not in the East. For decades the *Gustloff* and its awful fate were taboo, on a All-German basis, so to speak."[105]

Prominent journalists and public figures who participated in the subsequent discussion in the media on the fate of the expellees in general, and on Grass's novel in particular, seconded his claim: Volker Hage, the literary editor of the weekly magazine *Der Spiegel,* maintained that Grass had related "the history and effect of this all-German (Gesamtdeutsche) taboo."[106]

"The taboo was as sturdy as a German oak," wrote Wolfgang Büscher, a critic for *Die Welt.*[107] Other observers, among them the historian Karl Schlögel, avoided the term "taboo," but nevertheless argued that the expulsion story had long been suppressed, concealed, and even fallen into oblivion. In the weekly *Die Zeit,* Günther Franzen praised Grass's courage in writing on the topic.[108] Although this taboo claim was challenged by other historians and journalists,[109] the notion that these issues were silenced for many years is still widespread in today's Germany.

Grass argues in the book that the silencing of German suffering had actually brought about political extremism in the younger generation, and that, ostensibly, only the extreme right had addressed the subject. He repeated this claim in newspaper interviews he gave when the book was published. There, he said he sought to give a voice to the mute victims. Furthermore, he asserted, he wanted to remove the subject of the expulsion from the hands of the right, which used it manipulatively.[110] However, in the novella, Grass did more than present the supposedly mute voices of the victims of the *Wilhelm Gustloff.* His imagined victims express Nazi and antisemitic ideas and speech.

The story is constructed in such a way as to confirm his claim. Konrad (Konny) Pokriefke, a young and likeable boy, is the son of the narrator and the grandson of Tulla, a survivor of the ship (Tulla's character appeared in some of Grass's earlier books). He gets caught up in the web of the ship's story and of the extreme right. His journalist father, the narrator, has avoided these all his life, despite Tulla's entreaties that he tell the story. Konny conducts, via the internet, conversations with another odd-ball kid,

Wolfgang Stremplin, who identifies himself as David, a Jew. Konny, for his part, identifies with the Nazi leader Wilhelm Gustloff, whom he admires. All that interests him is to break the taboo against the ship's story, as well as the ostensible taboo in Germany against speaking of the advanced social aspects of the Nazi regime. Wolfgang's idol is David Frankfurter, the Jew who assassinated Gustloff. He needles Konny by celebrating the tragic fate of the *Wilhelm Gustloff*'s passengers as a Jewish victory over Nazism. Konny regards any mention of the Holocaust as Jewish provocation. The very existence of "David" drives him into a torrent of hatred against the Jews. Konny the antisemite and Wolfgang the philosemite both adopt the identities of their heroes and carry on their polemic over the internet. At the story's climax, the two boys meet at Gustloff's grave, and Konny murders Wolfgang "the Jew." But even this sickening murder does nothing to detract from Konny's image as a nice boy and, above all, as a victim. One reason is that Wolfgang, alias David, wrote a number of times in his chat exchanges with Konny that he was willing to let Konny murder him. Only after the murder does the reader learn that David was in fact a "fake Yid" (*falsche Jude*).[111] It may be that the "German David" actually sought to sacrifice himself as an atonement for the murder of the Jews, a kind of secular version of the self-sacrifice of Margarete Walker in Albrecht Goes's *Brandopfer* of 1954. Walker, it may be recalled, is a German woman who, during the war, tries to sacrifice herself to God in defiance and as atonement for the Nazis' murder of the Jews.[112]

The parents of Grass's two boys offer similar explanations for their sons' actions. David's father maintains: "[It] had probably been his purely theoretical scientific work at the nuclear research center and certainly also his overly detached attitude toward certain historical events that had resulted in the alienation between him and his son."[113] The two boys' drift into extremism is thus depicted as two facets of a single phenomenon: the silencing of discussion about the suffering of Germans during the war. The parents of both youngsters were members of the generation of 1968. The implication was that, if the past had been discussed from a national point of view that empathized with the motives of Hitler's followers and with German suffering, Konny would not have become a neo-Nazi.[114] And had Wolfgang been raised on "what happened when that ship went down. All those children,"[115] he would probably not have adopted "the name David and [have become] so obsessed with thoughts of atonement for the wartime atrocities and mass killings, which, God knows, were constantly harped on in our society, so that eventually everything Jewish became somehow sacred to him."[116]

In other words, he would not have become a fanatical philosemite, would not have admired Frankfurter the assassin and sanctified his act of murder, and would not have incited Konny to murder him. Grass seems to view this young German's identification with a persecuted Jew as something abnormal, not a natural human response to the Holocaust's horrors or a choice resulting from interest and curiosity. The concept that German suffering inflicted by the Allies somehow offset German guilt for the extermination of the Jews seems to have been, in this book, central to Grass's attitude toward the Nazi past. Had Wolfgang only known about the *Gustloff,* he would have understood that atrocities had not been committed against the Jews alone. The knowledge that the Germans, too, had endured immeasurable suffering would have moderated his extreme pro-Jewish attitude. Also unmentionable were the "positive" social aspects of Nazism, such as the establishment of an ostensibly socialist-egalitarian social order. This was no better exemplified by the *Wilhelm Gustloff* itself, a passenger ship with no class distinctions, built for the Nazi organization Strength Through Joy. In Grass's *Crabwalk,* the author peppered this "true" picture with material that the German public after 1945 termed the "positive side" of Nazism—social policies and the organized leisure activity of Robert Ley's Strength Through Joy organization, for which the *Gustloff* was built. The narrator, Tulla's son Paul, wonders:

> How did this state, legitimized by a questionable enabling act and the sole political party left in existence, manage within such a short time to induce all the workers and salaried employees organized into the German Labor Front not only not to protest, but even to cooperate, and soon to engage in mass rejoicing on command?

He responds:

> Partial credit can go to the activities of the Nazi organization Strength Through Joy, about which many survivors of those years continued to rave in private.[117]

Grass did not leave it at that. He put similar words into the mouth of Tulla Pokriefke, survivor of the *Gustloff,* the "classless ship." Nazi social policy, in her words, was egalitarian and advanced.[118] These claims were consistent with the central thesis of Götz Aly's *Hitlers Volksstaat* (Hitler's People's State). Aly attributed the Germans' support for Nazism to the perquisites the regime offered its citizens and its generous welfare policy.[119] He saw "in the National Socialist tax policy and social policy a social-democratic-leftist foundation."[120]

Yet Aly linked Nazi welfare policy and its social benefits to the atrocities of the Holocaust, offering a moral critique of the average German who was willing to turn a blind eye to injustice and expropriation in exchange for government handouts. Grass, however, offered no criticism of the "positive aspect" of Nazism, which he offered as a rational explanation for the mass support enjoyed by Hitler and his regime.

When he published his memoirs in the summer of 2006, Grass revealed for the first time, more than sixty years after the fact, that as a 17-year-old boy he had volunteered for and served in the Jörg von Frundsberg armored division of the Waffen-SS for some three months before being taken prisoner by the Allies. The elderly author stressed that, at his advanced age, he now wanted to tell the secret that had weighed on his conscience.[121]

Grass distanced himself from the extreme Nazi rhetoric of Konny and his grandmother, Tulla. However, through his narrator and the characters of Konny's father and Aunt Jenny, a close friend of Tulla's, he stated that although Tulla spoke a bit too bluntly, she touched on the truth. "That's always been Tulla's way. She says things other people don't wish to hear. Of course she sometimes exaggerates just a bit."[122] For example, she tells her coworkers at the cooperative factory where she works in the GDR that she is "the last of Stalin's loyalists," while in the sentence that immediately follows she lauds the classless Nazi leisure organization Strength Through Joy (which she calls by its German acronym, KdF) as a model of true Communism.[123] Grass pictures her as an exceptional figure whose insights derive from a penetrating and deep gaze ostensibly beyond the scope of most human beings. Yet her "wisdom" reflects provincial opinions widespread in her post-1945 German generation. Many Germans clung to their fond memories of the "positive aspects" of the Nazi regime, while denying all that was criminal and corrupt about this barbaric dictatorship. It seems that Grass, like the writer Martin Walser, assumed the right not only to present the Nazi past using a narrative itself contaminated with elements of the Nazi worldview, but also to present that narrative as a legitimate view that had hitherto not been expressed.[124]

In this tale, Grass is no longer the incisive social critic of *The Tin Drum* of 1959. That work was merciless in exposing the naked truth about German society in the time of the Nazis, and its protagonists' involvement in acts of evil. In his late work the elderly author has conformed, however, adopting the ostensibly silenced but quite conventional narrative of the society he lives in regarding the expulsions from the east and German torment. When Grass immersed himself in the spiritual world of Tulla Pokriefke, a woman his own age (born in 1927), and with the character of her grandson, the likeable neo-Nazi murderer Konny, he seemed in fact to be dealing with his own younger self. He tells what motivated him, like many other normative young Germans at the time, to become an avid Nazi, join the SS, and believe in Germany's final great victory.[125]

It is true that public discussion of the problematic aspects of the Germans' expulsions from the east, carried out under the auspices of the Allies, especially the Soviet Union, was a taboo in East Germany. The same was true of the rape of German women by Red Army soldiers. But, as we have seen, Communist Germany's official culture of memory fostered other aspects of German suffering and sense of national victimization by the Allies. As early as 1945, the Communist leadership viewed the soldiers of Nazi Germany as victims of fascism and militarism, not its servants. When the Communists forcibly co-opted the SPD into the Communist-dominated SED, that new party's leadership continued to take the same position until the German Democratic Republic came to an end. From 1949 and throughout the GDR's history, its ruling party consistently directed public attention to how the Germans had been victimized by the bombardments of the Allies. It equated their suffering with that of the targets of the Nazi extermination policy. This attention helped make Dresden, rather than the harder-hit Hamburg, the symbol of German victimhood—even outside Germany.

On January 21, 2005, Holger Apfel, leader of the extreme right National Democratic Party of Germany (NPD) faction in Saxony's state parliament (Landtag), made a provocative speech in a legislative session in Dresden, the state's capital. He called the Allied air raid on Dresden a "bombardment holocaust" (*Bomben-Holocaust*) and extolled the Communist state's policy of commemorating the bombings. He remarked that the Communists had given honorary Dresden citizenship to the British historian (and Holocaust denier) David Irving, who in 1963 wrote a book

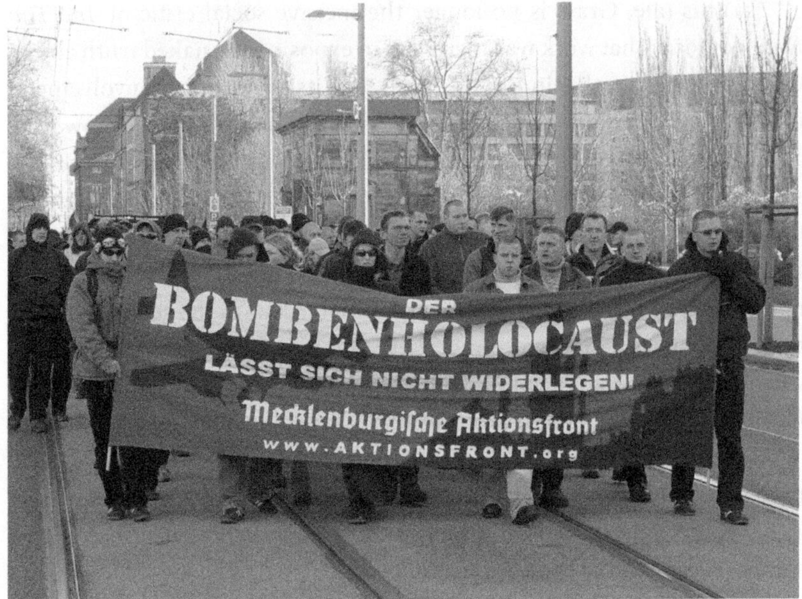

Figure 31. The "Bombardment Holocaust"—a far-right demonstration in Dresden, February 2005

about the attack on the city and presented it as a crime. That was the time, Apfel said, when one could still call an Allied crime a crime. He maintained that the president of the East German parliament, Johannes Dieckmann, had justly called the bombers of Dresden "American aerial gangsters."[126]

But East Germany was not alone in memorializing the bombing victims. Cities in the Federal Republic that were attacked also conducted official ceremonies on those anniversaries. The local press devoted whole pages to first-person stories, essays, and poetry, as well as to photographs of the destruction. The cities erected monuments to the dead. The anniversaries, especially those marking each decade, were not just local affairs. They had nationwide impact as a result of coverage by the national press. They opened television news shows and were also occasions for special programs in the broadcast media.

The expulsion of the Germans from Eastern Europe was never a taboo in West Germany, as discussed in chapter 6. True, Grass chose to depict post-1945 Germans as so consumed by guilt and remorse for the Nazis' crimes that they repressed their own suffering. His view was accepted by many who wrote about his book in Germany.[127] Yet this was far from the reality. In the wake of the war, in spite of widespread expressions of guilt feelings, most Germans felt persecuted. Rather than seeing themselves as persecutors, they believed themselves to have been the victims of the Nazis, who seduced them to follow Hitler into disaster. They also held that they were victims of the Allies, who conducted a ruthless and vindictive campaign.

Günter Grass lamented that the story of the *Wilhelm Gustloff* was suppressed—but that is hardly the case. The sinking of the "German Titanic" was made into a film in 1959. In his book, Grass even mentions the film *Night Fell over Gotenhafen,* directed by Frank Wisbar.[128] Gotenhafen is the German name of the Polish port of Gydnia, from which the *Gustloff* sailed on its last journey. This cinematic version of the story contradicts Grass's claim that the incident was silenced. His narrator, Paul Pokriefke, Konny's father, said that Tulla didn't like the film, because (as in the movie *Titantic*), "a love story had to be brought in as a filler . . . as if the sinking of the overcrowded ship weren't exciting, the thousands of deaths not tragic enough."[129] The fictional figure seems to serve as the author's mouthpiece.

Grass and Sebald do not claim, as the extreme right does, that the Allies and their German lackeys imposed such a taboo. In their view, it was a product of self-censorship growing out of a sense of guilt. Nevertheless, their claim is extremely problematic. The word "taboo" evokes a highly loaded political slogan of Germany's extreme right. After 1945, Germany's political discourse developed ways of circumventing sensitive and problematic issues such as antisemitism and favorable references to Nazism. Speakers who wished to air such ideas publicly employed a variety of euphemistic codes and phrases. The speakers could not be accused of Nazi sympathies on the basis of these locutions, but their real meanings were crystal clear to their target audiences.[130] This is exactly Norbert Frei's point. Such claims, he maintains, are scandalous, because "the extreme right profits from the fact that such talk has today made its way into the heart of German society"[131]—talk that once was heard mostly among neo-Nazis.

In such a political culture Grass and Sebald could easily be interpreted as confirming the extreme right's claim that any talk of German suffering, or of injustices inflicting on the Germans, had been proscribed.[132] This was the claim made by veteran Nazis and neo-Nazis, as well as conservatives, against the de-Nazification and reeducation policies instituted by the Allies in 1945. It linked up with the assertion that the Germans had been enslaved at the war's end. These groups still allege that in the Federal Republic's political culture it was forbidden to talk about Allied crimes and German suffering, while the Holocaust was given much more attention than it deserved. The Allies were said to have imposed these rules of political correctness on Germany. This served "foreign interests" (a familiar euphemism in these circles for "international Judaism"). And these rules are still in force, the right contends. German public figures and the German media implement them and, ostensibly, do not allow free and open expression of other views.[133]

"Flight and Expulsion" in the German Mass Media

In fact, the story of the *Gustolff* and the expellees reappeared in the German mass media several months before the controversy surrounding the appearance of Grass's book. In November 2001, Germany's Channel 2 (ZDF) broadcast *Die Große Flucht* (The Great Flight), Guido Knopp's four-part documentary series on the fate of the expelled Germans. The film included very brief, personal testimonies about German suffering, depicting the expellees as victims[134] of hatred, arbitrary retribution, hunger, crime, and murder who had passed through the fire of martyrdom. Background music, sometimes sentimental, sometimes dramatic, ornamented the story, which was interspersed with emotional narration. Some of the segments have a tendency to ignore the historical context: the German expulsion from the east was not an isolated phenomenon. It was preceded by a war of annihilation that Germany instigated as it exploited the issue of the German minorities in Eastern Europe. The chronology of the expulsion, as presented in the series, began with Jewish instigation for the murder of defenseless Germans. The program blurred the historical context of that time, and it also told a story notably similar to the Nazi and antisemitic narrative of the war.

Ilya Ehrenburg, the well-known Soviet-Jewish writer who, during the war, wrote for *Pravda* and the Red Army newspaper *Krasnaia Zweizda*, was portrayed in the first part of the series as a "hate-consumed journalist" and the leading provocateur who encouraged Red Army soldiers to commit atrocities against the German population in the territories occupied by Soviet forces: "At the beginning, official [Soviet] Party propaganda still distinguished between the Nazi leadership and the German population, while in his articles Ehrenburg turned the Germans into a nation of barbarians and criminals." As proof, the program quoted from a well-known leaflet composed by Ehrenburg in 1942, quite clearly in the context of the war of annihilation that Germany was conducting on Soviet territory, obviously referring to the invading German soldiers, not to the German civilians in the rear. At the time, the Red Army's entry into Germany was not in the cards:

> Attention, soldier! There, in Germany, hides the German who murdered your son. Who raped your wife, your daughter-in-law, and your sister. Who shot your father and mother and who burned your flock. Advance toward the enemy in everlasting hatred . . . the mother's eternal tears call you to merciless revenge.[135]

While the documentary did provide some context for this quote, in the first part of the series Knopp and his team focused on Ehrenburg personally. He alone and not the Red Army command was described as principally responsible for the atrocities committed against defenseless Germans. This was not the message given in all the program's segments. For example, the fourth installment, "The Hour of the Women," took a different tack. One of the witnesses, Christian Graf von Krockow, explained that the war crimes committed by Red Army soldiers were brought on, first and foremost, by the deliberate loosening of the harsh military discipline at the end of the war to which the soldiers had been held throughout it.[136]

Yet the depiction of the Jew (Ehrenburg) as pulling the strings behind the scenes in the war was disturbingly similar to the antisemitic narrative of the war provided by the Nazi propaganda machine, and to the Nazi doctrine of the war against Jewish Bolshevism. Such claims against Ehrenburg were also made—though of course in a much more vicious way—by Germany's extreme right as early as the beginning of the 1960s, and they continue to appear to this day in the expellee press.[137]

The source used by Knopp's researchers, and by the German media at the beginning of the new millennium, seems to have been a book by the American jurist and historian Alfred M. de Zayas. *Nemesis at Potsdam*, published in 1977, states that the behavior displayed by Red Army troops when they reached Germany cannot be explained as an explosion of revenge for the atrocities committed by the SS and the Einsatzgruppen on Soviet territory (note that in de Zayas's version of events, the Wehrmacht was not involved in atrocities). "On the other hand," de Zayas stresses, "Russian excesses in East Prussia were not simply a spontaneous eruption of retributive justice. The Red Army had been systematically incited by the propaganda of Ilya Ehrenburg, the fanatical anti-German author."[138]

De Zayas did not subject his sources to the kind of critical analysis incumbent on historians. His claim was based entirely on the hearsay testimony of German officers he interviewed in the 1970s, some thirty years after the event. They referred to the leaflet, which they said had been designed by Ehrenburg and disseminated by the Red Army not long before October 1944. In that month, Red Army soldiers allegedly murdered twenty-six German civilians, some of them infants, in the East Prussian village of Nemmersdorf. Some of the victims were women whom the soldiers had allegedly previously raped. De Zayas admitted that he had found no evidence for the leaflet's existence, yet he allegedly produced an English rendition of it, one that appeared frequently in German neo-Nazi publications.[139] However, de Zayas did not go to the trouble of informing his readers of the source:

> Kill. Nothing in Germany is guiltless, neither the living nor the yet unborn. Follow the words of Comrade Stalin and crush forever the fascist beat in its den. Break the racial pride of the German woman. Take her as your legitimate booty. Kill, you brave soldiers of the victorious Soviet Army.[140]

I believe that the phrase referring to breaking the racial pride of the German woman indicates the source of the forgery. This is not the language of Communism, but rather of *völkisch*-racial doctrine.

Later in the first segment, the narrator quotes from Goebbels's diary. Göring had reported to him the atrocities committed by Red Army soldiers in Nemmersdorf.[141] When the Wehrmacht retook the village, a few days after it fell to the Red Army, it discovered the bodies, including those of the raped women. The so-called massacre of Nemmersdorf is thus depicted in Knopp's first segment as a direct consequence of (the Jewish) Ehrenburg's incitement, and as a cause of the mass flight of Germans from the east.[142]

Goebbels hitched the event to the Nazi propaganda train. He sought to use fear of the Soviets to unite Germans behind the Nazi leadership at a fateful hour, to awaken in German soldiers a desire for "fanatical" revenge against the Russians, and to banish any thought of surrender to the enemy.[143] The bodies of the Nemmersdorf dead and those from other places were depicted in the *Wochenschau*, the newsreel shown in cinemas, at the beginning of November 1944, accompanied by the following voiceover:

> The Soviet gangs were given a free hand in Nemmersdorf and other places in East Prussia: women were violated, old people slaughtered, children murdered. . . . This record of beastly brutality may be Europe's final warning. The extent of the cruelty cannot be described. One of its manifestations: the murder of an innocent child with a shot to the head.

With the camera showing crosses on the victims' graves, the newscaster concluded his report: "These crosses mark merciless, bitter defiance. Nemmersdorf has aroused in German soldiers fanatical hatred."[144]

In a speech he gave in Görlitz (selections from which were broadcast on the weekly newsreel of March 16, 1945), Goebbels reiterated this theme. German forces that go into battle, he said, "will see themselves as participating in a religious ceremony. . . . All they will see will be the slaughtered children and violated women, and the call for vengeance will erupt from their throats."[145]

In his first installment, Knopp made use of the Nazi footage of the alleged massacre and the Nazi leadership's usage of these deeds, along with its demonization of Ehrenburg and exaggeration of his influence on Soviet forces. While it also referred to the Nazi propaganda machine's cynical and self-righteous manipulations, as well as the racist fantasies of the Nazis, Knopp's documentary presented his audience with a narrative very similar to the Nazi narrative of World War II: Germany fought for European civilization against international Judaism and its Bolshevik minions who plotted to destroy Europe and commit atrocities against the German population. In this way, by addressing the suffering and persecution of the Germans, the program granted public legitimacy to the Nazi view of the war.

Der Spiegel also published, over four weeks, a series of articles, reports, and testimonies under the title "Expulsion" (*Vertreibung*). The opening piece was titled "The Germans as Victims."[146] The headline of this first installment was "Daddy, Please Shoot Me!" The speaker is a girl seriously wounded by a Soviet tank that deliberately runs down the column of refugees in which she is walking. She explains her plea: "I have nothing to live for!"[147] *Der Spiegel* also presented the rape and murder of German women by Red Army troops in Nemmersdorf as an event of major significance: "There can be no dispute: On October 21, 1944, during the fourth year of the total war against the Soviet Union, Nemmersdorf saw a nation of murderers become a nation of victims."[148] This is typical of the current discourse on the Germans' suffering. Samuel Salzborn has remarked that it pictures the harsh experiences and suffering of German individuals as a collective experience of all Germans, which turned them into "a nation of victims."[149]

But it is bogus. The incident may have been a fabrication of Goebbels, or it may have been a real and horrifying war crime, if of limited proportions. Even if the latter is the case, the crime took place in a context—that of a war in which millions of defenseless civilians were murdered, as a matter of course, by German soldiers. This segment of *Der Spiegel*'s article also played down the Nazi regime's role in the evacuation of German civilians. It focused on "flight and expulsion," while passing in silence over the Nazi officials who fled, with their families, from the occupied territories in the east as the Red Army approached. The behavior of the Red Army in wartime was described in a way suggesting that the Soviet Union had conducted a war of annihilation against Germany.

Unlike Knopp's expulsion documentary, *Der Spiegel*'s writers did not relate how many were murdered and how many raped. They said that the numbers were in dispute. Nevertheless, they quoted testimonies at length.[150] Despite the great similarity between the *Der Spiegel* piece and Knopp's documentary, the context of the war that Germany waged against the Soviet Union was stressed more in the former than the latter. In both, Ehrenburg sowed hatred and incited Soviet soldiers to lash out at the Germans. However, *Der Spiegel* did not depict him as being solely responsible for producing this atmosphere. The writers pointed out other reasons for the soldiers' brutish behavior. They noted that Soviet generals loosened their iron discipline at the end of the war. They quoted operating orders handed down by the top Red Army command showing that Ehrenburg's style was hardly exceptional, and in fact expressed the Soviet Union's official war rhetoric. In the spirit of the times, in some ways they modeled the suffering German on the image of the Jewish victim of the Holocaust, making him out to be an innocent victim of war crimes and crimes against humanity.

Three months after Channel 2's series on expellees, Germany's Channel 1 (ARD) followed suit with its own. The title, "The Expellees: Hitler's Last Victims," clearly likened its subjects to victims of the Holocaust. The three segments were broadcast during prime time in February and March 2002 and were accompanied by a book.[151] Like the earlier series, Channel 1 began its story with the Nemmersdorf massacre and the flight from the east, and, similarly, it did not state how many of the raped women died. It simply asserted that "all the women and girls, no matter what their age, were murdered"[152]—a statement without basis in fact. Here, too, Ehrenburg was depicted as a culprit, but not as the only person responsible for the rape and murder.[153]

Ehrenburg and Nemmersdorf also appear on the margins of Grass's novel, where they serve as milestones in the German saga of suffering at the end of the war. Grass portrayed Nemmersdorf as "the epitome of horror," an essential event in the German flight from the east, repeating de Zayas's claim, based on Nazi propaganda's fictitious newsreel accounts, that Russian soldiers murdered the raped women and hung their bodies on the doors of a silo in Nemmersdorf.[154]

This narrative of German flight and expulsion from the east, which surfaced at the end of 2001 and the beginning of 2002, thus signaled a paradigm shift in how German political culture comprehended the Nazi period. Those who were engaged with the topic professed to be accurately depicting historical events,[155] but an examination shows that this approach was inspired by Nazi propaganda. The result was the presentation of limited and singular events, as terrible as they might have been, in a biased and manipulative way. They became an image of national suffering, meeting the needs of a Nazi regime on the edge of obliteration.

The television programs were accompanied by articles in the press and talk-show discussions, giving the expulsions, in this biased representation, an unprecedented visibility on the public agenda. The juxtaposition of the expulsion and the Holocaust was evident in the extreme right-wing press in Germany and Austria. Heinz Nawratil, a jurist and writer close to these circles, criticized Knopp's documentary in an interview with the extremist *Junge Freiheit* and claimed that the title "Flight and Expulsion" concealed "murder, terror, rape, torture, expulsion, and incarceration." He claimed that these crimes had caused the deaths of close to three million Germans, "a number sufficient to justify the term genocide [*Völkermord*]." Nawratil stressed that this genocide and the expulsions of the Germans were not a product of the war, but rather a crime that, morally, should be judged separately from the war.[156] The same linkage of the expulsion with Allied war crimes and crimes against humanity also appeared in the views of the moderate German right, though they did not use the term "genocide." "Ethnic cleansing," a term that gained currency in the Balkan wars of the early 1990s,[157] became a useful phrase that the right, as well as others like Social Democratic chancellor Gerhard Schröder,[158] could apply to two different outrages. Each person according to his particular worldview could interpret the term either as expulsion from a territory or as genocide. This construction legitimized the comparison of the Allied war crimes with those of the Nazis in German public discourse.

In July 2003, the Bundesrat (the upper house of Germany's parliament) decided to hold a national memorial day on August 5 (around the anniversary of the Potsdam agreement, similar to the original date of Homeland Day in the early years of the Federal Republic) for the victims of the expulsions, in a pattern similar to the national memorial day for the Holocaust that President Roman Herzog instituted some years earlier on the anniversary of the liberation of Auschwitz, January 27, 1945. A survey conducted by the Allensbach Institute for the conservative newspaper *Frankfurter Allgemeine Zeitung* on October 23, 2003, showed that 76.2 percent of Germans believed that they, as a national collective, were the victims of the war and were worthy of compassion.[159] The poll results did not say whether the respondents believed that Germans during the war were persecuted just as Europe's Jews, or whether they distinguished between these two categories at all.

The Public Debate on the Center Against Expulsions, 2000–2008

In her role as president of the Union of Expellees, Erika Steinbach founded in September 2000 a fund for the construction of a Center Against Expulsions in Berlin. The effort was led by Steinbach and Peter Glotz, a prominent former Social Democratic politician and editor of that party's intellectual journal, *Die Neue Gesellschaft-Frankfurther Hefte.*[160] Glotz was born in the Sudetenland to a German father and a Czech mother, but his forebears "naturally always saw themselves as Germans without ifs, ands, or buts."[161]

Working together, Steinbach and Glotz lent the initiative an allegedly nonpartisan character and thus enhanced its status with the public. In the summer of 2003, the project went into high gear with the opening of a well-marketed publicity campaign, which ignited an animated public debate in the German and Polish media over the founding of a center in Berlin devoted to the fate of German and non-German expellees in the twentieth century. It should be noted that, in June 1999, the Bundestag had voted to erect a monument to the memory of the Jews of Europe murdered by the Nazis. Glotz's and Steinbach's initiative came in the context of the German parliament's move to establish such a memorial in the heart of Berlin.

The center would serve as an archive and monument against expulsions. Ostensibly, it would oppose not just the removal of the Germans from the east but expulsions of anyone, anywhere. The fund's web site (www.z-g-v.de) opened with the following message: "Between 80 to 100 million people were expelled, driven out of their homes, or uprooted during the twentieth century." But the center's major interest was the fate of the more than 15 million Germans expelled from Eastern Europe. According to Steinbach, in excess of 2.5 million of them died as a result of torture, forced labor, or rape. The figures have no basis in fact,[162] but Steinbach used them to imply that this was a genocide. Other expellees' organizations echoed the equation. "Expulsion is Genocide" (*Vertreibung ist Völkermord*), read the slogan of the annual German Sudeten convention in Nuremberg on May 2006.[163] An examination of the chronicle of expulsions on the web site shows that the center includes 6 million Jews among these expellees. Of these, 5.86 million died during the expulsions. In other words, the Holocaust is an expulsion and the expulsion is a Holocaust. This juxtaposition, which can be found in many of Steinbach's public statements, places the eviction of the Germans under the rubric of "crimes against humanity," in a subheading that couples "expulsions and genocide." This is outrageous revisionism, not by denying the Holocaust, but by downgrading it with the implication that it was equaled by the suffering of the Germans. It seeks to compare an expulsion that did not include the planned murder of expellees (although some were murdered) to a systematic and deliberate genocide.

Steinbach and her supporters wanted the Center Against Expulsion to be established in Berlin. At the beginning of the new millennium they spoke of a building in the Kreuzberg quarter that had served as a bomb shelter in the Third Reich, and in which expellees had been given shelter after the war. When this did not succeed, Steinbach advocated housing the center in the Church of St. Michael in central Berlin, which had been damaged during the war and was not yet completely repaired. The Catholic Church opposed the idea, because it was not clear what the center's intentions were, and there was no broad public support for it.[164] The symbolism behind Steinbach's choice might reveal some of the thinking of the expellee leaders. The angel Michael, folklorist Elisabeth Fendl has shown, was frequently made the patron saint of expellee communities established in the 1950s in West Germany. Depicted as fighting a dragon, he was seen as a defender of the Germans from the forces of evil. During the Cold War, West Germans identified the Communists as the forces of evil responsible for the expulsion.[165]

Opponents of the project argued that the center was meant to serve as a counterweight to the recently dedicated memorial to murdered European Jewry in the German capital's center, close to the Brandenburg Gate. Steinbach and her fund demanded that the Federal Republic support their project as well. Chancellor Gerhard Schröder and Foreign Minister Joschka Fischer opposed the demand on principle, and also because of the damage it would do to Germany's relations with Poland and the Czech Republic. This position continued the memory policy of the SPD from Brandt's Ostpolitik.

In December 2000, an organization called Prussian Loyalty (Preußische Treuhand Gmbh) was founded in Germany. The head of its supervisory executive board, Rudi Pawelka, a central figure in the Union of Expellees (BdV) as well, wanted to conduct a legal battle, principally against Poland, in the European Union's courts, modeled on the activities of Jewish claims organizations. The goal would be to force the Poles to return real estate to its German owners. The organization opposed accepting compensation or any other solution, and insisted on the return of expropriated property. Here, too, the move was clearly based on the precedent set by Jewish organizations in their demand for the return of Jewish property in these countries. According to Pawelka, forfeiting property was tantamount to "a partial forfeiture of the right to a homeland (*Heimatrecht*)."

Prussian Loyalty was established as a corporation in which the East Prussian and Silesian expellee organizations, members in Steinbach's umbrella expellees' union, held most of the shares, though Steinbach took care to separate herself from the new organization's activities.

Steinbach's initiative also set off a lengthy controversy in Poland. Many Poles viewed a project that portrays the Germans as victims (of Polish persecutors, among others) as an attempt to twist history and obscure German crimes against their countrymen. In the summer of 2004, after she was accused of sabotaging Germany's foreign relations, Steinbach proposed a legal arrangement under which the German government would compensate the expellees. This would prevent deterioration of Germany's relations with its neighbors.[166] The members of Prussian Loyalty and other expellees, however, vigorously opposed the idea.[167] During the same summer, the Sjem (the Polish parliament) decided almost unanimously to instruct the Polish government to demand compensation from Germany for the enormous damage it wreaked on Poland during its occupation.[168]

In an interview in *Die Zeit* in August 2003, Foreign Minister Fischer said that the preoccupation with the Germans' expulsion had the effect of detracting from German guilt and distorting history. The origin of the expulsion was the self-destruction that Germans initiated with the Nazis' rise to power, the foreign minister stressed. The BdV did not have the authority to determine the German nation's historical consciousness, he added.[169] However, Edmund Steuber, then leader of the Bavarian Christian Social Union, and the future chancellor, Angela Merkel, then leader of the Christian Democratic Party, supported the initiative,[170] arguing that the federal government should provide funding for it.

Markus Meckel, a member of the Social Democratic Party and East Germany's last foreign minister, offered a counter-proposal, with the support of German and even some Polish intellectuals. He called for a European framework that would discuss the issue with Germany's neighbors rather than act unilaterally. A center devoted to expulsions, not focused just on Germans, could be established in Wrocław (the German Breslau), he suggested, or elsewhere on the Polish-German border.[171]

A public opinion poll conducted by the Bonn Historical Museum at the opening of an exhibit in 2005 titled "Flight, Expulsion, Integration" quantified the German public's positions on the establishment of a Center Against Expulsions. It showed that about a third of Germans believed the idea was a good one. However, 45 percent—a plurality—said that such an institute was unnecessary.[172]

The decision will ultimately be made by politicians, not by the public. Upon being elected chancellor in November 2005, Merkel issued a declaration of intentions in which she sought a compromise between the Union of Expellees' initiative and that of Markus Meckel:

> The Federal Republic will contribute to the preservation of the expellee's heritage. Its desire is to erect, in a spirit of conciliation, a prominent monument in Berlin to commemorate the injustice of the expulsion. This will be done in a European context. The joint declaration of the former president of Germany, Johannes Rau, and of the president of Poland, Aleksander Kwaśniewski, contains guarantees that will make it possible to find a common way to do this.[173]

Steinbach and her partners have worked with figures from all parts of the German political spectrum in promoting the center, among them well-known German Jews. Among the supporters listed on its web site are conservative professors such as Arnulf Baring and Horst Möller, as well as Joachim Gauck, who headed the authority responsible for the records of the East German Secret Police (Stasi); Otto Graf Lambsdorff of the Free Democratic Party; media historian Guido Knopp, the historian responsible for documentaries on Channel 2; and the Jewish-German professors Julius H. Schoeps and Michael Wolffsohn. The latter two have stated publicly that they as Jews have no reason not to support the establishment of a Center Against Expulsions in Berlin.[174] Another supporter is the Jewish-Hungarian novelist, Holocaust survivor, and Nobel Laureate Imre Kertész, and even a rabbi, Dr. Walter Homolka.

In September 2003, Steinbach reported that an Israeli professor, Moshe Zimmermann, had joined the center's academic board.[175] This was surprising given that, just two months earlier, Zimmermann had published in the *Süddeutsche Zeitung* a sharp critique of the Germans' current preoccupation with their suffering, and in particular against the character of the debate over the expellees' fate. He argued that the discussion was principally aimed at canceling out (*Aufrechnung*) German guilt and responsibility, with the aim of clearing the conscience of a collective charged with expelling others. According to Zimmermann, the current polemic over the expulsion of Sudeten Germans from Czechoslovakia at the end of the war was meant to serve as a counterweight to Germany's expulsion of ethnic Czechs from the Sudetenland after it took the region from Czechoslovakia in 1939. Steinbach and Glotz (who had been expelled from Sudetenland as a child) never spoke of this German action.[176] The center also announced that it would award a human rights prize named after the Jewish-German writer Franz Werfel, who wrote a novel about the Armenian genocide, *The Forty Days of Musa Dag*. Steinbach and her associates made a point of appointing Jewish figures to the prize committee. They included Ralph Giordano, who in 2002 was still a critic of the deportee organizations and their revanchist views,[177] and leftist leader Daniel Cohn-Bendit, a member of the Green Party faction in the European parliament. Whatever the motives of these Jewish figures, and even if they sought to defend Jewish causes by moderating problematic trends from within the organization, their very involvement in the fund is troubling. The German public perceives them as representing the victims of the Holocaust, and as such they enjoy moral standing. Yet it seems possible that those promoting the Center Against Expulsions are simply seeking Jewish legitimization of their ideology, with all its revisionist insinuations.

For example, Wilfried Rogasch, an active supporter of the center, maintained in an interview with a German radio station that suffering placed both Jewish and German victims on the same plane:

> Ralph Giordano, a member of our [Jewish] advisory committee, always says that humanism cannot be divided. If that is the case, from the victim's point of view it is entirely meaningless, and I'll put it in a somewhat provocative way, if a woman from East Prussia was raped and then murdered in 1944/45 or if a Jewish woman was sent by the Germans to the Auschwitz concentration camp and murdered there, I am convinced that the point of view of this victim is meaningless.[178]

Here Rogasch did not really examine death from the humanistic point of view, which takes the position of the victim facing death. Instead, his point is that in both cases a person died.[179] Rogasch used Giordano's words as a basis for relativizing the Holocaust. Germans of the extreme right have for years used Jewish statements to legitimize their positions and devalue the Holocaust. After the broadcast of this interview, Zimmermann announced his resignation from the Center Against Expulsions' academic board.

Two Different Exhibitions—Different Concepts?

In 2005 the historical museum (*Haus der Geschichte*)in Bonn opened an exhibition on the expulsion of the Germans from the east. Sponsored by Germany's president, Professor Horst Köhler, it evinced the new directions taken by the German public discourse, which viewed the expulsion not as a reaction to the collaboration of these German minorities with the Nazis in the destruction of Slavic nation-states during World War II, but as a link in a long chain of expulsions in the "century of expulsions." Likewise, it stressed that the Germans were the most numerous victims of this phenomena. The exhibition web site stated:

> In the first half of the twentieth century, between 60 and 80 million people in Europe alone were forced to leave their homelands. World War II, unleashed by Nazi Germany, gave a new and terrifying dimension to flight and expulsion. The hardest-hit people were the Germans, with up to 14 million refugees and expellees. . . . The term "century of expulsion" itself makes clear that the focus cannot be restricted to the end of World War II. Examples of forced resettlement and expulsion in Europe dating from the beginning of the twentieth century are illustrated here.[180]

The exhibition's accompanying book made the same point in a number of places, among them the opening article by the president of the *Haus der Geschichte* fund, Hermann Schäfer. Schäfer places the expulsion of the Germans in a historical context of "expulsions and dismantlement of ethnic complexities which were often during the twentieth century, a policy frequently used by the great powers. The overriding goal was the creation of ethnically homogenous states." He also noted that the Nazi policy of territorial expansion, which involved the violent displacement of nations, was a preface to the transfer of millions of Germans out of the region to the east of the Oder and Neisse Rivers.[181] Schäfer chose, in this context, to address only the expulsions carried out by the Germans during World War II—he failed to mention other German crimes, such as the mass murder of Poles and of the great majority of Polish Jewry. After all, the exhibition's conceptual pivot was "a century of expulsions," not "a century of genocides." Schäfer's cursory reference to this broad historical context of the expulsion of the Germans is elaborated in the following piece, written by the historian K. Erik Franzen, wholly devoted to placing the exhibition in the context of "a century of expulsions" in Europe. Franzen begins with a description of the deportation and flight of refugees from war zones, and continues with expulsions carried out by the Ottoman Empire during the Balkan wars, as well as the massacre of the Armenians and the Turkish-Greek population exchange after World War I. Franzen is confusing genocidal acts with expulsion, which is typical of the Center Against Expulsions. From there he goes on to the problem of the German minorities in Poland and Czechoslovakia after World War I and until their expulsion. At the end of the article, Franzen states his thesis: "Fundamentally, the forced population migrations of the first half of the twentieth century were based, over and above all else, on a principle of national homogenization. These measures were generally justified by states on the basis of the right to national self-determination." It seems, however, that he was not entirely comfortable with this statement, and with his numerous examples that fail to lend support to his claim. In discussing the expulsion of the Germans, he makes no reference to German *völkisch* ideology, with its inherently racist attitude toward the Slavic nations and its view, dating back to the nineteenth century, that Eastern Europe was Germany's natural area of expansion and colonization. Franzen fails to explain why, if Czechoslovakia's aim was ethnic purity, it did not expel the Germans from Sudetenland in 1919.[182] At several points in his article, Franzen qualifies his statements, including at the end. After stating and summarizing his thesis, he again chooses to equivocate: "Nevertheless, the forced migrations cannot be explained, in the context of World War II, solely on these grounds."[183]

Alongside articles by important scholars about issues addressed in the exhibition, the accompanying book also includes an article by Alfred de Zayas, the controversial historian and jurist whose problematic views are mentioned above.[184] De Zayas served on the Center Against Expulsion's scholarly committee.

The first part of the exhibition was devoted to the expulsion and murder of the Armenians by the Turks and to the population exchange between Greece and Turkey in 1923. The second part focused on German minorities. It opened with Germany's policy of conquest, and then segued immediately into the flight and expulsion that followed World War II. The sections that followed addressed various aspects of the absorption and integration of the refugees in the different German states—for example, the absorption of expellees in East Germany, the attitude of the Allies, housing, the attitude of the churches, expellee organizations and their activities, West Germany's *Ostpolitik*, and a large variety of other issues.

The exhibition in Bonn's historical museum presents interesting aspects of the absorption of the expellees and the problems they faced, but also embodies the revisionist approach dating from the mid-1990s, according to which there is no connection between the fate of the Germans of Eastern Europe and Germany's policy of conquest, Nazi crimes, and the collaboration of East European German minorities with Hitler.

This same idea was even more blatantly evident in an exhibition that opened a few months later. In August 2006, the Center Against Expulsions Fund opened an exhibit called "Forced Ways" (*Erzwungene Wege*) in the Kronprinzenpalais in central Berlin. The exhibit was part of its campaign to promote its views in the German public. The exhibit moved in the summer of 2007 to the Paulskirche in Frankfurt (the site where the all-German parliament convened in the "spring of nations" of 1848). According to Erika Steinbach, the Berlin exhibit was "a complete success," visited, she claimed, by 60,000 people and 130 school classes.[185]

The exhibit was devoted to the phenomenon of expulsion and flight in twentieth-century Europe. Its opening panel displayed the following text: "The implementation of the idea of an ethnically homogeneous nation-state is one of the principal reasons for the expulsion of ethnic groups and minorities in the twentieth century. Racism and antisemitism, alongside nationalism, were further driving forces behind expulsion and annihilation."

This text reflects the attempt by the fund's supporters, led by Steinbach, to obscure the distinction between the Holocaust committed again the Jews and the expulsion of Germans from Eastern Europe at the war's end. The same purpose was evident in other texts on display and in the very design of the exhibit. The expulsion of the Germans was presented as an integral link in a chain of expulsions that began with the massacre of Armenians by the Turks in World War I and which continued with the population exchange between Greece and Turkey in 1922–1923, through the Holocaust. The latter subject, which occupied a prominent and central place alongside the expulsion of the Germans, was termed "the expulsion of the Jews from Germany starting in 1933." The Nazis' annulment of the civil rights of German Jews and banishment of Jews from all areas of life was described as "the Nazi policy of Germanization." The final part of the exhibit was devoted to the mass murders in Bosnia-Herzegovina in the 1990s. Thus the exhibit, for all intents and purposes, positioned the expulsion of the Germans from the east as one link in a series of twentieth-century genocides. The expulsion of the Germans was a Holocaust, and the Holocaust was an expulsion.[186]

As one might expect, the exhibition was the subject of a public debate in the media, during which a variety of opinions about the political and historical conception at the exhibition's foundation were expressed.[187] Of course, many Germans are not a party to this focus on their people's suffering. Yet, while that position remains controversial, it is becoming more and more legitimate. And it is now becoming acceptable in circles that rejected it for the last thirty years.

The findings of the survey conducted by the Allensbach Institute for the *Frankfurter Allgemeine Zeitung* and the Polish newspaper *Gazeta Wyborcza* could be taken to show that most Germans today identify with the view of their nation as a victim of World War II. Those who oppose this view, and who fight it as part of a German struggle for shaping united Germany's memory of its Nazi past, seemed to be in a minority, according to this poll. However, the constant public discourse and debates on such issues show that there is no consensus in the German public about portraying the Germans who lived through the Nazi period and World War II as victims. One can always hear German voices who counter and challenge such convictions and who emphasize the uniqueness of the Holocaust and the exceptionality of the fate suffered by the Jews under the Nazi yoke, as opposed to that of the Germans.[188]

The End of the Debate on the Center Against Expulsions?

During Jaroslaw Kaczyński's tenure as prime minister of Poland (2005–2007), his country's relationship with Germany worsened as a result of the activity and demands of Erika Steinbach and her expellee organization and the Polish reactions to them. This led the SPD, which after the elections of 2005 became the senior partner in the coalition of Christian Democrat Angela Merkel, to advocate a Center Against Expulsions. In November 2007, Kaczyński was defeated and replaced by Donald Tusk.

Germany's culture minister, Bernd Neumann, quickly met with the new Polish leader and obtained his support for the center. Tusk's condition was that the center be established by the German government and not by the expellee organizations, and that its program differ from what those organizations proposed. The Poles insisted that the exhibition stress Germany's invasion of Poland and the crimes committed by Germany against civilians in occupied Poland. The Poles also demanded that Steinbach not be involved in the project.[189] Once the Poles' consent had been obtained, the German cabinet, with the consent of all parties in the coalition, resolved in March 2008 to establish a Documentation Center for the expulsions in Berlin, with the exhibition based on the one that appeared at the Haus der Geschichte in Bonn in 2005.

As noted, the perspective of that exhibit was hardly consistent with the Polish demands. The SPD opposed including Steinbach on the supervisory board, but the BdV insisted that she be a member.[190] In fact, three members of the BdV were nominated as supervisory board members, not only Steinbach but her two vice presidents. The foreign affairs advisor to the Polish prime minister, Wladyslaw Bartoszewski, who had been a prisoner at Auschwitz, equated Steinbach's nomination with the Vatican's choice of Bishop Richard Williamson, a Holocaust denier, as the papal delegate to Israel.[191]

At present, there still appear to be unbridgeable gaps not only about personnel but also the substance of the Bonn exhibition, based on the revisionist view of the expulsions and the Poles' demands. But the nature of the solution, in which the government has taken charge of a BdV initiative, shows that Merkel and her advisers are no less "Adenauer's grandchildren" than was Chancellor Helmut Kohl, as the historian Michael Schwartz called the previous CDU chancellor. Like the patriarch of the Federal Republic, they also seek to embrace expellee political leaders as a way of restraining their radicalization and preventing damage to Germany's diplomatic relations. It is not clear, however, whether Steinbach's plan for a Center Against Expulsion has been laid to rest. Even though there is now no need for a separate museum, Steinbach has announced that the fund she founded will continue to function.[192]

The trends of the 1990s and the early years of the new millennium seem to show that a significant part of the German public is fed up with being the guilty party of the Second World War. For them, that war was a saga of German torment. The persecutors were Nazis in the abstract, the Allies, and the peoples of Eastern Europe. The saga is interwoven with the Holocaust, because they are both about expulsion and murder. This position is then but a short distance from the offensive claim that the Germans also suffered an equivalent Holocaust that cut short the lives of millions of German women and children. Indeed, in his book, Jörg Friedrich insinuated that the Allied bombings of German cities were tantamount to a "German Holocaust," a notion heretofore used only in extreme-right and neo-Nazi publications.[193] These groups have escalated their use of such language. The sixtieth anniversary of the Dresden bombing was an excuse for the far right NPD faction in the city's parliament to get a lot of media play for one of its favorite terms, "bombing Holocaust" (*Bomben-Holocaust*).

This renewed German preoccupation with their victimhood indicates a resurgence of German national narratives purged of the moderation offered by World War II's victors and Nazism's victims. This new German account is based on a subjective memory of the war from the point of view of the average citizen in Nazi Germany and on conventions that merged in both parts of Germany during the Cold War. Such a citizen was certainly not an opponent of the regime and, indeed, appreciated its "positive aspects." He or she may well have been fond of Führer Adolf. Manifestations of this narrative, crystallized at the end of the war, have been heard publicly in Germany since the defeat in 1945, especially on the extreme right. However, the studies of Harald Welzer and others[194] show that this storyline has not been absent from intimate conversations in families and among friends. In contrast to Welzer, I have emphasized in this book that the contradiction between the intimate family memories and elements of official memory have not been especially large. The official cultures of memory and commemoration fashioned during the Cold War in both German states incorporated certain elements of the Nazi narrative, in a way that softened them. These official cultures viewed Germans who fell in battle as victims, and both explicitly and implicitly criticized the Allies' "criminal" conduct of the war while emphasizing German distress. This allowed some Germans to reject guilt and any demand for political responsibility.

The legitimacy of these elements has been challenged in the Federal Republic since the 1960s, but it never completely disappeared from the political culture.German cultures of memory and commemoration thus

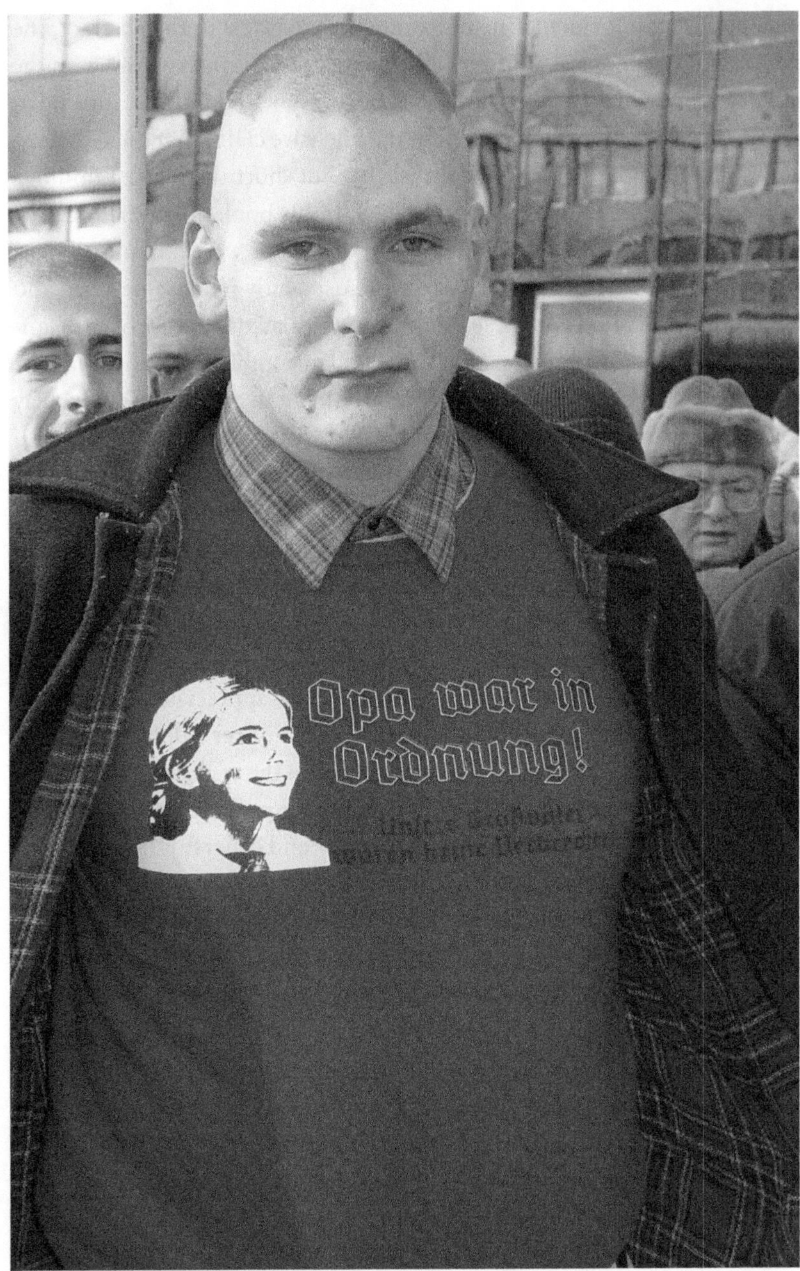

Figure 32. "Grandpa was ok. Our grandparents were not criminals." The message on the shirt of a far-right demonstrator in Dresden on the sixtieth anniversary of the city's bombing, in February 2005

display internal contradictions. Alongside their firm rejection of Nazism, these cultures contain revisionist elements derived from the Nazi view of the war that dissent from the narratives of the nations allied with the two Germanys during the Cold War.[195] This legitimized claims common in private German discourse on the experience of World War II, and in German feelings of hatred, animosity, and bitterness against the Allies. The Cold War moderated blunt public expression of the nationalist discourse, but it survived in private spaces and was bequeathed to the generations that followed.[196] This self-restraint toward the great powers disappeared at the end of the Cold War, and the narrative enjoyed a renaissance in the public discourse of united Germany.

All this occurred during a change of generations. Most Germans today do not have personal memories of the war. As a result, many do not see themselves as bearing any responsibility for events of the distant past. Certain Germans are not prepared to hear any more criticism of their parents' or grandparents' generation for having supported Hitler and his criminal regime. Some members of the second generation, who have now reached retirement age (and who are therefore the same age their parents were when they clashed in 1968), seem to want to retroactively and collectively clear their parents' generation of all responsibility for the Nazis' crimes, and to grant them the status of victims—a status that has become prestigious in Western political culture.[197]

A struggle is on in Germany over how the Nazi past will be remembered. Internalization of the feeling of suffering and the status of victim (which blurs the fundamental distinction between the Nazis' war targets and those of the Allies) is of political significance. In September 1990, Germany officially and finally recognized its current borders (the Oder-Neisse line) and abdicated all its territorial claims. However, the expulsion of the Germans from the east is still widely regarded as an unlawful and immoral act. Indeed, German politicians never acknowledge the necessity of the expulsions from their former Slavic states, as did the Allies following the end of the Cold War with their reaffirmation of the Potsdam agreement. Germany's eastern neighbors and observers around the world wonder about the significance of the German self-image of victims of Nazism and war. Might this common view, in certain future circumstances, be used to call into question the legitimacy of the geopolitical arrangements that have prevailed in central and eastern Europe since the end of

World War II? Insofar as the revisionist message hints that both Hitler and Churchill were in fact war criminals, guilty of crimes against humanity, then one may question the very legitimacy of the borders that Churchill and the other Allied leaders dictated at Potsdam. Germany's neighbors have still not forgotten the stubborn opposition West Germany expressed to the Potsdam agreement throughout the Cold War. The encouragement of the public discourse on the suffering of the Germans leads them to fear the potential political implications, which are evident in that discourse's history.[198]

Conclusion

The German state and German society have gradually distanced themselves from Nazi ideology and heritage since 1945. In a process that Konrad Jarausch has called "re-civilization," Germany has developed a modern civil society and, by doing so, has integrated itself into the democratic West.[1] West Germany accomplished this through a gradual but profound process of democratization and liberalization.[2] East Germany rejected Nazism by becoming an antifascist Soviet-aligned Communist dictatorship. Yet, Jarausch argues, even in this totalitarian state, opposition figures and groups adopted and internalized, if in a limited way, humanistic and democratic values. They attempted to create a civil sphere, untouched by the dictatorship. As in other Eastern European countries, the dissident culture that emerged alongside the official Communist culture served an alternative public sphere, an avant-garde that set the stage for the civil revolution of 1989.[3]

One of the manifestations of liberalization in West Germany's political culture was its citizens' growing readiness, beginning at the end of the 1950s, to listen to the Jewish narrative of the Holocaust. This process was reinforced by the change of generations—the coming of age of cohorts that bore no responsibility for the horrors of the past. For these young people, the subject was less charged. This process did not affect the whole society with the same magnitude. It seemed that, at least among the educated, new generations of Germans had internalized the narrative of the Holocaust, and with it the recognition that there was a fundamental difference between the experiences of the average German, as a soldier at the front and as a civilian in the rear during World War II, and those of the average European Jew. This awareness contradicted what was implied by the reconciliation narrative that had characterized the official cultures of memory of the two rival German states during the Cold War.

Nevertheless, the responses to the increasing presence of the Jewish narrative were not unequivocal. Some, even outside the radical right, viewed the Jewish narrative's penetration of Germany as the external imposition of a foreign perspective that ran counter to German experience. It has also met with mainstream (not only marginal) resentment that has also been directed against its promoters in the German political culture. The 1998 "Sunday speech" of Martin Walser at the Paulskirche in Frankfurt was only one expression of this phenomenon.

Liberalization was evident in a variety of areas. It was especially notable in West German political culture,[4] but also in social policy, medicine, the social sciences, and the humanities[5]—for example, in historiography addressing the Third Reich. Yet the Federal Republic's movement toward pluralism and integration into the West from the early 1960s onward also had its limits.

Memories of the war and of the Nazi past were slow to change, and the change was less pronounced than in the areas mentioned above.[6] This may come as no surprise, given that even some agents of liberalization and enlightened thinking about the Nazi past had themselves been socialized in the Third Reich and were members of the so-called "skeptical generation" born around 1930.[7] Their thinking about that period was thus on occasion ambivalent and contradictory. In some cases, this confusion could be seen clearly in their work and public activity. The writings and public statements of Günter Grass are paradigmatic of other German agents of liberalization of his generation.[8] On the one hand, "it was Günter Grass who, to his lasting credit, reminded his German readers that 'them' was us and confronted them with the sleaziness of evil in the average German town and household and heart of the Nazi period."[9] On the other hand, in the very same works the novelist might slip into antisemitic clichés and also express an anomalous attitude toward Jews out of his sense of guilt regarding the Holocaust. He could even wax lyrical about certain aspects of Nazism.[10]

Ambivalence about the past, and sometimes utter and unqualified identification with the stories of German suffering during and after the war, was manifest in an area that is less exposed to the public eye, one where emotion takes precedence over the historian's "cold sobriety" (*Broszat*), by which I mean the intergenerational transfer of memories of the Nazi past and the war. Recent studies on this subject indicate that the sense of victimization has persisted in families and the semi-public space. Furthermore, these sentiments tend to be phrased in the plural ("we, the Germans"), and apply the sense of victimization to the entire German public of the period in question.[11] The family picture of the war period focuses on how its members suffered from hunger, expulsion, abuse by the victors, and other evils, and this apparently has been passed on to children and grandchildren in a significant portion of German families. In some of these stories, the saga of the family's anguish does not begin in World War II but goes back to the 1920s. The torment and injustice the family endured are presented as a part of the German people's suffering, and as an explanation for why its members supported the Nazis.[12] The British historian Bill Niven believes that these findings "would seem to contradict the view that the 1968 generation had overcome such uncritical memory."[13]

German family memory—alongside trends in political culture and in the official cultures of memory in the two Germanys regarding World War II and its aftermath—contributed to the legitimacy and preservation of certain elements that were also present in the Nazi war narrative, and, for many Germans, to the solidification of ambivalent memories of the war and the Nazi past. Such memories perpetuated the tension within the collective German memory between the motif of guilt, whose most widespread manifestation in the West German political culture was the Jewish Holocaust narrative, and the motif of suffering expressed by the reconciliation narrative. This tension continued until the end of the Cold War.

The end of the Cold War made it theoretically possible, especially in East Germany, to conduct a free and public discussion of the war and its end. This discussion was not subject to the official ideology that had dictated its course in the past—for example, the portrayal of the Red Army as having liberated the Germans from the yoke of Nazism, or the equation of the Allied bombings with Nazism's crimes.[14] East Germans could now talk and write publicly about the rape of German women by Red Army soldiers, the persecution of Germans whom the military government and

Communist leadership viewed as rivals and enemies, and about the suffering of the ethnic Germans during their expulsion from the eastern territories. But for the most part, there was no change in the conventional wisdom about the Allied bombings of German cities, even if it seemed as if the Marxist veneer that had typified the subject in East Germany had fallen by the wayside. Similar verdicts on Allied air raids lingered in the private sphere in the West as well, throughout the Cold War years. However, due to the liberalizing trend in the West, a more refined version of the East German narrative on the Allied bombings became established in the Federal Republic's political culture, years before the Berlin Wall fell.

The East-West conflict automatically politicized the German discourse of suffering and, from the 1970s onward, may well have prevented a relatively small group on the West German left and some liberals from acknowledging or addressing their nation's suffering during and after World War II. They understood that acknowledging German suffering at the hands of the Red Army and the Slavic peoples (especially during the expulsion) was tantamount to denying German guilt.[15] Yet the government and the rest of the political spectrum were not so affected. The increase in attention to German suffering after the Cold War did not, by and large, create a sincere national narrative that integrated recognition of German suffering and loss with acceptance (though not minimizing) of German guilt and collective responsibility for the suffering of millions of Europeans without equating the two, as some Western observers wish to see.[16] In the previous chapters I have adduced a plethora of examples to demonstrate that many aspects of the current discourse about German suffering during the war do not take into account, frankly and with sufficient gravity, the issue of German guilt and responsibility. The analogy between German suffering and the Holocaust plays a central role in this discourse, and the new preoccupation with German victims has come, explicitly, at the expense of the Nazis' victims.[17]

German memory of World War II is today characterized by the parallel presence of ostensibly contradictory narratives: the reconciliation narrative alongside the narratives of the Nazis' various victims. Since the Cold War's end and Germany's reunification, the Jewish narrative's presence has increasingly manifested itself in the landscape of German memory, general culture, and political culture; the same is true of the persecution narratives of other groups of victims. The number of victims in these latter groups is relatively small, and for the most part they are Germans. Among them are the homosexuals, the victims of euthanasia, and Gypsies.

These narratives of the Nazis' heterogeneous victims underline, in a humanistic way, the uniqueness of the ordeal of the members of all these groups under the Nazi regime. Obviously, such phenomena either did not exist or were much more modest in the 1950s. Then, many of those involved in the crimes, especially those not involved in the direct physical murder of the victims, continued to hold their public service posts. Unlike their victims, they were admired and respected by their fellow Germans.[18] Nevertheless, the narrative of Soviet and Slavic victims of the war, whose numbers exceeded those of all the other groups mentioned above combined, has not to this day succeeded in penetrating German consciousness in a similar way, and its manifestations in the landscape of memory cannot be compared to that of other groups of victims. Perhaps this is an artifact of the demonization of "the Russians," which originated in Nazi propaganda and was continued by the anti-Bolshevik consensus in West Germany during the Cold War, as well as by family stories on both sides of the German-German border. No small number of Germans are in fact unwilling to recognize the former Soviet peoples as victims of the Nazi war, and to accept that Germans are collectively responsible for their suffering. Alternatively, they prefer to ignore the lack of reciprocity between the conduct of the Nazi war of extermination against the Soviet Union and the conduct of the Red Army toward the Germans. They prefer to justify the Nazi policy of murder as growing out of the harsh military campaign between two dictatorships.

This certainly is not the only phenomenon in German memory in which past trends come into play. A prominent development since the end of the 1990s has been a return to the mood of the 1950s, which saw the entire German collective of the Nazi and war years as victims. In the name of a universal concept that sees every sufferer as a victim, this view seeks to apply the status of innocent victims collectively to all the Germans, including the soldiers who loyally served the Führer and who, in doing so, committed crimes.

In this discourse, the German victims are often depicted in ways borrowed from the Jewish narrative of the Holocaust, which undoubtedly points to at least some of the motives behind it. It contains a claim that is often unstated, but sometimes made explicit, that Jewish and German suffering are identical manifestations of victimization: all were the victims of a horrible war and of belligerent, irresponsible rulers. The different ideologies held by the antagonistic forces are ostensibly indistinguishable in the face of the destruction and death they wreaked.

A discourse of German suffering, one that grants the Germans the status of victims, has thus reappeared in united Germany. The impression is that the previous consensus about the fundamental difference between the experiences of the Nazis' victims and those of the Germans—a matter of common wisdom in the political culture of the Bonn republic for thirty years—has weakened in recent years. This frame of mind, familiar from the 1950s, has once again become common in the Berlin republic. It is not only tolerated, but has actually become acceptable in circles that rejected it in the past, at least since the end of the 1970s.

The narrative of the bombing of German cities by the English-speaking Allies, of the expulsion of Germans from the east, and of the abuse they ostensibly suffered at the hands of the victors has been passed down from generation to generation. The discourse on German suffering after the end of the Cold War leads one to suspect that these memories might have found a place in German collective memory. Bill Niven's impression is that

> the depressing corollary of such conclusions is that memory of German perpetration, guilt and the suffering of Nazi victims, however intensely cultivated in school education or in acts of commemoration in the 1980s and the 1990s, did not percolate down to the level of family memory. Equally depressing is the thought that the current explosion of memory of German victimhood in the public realm might represent the triumph of the private over the public, of emotion over enlightenment, and of uncritical empathy over pedagogy.[19]

A not insignificant number of participants in the discourse of suffering completely remove questions of guilt and responsibility from their historical context and the circumstances in which they took place. This can be seen by the presence of claims whose origin lie in Nazi and *völkisch* narratives. Also disturbing is the fact that, alongside the amplification of this discourse, there has been a corresponding and relentless increase in antisemitism and racial violence and in anti-Americanism in Germany.[20] The phenomena may well be linked.

Furthermore, while the discourse calls up ghosts of the 1950s, it takes place in an utterly different political and social reality. When the Federal Republic was young, only a small minority disputed the consensus, and the representatives of central political movements spoke scandalously without encountering any response or criticism. At that time, German revisionism regarding the Potsdam treaty had very concrete political goals—the revision of Germany's eastern borders. The current revival of the mood of the 1950s is restricted for the time being to memory politics, and in some cases also to (usually unsuccessful) legal attempts to regain personal and collective German property in Eastern Europe. It has elicited a lively debate within a modern civil society, and has encountered opposition and even condemnation from well-known public figures, prominent historians, and various groups within the political culture. Nevertheless, in many circles, the discourse of suffering finds not only support but has become the fashionable view that participants in the discussion cannot comfortably dispute. German political culture and the German state still cultivate today a revisionist memory of central historical events of the twentieth century and the end of the Second World War, which contradict the memory of these same historical events in other national memories.

Today's Federal Republic of Germany is a stable democratic state. Today's German society has undergone profound political, cultural, and mental changes since the 1950s. An affluent Western society of a liberal and pluralist cast flourishes in the former West Germany. This atmosphere radiates into most parts of the country's east, where a younger generation molded by democracy has arisen, even if the older generations have not undergone socialization into the democratic regime. No longer can former Nazis be found in the country's elites as in the past.[21]

While neo-Nazis and the radical right[22] are actively involved in the current discourse of German suffering, their belligerent, aggressive style, which includes denial of the suffering of victims of the Nazis and of the Holocaust, has been rejected by the majority of participants in the discussion. Indeed, the parties of the extreme right (which are only in theory not neo-Nazi) have not succeeded in gaining enough votes to enter the federal parliament. However, since reunification they have succeeded in gaining representation in two state legislatures in the former East Germany—in Saxony (2004) and in Mecklenburg-Western Pomerania (*Vorpommern*) (2006). Some of the tens of thousands who voted for these parties of contemptible ideology were members of the lower strata of society whose plight had been neglected in the age of liberalization, rapid privatization, and cutbacks in the welfare state. It is clear today, however, that these people did not cast one-time protest votes, but in fact have a long history of identification with the ideas of the radical right. This voting pattern has become a fixture on the eastern German political landscape.[23] If the current trend continues, neo-Nazis might sit in the Bundestag in the not-too-distant future.

The NPD publicly displayed its contempt for the memory of the Nazis' victims when its faction walked out of the Saxonian Lantag in Dresden during a moment of silence observed as part of a Holocaust Memorial Day ceremony in January 2005. The walkout was widely covered by the international media. This scandal is a warning against underestimating the capability of such a small minority faction to influence German political culture. Even though the Federal Office for the Protection of the Constitution (*Verfassungsschutz,* the German security service) keeps an eye on the party, the NPD operates in the open and uses sophisticated means to disseminate its hate propaganda under the protection of the law, with the use of public funds.

It is difficult to predict whether the public discourse of Germans as a nation of World War II victims will become a fixture that will shape German memory of the war and will perhaps even find a place in the mainstream of German historical writing, when the last members of the generation that experienced the war have passed on. But institutionalization of the revisionist memory of the expulsion might well leave an imprint on German culture and memory.

This may be a temporary trend in the public mood and especially in published opinion, a counter-reaction to the ways of talking about Nazism that gradually took form among many educated West Germans since the beginning of the 1960s. That was itself a reaction to the discourse of the 1950s. Gerd Koenen called the period between 1967 and 1977 "our red decade."[24] That period continued to influence attitudes to Nazism during the 1980s, until reunification. If in the "red decade" these circles perceived the private as political and many chose to identify with anti-Nazi fighters and the Nazis' victims rather than with their parents, in the 1990s the pendulum swung the other way. Now the political has become private, and even the Nazi past, perceived and portrayed from the allegedly nonpolitical standpoint of its contemporaries (usually a member of the immediate family, best a grandmother, mother, or adult civilian, but sometimes also a Wehrmacht soldier) is discussed without the ostensibly anachronistic moral and political judgment of the "red decade." Perhaps this tendency will, like its predecessor, produce a counter-reaction that will return the discussion to a less sentimental and more critical track.

Either way, even if this is a temporary phenomenon, in the age of globalization this German revisionist history is being disseminated outside Germany at a rapid pace, reaching wider audiences than ever before, certainly in comparison with the 1950s.[25] So if the current wave comes to an end in Germany itself, it will still have an independent existence elsewhere. The discourse of universal suffering during World War II seems to be penetrating even Israel, a land regarding itself as the home of the Holocaust's victims. On a recent Holocaust Memorial Day, one of Israel's commercial television stations broadcast not only programs about the Holocaust, as had always been the practice, but also a film about Hiroshima. Apparently, the person responsible for the program thought that this nuclear catastrophe was also an integral part of the Holocaust.

NOTES

Introduction

1. Schwake 2008.
2. Oren 2002b.
3. Ibid.; Wimmer 2002.
4. "Begin: Ha-Metziyut Mar'eh she-Eskol u-Memshalto Ainam Mesugalim Lenahel 'Inyanei ha-Uma."
5. Conrad 1999, 186–290; 207–208.
6. See, for example, Hartmann 2004, 1–75.
7. Bartov 1991; Bartov 2005, 374–388.
8. Bartov 2005, 374–388; Bessel 2004.
9. Overmans 1999, 228, 265–266, 278–279; Blank 2004, 357ff.; Haar 2006: the number of victims of flight and expulsion from the territories east of the line of the Oder and Neisse Rivers is estimated to be 400,000, while about 16,000 Germans from Sudetenland were killed or died in the aftermath of World War II.
10. Corneliβen 2003, 548.
11. Fritzsche 2002, 140–162.
12. Jarausch and Sabrow 2002, 9ff.
13. Jarausch 2002, 140–162.
14. Diner 2000, 173–182.
15. Corneliβen 2002, 78ff: "The historian Peter Rassov: 'We are not poets, but we speak from within our people, for our people'"; Jessen 2002, 163: "The historian Paul Kluke, director of the Institute of Contemporary History in Munich (IfZ): 'In his writing, the historian is like a physician and teacher for his people.'"
16. Jessen 2002, 166–171.
17. Frei 2005c, 45–49; Broszat and Friedländer 1988, 7–8; 12–13; 20–22; 25–26; 29–30; 40–42. Friedländer (p. 41): "For us a kind of purely scientific distancing from that past, that is, a passage from the realm of knowledge strongly influenced by personal memory to that of some kind of 'detached' history, remains, in my opinion, a psychological and epistemological illusion." The historian Konrad Jarausch does not accept Friedländer's critique, in which he perceives a misunderstanding of the need

for emotional distance from the event and its detachment from the present, for the purposes of critical analysis; Jarausch 2002, 33.

18. Cornelißen 2003, 550.

1. Coping with Guilt

1. Volk 1983, vol. 4; 498: Dr. Kottmann ad den Diözesan Klerus, May 25, 1945.
2. Löffler 1988, vol. 2 (1939–1946), 1038.
3. Eberan 1983.
4. Breitman and Laquer 1994.
5. Janowitz 1946, 142; Laurie 1996, 180–181. The U.S. Overseas Office of War Information (OWI) avoided and played down reports on the Holocaust until the last month of the war; Breitman 1998, 155–158. For example, the BBC broadcast a report about the Nazi policy toward Jews on December 27, 1942.
6. Manoschek 1995, 475–503; Longerich 2006.
7. Reifahrth and Schmidt-Linsenhoff 1995.
8. Kulka and Jäckel 2004, 20–21.
9. Noelle and Neumann 1997, 187.
10. Kulka and Jäckel 2004; see, for example, the position taken by the important historian Martin Broszat in 1987:

> When viewed retrospectively, one historical fact most juxtaposed to the centrality of Auschwitz: namely, that the liquidation of the Jews was only feasible during the period of time in which it actually was carried out specifically because that liquidation was not in the limelight of events, but rather could largely be concealed and kept quiet. Such concealment was possible because this destruction involved a minority which even many years before had been systematically removed from the field of vision of the surrounding non-Jewish world as a result of social ghettoization. The ease with which the centrality of the "Final Solution" was carried out became a possibility because the fate of the Jews constituted a little noticed matter of secondary importance for the majority of Germans during the war.

Broszat and Friedländer 1988, 21. On the Holocaust and young German historians in the Federal Republic of Germany, see Berg 2003a.

11. Friedländer 1997, 310.
12. Mommsen 1988, 186.
13. Friedländer 1997, 308–310; Mommsen 1991, 237.
14. See, for example, Kulka and Jäckel 2004, 522.
15. Kershaw 1979, vol. 2, 339; Kulka and Jäckel 2004, 510.
16. Volk 1983, vol. 4, 210–215.
17. Portmann 1957, 246.
18. Meier 1968, 122. In December 1943, the Protestant bishop of Hanover, August Marahrens, wrote to the interior minister about the persecution of Christians of Jewish origin. He requested that the authorities see to it that "necessary political and policy measures not be stained with harsh injustice by irresponsible individuals, who will impose a burden on the conscience of our nation, which it will not be able to bear." It should be noted that Marahrens is a very controversial figure and his attitude to Nazism was equivocal. In 1939, he was among the signers of a document that

stated that the National Socialist worldview was incumbent on German Christians. See Mommsen 1988, 185–186; Vollnhals 1989, 30.

19. Kershaw 1981, 285.

20. Bankier 1992, 105.

21. Kershaw 1979, 341f. See the SD reports in Kulka and Jäckel 2004, 528; 531 (from Würzburg, July 27, 1943); 529 (from Weigolshausen, August 13, 1943); 531, 533, and 537 (from Schweinfurt, September 6, 1943, October 11, 1943, and 1944); 532 (from Rotenburg, October 22, 1943); and 546 and 547 (from Berlin, November 29, 1944, and March 31, 1945). See Stargardt 2007, 252.

22. Bankier 1992, 105, 147; Kulka and Jäckel 2004, 531. See also Brockmann 2004, 30.

23. Francois and Schulze 2001, 569.

24. Gordon 1984, 267; Kulka and Jäckel 2004, 544.

25. Mommsen 1991, 226.

26. Bankier 1992, 149–150; Geyer 1999, 131–132; Bankier 2004, 55–76; Stargardt 2007, 251.

27. Manoschek 1995, 79; Stargardt 2007, 265 emphasizes the regret of the harsh treatment of Jews, vis à vis the defeat.

28. Thiessen 2007, 74–76.

29. Niethammer 1990, 126ff.

30. Padover 1946, 95–96. Frau Ferwents, an old German teacher interviewed by Padover, asserted that "[the Jews] are the enemies of the German people and mankind," but maintained at the same time that "I believe what it says in the Bible: Thou shalt not kill, except in battle. The Jews were not at war with us, so we had no right to kill them."

31. Amishai-Maisels 1992, 180.

32. Golgotha (the Place of the Skull) is the site of the crucifixion in Jerusalem: Matthew 27:33; Mark 15:23; Luke 23:33.

33. Amishai-Maisels 1992, 180.

34. Niemöller 1946b, 9.

35. Wasserstein 1982, 146.

36. Jaspers 1946, 7.

37. Brockmann 2004, 25–28.

38. See Volkmer von Zühlsdorff in Broch 1986, 35.

39. Mann 1995, 58.

40. Wasserstein 1982, 249–250; Kochavi 2002, 20–26.

41. Janowitz 1946, 141.

42. Bodemann 1998, 63–72; Eberan 1983, 19ff.; Ruhl 1980, 148ff.; Jaspers 1946, 25; Chamberlin 1981, 420–438; Weckel 2005, 282–318.

43. Padover 1946, 111.

44. Posener 2002, 28–29; "Aufruf des ZK der KPD vom 11. Juni 1945." In Berthold and Diehl 1965, 191, 193.

45. See chapters 3 and 5.

46. Only a minority in the Catholic Church, such as Bishop Konrad Prysing of Berlin and the circle of Gertrud Luckner of Freiburg, accepted the guilt thesis; see Phayer 1996; Phayer 1995.

47. Löffler 1988, vol. 2, 1939–1946; e.g., 1032.

48. Prolingheuer 1987, 77ff.

49. The Jacobins were the extremist French revolutionary party that executed King Louis XVI and instituted the Reign of Terror.

50. Prolingheuer 1987, 77ff.

51. Moskowitz 1946, 10.

52. Friedländer 1997, 45–46.

53. See Niemöller's letter attacking Wurm's speech at Treysa, in which the bishop expressed his satisfaction with the Protestant Church's behavior during the Third Reich, Stuttgart D1, 225. Landeskirches Archiv.

54. *Kirchliches Jahrbuch*, 12.

55. EZA 1985/76: Niemöller 1946a, 6–7.

56. According to Bishop Otto Dibelius, Niemöller was responsible for inserting this sentence into the declaration; Vollnhals 1989, 35.

57. Greschat 1982, 100.

58. See, for example, a letter dated August 31, 1945, sent by the Catholic welfare organization, Caritas, the Interior Mission, and the German Red Cross to the Allied governing council: "According to the announcement of the Berlin Conference on July 17, 1945 [referring to the opening of the Potsdam conference], the Allies have no intention of destroying the German people. However, today in the German East actions are taking place that reveal that a large portion of the German nation is being annihilated [*Vernichtung*]." Volk 1983, vol. 6, 712.

59. See Barth's position on how the statement regarding guilt should have been formulated; Vollnhals 1989, 35f.

60. See the discussions of the question of guilt in the Protestant Church: Stern 1992, 303ff.; Greschat 1982.

61. Greschat 1982, 225f.

62. Posener 2002, 28.

63. Vollnhals 1989, 34.

64. Posener 2002, 34.

65. Weiss 1998, 241–242.

66. Zentralarchiv der Evang. Kirche in Hessen und Nassau 62/0540.

67. Weiss 1998, 241–242.

68. See the response of the Berlin Protestant clergyman, Provost Heinrich Grüber, to these charges. Grüber had been incarcerated by the Nazis at Sachsenhausen, and on Christmas 1949 visited the Germans imprisoned there by the Soviets. In his report, he refutes the charges that the treatment of the German prisoners resembled Nazi treatment of concentration camp prisoners, with which he was well acquainted. Zentralarchiv der Evang. Kirche in Hessen und Nassau 62/0592: Probst Heinrich Grüber, "Sachsenhausen 1940–1949."

69. Niemöller 1946c, 9.

70. Zentralarchiv der Evang. Kirche in Hessen und Nassau 35/377.

71. See Martin Niemöller's letter to his brother, Wilhelm, on this subject, November 9, 1945, Zentralarchiv der Evang. Kirche in Hessen und Nassau 62/0671.

72. Jaspers 2000, 112ff.

73. Vollnhals 1989, 52ff.

74. EZA: 79/2787, 35–42.

75. Niemöller 1946c, 44.

76. Stern 1992, 101f.

77. Jaspers 2000, 67.

78. Undset, *Neue Zeitung*, October 25, 1945; Glaser 1986, 75–76.

79. Jaspers 1965, 47ff.

80. Jaspers 2000, 57; Hartmann 2004, 1–75. Hartmann estimates that the number of criminals among the Wehrmacht's soldiers was some 150,000, but his findings are disputed by many historians. On this subject see Bartov 2005, 377; Bartov 1991, 152–166. On the involvement of police auxiliaries in crimes see Goldhagen 1996, 181–280; Browning 1998. On another aspect of broad public involvement in the theft of Jewish property, Bajohr estimated in his study on the Aryanization campaign in Hamburg that at least 100,000 inhabitants of the city and its surroundings purchased below-cost property in France and the Low Countries taken from Jews who were sent to their deaths at Auschwitz; see Bajohr 1997, 334; Bajohr 1998, 198–201; Aly 2005b, 139–158.

81. Jaspers 2000, 25f.

82. See, for example, a report by the Social Democratic Party in Exile (SOPADE) from December 1938 about such responses, in Peukert 1987, 59: "Berlin: . . . when the Jewish synagogue was burning . . . a large number of women could be heard saying, 'That's the right way to do it—it's a pity there aren't any more Jews inside, that would be the best way to smoke out the whole lousy lot of them.'—No one dared to take a stand against these sentiments."

83. Jaspers 2000, 34f.

84. Reichel 2001, 70–72; on Jaspers's behavior in a scandal regarding the de-Nazification process at the University of Heidelberg in 1945, see Clark 2002, 203–209.

85. Moeller 1996, 1008–1048; Benz 1990, 1–12; Diner 2000, 177–186; Foschepoth 1997, 73–78.

86. Niemöller 1946a, 5.

87. Herbert 2000, 4; Frei 2005c, 45–49.

88. Moskowitz 1946, 7–8.

89. Janowitz 1946, 141–146.

90. Dubiel 1999, 71ff.; Frei 2005c, 145–155.

91. Such arguments were also commonly used by top Nazi officials. Robert H. Lochner, who had interviewed many of them in 1945 as a member of OMGUS, testified in a 1998 interview to the National Security Archive: http://www.gwu.edu/~nsarchiv/coldwar/interviews/episode-4/lochner1.html: "They all had either of two explanations: a) they would have had to fear for their own life if they had refused to carry on, or b) they stayed because if they left a real Nazi would take their job." "I concluded that there had only been one Nazi in all of Germany and he was conveniently dead. All the others had been against it."

92. Posener 2002, 24–25; See also Giordano 1990, 33.

93. *Trends in German Public Opinion 1946–1949*, Office of U.S. High Commissioner for Germany Office of Public Affairs. Reactions Analysis Staff, Report No. 51, 2.4.1947, 149.

94. On the dimensions of public participation in looting of Jewish property, see note 79 above.

95. Greschat 1982, 113–114. Emphasis in original.

96. Very typical of this is Volkmar von Zühlsdorff's position. He rejected any claim about popular support for the anti-Jewish policy. Moreover, Zühlsdorff even

maintained that despite the terror of the Gestapo, 40 percent of the Germans risked their lives to help the persecuted Jews: Broch 1986, 111.

97. Thomas Mann to Agnes E. Meyer, March 29, 1945, April 24, 1945; Mann 1963, 421ff., 428ff.

98. Posener 2002, 138ff.

99. Middlebrook 1981, 352.

100. Goes 1954, 62.

101. Ibid., 70.

102. Weiss 1998, 455.

103. Ibid., 8.

104. Posener 2002, 28f.

105. Brendler 1997, 53–104.

106. Wolffsohn and Brechenmacher 1999, 288–290.

107. For an incisive critique of this phenomenon, see Geissel 1992, 13ff., 23–34.

2. Remembering National Suffering in World War II

1. On the victim motif in *völkisch* circles see Hahn 2005, 219–224.

2. Szarota 1998.

3. Rothfels 1960, 1ff.

4. For Hans-Christoph Seebohm's interpretation regarding the origins of World War II in 1919, see Eschenburg 1960a.

5. Deutsches Museum, Archiv NL Anton Zischka 184–190: A Lecture of Zischka at the Deutsche Haus in Palma de Majorca, May 15, 1940.

6. A number of literary pieces with the title *German Passion* appeared in Germany during the last years of the Weimar Republic and the early years of the Third Reich. All were written by *völkisch* authors and, while referring to various historical periods, all emphasized the suffering of the German people, for example, Hohlbaum 1924, Hahn 2005, Bazan 1934, and the trilogy of Edwin Erich Dwinger (1929–1932). In 1940 Dwinger published another title containing the term "passion" on the suffering and atrocities inflicted on Germans in Poland.

7. Euringer 1933, 23, 25, 27. Several other works with similar names were produced by nationalists and Nazis during the Weimar Republic; see Hahn 2005.

8. Deutsches Museum, Archiv NL Anton Zischka 184-083-Anton Zischka, "Die Hunnen von 1940," September 1942, 12.

9. Longerich 2006, 201f.

10. Domarus 2004, 2993.

11. Fritzsche 1998, 13–82.

12. Norbisrath 2000, 8–14. During the war's initial months, there were frequent rumors about an impending ceasefire or peace treaty. The pervasiveness of such rumors is an indication of how unpopular the war was and how much the German public wanted, as early as the autumn of 1939, to see it ended. See Boberach 1984, vol. 2, 339f. and 347f.: report on the interior-political situation in Nazi Germany (Nos. 2, 3), October 11, 13, 1939.

13. From a propaganda film on the bombing of Warsaw and the conquest of Poland: *Feuertaufe. Der Film vom Einsatz unserer Luftwaffe im polnischen Feldzug*, a film by Hans Bertram, 1939/1940.

14. Domarus 2004, 2993; Bundesarchiv Koblenz: Sammlung Oberheitmann—Zsg. 109, Vertraulich Informationen (V.I.) des Reichsministerium für Volksaufklärung und Propaganda für die Presse No. 163/43, July 4, 1943; No. 157/43; No. 212/43, August 31, 1943, Bl. 73; Süβ 2007, 212ff.

15. Geyer 1999, esp. 131–132.

16. Kochavi 2002, 138ff., 164–171, esp. 167.

17. Borsdorf and Jamin 1989; Groehler 1992b.

18. DRA 2945653 PK-Bericht: Dresden nach den alliierten Bombenangriffen, February 20, 1945; see Süβ 2007, 212–216, about the change that had taken place in the reporting of the Nazi press about the Allied attack on Dresden; "Trotz Terror: Wir bleiben hart," *Der Freiheitskampf (Dresdner Zeitung)* February 16, 1945: "British aerial gangsters have in three terror attacks destroyed irreplaceable memorials and cultural buildings, such as the Dresden residential quarters." See the response to Nazi propaganda by Golo Mann, son of Thomas Mann, then a U.S. soldier, in an American propaganda broadcast to Germany: Mann 2005, Lahme 2005.

19. Brandt 1971, 109; Robert Lochner reported on a similar impression (National Security Archive: http://www.gwu.edu/~nsarchiv/coldwar/interviews/episode-4/lochner1.html): "After a certain level of intensive and indiscriminate bombing a sort of identification sets in between the Nazis and the non-Nazis. The non-Nazis shake their fists as angrily at the planes, who obviously cannot make a distinction between them and the Nazis."

20. Prenzlauer Berg Museum des Kulturamtes Berlin Prenzlauer Berg 1996, 70f.

21. See, for example, *Die Deutsche Wochenschau* of March 22, 1945.

22. Johr 2005, 48ff.

23. Niethammer 1990, 126ff.; Grossmann 1997, 33–52; Hörning 1985, 327–344; Moeller 1996, 1037ff.; Heineman 1996; Mühlhäser 2001.

24. Jünger 1980, 498 (June 30, 1945).

25. See also Bessel 2004, 183ff.

26. Schieder et al. 1955, 23E.

27. Schwartz 2008, 128.

28. Haar 2007; Haar 2006; Moeller 1996, 1008–1048; Auerbach 1995, 285–286; "Die Deutschen als Opfer," 50; personal reports of the suffering of ordinary Germans are documented in a monumental four-volume work, Kempowski 1999, vol. 3, 54ff.

29. "6 Millionen ermordete Deutsche."

30. Kossert 2008, 71–86, although the title he gave the chapter dealing with the attitudes of the West Germans to the expellees reads: "German Racism against German Expellees." Only a small number of the examples he mentions are typical of racist character. Most of the examples reflect rejection toward the expellees based on social grounds, fears of the economic implications of their arrival for the native German population, and unwillingness to share with them the relatively limited quantity of goods and work places. Nevertheless, there is no doubt that Kossert portrays a clear lack of Christian charity among fellow Germans toward the expellees.

31. For example, Hoffmann and Schwartz 1999; Schraut and Grosser 1996.

32. Wierling 1990, 195–197.

33. Schwartz 2008, 101–102.

34. Habenicht 1996, 225.

35. Ibid., 123.

36. Schildt 2007, 224–225.

37. Niemöller 1946b, 5; see Barnett 1992, 155ff. and esp. 159 about the attitudes during the war and its aftermath of leading members of the Confessing Church toward the war itself, service in the Wehrmacht, and fallen soldiers. Many tended to make distinctions between National Socialism and the patriotic duty to serve their nation at war; see Barnett 1992, 162ff.

38. Dorothee Wierling and Harald Welzer stress the central place of suffering and the sense of German victimhood in the experiences of the postwar generation both in Communist East Germany and in the Federal Republic, and the intergenerational transfer of this content: Wierling 2002a, 21–23; Welzer, Moller, and Tschuggnall 2002, 86–91, 141, 205.

39. See Welzer 2005, 198–215.

40. Overmans 1999, 228, 265; Biess 2006, 19ff.

41. Adorno 1956, 121–324.

42. Stern 1992, 28–29. Similar reactions were registered in early public opinion surveys of the U.S. occupation forces. At least some of the returning POWs interviewed about their responses to Allied films depicting concentration camps such as *Mills of Death* voiced the opinion "that all the dead bodies 'were all killed by Anglo-American bombs and anti-aircraft shells,'" and "conditions in concentration camps were no worse than those imposed on refugees from the east." OMGUS, Daily Intelligence Digest no. 158, May 2, 1946, "Reactions to KZ Film," National Archive, OMGUS, Information Control Division, Opinion Surveys Branch, box 146, file 20, "Daily Intelligence Digest, 1 April–20 June 1946." I am grateful to Robert G. Moeller for referring me to these documents.

43. Kucklick 2003, 147.

44. Landeskirchliches Archiv Stuttgart: D1.225, April 20, 1946.

45. See Rosenberg's comparison of Auschwitz and Majdanek with the expulsion of the Germans from the east: Hahn and Hahn 2005, 199; "What the Allies did to the Germans is no less horrible than the killing of those Jews. The bombings of cities in which men, women and children went up in phosphorous flames are things done by the Allies"; see, e.g., Karl Dönitz in Goldensohn 2004, 66. And see Martin Heidegger's letter to his former student, Herbert Marcuse, January 20, 1948, http://www.marcuse.org/herbert/pubs/40spubs/47MarcuseHeidegger.htm#mh, in which he defended himself against Marcuse's accusation that he had collaborated with the Nazis. With regard to Nazism's crimes, the philosopher argued that after 1945 the Allies had done the same to the Germans from the east, and that the only difference was that the Nazis had concealed the bloody terror they inflicted on the German people, whereas the Allies acted openly, with the knowledge of the world's public. For Ernst Jünger's comparison of Nazi atrocities to the deportation of Germans from the east, see Jünger 1980, 473–474, 498, 580; Brockmann 2004, 30. However, in summer 1943, "Jünger confirmed the existence of a deeply felt sense of communal guilt in a journal entry he made."

46. Volk 1978, 1071:

> For long weeks, representatives of the American press and American soldiers arrived in Dachau and immortalized the horrors in photographs and films, with the goal of showing the entire world, down to the furthest Negro village (*Negerdorf*), the shame and disgrace of the German people. If they were to present

> the terrible suffering caused by the American and British aerial bombardment of Munich and other cities, those pictures would be just as disturbing. I mean that, just as they did at Dachau, it was possible to photograph and film tens of thousands of dead bodies lying in the streets and at the entrances to the cellars, after being buried under them, burned, or torn to pieces in the aerial bombings. Humanity would be no less shocked by the sight of these horrors.

47. Conway 1987, 611; see also note 45 to chapter 1.

48. For more on the correspondence between Volkmar von Zühlsdorf and Hermann Broch, see Broch 1986, 110; Aschheim 1996, 85–96, esp. 91. In many of Zühlsdorff's letters to Broch he reiterates his claim that the Allies were pursuing a criminal Nazi extermination policy against the German people; see, for example, Broch 1986, 63, 65. He attributed a decisive influence to Jewish figures in the United States such as Secretary of the Treasury Henry Morgenthau and Bernard Baruch with regard to Allied policy toward Germany and the Germans, and argued that Morgenthau sought to kill 20 million German; see Broch 1986, 112. In one of his letters he called this "Roosevelt-Morgenthau Nazism"; see Broch 1986, 139; see also Aschheim 1996, 91ff.

49. Berg 2003b.

50. Bundesarchiv Berlin, DY 55 V278/2/13 Bl. 8 Dr. Hanns Lilje, November 1945.

51. Hahn 2005, 226, 299; see also 224–229, as well as Alfred Andersh in the newspaper *Der Ruf*, December 1946, quoted in Briegleb 2003, 240:

> The German guilt account is gradually beginning to close. The basic guilt for the war borne by the German leadership, and the crimes it committed, has been compensated for, certainly not by deliberate acts of revenge, but rather through the surfeit of suffering that has come upon Germany, apparently as a natural consequence of such utter guilt. The physical and psychic implications of bombardments belong to this, as do the expulsion of 10 million Germans from their homes in the east, the state of nourishment and the black market, the cold, and the diseases that assail us under its auspices, and the Babylonian captivity of millions of former soldiers. The destruction or paralysis of industry. . . .

52. Schildt 2007, 233.

53. Löffler 1988, vol. 2 (1939–1946), 1100.

54. Niemöller 1946b, 13.

55. For example: A title of a bulletin of German expellees from Karlovi-Vary (Karlsbad) in Czechoslovakia: Zimmer 1949, 3. On June 30, 1945, Ernst Jünger wrote in his diary (Jünger 1980, 49): "We know that there [in the east] one of the greatest passions is taking place." And see "Deutsche Passion," the title of a newspaper article (Klausing 1946) that attributed the term to the bombing and destruction of the city of Pforzheim, as well as Reichengbergert 1948.

56. Zentralarchiv der Evangelischen Kirche in Hessen und Nassau 62 Akzi 0722 Helmuth Thielicke, "Karfreitag 1947—Die Passion ohne Gnade."

57. For example, Evangelische Zentralarchiv in Berlin: 666/ 90 Pfarrer Rudolf Weckerling, "Evangelische Morgenfeier," RIAS Berlin, October 8, 1950; Weckerling was a young member of the Confessing Church during the Third Reich; see Barnett 1992, 161.

58. Melendy 2005, 108, 123.

59. Reimann 1954, 258.

60. Zentralarchiv der evangelischen Kirche in Hessen und Nassau 62/0003: Otto von Harling to Martin Niemöller, November 8, 1947.

61. Stern 1992, 276ff.

62. *Kirchliches Jahrbuch* 1949, 224–227.

63. Rubenstein and Roth 2003, 338–339. See Kulka and Jäckel 2004, 539, and a similar statement from the Catholic bishop of Eichstätt, Dr. Michael Rackl, in March 1944.

64. Stern 1992, 279f.

65. *Kirchliches Jahrbuch* 1949, 5–7.

66. Barnett 1992, 159–161.

67. Rieth 1955.

68. Holze 1992, 14f.

69. Plagemann 1986, 164; Schoenfeld 2000, 129.

70. Spence 1962.

71. Eich and Vastag 2002, 23 (Essingen/Ostalbkreis), 69 (Uhingen, Kreis Göppingen).

72. Schirmer 1988, 164, 306.

73. Ibid.

74. Kappel 2005, 30.

75. "Der Turm der alten Kirche soll an das Gericht Gottes erinnern, das in den Jahren des Krieges über unsere Volk herein brach."

76. Grünberg 1997, 47–60.

77. Volk 1983, vol. 4 (1943–1945), 178.

78. Padover 1946, 118: "No one criticized aggression as such. The only criticism was of aggression that failed. Hitler is blamed for losing the war, not for starting it."

79. For the origins of ties between Christians in war-damaged cities (Coventry and Dresden), see "Weihnachtsworte an Coventry"; "Eine christliche Aktion in England." See an article in *Neues Deutschland* about the initiation connections, with a politically leftist bent, between unions and cities councils: Richter 1965, 5; Neutzner 2005, 154–155. With regard to the missive sent by Poland's Catholic bishops to their German colleagues in 1965, in which the authors granted forgiveness for the crimes committed by Germany in Poland, and also asked for forgiveness for the deportation of the Germans, see Heller 1992.

80. Germany's newspapers and politicians regularly complain that the British view of their country and citizens has not changed since World War II. See the grievance of Matthias Matussek, a journalist who served as *Der Spiegel* correspondent in Britain, after the ceremonies marking the sixtieth anniversary of the war's end, "My personal VE Day," http://www.opendemocracy.net/themes/article-2-2485.jsp. See also an article in *Bild*, Germany's largest magazine: "Briten beschimpfen Deutsche."

3. German Memory and Remembrance of the Dead from 1945 to the 1960s

1. On master narratives, see Jarausch and Sabrow 2002, 3–9.

2. See, for example, Dregger 1986, a speech by Alfred Dregger, chairman of the CDU/CSU parliamentary faction in Bonn, on the public popular memorial day.

3. Kittel 2007, 31–57. Kittel vividly describes the ambivalent process of change which has taken place since the late 1950s in the West German media regarding the

expulsion of the Germans from the east, a central component of the German narrative of suffering following World War II. However, he sees the change deriving from a German response to the aggressive Soviet measures since 1956, totally disregarding the penetration of the Jewish narrative and the growing awareness of the suffering the Germans inflicted on Russians, Poles, and Czechs in this process.

4. Frei 2008, 79ff.
5. Schildt 1998, 45ff.; Lemke 1993, 153–174.
6. "Minister Oberländer unter schwerem Verdacht."
7. Hoffman 1964.
8. Schwarz 1959; Becker 1960.
9. Laak 2002, 163–193.
10. Foreign Minister Vyacheslav Molotov repeated these words at a meeting of foreign ministers in Paris, July 10, 1946; Eberan 1983, 20.
11. See Pieck's speeches from 1942 to 1945: Pieck 1979, 90–92, 271–275, 363–366.
12. Fulbrook 1998, 55–56; Janowitz 1946, 146.
13. "Schaffendes Volk in Stadt und Land! Mäner und Frauen! Deutsche Jugend!" (Aufruf des ZK der KPD vom 11 Juni 1945), in Berthold and Diehl 1965, 191ff.; Hass 1999, 1100–1112.
14. "Erste Vollsizung des Hauptausschusses 'Opfer des Faschismus'"; "Zuschriften aus dem Leserkreis: Opfer des Faschismus"; Groehler 1992, 42–43.
15. Emmerich 1997, 133f.; Braese 2001, 480–483.
16. Weckel 2000, 105–115; Hartewig 2000, 240; see also Stern 2005, 178ff.
17. Berthold and Diehl 1965, 129ff.
18. Ibid., 191, 201.
19. For a characteristic treatment of the service of one of the party's leaders, Ernst Thälmann, in the Weimar Republic, in the imperial army in World War I, and in the October program of the Spartacists, see Thälmann 1935, 25; Berthold and Diehl 1965, 101–106.
20. Blaensdorf, 1995, 27ff.; Staritz 1995, 214–215.
21. Wierling 2002a, 21–23; Wierling, 2002b, 47–59.
22. Welzer, Moller, and Tschuggnall 2002, 86–91.
23. Danyel 1999a, 186. See also: Leonhard 1957, 357ff.
24. Memorandum der Kommission des ZK der KPdSU(B) in Bonwetsch, Bordjugov, and Naimark 1998, 275.
25. Amos 1999, 19–30.
26. Danyel 1999b, 1145f.; Danyel 1995, 42ff.
27. On the process of the Communist Party's "demise" in West Germany after 1945, see Major 1997.
28. Lemke 2001, 114–120.
29. Wenzke 1999, 1117f.; Daniel 1999b, 1142f.
30. Hoffmann et al. 1993, 48.
31. Danyel 1999a, 182–184, 194.
32. Nationalrat der Nationalen Front der demokratischen Deutschland, 15. In his speech to the Reichstag on January 30, 1933, Adolf Hitler expressed similar sentiments: "France for the French, England for the English, America for the Americans, and Germany for the Germans." See Friedländer 1997, 310.
33. "Unser Künstlerporträt: Martin Hellberg," 5.

34. Lemke 2001, 120ff.; Gassert 1997, 309ff., esp. 363; Diner 2002, 90ff., 125.

35. On this subject, see the treatment of the Paul Merker episode in Herf 1997, 106–161.

36. Norden 1952, 207. Norden was a hyper-assimilated Jew (his father was a rabbi). See Podewin 2001, esp. 13–36; Herf 1997, 175–176.

37. Volksbund Deutsche Kriegsgräberfürsorge e.V 1952, 5: "They fought, doubted, suffered for us, they died for us. They were people like us."

38. Biess 2006, 126–152.

39. Seghers 1981, 214.

40. Bundesarchiv-Filmarchiv: *Das verurteilte Dorf* 1952; Schittly 2002, 62–64.

41. Behrenbeck 2003, 52.

42. "Gefallenen-Schändung."

43. The Volksbund was responsible for military cemeteries in the Federal Republic, but was not allowed to act in the GDR. However, the organization's headquarters in the Federal Republic offered unofficial assistance to private individuals in the GDR who cared for the graves of German soldiers killed in World War II. After reunification, the Volksbund opened branches in the east.

44. Pietsch, Potratz, and Stark 1995, 58–76.

45. Biess 2006, 130–134.

46. Groehler 1994, 282–285; Goschler 1993, 93–96.

47. Goschler 1993, 96; Kessler and Peter 1995, 611–632, esp. 614–615.

48. Azaryahu 1991.

49. Institut für Denkmalpflege in der DDR 1974; Frank 1970.

50. For Buchenwald, see Overesch 1995.

51. Reichel 1995, 129–149; Fulbrook 1998, 28–35; Kessler and Peter 1995, 623–624.

52. Stölzl 1993, 77–78.

53. Landesarchiv Berlin: C. Rep. 101 No. 351, Magistrat von Gross Berlin, Abt. Aufbau Herren Oberbürgermeister Ebert 11.8.1950.

54. Bundesarchiv Berlin: DY 30 /JIV 2/3 A/167 Prottokol No. 57 der Sitzung des Sekretariats des ZK am April 5, 1951, Bl. 73.

55. Landesarchiv Berlin: C. Rep. 100-05 No. 1119 Beschlusprotokoll der 39.(ordentlichen) Magistratsitzung am February 12, 1960. Bl. 7; Der Oberbürgermeister January 28, 1960, Bl. 73.

56. Landesarchiv Berlin: C. Rep. 901 No. 374, Heinrich Starck An SED Landesvorstand Gross-Berlin, September 16, 1949.

57. Landesarchiv Berlin: C. Rep. 907-04 Nr. 388; Reichel 1995, 231–246; Combe 1992, 141; Assmann and Frevert 1999, 163–166.

58. Stern 1990, 49–50.

59. On the sculpture, see Hoffmann-Curtius 1999, 272–281.

60. On Elkan and his work, see Menzel-Severing 1980.

61. StA Frankfurt: 380 Der Oberbürgermeister an die freie Deutsche Kultur Gesellschaft, December 12, 1945.

62. "Den Unvergessenen."

63. StA Frankfurt: S1 75 Nr. 25, "Ansprach (Eberhard Beckmanns) zur Einweihung des Opferdenkmals von Elkan," April 18, 1946, 6.

64. StA Frankfurt: 2.297, "Denkmal für die Opfer des Faschismus," September 10, 1946; Magistrat Beschluβ, September 13, 1946.

65. "OdF Mahnmal in Frankfurt geschändet" *Frankfurter Rundschau* Nr. 212, September 12, 1949.

66. Billerbeck 1971, 177.

67. Adenauer 1967, 18.

68. Moeller 2001a, 23f.

69. Moeller sarcastically refers to it as *Opferausgleich,* a reference to the *Lastenausgleich*—shared war burden—policy that Adenauer instituted in 1952 to provide aid to those who had suffered injury or loss during the war; Moeller 2001b, 29–30.

70. Deutscher Bundestag, 6. Sitzung vom 21. 9.1949, Stenographische Berichte, vol. 1, 36; Moeller 1996, 1014–1015.

71. Shafir 1987, 51; Jelinek 1990, 77–102.

72. Segev 1994, 201–205; for the text of his speech see Vogel 1967, 35.

73. "Und das Heimweh der Leute nach Deutschland," 41; Elon 1966.

74. "Begin: Ha-Metziyut Mar'eh"; Elon 1966.

75. Konrad Adenauer an Pastor Dr. Bernhard Custodius, Bonn, February 23, 1946, in Adenauer 1983, 172f.

76. Herf 1997, 213ff.

77. Buscher 1990.

78. On Schumacher's support for the integration of people with Nazi pasts, especially young people, both in his party and in the civil service, see Edinger 1967, 135–136. He went so far as to advocate the acceptance of Waffen SS veterans into the SPD; see Buscher 1990, 265.

79. Frei 2002b.

80. Ibid., 310.

81. Heuss 1964, 122.

82. Fischer 1949.

83. For example, Heuss 1940, 20; see also Zühlsdorff's verdict on Heuss in Broch 1986, 145.

84. Heuss 1955, 401.

85. Heuss 1964, 122.

86. For example, Heuss 1967, 54; Stern 1992, 249.

87. On the young Federal Republic's "policy of the past," the sweeping amnesties and the integration of Nazi sympathizers into society, see Frei 2002b. On the prevailing mentality regarding the Nazi past and the war, see in particular Moeller 2002, 123–170.

88. Bald 2005, 18–29.

89. Frohn 1996, 490ff.

90. Frei 2002a, 143–149; Bald 2005, 29–32.

91. Benz 1990, 11; Bald 2005, 30–32; on the popularity of the Wehrmacht generals' position among the German public see Geyer 2001, 283ff.

92. Abenheim 1988, 70; Frei 2002a, 147; Deist 1999, 213; Bald 2005, 34–35.

93. Eisenhower 1948, 280.

94. *Verhandlungen des Deutsche Bundestages I,* 11141.

95. Adorno 1986, 90.

96. Schildt 1999, 106; Kraushaar 1996, 495f.

97. Groh 2000, 56; on the trivialization of German war crimes and war criminals in the early Federal Republic see Schildt 1998, 283ff.; Herbert 1998, 109–112.

98. At this time, the Social Democrats also supported an amnesty for Nazi war criminals, see Buscher 1990, 266–271.

99. Goda 2007, 131.

100. Siegfried 2000, 187ff.; see also Helmut Peitsch's fascinating article on another quantifiable phenomenon—the decline in popularity of antifascist literature in West Germany and the rise in sales of apologetic works by Wehrmacht generals in and around 1950. These works were depicted as authentic and objective accounts of the behavior of these officers and of the Wehrmacht during the war, as opposed to the picture painted by the Nuremburg trials: see Peitsch 1989, 54–59.

101. See the results of a survey conducted in 1992 on this issue: 62 percent of those polled agreed that "46 years after the war's end, we no longer have to speak so much about the persecution of the Jews, and we should finally draw a line over the past." "Mehr verdrängt als bewältigt," 68.

102. Reichel 2001, 182–198.

103. Bodemann 1998, 57–59; Reichel 1995, 154ff.

104. See, for example, the depiction of the Bolshevik enemy's brutality in a propaganda pamphlet containing soldiers' letters from the front in Diewege 1941.

105. Heuss 1955, 402–403.

106. "Fahnen der Trauer wehten am Niederrhein," 77–78.

107. "Soldatenfriedhof Hürtgenwald eingeweiht."

108. Frei 2005a.

109. Ibid.

110. Letter by Marcks to Straus, January 12, 1946, Semrau 1995, 166.

111. Marcks's letter to his friend Felix Weize, June 4, 1946, Semrau 1995, 87.

112. HH Hamburg-Denkmalschutzamt 39–430.308.1 Kulturrat der Hansestadt Hamburg an den Senat, July 7, 1947.

113. Marcks to Grzimek, January 2, 1947, Semrau 1995, 220.

114. On Marcks and his work, see Marcks 1988.

115. Historisches Archiv, Stadt Köln: Acc. 177 Nr. 69.

116. Hoffmann-Curtius 2002, 387; Becker-Jákli 2002, 125, 139.

117. For the Mannheim City Council's discussions of erecting the memorial, see chapter 4.

118. The decision of the Bochum City Council to erect the monument: StA Bochum: BO 41/47 "Auszug aus der Niederschrift No. 30 über Sizung des Kulturausschusses der Stadt Bochum," March 26, 1952.

119. Papenbrock 1998, 231–246.

120. StA Mülheim 90/5 Bl. 16 aus dem Beschlußprotokoll über die Sitzung des Rates der Stadt, October 7, 1954.

121. "Den Opfern der Gewalt," *Mitteilungen der Stadtverwaltung Frankfurt a.M.*, no. 46 (14.11.1959), 443.

122. On Marcks's memorials, see Manske 1989, 271–291.

123. Historisches Archiv, Stadt Köln: Best. 2 Oberbürgermeister No. 1361–1370, Bl. 1–3; "Der Trümmerberg auf dem Birkenkopf."

124. Frei 2004; "Kunst auf dem Wallberg 'fehl am Platz.'"

125. Merritt and Merritt 1970, 32; FO 1005/ 1868 Public Opinion Record Office. Political Division C.C.G. Bielefeld. "Attitude to National-Socialism in the British Zone—April 1948," 99. I am grateful to Prof. Werner Bergmann of the Technical

University Berlin's Center for Anti-Semitism Research for calling these figures to my attention.

126. Aly 2005a.

127. Schildt 2007, 224.

128. Margalit 2002a, 114–115, 126n94.

129. Frei 1995, 127ff.

4. Memorial Days in West Germany and Their Metamorphosis, 1945–2006

1. Petersen 1998, 17–28.

2. See Dönhoff 1946.

3. Evangelisches Zentralarchiv in Berlin 1/ A2/650 Asmussen D.D., Rat der EKD an der Ev. -ref. Landeskirche Aurich 3.3.1946.

4. Evangelisches Zentralarchiv, Berlin EZA 1/A2/650 Ev.-Lutherisches Landeskirchenamt Sachsens Dresden, an die Deutsche Evangelische Kirche Kirchenkanzlei 15.7.1941.

5. Evangelisches Zentralarchiv in Berlin 1/ A2/650 Ev.-ref Landeskirche Aurich an der Kanzlei der EKD, February 26, 1946.

6. For example, Frey 1941.

7. Evangelisches Zentralarchiv, Berlin EZA 1/A2/651 Ev. Oberkirchenrat A.u. H.B. Wien an die Deutsche Evangelische Kirchenkanzlei, December 21, 1942.

8. StA Hamburg, SKII 4634, Herren Senatssyndikus Dr. Sieveking, November 15, 1945, Bl. 1–2; Senatskanzlei an das Garten- und Friedhofsamt, July 1, 1953.

9. Petersen 1998, 9–16.

10. Ibid., 20f.

11. See the correspondence on this: Volksbund Deutsche Kriegsgräberfürsorge e.V.—Landesverband Hamburg, Alte Akten 1915–1968; "Die Wehrmacht sorgt für alle Soldatengräber," *Völkischer Beobachter,* October 18, 1940.

12. Volksbund Deutsche Kriegsgräberfürsorge e.V.—Landesverband Hamburg, Tätigkeitsberichte 1946–1988, Monatsberichte 1946–1947.

13. Volksbund Deutsche Kriegsgräberfürsorge e.V.—Landesverband Hamburg, Tätigkeitsberichte 1946–1988, Monatsberichte 1946–1947.

14. Goschler 1992, 220; Herf 1997, 224.

15. StA Hamburg SK II 1628, Protokoll, 12.10.1945, Bl. 1.

16. Foschepoth 1997, 73ff.

17. StA Hamburg SK II 1628, Bl. 18–25.

18. HH Hamburg-Denkmalschutzamt 39-430.308.1 Bürgermeisteramt to the Denkmalschutzamt, October 15, 1945.

19. HH Hamburg-Denkmalschutzamt 39-430.308.1 Senatkanzlei, December 19, 1947.

20. StA Hamburg SK II 1628, "Aufruf zur Gedenkwoche," September 11, 1947.

21. Schoenfeld 2000, 136.

22. Schneider 1997, 26.

23. Ibid., 26; 29ff.; Stobwasser 2000, 36–42.

24. Bundesarchiv Berlin (BA): Protokol No. 85 der Sitzung des Sekretariat des ZK am 12.7.1951, SAPMO, DY 30/J IV/2/3/214, Bl. 6.

25. Reuter and Hansel 1997, 466–519.

26. StA Hamburg, SKII 1628 Bl. 4/1–4/2. Karl Kühne SPD-Hamburg an der Herrn Bürgermeister, August 2, 1948; Auszug aus der Niederschrift ueber die 58. Senatssitzung, August 10, 1948.

27. StA Hamburg, SKII 1628 Der Ministerpräsident des Landes Schleswig-Holstein an Herrn Bürgermeister Brauer 18.8.1948; Bürgermeister Brauer an Ministerpräsident Lüdemann, August 21, 1948.

28. StA Hamburg, SKII 1628, Philip Auerbach, Der Präsident des Bayerischen Landesentschädigungsamtes an den Präsident des Senates Herrn Brauer, July 3, 1950.

29. StA Hamburg SKII 1628 Bl. 6/25 Aktionsausschuss des BVN zur Vorbereitung des Gedenktages für Alle Opfer der Unmentschlichkeit am 10. September 1950, Mitteilung No. 1 August 1950.

30. Petersen 1998, 32.

31. "Volkstrauertag—heute wie vor 28 Jahren" *Kriegsgräberfürsorge* März 1950 Jg. 26, No. 3, 18.

32. Goschler 1992, 218; StA Hamburg, SKII 1628, Der Bundesminister des Innern an die Herren Innenminister der Länder, June 13, 1950.

33. StA Hamburg, SKII 1628 Arbeitsgemeinschaft der Innenministerium der Bundesländer Arbeitskreis I "Staatsrecht, Verwaltung und Verwaltungsgerichtsbarkeit am 17./18. Juli 1950 in Berlin," 27–30.

34. Bundesarchiv Koblenz: B 122 / 2238 Der Bundesminister des Innern to Staatssekretär des Innern im Bundeskanzleramt, August 14, 1950; B136 / 3003.

35. Bundesarchiv Koblenz: B 122 / 2238 Der Bundesminister des Innern, August 18, 1950; B106 77151 Abteilungsleiter I, August 21, 1950.

36. Bundesarchiv Koblenz: B 122 / 2238 "Bemerkungen [Bundespräsident Heuss] zur Frage eines Gedenktages am 3. September," 14.8.1950; Bundesarchiv Koblenz: B 136 / 3003 Der Bundesminister des Innern to Staatssekretär des Innern im Bundeskanzleramt, August 18, 1950; B106/77151 Abteilungsleiter I, August 15, 1950.

37. StA Hamburg: SKII A.z. 020.62-6 Sig. 1630 Der Bundesminister des Innern an die Senatskanzlei Hamburg, August 18, 1951.

38. Petersen 1998, 32–33.

39. Bekantmachung der Bayer. Ministerpräsident Dr. Hans Ehard, October 30, 1951.

40. Weckerling 1947.

41. Goschler 1992, 217–221.

42. Heuss 1955, 388; Bundesarchiv Koblenz: B 122 / 2238 p. 5.

43. Goschler 1992, 220.

44. Goschler 2005, 876.

45. Stadtarchiv Mannheim: Nachlaβ Hermann Heimerich Zug. 24/1972 Nr. 299: Gedächtnisrede OB Dr. Heimerich, September 12, 1948.

46. Stadtarchiv Mannheim: Ratsprotokol 29.8.1950. On the Mannheim monument, see Peters 2002, 65–78.

47. Stadtarchiv Mannheim: Protokol der Verwaltungsausschuses, June 11, 1952.

48. Volksbund Deutsche Kriegsgräberfürsorge 1987.

49. Staatsarchiv Hamburg: SKII 020.62–8 3974: "Ansprache Max Brauers anlässlich des Volkstrauertages am 16. November 1952," Bl. 23ff.

50. Staatsarchiv Hamburg: SKII 020.62-8 3975: "Rundfunkansprache von Bürgermeister Max Brauer anlässlich des Volkstrauertages am 16. November 1958."

51. "Wir Toten sind gröβere Heere."

52. Goes 1956, 10.

53. Volksbund Deutsche Kriegsgräberfürsorge e.V 1987, 50–51.

54. Kantsteiner 2003b, 278–297.

55. Grosser in Volksbund Deutsche Kriegsgräberfürsorge 1987, 68–69.

56. See, for example, a typical statement of Grosser in an interview with Doerry 2008, 133: "But the Allies committed the basic error. They collectively accused the Germans. Instead of saying: 'You are also victims,' exactly what the case was, 'and we accuse now with you the main responsible persons,' suddenly everyone was accused."

57. Schmid in Volksbund Deutsche Kriegsgräberfürsorge 1987, 93.

58. Renger in ibid., 118.

59. Puvogel, Stanowski, and Graf 1995.

60. Margalit 2002b.

61. Ibid., 169–171, 180–192.

62. Schmid in Volksbund Deutsche Kriegsgräberfürsorge 1987, 97.

63. Kohl in ibid., 125.

64. Dregger 1986.

65. http://www.bundespraesident.de/Die-deutschen-Bundespraesident/Roman-Herzog/Reden-,11072.11991/Ansprache-von-Bundespraesident.htm?global.back=/Die-deutschen-Bundespraesident/Roman-Herzog/-%2c11072%2c9/Reden.htm%3flink%3dbpr_liste

66. Ralf Feldmann, November 19, 2006: http://www.bo-alternativ.de/VVN/dokumente/2006_11_Volkstrauertag_Rede.pdf.

5. The Bombing of Germany's Cities and German Memory Politics, 1945–1989

1. Grayling 2007, 129–135; Reinhard 2005, 15–17.

2. See the classic studies: Webster and Frankland 1961; Boog 1992, 329–349; Boog 2001; Blank 2004. For articles on the public debate in Britain and Europe, see Kettenacker 2003; Moeller 2006, 106–109, presents a rich bibliography on this issue.

3. Webster and Frankland 1961, 144–166.

4. Ibid., 167–188.

5. Grayling 2007, 184.

6. Webster and Frankland 1961, 340–343.

7. Overy 2003a, 185.

8. Overy 2003b, 42.

9. Overy 2003a, 183–187.

10. See, for example, a prima facie conclusion reached by Robert Lochner, a member of the team which prepared the U.S. Strategic Bombing Survey, regarding the effectiveness of the Allied bombardment policy: http://www.gwu.edu/~nsarchiv/coldwar/interviews/episode-4/lochner1.html:

Q:What was your assessment of the effectiveness of allied bombing of Germany?

A:Categorically that you can't win a war by trying to destroy the cities. The Nazis of course had done a fantastic job in keeping production going. I visited personally whole factories they had built under forests, so that they were obviously immune to air attack. And it was known after the war that in virtually all fields of production, production still was going up. Of course in the fatal field of gasoline for airplanes, they didn't produce anything any more, so that the famous Stukas in the end were sitting ducks for American air attacks on the airplane. They couldn't fly them any more. But in other fields as I say, the production in many ways was still going up.

11. For example, *The Strategic Air War against Germany 1939–1945* (Cox 1998), 161:

> Three major factors were associated in Germany's defeat. The first and most obvious was the overrunning of her territory by the armies of the Allies. The second was the breakdown of her war industry, which was mainly a consequence of the bombing of her communications system. The third was the drying-up of her resources of liquid fuel, and the disruption of her chemical industry, which resulted from the bombing of synthetic oil plants and refineries.

12. Blank 2004, 357ff.

13. Grayling 2007, 179–208. On Vera Brittain, see Grayling 2007, 181–189; Brittain herself wrote:

> Nazism and fascism themselves are typical results of resentment and humiliation. That is why I keep on insisting that you cannot defeat an armed doctrine by bombs and tanks. All you can do is temporarily conquer the men and women enslaved to this doctrine. If you kill them the idea passes to others, rising like a phoenix from their ashes. You may thrust a doctrine underground by victorious might but you will not destroy it. (Brittain 2005, 33)
>
> Supposing instead that we were to offer by every broadcasting device available, an immediate armistice or "people's peace," coupled with food for starving, suggestions for reciprocal disarmament, and generous undertakings to share the rich resources still within our control? This might not influence the German and Japanese militarist, whose power flourishes on Allied ruthlessness, but would remove from the German and Japanese people their main reason for supporting their present leaders. A great magnanimous gesture is not merely one way of ending a war; it is the only way to end it without sowing the seeds of another conflict. (Brittain 2005, 28).

14. Grayling 2007, 179.

15. Stadtarchiv Dresden: 4.1.4, Nr. 955 Bl. 50, January 25, 1946.

16. Weidauer 1946.

17. Der Rat der Stadt Dresden an die Dresdner Bevölkerung, *Saechsische Volkszetung*, February 13, 1946, 6.

18. Stadtarchiv Dresden: 4.1.4, Nr. 955 Bl. 19, February 14, 1946; February 18, 1946.

19. Bundesarchiv -Filmarchiv-*Dresden*. A DEFA Film of Richard Groschopp, 1946.

20. Bundesarchiv -Filmarchiv-*Dresden warnt und mahnt*. A DEFA Film of Heino Brandes, 1951.

21. "Aufruf des ZK der KPD vom 11.Juni 1945." In Berthold and Diehl 1965, 193.

22. Diner 2002, 126–127; Herf 1997, 106.

23. "Be-Ehad be-Mai 1967" Andut, 3rd year, no. 9, May 1, 1967, p. 1. Norden 1947.

24. "Westmaechte ermutigten Hitler," 1, 3.

25. BA Berlin: Nachlaβ Albert Norden NY 4217 /29, "Die nationale Front im Kampf gegen den amerikanische Imperialismus," Bl. 106–108, published as Norden 1949.

26. Weidauer 1949.

27. Sächsiches HStA Dresden, A/419 Bl. 3. SED Abt. Massenagitation Sekretariatsvorlage, January 12, 1950.

28. Sächsiches HStA Dresden, A/419 Bl. 33, Gerhard Eisler an den Landesverband der SED Land Sachsen, January 21, 1950.

29. On the establishment and goals of this group, see Amos 1999, 19–30.

30. Nationale Front des demokratischen Deutschland 1950.

31. Sächsiches HStA Dresden, A/419 Bl. 38; 42.

32. Ibid., 22.

33. "Dresden mahnt: Erzwingt den Frieden!"; DEFA -Wochenschauen *Der Augenzeuge* No. 8, 1950/2.

34. Goebbels 1943, 344–350; Gassert 1997, 363; Bundesarchiv Koblenz: Sammlung Oberheitmann-Zsg. 109, Vertraulich Informationen (V.I.) des Reichsministerium für Volksaufklärung und Propaganda für die Presse No. 163/43, July 4, 1943; Süβ 2007, 212ff.

35. Kurt Maetzig's famous DEFA film *die Rat der Göter* (1949/1950) portrayed a conspiracy of American big capital with the German chemical concern IG Farben and a high-ranking Wehrmacht officer, all of whom together planned the Second World War in pursuit of economic profits. For this propagandistic docu-thriller (and typical Cold War work), Maetzig and screenwriter Friedrich Wolf were decorated with the GDR national prize first class.

36. Bundesarchiv Koblenz: Sammlung Oberheitmann—Zsg. 109, V. I. No. 163/43, July 4, 1943.

37. "Dresden mahnt zum Frieden," 1; "100,000 Dresdner demonstrierten," 1.

38. Sächsiches HStA Dresden, A/419 Bl. 075.

39. Bundesarchiv Berlin Berlin (BA) Protokoll No. 27 der Sitzung des Sekretariats des ZK am, December 15, 1954. SAPMO, DY 30/J IV 2/3/449; Bl. 17.

40. Bundesarchiv Berlin (BA): "Politische Richtlinien zum 10. Jahrestag des amerikanischen Terrorangriffes auf Dresden," January 29, 1955. SAPMO NY 4090/517, Bl. 200–204.

41. Kraushaar 1996, vol. 3 (1953–1956), 1135.

42. Archiv der Gedenkstaete Sachsenhausen AS, KAW, K5/M2, Bl. 133–134, Arbeitkopie aus Unterlagen des Komitees der Antifaschistischen Widerstandkämpfer der DDR.

43. Bundesarchiv-Filmarchiv-*Dresden mahnt Deutschland*. A DEFA Film 1955.

44. Bundesarchiv-Filmarchiv-*Dresden—Erinnerung und Mahnung*. A DEFA film of Max Jaap, 1965.

45. On the anniversary of the Dresden bombing in East Germany's final years, see Neutzner 2005, 128–163.

46. "Weltkrieg, zweiter" *Meyers Neues Lexikon* (1964), vol. 8, 698.

47. Zimmering 1959, 16.

48. Weidauer 1965, 50–62.

49. Groehler 1975, 458f.; Groehler 1988, 268–272.

50. "Tausende protestierten gegen schmutzigen Krieg"; Neutzner 2005, 153.

51. "Dresden 20 Jahre danach."

52. "Im Bewuβtsein der Kraft unseres freien Volkes schreiten wir mit Optimismus voran."

53. Gassert 1997, 326; Diner 2002, 90ff.; Haury 2002, 350ff.

54. Dresden: "Diese Häuser sind durch Anglo-Amerikanischen Bombenterror am 13.–14. Februar 1945 zerstört und von Aktivisten für Aktivisten unter Förderung des Oberbürgermeister Waidaur 1949–1950 wiederaufgebaut worden" (These houses were devastated by Anglo-American bomb-terror on February 13 and 14, 1945, and rebuilt by activist and for activists under the sponsorship of Mayor Waidaur 1949–1950.); I am grateful to Dr. Ruth Röcher of Chemnitz for having drawn my attention to this inscription. Ohlsdorfer Friedhof Hamburg: "Zum Gedenken an meine Liebsten, sie sind dem; Terrorangriff auf Hamburg zum Opfer gefallen . . . (In memory of my dearest, they fell as victims to the terror attack on Hamburg.)"

55. Gretschel 1995; Diner 2002, 127f.: "Die Frauenkirche in Dresden in Februar 1945 zerstört durch angloamerikanische Bomber. Erbaut von Georg Bähr 1726–1743. Ihre Ruine erinnert an Zehntausende Tote und mahnt die Lebenden zum Kampf gegen die imperialistische Barbarei Für Frieden und Glück der Menschheit."

56. The editors' response to a letter from a reader, Margaret Wundland, *Neues Deutschland*, no. 27, February 2, 1955.

57. "Bomben darauf?"

58. "Der 3. Februar 1945 mahnt zu Kampf die Pariser Kriegspakte."

59. Kucklick 2003, 147.

60. Wendler 1950.

61. "Nie wieder eine Schreckensnacht!," 1.

62. On Louis Fürnberg and his worldview during his Palestinian period, see Gordon 2004, 37, 52, 54, 142.

63. This is a common estimation, though unfounded. Brunswig 1978, 402, estimates the total number of dead in Hamburg as 45,000.

64. "Mahnmal, das kein Mahnmal ist," *Hamburger Volkszeitung* o. 175, July 29, 1952: "Was hier geschah [die Luftangriff an Hamburg in Juli 1943], war Mord, Massenmord an unschuldigen Frauen und Kindern."

65. "Propaganda rettet Dresden nicht."

66. On this, see Keil and Kellerhoff 2002, 144–146.

67. H.G., "Die Bomben auf Freiburg," 36; Hippler 1994, 224–225. According to Hippler, the director of the Nazi film *The Eternal Jew*, 253,000 people were killed in the bombing of Dresden. He rejected the official estimate of 30,000 as the lie of a conspiracy that sought to minimize the extent of the aerial massacre.

68. "Stellungnahme der USA zu den Luftangriffen auf Dresden."

69. Reichert 1994, 59–62.

70. Rodenberger 1952; "Inferno—empfunden, aber nicht gestalten."

71. Rahms 1955.
72. "Dresdner gedachten ihrer Heimat"; "Dresden—die verschwundene Stadt."
73. "Dresden war schliemer als Hiroshima."
74. Irving 1964.
75. Irving 1963, "Author's note"; "Historiker Irving korrigierte sich"; "der Angriff auf Dresden."
76. Hofmann 1964.
77. Schneider 1965.
78. I am grateful to my colleague Dr. Oren Meyers for referring me to this work: Zelizer 1998, 89ff., 110ff.
79. "Die Bombennaechte von Hamburg."
80. Bucerius 1993; Biermann 2003, 246.
81. Brenner 2001, 86, 88.
82. Klemperer 1995, 667ff.
83. Boberach 1984, vol. 14, 5545–5546.
84. Ibid., 5562ff.
85. Timm 2003, 27.
86. Goering bragged publicly in 1940 that "if enemy aircraft succeed in getting through German air defenses, my name will no longer be Goering, it will be Meyer." So the German public began calling him Meyer. Deutsches Volksliedarchiv, Freiburg: Gr. II 2. Weltkrieg M 300:

> Auf Vergeltung warten wir
> Dass es England geht wie hier,
> Hilf der Meyer doch, O Gott
> Jetzt in dieser grossen Not
> Gib ihm doch den richt'gen Geist
> Dass er wieder Göring heist.

87. "Als Hamburgs Pulsschlag stockte," 3.
88. "Verzeihen aber nicht Vergessen," 3.
89. "Nie wieder Hiroshima—nie wieder Bomben auf Hamburg," 1.
90. "Die Tote mahnen die Lebenden," 1.
91. Oppenheimer 2004, 354.
92. Ibid., 353, 373.
93. Denkmalschutzamt Hamburg: 39-430.302 Ehrenmal für die Bombenopfer in Ohlsdorf—"Grabmal für die Opfer des Bombenkrieges," January 7, 1950.
94. *Das Mahnmal für die Opfer des Bombenkrieges*, 28–30.
95. Manske 1989, 286.
96. Marcks 1988, 144.
97. Manske 1989, 286.
98. Denkmalschutzamt Hamburg: 39–430.302 Ehrenmal für die Bombenopfer in Ohlsdorf—Drucksache für die Senatssitzung: Berichtstatter Senator Landahl, 2.
99. "Schliemmer als die Atombombe," 3.
100. Irving 1963, 76.
101. For example, Hastings 1987; Best 1980, 108–109, 279–284.
102. For example, the dialogue between Bishop Bell and Churchill: Hochhuth 1968, 190ff.

103. "Hamburg, die unverzagte Stadt," 10.

104. "Feuer fill von Himmel," 1–2.

105. Ibid.

106. Schmidt, 1973, 28.

107. Hoffmann 1983, 7.

108. Noelle and Neumann 1956, 137; Noelle and Neumann 1957, 142.

109. "Mehr verdrängt als bewältigt," 61.

110. Noelle and Neumann 1956, 137, 202.

111. Adorno 1956, 121–324; Jordan 1956, 16–17.

112. Adorno 1986, 116. "Wer Adolf will," 34: "Today the NPD [a party of the extreme right] counts the blood of Dresden against Auschwitz. The party doubts that the victims of the bombings were killed in a more humane way than were the Jews." Such opinions were not the lot of the extreme right alone.

6. Flight and Expulsion in German Political Culture and Memory since 1945

1. Schwartz 2008, 114. As early as 1949, even some noncommunist West German observers were persuaded of the Communists' putative success in solving the refugees' problems; see Schwartz 2008, 110.

2. Ibid., 146.

3. The Hallstein doctrine disintegrated in 1967 with West Germany's recognition of Yugoslavia; see Gassert 2006, 587–588.

4. Ahonen 2003, 17–18.

5. Bayer. HSTA: Flüchtlingswesen: Allgemeiner Schriftverkehr 30674, Vol. 2, March 1948–July 1949: C. A. Macartney, "A Report on the German Refugees' Problem of 28 June 1948." In this report, composed at the request of the American military government, a well-known British historian based his findings on the impressions he gained in a special visit to the American occupation zone. The document addresses the prospects of the assimilation of the refugees within the indigenous population, and echoes the concern of the authorities that the refugees would become radicalized. See 6; on Adenauer's fear that the expellees would be radicalized, see Ahonen 2003, 94.

6. "Verbot der Flüchtlingsparteien"; Bauer 1982.

7. Weiβ 1995, 244–264; Ahonen 2003, 24ff.

8. Ahonen 2003, 26–27; Stöver 2002; Stöver 2005, 897–898; Foschepoth 1995, 88–99; Gausmann 2001, 154.

9. Bayer. HSTA, RG 260 OMGUS. OMGB-ID 10/70-3/ 23, Alfred Noske, "Flüchtlingsproblem," February 21, 1947, 4.

10. Bayer. HSTA, RG 260 OMGUS. OMGB-ID 10/70-3/ 23, Pierre M. Purves, "Luftpost aus Amerika," February 21, 1947.

11. Bayer. HSTA StK 30 131: OMGUS Office of the military Governor, "Länderrat Draft Law concerning the reception and Integration of German Expellees," January 24, 1947.

12. Stöver 2005, 897–911.

13. For example, Kossert 2008, 71–79.

14. Kössler 2005, 80–81; Connor 1995, 133–168.

15. In 1946, the Soviet occupiers imposed a union of the Social Democratic Party (SPD) and the much smaller Communist Party (KPD) in its zone of occupation, creating the SED.

16. Bayer. HSTA RG OMGB 10/108-3/22 Monthly Political Report, July 31, 1946.

17. *Lebensraum*—literally, "living space"—is a concept that developed in Germany in the late nineteenth century. It became a core element in the Nazi ideology. The German people must create for themselves a "living space" in the east in order to secure their future survival.

18. Bayer. HSTA RG OMGB 10/108-3/22 Monthly Political Report, July 31, 1946.

19. Bayer. HSTA RG 260 OMGB OMGB-ID 10/70-3/ 23, "District refugee Conference arranged by the Communist Party in Munich on February 16, 1947," 1.

20. Ibid., 5.

21. Ibid.; Hadek 1947.

22. Bayer. HSTA RG 260 OMGB OMGB-ID 10/70-3/ 23, "District refugee Conference arranged by the Communist Party in Munich on February 16, 1947," 5; Hadek 1947, 3.

23. For similar KPD positions in Lower Saxony (Niedersachsen), see Grebing 1990, 34–35.

24. Institut für Zeitgeschichte, München, OMGUS Files: POLAD 773/ 33 Report of the American Consulate in Munich on Wilhelm Pieck's Speech, March 20, 1947.

25. Gausmann 2001, 137–154; Bayer. HSTA: Flüchtlingswesen: Allgemeiner Schriftverkehr 30674, Vol. 2, March 1948–July 1949: A Report on the German Refugees' Problem of Professor C. A. Macartney of 28 June 1948, 6 ("It has been reported to me that Communist agents already told certain expellees that the Soviet Union would be able to draw the borders of a Communist united Germany east of [the Oder-Neisse line], and to secure [by that] the return home of at least the Selesians").

26. Anderson 2001, 40–45.

27. Grebing 1990, 34–35; Bayer. HSTA: Flüchtlingswesen: Allgemeiner Schriftverkehr 30674, Vol. 2, March 1948–July 1949: A Report on the German Refugees' Problem of Professor C. A. Macartney of 28 June 1948, 6 ("the expellees in general, at the present, are extremely anticommunist").

28. Bayer. HSTA RG 260 OMGUS. OMGB 10/70-3/23 A Report on the refugees' conference, February 21, 1947.

29. Melendy 2005, 107–125.

30. Bayer. HSTA RG 260 OMGUS. OMGB 15/102-2/21. Donald T. Shea, Director of the Intelligence Division to the Land Director, "Egon Hermann KPD Meeting at Dachau," August 8, 1949.

31. Bayer. HSTA Stk 10993 Anklage von ders. Gegen die Verfassung: "Flüchtlingsversammlung Der KPD am 31. Juli 1949 in Kulmbach."

32. Bayer. HSTA Stk 10993 Anklage von ders. Gegen die Verfassung: Report of Marr, Krim. Ob. Komm. March 1950. The last document in this file is from 1950. By then, Hermann's very limited success among the expellees had probably brought an end to his employment with the KPD.

33. Schwartz 2008, 102–103.

34. Bundesarchiv Koblenz. Nachlaß Seebohm 178/2a: A letter of Walter Ulbricht, the Chairman of the State Council of the GDR to Chancellor Erhard, May 26, 1964, 21ff.

35. Schwartz 2008, 107–108. This egalitarian principle also guided Communist policy regarding the victims of Nazi persecutions; see Goschler 1993.

36. Ther 1998, 157–159, 179–180, 250–251; Schwartz 2008, 107–110.

37. Ther 1998, 159–163.

38. Ibid., 175.

39. Ibid., 179–183, 230.

40. Ibid., 163–164.

41. Ibid., 164, 168, 181, 239.

42. Ibid., 239–240; Schwartz 2008, 117–118.

43. Ther 1998, 334.

44. For articles on the absorption of refugees in the Federal Republic, see Ahonen 2003 and the collection in Benz 1995; Schraut and Grosser 1996; Hoffmann and Schwartz 1999.

45. Schwartz 2008, 101, 103.

46. Ibid., 118f.

47. Ibid., 105, 130.

48. Ibid., 128.

49. Ibid., 126f.

50. Stickler 2004, 33–98.

51. Ahonen 2003, 29.

52. On the history of these organizations and on the political intrigues in the long way to their unification, see Stickler 2004, 33–97.

53. Ahonen 2003, 53, 99, 113.

54. Schwartz 2008, 145–146; Ahonen 2003, 258–259; Kittel 2007, 79–80.

55. Bundesarchiv Koblenz: B136 (Bundeskanzleramt)/ 2712 Der Bundesminister für gesamtdeutsche Fragen, February 1, 1955 Bl. 27.

56. Stickler 2004.

57. Ahonen 2003, 44–46.

58. On the meaning of the expellee organizations' demand for a homeland (*Recht auf die Hiemat*), see Stickler 2004, 357–369, 433.

59. Stickler 2004, 325–332; Kossert 2008, 183.

60. See a short interview that Jacksch gave to an Israeli journalist in the early 1960s: Elyashiv 1964; see also Martin 1996.

61. See, for example, Stickler 2004, 387–394.

62. Connor 2006, 193.

63. Kraft 1955, 2.

64. Bissinger 1970, 176–178. Bissinger's article, published at the time that Germany signed its treaty with Poland, presents the metamorphosis in West German public opinion on the issue of the German territories in the east, from the beginning of the 1950s through 1970. By the latter date, 72 percent of the German public believed that Germany had lost these territories forever, while only 11 percent continued to believe that the lands would return to German sovereignty some day. This represents a complete reversal of public sentiment—in 1953, only 11 percent believed that the territories had been lost forever, while 66 percent believed that they would again be German eventually.

65. On the expellee organizations, see note 30.

66. Ahonen 2003, 95.

67. Foschepoth 1995, 106.

68. On Adenauer's non-committed policy toward the Sudeten see Ahonen 2003, 95–96; BA Koblenz NL Seebohm 178/2a, 99, Chancellor Kiesinger to Minister Seebohm, August 7, 1967.

69. Noelle and Neuman 1997, 482–483.

70. Ibid., 482.

71. Ahonen 2003, 92–94.

72. Adenauer 1967, 17; Franz Richter was the alias of Fritz Rößler, a Nazi activist from Saxony, who settled after the war in Lower Saxony and presented himself as a Sudeten German.

73. Die Kabinettprotokolle der Bundesregierung 1949, 317–318.

74. Ahonen 2003, 110–112; Frohn 1996, 494–499; Foschepoth 1995, 106–110.

75. Ahonen 2003, 92.

76. Ibid., 92–93.

77. "Kanzler glaubt an Rückkehr der Schlesier."

78. Haar 2007, 260f.

79. Foschepoth 1995, 107. In November 1950, the three high commissioners of the Western Allies told Adenauer in an unequivocal manner that when they spoke of the reunification of Germany they meant only the inclusion of the Soviet Occupation Zone (GDR).

80. "Die Flüchtlingsnot—ein Weltproblem."

81. Ahonen 2003, 96; Kittel 2007, 77.

82. "Kritik an Oberländers Personalpolitik"; Miska 1954.

83. For example, in his message to the expellees on Homeland Day 1956, he referred to "the living space (*Lebensraum*) that the Germans procured through labor and sacrifice"; "Der Bundesminister für Vertriebenenund Flüchtlinge."

84. Frankfurter Rundschau Archiv: Mappe Theodor Oberländer: Speech of Oberländer at the Bavarian Radio November 5, 1954.

85. Ahonen 2003, 1001; BA-Koblenz: B 136 / 2712 /830 Bl. 40–41 Ministerialdirektor Dr. Janz to the Adenauer, July 7, 1955.

86. "Minister Oberländer unter schwerem Verdacht"; see the Protocolls of the Oberländer trial in the GDR: *Der Oberländer Prozess* 1960. Also see Wachs 2000, 377–379, where the author rejects the East German accusations against Oberländer as SED manipulation. Some of Wachs's arguments for Oberländer's innocence do not sound very persuasive, however: see esp. p. 487.

87. Aly tells the story of Oberländer's surprising acquittal after reunification: Aly 1999a, 99–106; for a critique of Aly's position, see Wachs 2000, 487.

88. "Seebohm löst Lodgman."

89. For example, "Hochkomissare protestiere gegen Seebohm Ausführungen"; "New York gegen Seebohm"; also, his speech at the 150th anniversary of Marienbad's celebrations in 1958, in Bad Homburg, in the presence of senior government officials, "Heimatrecht ist ein Teil des Völkerrecht"; Stöver 2005, 899–900.

90. Frankfurter Rundschau Archiv: Mappe Hans-Christoph Seebohm: "Presenotiz Bundesminister Dr. Seebohm zur Frage der Grenzen von 1937," undated, but apparently from 1951; "Alliierte Kritik an Seebohm-Rede."

91. Eschenburg 1960a.

92. Sudetendeutsches Archiv: Seebohm 16/1a SL-Reden und Veröffentlichungen: "Hat das Münchener Abkommen Konsequenzen für das sudetenproblem?" February 20, 1965, 3–6; Kanzlei des Sprechers 1/ C "Unsere Heimkehr ins Reich!" August 12, 1963.

93. Sudetendeutsches Archiv: Kanzlei des Sprechers B9/46: Rede des Sprechers Dr. Ing. Hans-Christoph Seebohm auf der Hauptkundgebung des XV. Sudetendeutschen Tages zu Pfingsten 1964 in Nürenberg (Marz 17, 1964) 22: "Especially there is no reason whatsoever to declare that the Munich treaty and the treaty between Prague, Paris, and London have no validity according to international law. From the point of international law, it is an agreement that without reproach came about. That should not prevent one from establishing that the German side [participating in this treaty] was a totalitarian and criminal regime."

94. For example: Bundesarchiv Koblenz: Nachlass Seebohm 178 /18: "Kolonialstatus oder Selbstbestimungsrecht, welchem Weg wählt Deutschland für Europa?" May 5, 1959, 3–5; NL 178/14: "Die Verantwortung des Akademikers gegenüber der wiedervereinigung," May 31, 1957.

95. Sudetendeutsches Archiv, München, Kanzlei des Sprechers B9-45; Rede des Sprechers Dr. Ing. Hans-Christoph Seebohm auf der Hauptkundgebung des Sudetendeutschen Tages in Stuttgart, Pfingsten 1963, 11–12.

96. Frankfurter Rundschau Archiv: Mappe Hans-Christoph Seebohm: "Pressenotiz Bundesminister Dr. Seebohm zur Frage der Grenzen von 1937," undated MS from 1951. Seebohm referred to a similar solution a few more times before the end of his political career; see, for example, Sudetendeutsches Archiv: Seebohm 16/1a SL-Reden und Veröffentlichungen: "Hat das Münchener Abkommen Konsequenzen für das sudetenproblem?" February 20, 1965, 8.

97. Sudetendeutsches Archiv: Seebohm 16/1a SL-Reden und Veröffentlichungen: "Hat das Münchener Abkommen Konsequenzen für das sudetenproblem?" February 20, 1965. 6: "[The act of expulsion] is also illegal on the basis of the Declaration of Human Rights, the Atlantic Charter, the Declaration of the Nuremberg Tribunal, and all the great international decisions."

98. See, for example, Lemberg's explanation of why Slavs were incapable of ruling: Hahn n.d.

99. "Seebohm dementiert Regierung"; "Seebohm verteidigt erneut das Münchener Abkommen."

100. "Klärung dringend nötig"; Henrich 1951.

101. "Seebohm vor Sudetendeutschen"; Goschler 2005, 141; "Scharfe Kritik an Seebohm."

102. See Sudetendeutsches Archiv: Seebohm 7/69 Bundeskanzler, on Brentano's rejection of Seebohm's wish that the German foreign minister raise the South Tyrolean issue in a meeting with the Italian prime minister. Brentano to Seebohm, November 29, 1955.

103. "Kanzler beschwichtigt Rom."

104. "Wenig beglückt"; "Besorgnis über Südtirol."

105. "Holländische Kritik an Seebohm"; "Seebohm muβ sich verantworten."

106. For example, the attacks in the weekly *Zeit*: Eschenburg 1960a; Eschenburg 1960b; Eschenburg 1960c.

107. Stickler 2004, 167f.; Adenauer 1995, 34, 401–402; in a letter from October 1953, Adenauer told Seebohm that, to be reappointed to the cabinet, he would have to refrain from making any further political speeches.

108. "Adenauer prüft Seebohm-Rede."

109. "Kanzler verurteilt Seebohm-Rede"; "Spiel mit Zahlen."

110. See "Trybuna Ludu."

111. Ahonen 2003, 94.

112. See the comments of Chancellor Adenauer and his successor, Erhard, on this issue: Ahonen 2003, 170; Kittel 2007, 77.

113. Ahonen 2003, 141–143.

114. Stickler 2004, 106–109.

115. Ibid., 112–117; Kittel 2007, 31–57; http://www.ekd.de/EKD-Texte/lage_der_vertriebenen_1.html.

116. "Das Memorndum der Acht. Wissenschftler warnen vor selbst Gefälligkeit und Illusionen"; Greschat 2000; Ahonen 2003, 166–167.

117. Raiser, von Bismarck, and von Weizsäcker 1962.

118. Ibid.

119. Ahonen 2003, 7–8.

120. Stickler 2004, 244.

121. See Elon 1964: "I never demanded the renewal of the 1937 borders. I didn't ever do so; after all, I'm no fool! We'll get to peace negotiations and we'll see what the other side can agree to."

122. Stickler 2004, 395.

123. "Erhard warnt vor Verzicht auf Ostgebiete."

124. "Minister Seebohm im Gegensatz zur Bundesregierung"; "Seebohm muß sich verantworten."

125. "Seebohm dementiert Regierung"; "Seebohm verteidigt erneut das Münchener Abkommen."

126. Ahonen 2003, 203–204. The text: www.ekd.de/EKD-Texte/45952.html.

127. Bissinger 1970, 176–178; another poll, conducted by the Emnid institute in June 1967, was more ambiguous. It found that 51 percent of Germans opposed the recognition of the Oder-Neisse line as Germany's eastern border; see Gassert 2006, 582–583.

128. Gassert 2006, 582–583.

129. "Brandt: Deutschlandpolitik nicht ohne Vertriebene"; see Ahonen 2003, 219, regarding Brandt's statement on the validity *ex tunc* of the Munich Pact of 1938.

130. Stickler 2004, 236ff.

131. Bissinger 1970, 176–178.

132. Ahonen 2003, 54f., 203ff.

133. Ibid., 244; Kittel 2007, 111–114.

134. Stickler 2004, 270–279.

135. Ahonen 2003, 251–253.

136. Schwartz 2008, 134; Ahonen 2003, 256–260.

137. Schwartz 2008, 135.

138. On the expellee organizations, see Stickler 2004; Ahonen 2003; Salzborn 2000; and Seebohm: Sudetendeutsches Archiv: Seebohm 16/1a SL-Reden und Veröffentlichungen, "Hat das Münchener Abkommen Konsequenzen für das Sudetenproblem?," February 20, 1965, 6: "This act of violence is illegal according to in-

ternational law. The applied methods there are equivalent to the attributes which characterizes benocide." A typical headline in a periodical of the organization of German expellees from Pomerania was "No! Never! Our Thoughts on the Occasion of the Anniversary of the Potsdam Crime"; see Stubbe 1950; Haar 2007, 256.

139. Kittel 2007, 9, 184.

140. Ahonen 2003, 256–257.

141. Ibid., 262–263.

142. Ibid., 263.

143. BA Koblenz; B 234/627: Jacob Kaiser's speech, September 10, 1955, 17.

144. Kittel 2007.

145. Ibid., 176.

146. Weiβ 1995, 258–262.

147. Lau 2003, 50; Ohliger 2000.

148. Haar and Fahlbush 2005.

149. On Theodor Schieder and his activity on the Jewish issue, see Heim and Aly, 1994, 45–70; Aly 1999a, 169–178; Aly 1999b, 163–182.

150. Haar 2007, 256.

151. Ibid., 260ff.

152. Schieder et al. 1955, 24E.

153. Beer 1998; Beer 1999, 287–289.

154. Kittel 2007, 118–119; Kossert 2008, 189.

155. http://www.bund-der-vertriebenen.de/infopool/inmemoriam.php3.

156. Kossert 2008, 287.

157. Kittel 2007, 147–149.

158. Kossert 2008, 274–290.

159. Ibid., 290–299.

160. Kittel 2007, 169.

161. http://www.alfreddezayas.com/books.shtml, accessed October 21, 2007.

162. "Becher will nach 'Holocaust' Sendungen zur Vertreibung"; Sudetendeutsches Archiv: Der Kanzlei des Sprechers B19/ 6.: Sudetendeutsche Landesmannschaft, Kreisgruppe Nürenberg-Stadt to the Sudetendeutsche Landesmannschaft Bundesverband, Munich, February 16, 1979; Kittel 2007, 157, portrays Becher's reaction as a more widely held position among the German spectators of *Holocaust*. This seemed to be a typical rejection mechanism against the agony of the German-Jewish Weiss family depicted in the series.

163. Regarding Schönhuber's position on left-wing and liberal influence on the German media, see "Die Schwächen der liberalen Anpasser."

164. Kittel 2007, 158–159.

165. Fritzsche 2002, 80.

166. Kittel 2007, 159.

167. Herf 1980, 30–52.

7. The Resurgence of the German Sense of Victimization since Reunification

1. Diner 1983, 100ff., 102n29.

2. Moller 1998.

3. "*Historikerstreit*" 1987.

4. Levkov 1987; Hartman 1986; Herf 1997, 353f.
5. "*Historikerstreit*" 1987, 42.
6. Azaryahu 1999, 341–354; Ritscher 1995, 163–180.
7. Seewald 2004; Zekri 2003a; Zekri 2003b; Frei 2005b, 361–363.
8. Aly 2003b.
9. Deutscher Bundestag, Drucksache 15/3048 Plenarsitzung No. 114 (June 17, 2004).
10. Erb 2003, 155–161.
11. Ibid., 161–164.
12. Moeller 2001a, 2.
13. Zekri 2002; on Vollmer's former radical years as Maoist see Aly 2008, 13–16.
14. Hahn and Hahn 2004.
15. Brandes 2005, 87. Beneš consolidated his demand for expulsion of the Sudeten Germans only in 1940.
16. Vollmer 1997a.
17. For example, Vollmer 1997b; Vollmer 2002; see also Hahn and Hahn 2004.
18. For example, Altmeyer 2003; Aly 2003a; Ther 2003.
19. Erb 2003, 168–169. See Fischer's own interpretation of these events in Fischer 2007, 161-187.
20. Erb 2003, 169.
21. Lau 2004.
22. See similar statements by Hans-Christoph Seebohm in 1960: BA Koblenz NL Seebohm 178/18 H.-C. Seebohm, Sudetendeutsche Landsmanschaft. Gedanken aus dem Vortrag in Siegen, May 15, 1960; Franz Josef Strauβ in *Deportation* 1985, 1.
23. Steinbach, "Opfer und Täter."
24. Rogalla 1998.
25. Kittel 2007, 104–107, esp. 105.
26. Schily 1999.
27. Salzborn 1999.
28. http://www.bundeskanzler.de/Reden-.7715.11806/Rede-von-Bundeskanzler-Gerhard-Schroeder-anlaess . . . htm (last accessed August 19, 2004).
29. Jelpke 2002.
30. See the speech of Professor Dr. Guido Knopp during the celebration of the fiftieth anniversary jubilee for the enactment of the Federal Expellees Law *(Bundesvertriebenengesetz [BVFG])*, May 6, 2003, http://www.bund-der-vertriebenen.de/presse/index.php3?id=45.
31. "Tschechiens Ministerpräsident verteidigt Vertreibung," *Spiegel Online*, May 18, 2002, http://www.spiegel.de/politik/deutschland/0,1518,196846,00.html. See the historian Jan Pauer's article on the connection between the orders confiscating German property in Czechoslovakia, issued by that country's president, Eduard Beneš, and the Potsdam agreements, and the current demand by right-wing groups in Austria and Germany for the retroactive revocation of Beneš's decrees and the Potsdam agreements; Pauer 2002.
32. Schlink 1999.
33. Welzer 2004, 53–64, esp. 55.
34. Schlink 1999, 128.
35. Ibid., 125–126.
36. Ibid., 117–118.

37. Ibid., 138.

38. Ibid., 171.

39. Ibid., 105–106.

40. Schlink's position complies with the current conservative challenge against the alleged "cultural hegemony" of the 1968 generation and its claim to an "exclusive right to interpret the past." See Taberner 2006, 166–168.

41. Bartov 2000, 34.

42. Sander and Johr 1992, 5, conclude that at least 100,000 women were raped in Berlin and 2 million women in the whole eastern region between December 1944 and the end of 1945, but here, too, that is an estimate and not based on solid data.

43. Anonymous, *Eine Frau in Berlin.* A film of Max Färberböck 2008.

44. Anonymous 1955, 95.

45. Marek served in the propaganda unit of the Wehrmacht during the war. As an editor for the publisher Rowohlt after the war, he rejected, ostensibly on literary grounds, autobiographical works by antifascists about their experiences in concentration camps. See Peitsch 1989, 56–57.

46. Anonymous 1955, 94: "I know that they are human beings like ourselves, although—so it seems to me—on a lower level of development, a nation younger, still closer to their origins than we are. I imagine that the Teutons behaved in very much the same way when they invaded Rome and grabbed the perfumed, coiffed, mani- and pedicured conquered Roman ladies."

47. Bisky 2003, 16; http://hsozkult.geschichte.hu-berlin.de/rezensionen/2003-4-138.

48. Moeller 2001a, 163–164.

49. Niven 2003, 143–174; Hamburger Institut für Sozialforschung 1999.

50. Embacher, Lichtblau, and Sandner von Residenz 1999; Hamburger Institut für Sozialforschung 1999.

51. *So Weit die Füsse tragen.* A Film of Hardy Martins (FRG), 2001.

52. Bauer 2003; *So Weit die Füsse tragen.* A Film of Fritz Umgelter (FRG), 1959.

53. Bauer 2003, 261–264; *So Weit die Füsse tragen.* A Film of Fritz Umgelter (FRG), 1959, Part 6.

54. The first in the series was "Wir leben wie Tiere in Erdlöcher," *Bild* (November 25, 2003), 13. The final one was "Die Tränen werden schwinden, die Kerzen heller glühen," *Bild* (November 30, 2003), 12.

55. On the nature of Knopp's broadcasts, see Kansteiner 2003a, 626–648.

56. Kansteiner 2003b.

57. Keilbach 2002, 127–141, esp. 136.

58. Sebald was killed in an automobile accident in 2001.

59. Schlant 1999, 224–234.

60. The most notable of these is *The End. Hamburg 1943*, by Hans Erich Nossack, 1961. It was written in the autumn of 1943, and documents the author's experiences in Hamburg during the summer of that year.

61. I have translated this myself because, in the published English version, the translator softened Sebald's words by using "destruction" instead of "annihilation." The German original is Sebald 2001, 11–12; the published English translation is Sebald 2004, 4.

62. Sebald 2004, 10.

63. Ibid., 13–14; Nossack 1961, 32–33.

64. Niven 2006, 112.

65. Sebald 2004, 19.

66. Güntner 1998.

67. Zimmering 1954; five editions totaling 65,000 copies had been printed by 1959.

68. A few other prominent examples from East German literature on the Dresden firebombing are Panitz 1979; Panitz 1980; Czechowski 1990.

69. For Schirrmacher's position on the Walser-Bubis polemic, see Eshel 2000, 340–344, 352–354.

70. Schirrmacher 1998. Other articles in this discussion were published in *Deutsche Literatur Jahresüberblick* 1999, 249–290.

71. Hage 1998.

72. Forte 2002, 10–11, 33, 49.

73. Forte 1998.

74. Niven 2006, 13–14; Taberner 2006, 173–175; Forte 2002, 50–52.

75. Forte 2002, 34–35.

76. Sebald 2004, 103.

77. Grass, Milosz, Szymborska, and Venclova 2001, 30–34.

78. See, for example, his article Friedrich 1993a, 57–77.

79. Friedrich 1984, 17.

80. Friedrich 2006.

81. Friedrich 1993b; for a critique of this book's thesis, see Heer 2004, 274–306.

82. Friedrich 2006, 91.

83. Friedrich 2002a, 93, 311, 359, 388.

84. A total of 79,265 American air crewmen were killed in the line of duty, composing 26.4 percent of the 300,000 American soldiers killed in the war. The British air crews' losses numbered 79,281, composing 23.3 percent of the 340,000 British soldiers killed in action. See "The United States Strategic Bombing Survey. Summary Report (European War) September 30, 1945," http://www.anesi.com/ussbs02.htm.

85. Messenger 1984, 188, 209–211.

86. See Süß 2007, 212ff.

87. Friedrich 2002a, 533ff.

88. Overy 2003a, 183–187.

89. The series appeared daily. The first installment was "Der Feuertodderdeutsche Städte. Brand-Bomben prasseln nieder wie ein Wasserfall," *Bild*, September 18, 2002, 13.

90. See, for example, a characteristic British critique: Barnett 2003, 171–176. For a German critique of the book, see Ullrich 2002.

91. For example, Platthaus 2002; see also Friedrich 2002b.

92. Friedrich 2003.

93. For the major positions in the public debate elicited by the series in *Bild* and by the book in Germany and Britain, see Kettenacker 2003. Even though the historian Hans-Ulrich Wehler rejected Friedrich's use of Holocaust terminology, he himself adopted the term "murder" (*Ermordung*) in referring to the Allied bombings; Wehler 2002.

94. Grünbein 1999, 143–153; I was introduced to Grünbein's poetry by Prof. Amir Eshel of Stanford University, to whom I am grateful. However, I dispute Eshel's view

of how Grünbein treats the war and the Nazi past in this particular poem; see Eshel 2001, 407–416. Grünbein's recent book, *Porzellan,* is also dedicated to the destruction of Dresden; see Grünbein 2005.

95. Keil and Kellerhoff 2002, 135–138; *Dresden—Fall und Aufstieg einer Stadt.* A Film of Carl-Ludwig Paeschke and Dieter Zimmer (ZDF), 1995.

96. Grünbein 1999, 151.

97. Ibid., 149; he engages with this issue also in Grünbein 2005, 109.

98. "Sollte die erste Atombombe auf Dresden fallen?"

99. "Dresden als Ziel für Atombombe." Heisenberg worked for the Germans and participated in the attempt to develop a Nazi nuclear bomb. Fuchs, on the contrary, worked for the Allies.

100. Grünbein 1999, 150.

101. Eshel 2001, 413.

102. Grass 2002.

103. Hage 2002, 184–190.

104. See Hahn and Hahn 2002, 19; Faulenbach 2002, 44–54.

105. Grass 2004, 29, 50.

106. Hage 2002, 185.

107. Büscher 2002.

108. Medicus 2002; Kellerhoff 2002; Günter Franzen 2002; Schlögel 2002.

109. Wittstock 2002; Frei 2005b, 358; Michaelsen and Hinz 2002; Fuhr 2002; Güntner 2002. Even Erika Steinbach rejects the notion that Grass's book broke a taboo. See Hass 2002 and also Moeller 2003, 151.

110. "Grass: Kein Anlass für irgendwelche Denkmäler."

111. Grass 2004, 195.

112. See chapter 1.

113. Grass 2003, 198–199.

114. Ibid., 202f., 225: Konny: "But if you had given me the *Gustloff* for my birthday when I was thirteen or fourteen, I wouldn't have to make up for missing out on this kid's stuff."

115. Grass 2003, 200.

116. Ibid., 199.

117. Ibid., 37–38.

118. Ibid., 49–50.

119. Aly 2005b.

120. Aly 2005a.

121. "Warum ich nach sechzig Jahren mein Schweigen breche"; Schirrmacher 2006.

122. Grass 2003, 39.

123. Ibid.

124. Eshel 2000, 333–339.

125. Grass 2006; see also Margalit 2007.

126. http://www.npd-fraktion-sachsen.de/fra_dokumente/2005/ApfelDresden1302-2.pdf.

127. See, for example, the sympathetic treatment of the book by the journalist Thomas Medicus and the historian Karl Karl Schlögel: Medicus 2002; Schlögel 2002.

128. See in particular an as yet unpublished article by Robert G. Moeller analyzing the film: Moeller n.d.; Kossert 2008, 269–274.

129. Grass 2003, 119.

130. See Wodak 1990.

131. Frei 2005b, 358; Güntner 2005.

132. Frei 2005b, 358.

133. In a speech given on January 21, 2005, the NPD representative in the Saxon state parliament in Dresden called the Federal Republic "the Canossa Republic of reeducation"; http://www.npd-fraktion-sachsen.de/fra_dokumente/2005/Gansel-Dresden1302.pdf.

134. The series has since appeared in book form: Knopp 2001.

135. Ibid., 34–36.

136. Graf von Krockow wrote a well-known book about his family's experience in the war, with the same title as this installment in Knopp's documentary: Krockow 1997.

137. Knopp 2001, 35ff.; Jahn 1997, 67–82; in 1960, and with even greater force in 1962, Gerhard Frey's extreme right-wing newspaper *Deutsche Soldaten Zeitung* embarked on an attack on Ehrenburg and on the plans to publish his works in Germany. The newspaper depicted him as a murderer and stressed his Jewish origins; see "Ilja Ehrenburg der Europäer"; "Tötet alle Deutsche," 1; "Ein Mörder wird verlegt," 1; "Als der rote Terror Deutschland erreichte"; "Was Graf Büllow und Ehrenburg verbindet."

138. De Zayas 1989, 65.

139. Jahn 1997, 7, 77.

140. De Zayas 1989, 201n11.

141. Schieder's anthology of oral testimonies includes two from Nazi officials about the number of civilians killed in Nemmersdorf. One puts the total at sixty-two, the other at seventy-two. However, both testimonies are questionable. One is not dated; the other was recorded in 1953. See Schieder et al. 1955, 5, 8; and de Zayas 1977, 61–65. De Zayas added to the foundation laid by Schieder eyewitness testimonies from Nazi functionaries whose reliability seems, on the face of it, to be most problematic. Thus he granted scholarly legitimacy to a narrative widespread in the neo-Nazi and expellee press, which presented Ehrenburg, an "avenging Jew," in the spirit of Goebbels's propaganda, as the person directly responsible for inciting Soviet soldiers to murder Germans and rape their wives in Nemmersdorf; see Fisch 1997, who presents new testimonies about the event and disproves the charge of rape. Knopp and his staff, along with a part of the German media, based their material on de Zayas's depiction.

142. Knopp 2001, 38ff.

143. *Die Deutsche Wochenschau*, November 2, 1944; Knopp 2001, 43.

144. *Die Deutsche Wochenschau*, November 2, 1944. The term "fanatical" had a positive connotation in the Third Reich, as noted by Klemperer: Klemperer 1975, 77–83.

145. *Die Deutsche Wochenschau*, March 16, 1945.

146. Noack 2002, 36–39.

147. Darnstaedt and Wiegrefe 2002, 40–60, esp. 43.

148. Ibid., 41.

149. Salzborn 2003, 33ff.

150. Fisch 1997.

151. Erik K. Franzen 2002.

152. Ibid., 41.

153. Ibid., 99f.

154. Grass 2003, 103–107; the quotation comes from 107.

155. Martin Walser professed to present an authentic view of the Nazi past, from which he omitted the Holocaust and Nazi crimes on the grounds that they were not known to the German public until after the war. See Eshel 2000, 333–339.

156. Schwartz 2001; Nawratil 2005, esp. 70–76, on his estimation of the number of victims in the expulsion of Germans.

157. Naimark 2002, 2–5; and see Hahn and Hahn 2005, 197–217.

158. See, for example, Schroeder's use of the term in his speech on Homeland Day (*Tag der Heimat*) before German expellee organizations in September 2000: "The awful term 'ethnic cleansing' still rings in our ears" (Das böse Unwort von der "ethnischen Säuberung" haben wir alle noch im Ohr). http://www.bundeskanzler.de/Reden-.7715.11806/Rede-von-Bundeskanzler-Gerhard-Schroeder-anlaess . . . htm (last accessed August 19, 2004). Nevertheless, it should be emphasized that the chancellor did not intend to equate the expulsion of the Germans and the Holocaust. That was, however, the intention of Götz Aly and other Germans who used this term; see Aly 2003a, 28–41.

159. "Umfrage: Polien zweifeln an Deutschen."

160. Glotz died in 2005 following a serious illness.

161. Glotz 2003, 25; see the critique of the book in Hahn and Hahn 2004, esp. 73–74.

162. Haar 2007.

163. Broder 2006; Schulze Wessel 2006. In an interview with Marcus Schmidt, Alfred de Zayas supported the use of this slogan at the German Sudeten convention: Schmidt 2006, 6.

164. Füllig 2005.

165. Fendl 2003, 62–65.

166. Graw 2004; Arning 2004.

167. "Pawelka: Preuβische Treuhand reicht im Herbst ein."

168. "Der polnische Beschluss zur Kriegsentschädigungim Wortlaut."

169. "Was haben wir uns angetan?"

170. "Pro und Contra Vertriebenen-Zentrum."

171. Ther 2003.

172. Kellerhoff 2005; Petersen 2005, 58ff.

173. http://www.bundesregierung.de/regierungserklaerung-,413.926301/Regierungserklaerung-von-Bunde.htm.

174. Interview with Julius H. Schoeps: "Jede Vertreibung ist zu verurteilen."

175. Facius 2003.

176. Zimmermann 2003.

177. Giordano 2002. And see his apologetic piece explaining his change of heart: Giordano 2003.

178. http://www.dradio.de/dlf/sendungen/kulturheute/464778/.

179. Diner 2006. Diner, a historian, spoke before the Saxonian parliament in Dresden on January 27, Holocaust Memorial Day. He disputed the claim that there is no real difference between the death of a Jew in Auschwitz and the death of a German civilian in the Allied bombings. By telling a story that took place in an extension of a concentration camp near Dresden during the bombing of that city, he showed that, from the point of view of a victim facing death, there is a significant difference

between the death sentence imposed by the Nazis on all Jews, simply for having been born Jews, and being suddenly and arbitrarily killed in the Allied bombings.

180. http://www.hdg.de/index.php?id=6425&no_cache=1&L=1&Fsize=2&tx_ttnews[tt_news]=171&tx_ttnews[backPid]=116.

181. Schäfer 2006, 10.

182. Piskorski 2005, 25.

183. Franzen 2006, 35.

184. De Zayas 2006, 180–187.

185. Steinbach's speech on *Haimat* day, August 18, 2007: http://www.bund-der-vertriebenen.de/presse/index.php3?id=597.

186. http://erzwungenewege.z-g-v.de/einfuehrung.htm.

187. Kellerhoff 2007; Hofman 2007; Zekri 2007; Mönch 2007; Speicher 2007; Semler 2007.

188. "Umfrage: Polen zweifeln an Deutschen," 2.

189. Flückiger and Wigura 2008.

190. Graw 2008; Fuhr 2008.

191. "Polen fühlt sich provoziert"; "Vertriebenen Bund nominiert Erika Steinbach"; Neukirch and Paul 2009.

192. "Umstrittenes Vertriebenenzentrum kommt doch."

193. See, for example, the chapter called „The Holocaust of Dresden" in a book by a writer from the extreme right, in which he (typically) supports his position with quotes from David Irving and the British press: Schwinge 1978, 55.

194. See, for example, the film by director Malte Ludin, son of the Nazi war criminal Hans Ludin, which portrays how three generations have confronted the father's deeds: *2 oder 3 Dinge, die ich von ihm weiß* (2005).

195. See, for example, the Federal Republic's intention, during the 1950s, to use the issue of the expellees as a bargaining card with the superpowers against claims for reparations and territory likely to be presented in negotiations for a European peace treaty. The expulsion of the Germans was termed "a crime against the German people." Beer 1998, 345–389.

196. Welzer, Moller, and Tschuggnall 2002.

197. Hirsch 2004, esp. 12 and 16.

198. According to Schulze Wessel 2006, 38 percent of the Czechs believed that the German government would one day demand the Sudetenland or compensation for loss of the territory.

Conclusion

1. Jarausch 2006.
2. Herbert 2002; Jarausch 2006; Doering-Manteuffel 2000; Scheibe 2002.
3. Jarausch 2006, 42–43, 101, 196–205.
4. See Doering-Manteuffel 2000; Scheibe 2002.
5. Herbert 2002. See also the various articles in this book.
6. Ibid., 17.
7. Ibid., 43–45; Moses 1999.
8. Herbert 2002, 44; Moses 1999.
9. Angress 1985, 222.

10. Margalit 2007.

11. Weissmark 2004, 59–60, 62–63, 86, 90; see also Welzer 2002; Wittlinger 2006, 74–75; Wierling 2002b, 47–59.

12. For example, Weissmark 2004, 59, 99.

13. Niven 2006, 20.

14. Ibid., 4.

15. For example, Altmeyer 2003; the author attributes this pattern in fact to all Germans.

16. Moeller 2005b, 171–175.

17. Schmitz 2006.

18. See Herbert 1998, 111–112, on Adenauer's distinction between the "real criminals," who were "a-socials," and others who were convicted of crimes connected to the pursuit of the war—such as senior officers who "only" planned and ordered mass murder but did not actively carry it out.

19. Niven 2006, 20; see also how Norbert Frei evaluates this phenomenon: Frei 2005b, 358–359.

20. *Bundesministerium des Innern* 2007, 31–37.

21. Herbert 1998.

22. Unlike the neo-Nazis, the radical right accepts constitutional principles. Such parties are thus permitted to participate in elections. In practice, there is a clear connection between these extremist parties and the neo-Nazi scene. Neo-Nazi influence in the extreme rightist National Democratic Party (NPD) has grown in recent years. The Federal Office for the Protection of the Constitution report of 2006 even notes that the NPD faction in the Mecklenburg-Western Pomeranian Landtag includes a number of neo-Nazis; see *Bundesministerium des Innern* 2007, 49.

23. See Minister of the Interior Wolfgang Schäuble in the introduction to the Federal Office for the Protection of the Constitution Report (*Bundesministerium des Innern* 2007, 9): "Rightist extremism is a steadily growing problem [in Germany]"; "The level of support for the NPD in some Western Pomeranian communities exceeds 30 percent." Bundes Ministerium 2007, 49.

24. Koennen 2001.

25. For example, the appearance of Friedrich's book in English in 2006, and Nicholson Baker's *Human Smoke* in 2008, which seems to be inspired by Friedrich.

BIBLIOGRAPHY

Archival Sources

Bundesarchiv Koblenz

B 122 / 2238

Bundespräsidialamt: Staatsfeiertage, Staatstrauertage, Gedenktage. Gestaltung, Abhaltung, Teilnahme des Bundespräsidenten 1949–1959.

B136 / 3003

Bundeskanzleramt: Nationaler Gedenktag des deutschen Volkes am 7. September 1950. 1950–1954.

B136 Bundeskanzleramt / 2712

Bundeskanzleramt: Der Bundesminister für gesamtdeutsche Fragen Bd. 4: Zehnjahresgedenken an Flucht und Vertreibung der Ostdeutschen 1954–1955.

B106 / 77151

Bundes Ministerium des Innern: Nationaler Gedenktag des deutschen Volkes am 7. September 1950. Vol. 1–1950.

B 234 / 627

Tag der Deutschen 1955.

Zsg. 109

Sammlung Oberheitmann—Vertraulich Informationen V. I. des Reichsministerium für Volksaufklärung und Propaganda für die Presse.

NL 178/2a Nachlaß Hans-Christoph Seebohm

/14

/18

Bundesarchiv Berlin

DY 55 V278/2/13

DY 30 /J IV/ ⅔ A/167 Protokolle der Sitzungen des Sekretariats des ZK

DY 30 /J IV/2/3/214

DY 30/J IV 2/3/449

NY 4090/517

NY 4217 /29 Nachlaß Albert Norden

Bundesarchiv –Filmarchiv Berlin

Dresden. Ein DEFA Film von Richard Groschopp 1946.
Dresden warnt und mahnt. Ein DEFA Film von Heino Brandes 1951.
Dresden mahnt Deutschland. Ein DEFA Film 1955.
Dresden—Erinnerung und Mahnung. Ein DEFA Film von Max Jaap 1965.
Sächsiches HStA Dresden
A/419
Bay. HSTA
Flüchtlingswesen: Allgemeiner Schriftverkehr 30674 Vol. 2, March 1948.
July 1949
RG 260 OMGUS. OMGB-ID 10/70–3/ 23, 1947
RG 260 OMGUS. OMGB 10/108–3/22
RG 260 OMGUS. OMGB 15/102–2/21
Staatskanzlei 30 131
Staatskanzlei 10 993
STA Hamburg
SKII 4634 020.62.-2 Politische Gedenktage und Feiern. Einzelfälle. Gefalleneehrungen am Totensonntag 1945–1958.
SKII 1628 020.62–6 Gedenkfeiern für die Opfer des NS. 1945–1953.
SKII 1630 020.62–6 Nationaler Gedenktag des deutschen Volkes am 7. September 1950. 1950–1952.
SKII 3974 020.62–8 Volkstrauertag. Verbreitung und Gestaltung der Feiern. 1950–1955.
SKII 3975 020.62–8 Volkstrauertag. 1956–1960.
HH Hamburg-Denkmalschutzamt
39–430.308.1: KZ-Opfer Ehrengedächtnismal Urnengedenkstätte Ohlsdorfer Friedhof v. 27.7.1946
39–430.302: Ehrenmal für die Bombenopfer in Ohlsdorf
Landesarchiv Berlin
C. Rep. 101 Nr. 351, Magistrat von Gross Berlin
C. Rep. 100–05 Nr. 1119
C. Rep. 901 Nr. 374
C. Rep. 907–04 Nr. 388
Stadtarchiv Bochum: BO 41/47 Kulturant: Mahnmal für die Kriegsopfer der Stadt Bochum 1952–1956.
Stadtarchiv Dresden
4.1.4, Nr. 955
4.1.4, Nr. 980
Stadtarchiv Frankfurt
380 Kulturamt Wiederaufstellung des Denkmals "Den Opfern" des Bildhauers Benno Elkan an der Kaiserstr. / Ecke Taunusanlage. 1945–1946.
S1 75 Nr. 25: Nachlaβ Beckmann, Eberhard 1945–1946.
2.297: Magistratsakten Errichtung eines Mahnmals für das unbekannte Zerstörung Frankfurts 1946–1969.
Historisches Archiv, Stadt Cologne: Acc. 177 Nr. 69
Best. 2 Oberbürgermeister Nr. 1361–1370
Stadtarchiv Mannheim: Nachlaβ Hermann Heimerich Zug. 24/1972 Nr. 299
Stadtarchiv Mülheim: 90/5 Bauverwaltungsamt. Ehrenmal für die Opfer des Zweiten Weltkrieges.

Stadtarchiv Pforzheim
1585 Austellungswesen: Kunstaustellung "Pforzheim vor u. nach der Katastrophe von 23.2.1945," 1946.
ZGS 1 657 Zeitungsausschnitte: Grossangriff 23.2.1945.
Evangelisches Zentralarchiv in Berlin
1/A2/650
1/A2/651
Zentralarchiv der Evangelischen Kirche in Hessen und Nassau
35 / 377
62 / 0003 Nachlaβ Martin
0540
0592
0671
Niemöller
Landeskirchliches Archiv Stuttgart: D1.225 Nachlaβ Theophil Wurm.
Archiv der Gedenkstäte Sachsenhausen AS, KAW, K5/M2.
Deutsches Rundfunkarchiv, Wiesbaden
2945653—PK-Bericht: Dresden nach den alliierten Bombenangriffen, 20.2.1945.
Deutsches Volksliedarchiv, Freiburg: Gr. II 2. Weltkrieg M 300
Frankfurter Rundschau Archiv, Mappe Hans-Christoph Seebohm: "Pressenotiz Bundesminister Dr. Seebohm zur Frage der Grenzen von 1937" (undated, but apparently from 1951) Mappe Theodor Oberländer: "Oberländer-Rede über den bagerischen Rundfunk" 5.11. 1954.
Institut für Zeitgeschichte, Munich: OMGUS Files: POLAD 773/ 33
Sudetendeutsches Archiv
H.-C. Seebohm 7/69
16/1a Sudetendeutsche Landesmannschaft -Reden und Veröffentlichungen.
Kanzlei des Sprechers 1/ C
B 9 / 45
B 9 / 46
B 19 / 6 Sudetendeutsche Landesmannschaft
Volksbund Deutsche Kriegsgräberfürsorge e.V.—Landesverband Hamburg, Alte Akten 1915–1968
Tätigkeitsberichte 1946–1988
Institut für Zeitgeschichte, München, OMGUS Files: POLAD 773 / 33
Deutsches Museum, Archiv, Munich: NL Anton Zischka 184–083–Anton Zischka, "Die Hunnen von 1940," September 1942, p. 12.
Public Record Office, London: FO 1005/1868 Public Opinion Research Office. Political Division C.C.G. Bielefeld. Report no. 5, June 1948. Attitude to National Socialism in the British Zone.
National Archive, Washington, D.C.: OMGUS, Information Control Division, Opinion Surveys Branch, box 146, file 20, Daily Intelligence Digest, April 1–June 20, 1946.

Other Sources

Abenheim, Donald. 1988. *Reforming the Iron Cross: The Search of Tradition in the West German Armed Forces.* Princeton, N.J.: Princeton University Press.

Adenauer, Konrad. 1967. *Bundestagreden.* Bonn: AZ Studio.

———. 1983. *Briefe 1945–1947.* Ed. Hans Peter Mensing. Berlin: Siedler.

———. 1995. *Rhöndorfer Ausgabe. Briefe 1953–1955.* Ed. Hans Peter Mensing. Berlin: Siedler.

"Adenauer prüft Seebohm—Rede." 1960. *Frankfurter Rundschau,* September 22.

Adorno, Theodor W. 1956. "Schuld und Abwehr." *Soziologische Schriften* II, 2. Frankfurt a.M.: Suhrkamp. 121–324.

———. 1986. "What Does Coming to Terms with the Past Mean?" In *Bitburg in Moral and Political Perspective,* ed. Geoffrey H. Hartman. Bloomington: Indiana University Press. 114–129.

Ahonen, Pertti. 2003. *After the Expulsion: West Germany and Eastern Europe 1945–1990.* Oxford: Oxford University Press.

"Alliierte Kritik an seebohm-Rede." 1951. *Kurier,* December 5.

"Als der rote Terror Deutschland erreichte." 2004. *Preußische Allgemeine Zeitung,* October 16.

"Als Hamburgs Pulsschlag stockte." 1947. *Hamburger Echo,* no. 58, July 22. 3.

Altmeyer, Martin. 2003. "Deutsche Täter-deutsche Opfer." *Tageszeitung,* August 18.

Aly, Götz. 1999a. *Macht-Geist-Wahn: Kontinuitäten deutschen Denkens.* Frankfurt a.M.: Fischer.

———. 1999b. "Theodor Schieder, Werner Conze oder die Vorstufen der physischen Vernichtung." In *Deutsche Historiker im Nationalsozialismus,* ed. Winfried Schulze and Otto G. Oexle. Frankfurt a.M.: Fischer. 163–182.

———. 2003a. "Dafür wird die Welt büßen." In *Rasse und Klasse: Nachforschungen zum deutschen Wesen.* Frankfurt a.M.: Fischer. 28–41.

———. 2003b. "Europas selbstzerstörung." *Süddeutsche Zeitung,* July 24.

———. 2005a. "Wie die Nazis Ihr Volk kauften." *Die Zeit,* June 15.

———. 2005b. *Hitlers Volksstaat: Raub, Rassenkrieg und nationaler Sozialismus.* Frankfurt: Fischer.

———. 2008. Unser Kampf. 1968- ein irritierter Blick zurïck. Frankfurt: Fischer.

Amishai-Maisels, Ziva. 1992. *Depiction and Interpretation: The Influence of the Holocaust on the Visual Arts.* Oxford: Pergamon.

Amos, Heike. 1999. *Die Westpolitik der SED 1948/49–61: "Arbeit nach Westdeutschland" durch die Nationale Front, das Ministerium für Auswärtige Angelegenheiten und das Ministerium für Staatssicherheit.* Berlin: Akademie.

Anderson, Sheldon. 2001. *A Cold War in the Soviet Bloc: Polish–East German Relations 1945–1962.* Boulder, Colo.: Westview Press.

Angress (Klüger), Ruth K. 1985. "A 'Jewish Problem' in German Postwar Fiction." *Modern Judaism* 5, 3 (October): 215–233.

Anonymous. 1955. *A Woman in Berlin.* Introduction by C. W. Ceram. Trans. James Stern. London: Secker & Warburg.

———. 2003 [1959]. *Eine Frau in Berlin: Tagebuchaufzeichnungen vom 20. April bis 22. Juni 1945.* Frankfurt a.M.: Eichborn.

Arendt, Hannah. 1963. *Eichmann in Jerusalem: A Report on the Banality of Evil.* London: Faber and Faber.

Arning, Matthias. 2004. "Abschied von Gestern." *Frankfurter Rundschau,* August 7.

Aschheim, Steven E. 1996. *Culture and Catastrophe: German and Jewish Confrontations with National Socialism and Other Crises.* London: Macmillan.

Assmann, Aleida, and Ute Frevert. 1999. *Geschichtvergessenheit: Vom Umgang mit deutschen Vergangenheiten nach 1945*. Stuttgart: Deutsche Verlags-Anstalt.

Auerbach, Hellmut. 1995. "Literatur zum Thema: Ein kritischer Überblick." In *Die Vertreibung der Deutschen aus dem Osten: Ursachen, Ereignisse, Folgen*, ed. Wolfgang Benz. Frankfurt a.M.: Fischer. 285–286.

Azaryahu, Maoz. 1991. *Von Wilhelmplatz zu Thälmanplatz: Politische Symbole im öffentlichen Leben der DDR*. Gerlingen: Bleicher.

———. 1999. "Commissioned Memory: Politics of Commemoration in Contemporary Germany." *Tel Aviver Jahrbuch für deutsche Geschichte* 28: 341–354.

Bajohr, Frank. 1997. *"Arisierung" in Hamburg: Die Verdrängung der jüdischen Unternehmer 1933–1945*. Hamburg: Christians.

———. 1998. "The Beneficiaries of 'Aryanization': Hamburg as a Case Study." *Yad Vashem Studies* 26: 173–202.

Baker, Nicholson. 2008. *Human Smoke: The Beginnings of World War II, the End of Civilization*. New York: Simon & Schuster.

Bald, Detlef. 2005. *Die Bundeswehr. Eine kritische Geschichte 1955–2005*. München: C. H. Beck.

Bankier, David. 1992. *The Germans and the Final Solution: Public Opinion under Nazis*. Oxford: Basil Blackwell.

———. 2004. "The Secret and the Exposed in Nazi Wartime Propaganda" (Heb.). *Dapim—Studies on the Shoah* 18, 55–76.

Barnett, Corelli. 2003. "Die Bombardierung Deutschlands war kein Kriegsverbrechen." In *Ein Volk von Opfern: Die neue Debatte um den Bombenkrieg 1940–45*, ed. Lothar Kettenacker. Berlin: Rowohlt. 171–176.

Barnett, Victoria. 1992. *For the Soul of the People: Protestant Protest against Hitler*. Oxford: Oxford University Press.

Bartov, Omer. 1991. *Hitler's Army: Soldiers, Nazis, and War in the Third Reich*. New York: Oxford University Press.

———. 2000. "Germany as Victim." *New German Critique* 80 (Spring-Summer): 29–40.

———. 2005. "The Controversy over the Exhibition 'Crimes of the Wehrmacht': Documentation and Politics." In *Memory and Amnesia: The Holocaust in Germany* (Heb.), ed. Gilad Margalit and Yfaat Weiss. Tel Aviv: Hakibbutz Hameuchad. 372–395.

Bauer, Franz J. 1982. *Flüchtlinge und Flüchtlingspolitik in Bayern 1945–1950*. Stuttgart: Klett-Cotta.

Bauer, Josef. M. 2003. *As Far as My Feet Will Carry Me*. New York: Carroll & Graf.

Bazan, Heinrich Banniza von. 1934. *Deutsche Passion: Ein myth. Spiel in 2 Bildern*. Potsdam: Voggenreiter.

"Becher will nach 'Holocaust' sendungen zur Vertreibung." 1979. *Frankfurter Rundschau*, February 5.

Becker, Kurt. 1960. "Lehren aus den Fall Oberländer." *Die Welt*, April 11.

Becker-Jákli, Barbara, ed. 2002. *Ich habe Köln doch so geliebt. Lebensgeschichten jüdischer Kölnerinnenund Kölner*. Cologne: Emons.

"Be-Ehad be-Mai 1947 Yipaqed Ma'amad Ha-Po'alim Ha-'Ivry be-Milhamto le-Herut ha-'Am ve-le-Sotzializm!" *Ahdut* 3, 9 (11 Iyyar 1947): 1.

Beer, Mathias. 1998. "Im Spannungsfeld von Politik und Zeitgeschichte." *Vierteljahreshefte für Zeitgeschichte* 46: 345–389.

———. 1999. "Der 'Neuanfang' der Zeitgeschichte nach 1945. Zum Verhältnis von nationalsozialistischer Umsiedlungs- und Vernichtungspolitik und der Vertreibung der Deutschen aus Ostmitteleuropa." In *Deutsche Historiker im Nationalsozialismus,* ed. Winfried Schulze and Otto G. Oexle. Frankfurt a.M.: Fischer. 274–301.

"Begin: Ha-Metziyut Mar'eh she-Eskol u-Memshalto Ainam Mesugalim Lenahel 'Inyanei ha-Uma." 1966. *Ha'aretz,* May 19.

Behrenbeck, Sabine. 2003. "Between Pain and Silence: Remembering the Victims of Violence in Germany after 1949." In *Life after Death: Approaches to a Cultural and Social History of Europe during the 1940s and the 1950s,* ed. Richard Bessel and Dirk Schumann. New York: Cambridge University Press.

Benz, Wolfgang. 1990. "Postwar Society and National Socialism: Remembrance, Amnesia, Rejection." *Tel Aviver Jahrbuch für deutsche Geschichte* 19: 1–12.

———, ed. 1995. *Die Vertreibung der Deutschen aus dem Osten: Ursachen, Ereignisse Folgen* 2. Frankfurt a.M.: Fischer.

Berg, Nicolas. 2003a. *Der Holocaust und die Westdeutschen Historiker: Erforschung und Erinnerung.* Göttingen: Wallstein.

———. 2003b. "Eine deutsche Sehnsucht." *Die Zeit,* November 6.

Berthold, Lothar, and Ernst Diehl, eds. 1965. *Revolutionäre deutsche Parteiprogramme vom kommunistischen Manifest zum Programm des Sozialismus.* Berlin: Dietz.

"Besorgnis über Südtirol." 1958. *Frankfurter Rundschau,* April 18.

Bessel, Richard. 2004. *Nazism and War.* New York: Random House.

Best, Geoffrey. 1980. *Humanity in Warfare: The Modern History of the International Law of Armed Conflicts.* London: Methuen.

Biermann, Wolf. 2003. "Die Rettung." In *Hamburg 1943: Literarische Zeugnisse zum Feuerstrurm,* ed. Volker Hage, Frankfurt a.M.: Fischer. 246–252.

Biess, Frank. 2006. *Homecoming: Returning POWs and the Legacies of Defeat in Postwar Germany.* Princeton, N.J.: Princeton University Press.

Billerbeck, Rudolf. 1971. *Die Abgeordenten der ersten Landtage (1946–1951) und der Nationalsozialismusk.* Düsseldorf: Droste.

Bisky, Jens. 2003. "Wenn Jungen Weltgeschichte spielen, haben Mädchen stumme Rollen." *Süddeutsche Zeitung,* September 24.

Bissinger, Manfred. 1970. "Frage an die Bundesbürger: Liegt Polens Grenze an Oder und Neiße?" *Stern* 22: 176–178.

Blaensdorf, Agnes. 1995. "Die Einordnung der NS-Zeit in das Bild der eigenen Geschichte." In *Schwieriges Erbe: Der Umgang mit Nationalsozialismus und Antisemitismus in Oestreich, der DDR und der Bundesrepublik Deutschland,* ed. Werner Bergmann et al. Frankfurt a.M.: Campus.

Blank, Ralf. 2004. "Kriegsalltag und Luftkrieg an der "Heimatfront." In *Die deutsche Kriegsgesellschaft 1939 bis 1945. Das Deutsche Reich und der Zweite Weltkrieg,* vol. 9, part 1, ed. Jörg Echternkamp. München: Deutsche Verlags-Anstalt. 357–461.

Boberach, Heinz. 1984. *Meldungen aus dem Reich. Die geheimen Lageberichte des Sicherheitsdienstes der SS.* Herrsching: Pawlak Verlag.

Bodemann, Michal Y. 1998. "Eclipse of Memory: German Representation of Auschwitz in the Early Postwar Period." *New German Critique* 75 (Fall): 63–72.

"Bomben darauf?" *Märkische Volksstimme.* 1945. April 14.

Bonwetsch, Brend, Gennadij Bordjugov, and Norman M. Naimark, eds. 1998. *Sowjetische Politik in der SBZ 1945–1949. Dokumente zur Tätigkeit der Propagandaverwaltung Informationsverwaltung der SMAD unter Sergej Tjulpanov*. Bonn: Dietz.

Boog, Horst, ed. 1992. *The Conduct of the Air War in the Second World War: An International Companion*. New York: Berg.

———. 2001. "Strategischer Luftkrieg in Europa und Reichsluftverteidigung 1943–1944." In *Das Deutsche Reich in der Defensive. Das Deutsche Reich und der Zweite Weltkrieg*, vol. 7, ed. Horst Boog, Gerhard Krebs, and Detlef Vogel. Stuttgart und München: Deutsche Verlags-Anstalt. 3–411.

Borsdorf, Ulrich, and Mathilde Jamin, eds. 1989. *Überleben im Krieg: Kriegserfahrungen in einer Industrieregion 1939–1945*. Hamburg: Rowohlt.

Braese, Stephan. 2001. "Unmittelbar zum Krieg: Alfred Andersch und Franz Fühmann." In *Nachkrieg in Deutschland*, ed. Klaus Naumann. Hamburg: Hamburger Edition. 472–497.

Brandes, Detlef. 2005. *Der Weg zur Vertreibung, 1938–1945: Plane und Entscheidungen zum "Transfer" der Deutschen aus der Tschechoslowakei und aus Polen*. München: R. Oldenbourg.

"Brandt: Deutschlandpolitik nicht ohne Vertriebene." 1965. *Frankfurter Rundschau*. June 28.

Brandt, Willy. 1971. *In Exile. Essays, Reflections, and Letters, 1933–1947*. Trans. R. W. Last. London: Oswald Wolf.

Breitman, Richard. 1998. *Official Secrets: What the Nazis Planned, What the British and Americans Knew*. New York: Hill and Wang.

Breitman, Richard, and Walter Laqueur. 1994. *Breaking the Silence: The German who Exposed the Final Solution*. Hanover, N.H.: Brandeis University Press.

Brendler, Konrad. 1997. "Die NS-Geschichte als Sozialisationsfaktor und Identitätsballast der Enkelgeneration." In *"Da ist etwas kaputtgegeangen an den Wurzeln. . . ." Identitätsformation deutscher und israrelischer Jugendlicher im Schaten des Holocaust*, ed. Dan Bar-On, Konrad Brendler, and A. Paul Hare. Frankfurt a.M.: Campus. 53–104.

Brenner, Henny. 2001. *"Das Lied ist aus." Ein jüdisches Schicksal in Dresden*. Zürich und München: Pendo.

Briegleb, Klaus. 2003. *Mißachtung und Taboo. Eine Streitschrift zur Frage: "Wie antisemitisch war die Gruppe 47?"* Berlin und Wien: Philo.

"Briten beschimpfen Deutsche." 2004. *Bild*, October 29.

British Bombing Survey Unit. 1998. *The Strategic Air War against Germany*. London: F. Cass.

Brittain, Vera. 2005. *One Voice: Pacifist Writing from the Second World War*. London: Continuum.

Broch, Hermann. 1986. *Briefe über Deutschland 1945–1949. Die Korrespondenz mit Volkmar von Zühlsdorff.*, ed. Paul Michael Lützeler. Frankfurt a.M.: Suhrkamp.

Brockmann, Stephen. 2004. *German Literary Culture at the Zero Hour*. New York: Camden House.

Broder, Henryk M. 2006. "Der Holocaustneid. Die Sudetendeutschen wollen auch Opfer eines Völkermordes sein." *Tagesspiegel*, May 31.

Broszat, Martin, and Saul Friedländer. 1988. "A Controversy about the Historicization of National Socialism." *Yad Vashem Studies* 19 (Fall): 1–47.

Brunswig, Hans. 1978. *Feuersturm über Hamburg. Die Luftangriffe auf Hamburg im 2. Weltkrieg und Ihre Folgen.* Stuttgart: Motorbuch Verlag.

Browning, Christopher R. 1998. *Ordinary Men: Reserve Police Battalion 101 and the Final Solution in Poland.* New York: Harper Perennial.

Bucerius, Gerd. 1993. "'Endlich', rief ich immer Wieder, 'Endlich'," *Welt,* July 18.

Bundes Ministerium des Innern, ed. 2007. *Vergassungsschutzbericht 2006.* Bonn: BMI. In http://www.bmi.bund.de/Internet/Content/Common/Anlagen/Broschuren/2007/Verfassungs Schutzbericht_2006_de,templated=raw,property=publication File.pdf/Verfassungsschutzbericht_2006_de.pdf.

Buscher, Frank M. 1990. "Kurt Schumacher, German Social Democracy and the Punishment of Nazi Crimes." *Holocaust and Genocide Studies* 5, 3: 261–273.

Büscher, Wolfgang. 2002. "Vertrieben. Verdrängt. Vergessen?" *Die Welt,* February 5.

Chamberlin, Brewster S. 1981. "Todesmühlen: Ein frueher Versuch zur Massen-'Umoooerziehung' im besetzten Deutschland 1945–1946." *VfZ* 29: 420–438.

Clark, Mark W. 2002. "A Prophet without Honour: Karl Jaspers in Germany, 1945–1948." *Journal of Contemporary History* 37, 2: 197–222.

Combe, Sonia. 1992. "Gedenkfeiern zur Überwindung der Nazi-Vergangenheit." In *Die Wiedergefundene Erinnerung: Verdraengte Geschichte in Osteuropa,* ed. Annette Leo. Berlin: Basis Druck. 137–158.

Connor, Ian. 1995. "Flüchtlinge und die politischen Parteien in Bayern 1945–1950." *Jahrbuch für Deutsche und Osteuropäische Volkskunde* 38: 133–168.

———. 2006. "German Refugees and the SPD in Schleswig-Holstein, 1945–1950." *European History Quarterly* 36, 2: 175–199.

Conrad, Sebastian. 1999. *Auf der Suche nach der verlorenen Nation: Geschichtsschreibung in Westdeutschland und Japan, 1945–1960.* Göttingen: Vandenhoeck & Ruprecht.

Conway, John S. 1987. "How Shall the Nations Repent? The Stuttgarter Declaration of Guilt, October 1945." *Journal of Ecclesiastical History* 38, 4: 596–622.

Corneliβen, Christoph. 2002. "Die wiederentstandene Historismus: Nationalgeschichte in der Bundesrepublik der fünfziger Jahre." In *Die historische Meistererzählung: Deutungslinien der deutschen Nationalgeschichte nach 1945,* ed. Konrad H. Jarausch and Martin Sabrow. Göttingen: Vandenhoeck & Ruprecht. 78–107.

———. 2003. "Was heiβt Erinnerungskultur? Begriff—Methoden—Perspektiven." *Geschichte in Wissenschaft und Untericht* 10: 548–563.

Cox, Sebastian. 1998. *The Strategic Air War against Germany, 1939–1945: The Official Report of the British Bombing Survey Unit.* London: Frank Cass.

Crew, David F. 2007. "Sleeping with the Enemy? A Fiction Film for German Television about the Bombing of Dresden." *Central European History* 40: 117–132.

Czechowski, Heinz. 1990. *Auf eine im Feuer versunkene Stadt. Gedichte und Prosa 1958–1988.* Halle-Leipzig: Mitteldeutscher Verlag.

Danyel, Jürgen. 1995. "Die Opfer- und Verfolgenperspektive als Gründungskonsens? Zum Umgang mit der Widerstandtradition und der Schuldfrage in der DDR." In *Die geteilte Vergangenheit: Zum Umgang mit Nationalsozialismus und Widerstand in beiden deutshen Staaten,* ed. Jürgen Danyel. Berlin: Akademie. 31–46.

———. 1999a. "Die SED und die 'kleinen Pg's': Zur politischen Integration der ehemaligen NSDAP-Mitglieder in der SBZ/DDR." In *Helden Täter und Verräte: Studien zum DDR—Antifaschismus*, ed. Annette Leo und Peter Reif-Spirek. Berlin: Metropol. 177–196.

———. 1999b. "Die Erinnerung an die Wehrmacht in beiden deutschen Staaten. Vergangenheitspolitik und Gedenkenrituale." In *Die Wehrmacht. Mythos und Realität Im Auftrag des Militärgeschichtlichen Forschungsamtes*, ed. Rolf-Dieter Müller and Hans-Erich Volkmann. München: R. Oldenbourg. 1139–1149.

Darnstaedt, Thomas, and Klaus Wiegrefe. 2002. "Vater, erschiess mich!" *Der Spiegel*, March 25. 40–60.

Das Mahnmal für die Opfer des Bombenkrieges. 1992. Hamburg: Förderkreis Ohlsdorfer Friedhof e.V. 28–30.

"Das Memorndum der Acht. Wissenschftler warnen vor selbst Gefälligkeit und Illusionen." 1962. *Die Zeit*, no. 9, March 2.

de Zayas, Alfred M. 1977. *Nemesis at Potsdam. The Anglo-Americans and the Expulsion of the Germans: Background, Execution, Consequences*. London: Routledge.

———. 1989. *Nemesis at Potsdam: The Expulsion of the Germans from the East*. Lincoln: University of Nebraska Press.

———. 1994. *A Terrible Revenge: The Ethnic Cleansing of the East European Germans, 1944–1950*. New York: St. Martin's.

———. 2006. "Vertreibung und Völkerrecht." In *Flucht, Vertreibung, Integration*, ed. Stiftung Haus der Geschichte der Bundesrepublik Deutschland. Bonn: Kerber. 180–187.

Deist, Wilhelm. 1999. "The Wehrmacht at War." In *The Third Reich. A Historical Reassessment*, ed. Moshe Zimmermann. Jerusalem: Magnes. 197–214.

Den Kämpfer für Frieden und Freihit Ernst Thälmann. 1935. Moskau: Verlagsgenossenschaft ausländischer Arbeiter in der UdSSR.

"Den Unvergessenen." 1946. *Frankfurter Rundschau*, April 23.

Deportation, Flucht und Vertreibung. Ein Rückblick nach 40 Jahren. 1985. München: Bayerisches Staatsministerium für Arbeit and Sozialordnung.

"Der Angriff auf Dresden." 1966. *Frankfurter Allgemeine Zeitung*, July 8.

"Der Bundesminister für Vertriebenenund Flüchtlinge." 1956. *Der Vertriebene*, no. 17, September 1.

"Der 3. Februar 1945 mahnt zu Kampf die Pariser Kriegspakte." 1955. *Neues Deutschland*, February 3.

"Der Feuertodderdeutsche Städte. Brand-Bomben prasseln nieder wie ein Wasserfall." 2002. *Bild*, November 18.

"Der polnische Beschluss zur Kriegsentschädigungim Wortlaut." 2004. *Die Welt*, September 13.

Der Oberländer Prozess. Gekurztes Protokol der Verhandlung vor dem Obersten Gericht der Deutschen Demokratischen Republik von 20.-27. und 29.4.1960. Berlin: Ausschuss für Deutsche Einheit.

Deutsche Literatur 1998 Jahresüberblick. 1999. Stuttgart: Philipp Reclam.

"Die Bomben auf Freiburg." 1955. *Nation Europa* 6 (June): 36.

"Die Bombennaechte von Hamburg." 1946. *Hamburger Echo*, July 20.

"Die Deutschen als Opfer." 2002. *Der Spiegel*, March 25, 36–40.

"Die Flüchtlingsnot—ein Weltproblem." 1955. *Frankfurter Rundschau,* April 4.

Die Kabinettprotokolle der Bundesregierung. 1949. Vol. 1: 317–318.

"Die Schwächen der liberalen Anpasser." 1977. *Münchner Merkur,* April 23.

"Die Tote mahnen die Lebenden: Kämpf für den Frieden!" 1950. *Hamburger Volkszeitung,* no. 169, July 25. 1.

"Die Tränen werden schwinden, die Kerzen heller glühen." 2003. *Bild,* November 30.

"Die Wehrmacht sorgt fuer alle Soldatengraeber." 1940. *Völkischer Beobachter,* October 18.

Diewerge, Wolfgang. 1941. *Deutsche Soldaten sehen die Sowjetunion: Feldpostbriefe aus dem Osten.* Berlin: Limpert.

Diner, Dan. 1983. "The 'National Question' in the Peace Movement: Origins and Tendencies." *New German Critique* 28: 86–107.

———. 2000. *Beyond the Conceivable: Studies on Germany, Nazism, and the Holocaust.* Berkeley: University of California Press.

———. 2002. *Feindbild Amerika: Über die Beständigkeit eines Ressentiments.* München: Propylän.

———. 2006. "Tod ist nicht gleich Tod." *Die Welt,* February 4.

Doering-Mantteuffel, Anselm. 2000. "Westernisierung, Politisch-ideeller und gesellschftlicher Wandel in der Bundesrepublik bis zum Ende der 60er Jahre." In *Dynamische Zeiten: Die 60er Jahre in den beiden deutschen Gesellschaften,* ed. Axel Schildt, Detlef Siegfried, and Karl Christian Lammers. Hamburg: Christians. 311–341.

Doerry, Martin. 2008. *"Nirgendwo und überall zu Haus." Gespräche mit Überlebenden des Holocaust.* München: Goldmann.

Domarus, Max, ed. 2004. *Hitler: Speeches and Proclamations 1932–1945.* Vol. 4: *The Years 1941 to 1945.* Wauconda, Ill.: Bolchazy-Carducci.

Dönhoff, Marion Gräfin. 1946. "Totengedenken 1946." *Die Zeit,* March 21.

Dregger, Alfred. 1986. "Alle toten des Krieges verdienen die gleiche Ehrfurcht." *Frankfurter Allgemeine Zeitung,* November 17.

"Dresden als Ziel für Atombombe." 1965. *Frankfurter Rundschau,* February 9.

"Dresden—die verschwundene Stadt." 1955. *Frankfurter Rundschau,* February 15.

"Dresden mahnt: Erzwingt den Frieden!" 1950. *Neues Deutschland,* February 14.

"Dresden mahnt zum Frieden." 1951. *Neues Deutschland,* February 14. 1.

"Dresden war schliemer als Hiroshima." 1955. *Kasseler Post,* February 11.

"Dresden 20 Jahre danach." 1965. *Freie Presse,* February 13.

"Dresdner gedachten ihrer Heimat." 1955. *Frankfurter Rundschau,* February 14.

Dubiel, Helmut. 1999. *Niemand ist frei von der Geschichte: Die nationalsozialistische Herrschaft in den Debatten des Deutschen Bundestages.* München: Carl Hanser.

Dwinger, Edwin Erich. 1929. *Die Armee hinter Stacheldraht: Das Sibirische Tagebuch.* Jena: E. Diederichs.

———. 1930a. *Zwischen Weiβ und Rot: Die russische Tragödie 1919–1920.* Jena: E. Diederichs.

———. 1930b. *Wir rufen Deutschland: Heimkehr und Vermächtnis; 1921–1924.* Jena: E. Diederichs.

———. 1940. *Der Tod in Polen: Die volksdeutsche Passion.* Jena: Diederichs.

Eberan, Barbro. 1983. *Luther? Friedrich "der Grosse"? Wagner? Nietzsche? . . . ? . . . ? Wer war an Hitler schuld? Die Debatte um die Schuldfrage 1945–1949.* München: Minerva.

Edinger, Lewis J. 1967. *Kurt Schumacher. Persönlichkeit und politisches Verhalten.* Köln und Opladen: Westdeutscher Verlag.

Eich, Heinrich, and Hans Vastag. 2002. *Dem Vergessen Entrissen. Gedenkstätten und Mahnmale der Vertriebenen, Flüchtlinge und Aussiedler in Baden-Württemberg.* Stuttgart: Bund der Vertriebenen.

"Ein Mörder wird verlegt." 1962. *Deutsche Soldaten Zeitung* 33, August 24. 1.

"Eine christliche Aktion in England." 1947. *Die Kirche. Evangalische Wochenzeitung* 18, March 30.

Eisenhower, Dwight D. 1948. *Crusade in Europe.* New York: Doubleday.

Elon, Amos. 1964. "Siha 'im Dr. Adenauer: 'Ani Hayyiti Masdir et 'Inyan ha-Mad'anim.'" *Ha'aretz,* November 6. 11.

———. 1966. "Adenauer: Ain Adam Zaken mi-Lilmod Davar Hadash." *Ha'aretz,* May 5.

Elyashiv, Vera. 1964. *Deutschland kein Wintermärchen. Eine Israeli sieht die Bundesrepublik.* Wien: Econ.

Embacher, Helga, Albert Lichtblau, und Günther Sandner von Residenz, eds. 1999. *Die Wehrmachtaustellung. Dokumentation einer kontroverse.* Bremen: Edition Temmen.

Emmerich, Wolfgang. 1997. *Kleine Literaturgeschichte der DDR.Erweitere Neuausgabe.* Leipzig: Kiepenheuer.

Erb, Scott. 2003. *German Foreign Policy: Navigating a New Era.* Boulder, Colo.: Lynne Rienner.

"Erhard warnt vor Veryicht auf Ostgebiete." 1964. *Frankfurter Rundschau,* March 23.

"Erste Vollsizung des Hauptausschusses 'Opfer des Faschismus.'" 1945. *Deutsche Volkszeitung,* no. 17, July 1.

Eschenburg, Theodor. 1960a. "Des Ministers Betrachtungen." *Die Zeit,* March 18.

———. 1960b. "Unbelehrbar, Herr Minister?" *Die Zeit,* April 14.

———. 1960c. "Seebohms Fall." *Die Zeit,* June 3.

Eshel, Amir. 2000. "Vom eigenen Gewissen: Die Walser-Bubis Debatte und der Ort des Nationalsozialismus im Selbstbild der Bundesrepublik." *Deutsche Vierteljahresschrift für Literaturwissenschaft und Geistesgeschichte* 2 June. 333–360.

———. 2001. "Diverging Memories? Durs Grünbein's Mnemonic Topographies and the Future of the German Past." *German Quarterly* 74, 4 (Fall): 407–416.

Euringer, Richard. 1933. *Deutsche Passion 1933.* Oldenburg: Gerhard Stalling.

Facius, Gernot. 2003. "Überraschender Gegenwind. Nach anfänglichem Wohlwollen kippte die Stimmung gegen das Zentrum." *Die Welt,* September 29.

"Fahnen der Trauer wehten am Niederrhein." 1950. *Kriegsgräberfuersorge* 26, 10 (October): 77–78.

Faulenbach, Bernd. 2002. "Die Vertreibung der Deutschen aus den gebieten jeneseits von Oder und Neiβe." *Aus politik und Zeitgeschichte* B 51: 44–54.

Fendl, Elisabeth. 2003. "'Auch die Seele braucht eine Heimat!' Kirchengebäude in Heimatvertriebenen Gemeinde als Orte der Identifikation." *Jahrbuch für Deutsche und Osteuropäiche Volkskunde* 45: 53–80.

"Feuer fill von Himmel." 1993. *Hamburger Abendblatt, Wochenende Journal*, no. 164, July 17–18. 1–2.

Fisch, Bernhard. 1997. *Nemmersdorf, Oktober 1944. Was in Ostpreußen tatsächlich geschah.* Berlin: Editionost.

Fischer, Alfred Joachim. 1949. "Theodor Heuss berichtet aus seinem Leben." *Neue Zeitung*, September 13.

Fischer, Joschka. 2007. *Die rot-grünen Jahre. Deutsche Außenpolitik - vom Kosovo bis zum 11. September.* Cologne: Kiepenheuer und Witsch.

Flückiger, Paul, and Karolina Wigura. 2008. "Verständigung aus heiterem Himmel." *Die Welt*, February 7.

Forte, Dieter. 1998. *Der Junge mit den blutigen Schuhen*. Frankfurt a.M.: Fischer.

———. 2002. *Schweigen oder Sprechen*. Frankfurt a.M.: S. Fischer.

Foschepoth, Josef. 1995. "Potsdamm und danach: Die Westmächte, Adenauer und die Vertriebenen." In *Die Vertreibung der Deutschen aus dem Osten. Ursachen, Ereignisse Folgen*, ed. Wolfgang Benz. Frankfurt a.M.: Fischer. 86–113.

———. 1997. "German Reaction to Defeat and Occupation." In *West Germany under Construction: Politics, Society, and Culture in the Adenauer Era*, ed. Robert Moeller. Ann Arbor: University of Michigan Press. 73–78.

Francois, Etienne, and Hagen Schulze, eds. 2001. *Deutsche Erinnerungsorte*. München: Beck.

Frank, Volker. 1970. *Antifaschistische Mahnmäle in der DDR: Ihre künstlerische und Architektonische Gestaltung.* Leipzig: VEB E.A. Seemann.

Franzen, K. Erik. 2002. *Die Vertriebenen: Hitlers letzte Opfer.* München: Ullstein.

———. 2006. "Zwangsmigrationen im 20. Jahrhundert bis zum Zweiten Weltkrieg." In *Flucht, Vertreibung, Integration*, ed. Stiftung Haus der Geschichte der Bundesrepublik Deutschland. Bonn: Kerber. 29–35.

Franzen, Günter. 2002. "Der alte Mann und sein Meer." *Die Zeit*, no. 7, February 7.

Frei, Norbert. 1995. "NS-Vergangenheit unter Ulbricht und Adenauer: Gesichtspunkte einer vergleichenden Bewältigungsforschung." In *Die geteilte Vergangenheit. Zum Umgang mit Nationalsozialismus und widerstand in beiden deutschen Staaten*, ed. Jürgen Danyel. Berlin: Akademie. 125–132.

———, ed. 2002a. *Karrieren im Zwielicht: Hitlers Eliten nach 1945*. Frankfurt a.M.: Campus.

———. 2002b. *Adenauer's Germany and the Nazi Past: The Politics of Amnesty and Integration*. New York: Columbia University Press.

———. 2005a. "'Erlöst und vernichtet in einem.' Das Kriegsende im Gedächtnis der deutschen." *Neue Zürcher Zeitung*, May 14.

———. 2005b. "Wie aus Täter Opfer werden." *Blätter für deutsche und internationale Politik* 3: 356–364.

———. 2005c. *1945 und Wir. Das Dritte Reich im Bewusstsein der Deutschen.* München: C. H. Beck.

———. 2008. *1968. Jugendrevolte und globaler Protest.* München: Deutscher Taschenbuch Verlag.

Frei, Thomas. 2004. "Wallberg schreibt Geschichte." *Pforzheimer Zeitung*, July 25.

Frey, V. A., ed. 1941. *Tapfere Trauer: Ein Gedenken für Unsere Gefallenen.* Stuttgart und Berlin: Truckenmüller Verlag.

Friedländer, Saul. 1997. *Nazi Germany and the Jews.* Vol. 1: *The Years of Persecution, 1933–1939.* New York: HarperCollins.

Friedmann, Jan, and Jörg Später. 2002. "Britische und deutsche Kollektivschuld-Debatte." In *Wandlungsprozesse in Westdeutschland. Belastung, Integration, Liberalisierung 1945–1980,* ed. Ulrich Herbert. Göttingen: Wallstein. 53–90.

Friedrich, Jörg. 1984. *Die kalte Amnestie: NS-Täter in der Bunderepublik.* Frankfurt a.M.: Fischer.

———. 1993a. "Confronting the Past: The Attitude toward Nazi War Criminals in the Federal Republic" (Heb.). In *"Normal" Relations: Israeli-German Relations,* ed. Moshe Zimmermann and Oded Heilbronner. Jerusalem: Magnes. 57–77.

———. 1993b. *Das Gesetz des Krieges. Das deutsche Heer in Rußland 1941 bis 1945: Der Prozeß gegen dei Oberkommando der Wehrmacht.* München: Piper.

———. 2002a. *Der Brand: Deutschland im Bombenkrieg 1940–1945.* Berlin: Propyläen.

———. 2002b. "Ein Kriegsverbrechen? Das muss jeder für sich selbst entscheiden." *Die Welt,* November 21.

———. 2003. *Brandstätten: Der Anblick des Bombenkrieges.* Berlin: Propyläen.

———. 2006. *The Bombing of Germany 1940–1945.* Trans. Allison Brown. New York: Columbia University Press.

Fritzsche, Peter. 1998. *Germans into Nazis.* Cambridge, Mass.: Harvard University Press.

———. 2002. "Volkstümliche Erinnerung und deutsche Identität nach dem Zweiten Weltkrieg." In *Verletztes Gedächtnis. Erinnerungskultur und Zeitgeschichte im Konflikt,* ed. Konrad H. Jarausch and Martin Sabrow. Frankfurt: Campus. 75–98.

Frohn, Axel. 1996. "Adenauer und die Deutschen Ostgebiete in den Fünfziger Jahren." *Vierteljahrhefte für Zeitgeschihte* 44: 485–525.

Fuhr, Eckhard. 2002. "Ein Anfall von Nostalgie. Interview mit der Historiker Hans Ulrich Wehler." *Die Welt,* February 22.

———. 2008. "Kultursminister Neumann löst Spannung." *Die Welt,* March 19.

Fulbrook, Mary. 1998. *German National Identity after the Holocaust.* Cambridge: Polity Press.

Füllig, Thomas. 2005. "Erzbistum will kein Vertriebenenzentrum." *Die Welt,* August 16.

Gassert, Philipp. 1997. *Amerika im Dritten Reich: Ideologie, Propaganda, und Volksmeinung 1933–1945.* Stuttgart: Franz Steiner.

———. 2006. *Kurt Georg Kiesinger 1904–1988. Kanzler zwischen den Zeiten.* München: Deutsche Verlags-Anstalt.

Gausmann, Ulrich. 2001. "Für Volk und Vaterland." Eine hitorisch-soziologische Studie über die Politik der Kommunistischen Partei Deutschlands zur nationalen Frage 1945–1949. Diss., University of Paderborn.

"Gefallenen-Schändung." 1950. *Hamburger Freie Presse,* November 15.

Geissel, Eike. 1992. *Die Banalität der Guten: Deutsche Seelenwanderungen.* Berlin: Edition Tiamat.

Gerlach, Wolfgang. 1987. *Als die Zeugen schwiegen: Bekennende Kirche und die Juden.* Berlin: Institut Kirche und Judentum.

Geyer, Michael. 1999. "'There Is a Land Where Everything Is Pure: Its Name Is Land of Death': Some Observation on Catastrophic Nationalism." In *Sacrifice and Na-*

tional Belonging in Twentieth-Century Germany, ed. Greg Eghigian and Matthew Paul Berg. College Station: Texas A& M University Press, 118–147.

———. 2001. "Der Kalte Krieg, Die Deutschen und die Angst. Die westdeutsche Opposition gegen Wiederbewaffung und Kernwaffen." In *Nachkrieg in Deutschland*, ed. Klaus Naumann. Hamburg: Hamburger Edition. 267–318.

Giordano, Ralph. 1990. *Die zweite Schuld oder Von der Last Deutscher zu sein*. München: Knaur.

———. 2002. "Der böse Geist der Charta." *Die Welt*, February 9.

———. 2003. "Ein Herz für den geschlagenen Feind." *Frankfurter Allgemeine Zeitung*, no. 28, July 13.

Glaser, Hermann. 1986. *The Rubble Years: The Cultural Roots of Postwar Germany 1945–1948*. New York: Paragon House.

Glotz, Peter. 2003. *Die Vertreibung. Böhmen als Lehrstück*. Berlin: Ullstein.

Goda, Norman J. W. 2007. *Tales from Spandau: Nazi Criminals and the Cold War*. New York: Cambridge University Press.

Goebbels, Joseph. 1943. "Der Luft- und Nervenkrieg." *Das eherne Herz: Reden und Aufsätze aus den Jahren 1941/42*. München: Eher.

Goes, Albrecht. 1954. *Das Brandopfer*. Frankfurt a.M.: S. Fischer.

———. 1956. *Das Dreifache Ja: Rede zum Volkstrauertag*. Frankfurt a.M.: Fischer.

Goldensohn, Leon. 2004. *The Nuremberg Interviews: An American Psychiatrist's Conversations with the Defendants and Witnesses*, ed. Robert Gellately. New York: Alfred A. Knopf.

Goldhagen, Daniel J. 1996. *Hitler's Willing Executioners: Ordinary Germans and the Holocaust*. New York: Alfred A. Knopf.

Gordon, Adi. 2004. *"In Palestine. In a Foreign Land": The Orient. A German-Language Weekly between German Exile and Aliyah* (Heb.). Jerusalem: Magnes.

Gordon, Sarah. 1984. *Hitler, Germans, and the "Jewish Question."* Princeton, N.J.: Princeton University Press.

Goschler, Constantin. 1992. *Wiedergutmachung: Westdeutschland und die Verfolgten des Nationalsozialismus 1945–1954*. München: R. Oldenbourg.

———. 1993. "Paternalismus und Verweigerung: Die DDR und die Wiedergutmachung für jüdische Verfolgte des Nationalsozialismus." *Jahrbuch für Antisemitismusforschung* 2. 93–117.

———. 2005a. *Schuld und Schulden. Die Politik der Wiedergutmachung für NS-Verfolgte Seit 1945*. Göttingen: Wallstein.

———. 2005b. "'Versöhnung' und 'Viktimisierung'. Die Vertriebenen und der deutsche Opferdiskurs." *Zeitschrieft für Geschichtswissenschaft* 53, 10: 873–884.

Grass, Günter. 2002. *Im Krebsgang: eine Novelle*. Göttingen: Steidl.

———. 2004. *Crabwalk*. Trans. Krishna Winston. Orlando: Harcourt, Harvest Books.

———. 2006. *Beim Häuten der Zwibel*. Göttingen: Steidl.

Grass, Günter, Milosz Czeslav, Wislawa Szymborska, and Tomas Venclova. 2001. *Die Zukunft der Erinnerung*. Göttingen: Steidl.

"Grass: Kein Anlass für irgendwelche Denkmäler." 2003. *Die Welt*, January 12.

Graw, Ansgar. 2004. "Vertriebene fordern vom Kanzler nationales Entschädigungsgesetz." *Die Welt*, August 3.

———. 2008. "Ein Paar Beschlüsse, ein wenig Streit und dann Osterfriede." *Die Welt*, March 20.

Grayling, A. C. 2007. *Among the Dead Cities: Is the Targeting of Civilians in War Ever Justified?* London: Bloomsbury.

Grebing, Helga. 1990. *Flüchtlinge und Parteien in Niedersachsen. Eine Untersuchung der politischen Meinungs- und Willensbildungsprozesse während der ersten Nachkriegszeit 1945–1952/1953.* Hannover: Hahnsche Buchhandlung.

Greschat, Martin. 1982. *Die Schuld der Kirche: Dokumente und reflexionen zur Stuttgarter Schulderklärung vom 18./19. Oktober 1945.* München: Chr. Kaiser.

———. 2000. "'Mehr Wahrheit in der Politik!'. Das Tübinger Memorandum von 1961." *VfZ* 48: 491–513.

Gretschel, Mathias. 1995. *Die Dresdner Frauenkirche.* Hamburg: Ellert & Richter.

Groehler, Olaf. 1975. *Geschichte des Luftkrieg 1910–1970.* Berlin: Militärvetrlag der DDR.

———. 1988. *Kampf um die Luftherrschaft.* Berlin: Militärvetrlag der DDR.

———. 1992a. "Der Holocaust in der Geschichtsschreibung der DDR." In *Zweierlei Bewaeltigung: Vier Beitraege ueber den Umgang mit der NS-Vergangenheit in den beiden deutschen Staaten,* ed. Ulrich Herbert and Olaf Groehler. Hamburg: Ergebnisse. 41–66.

———. 1992b. "The Strategic Air War and Its Impact on the German Civilian Population." In *The Conduct of the Air War in the Second World War: An International Companion,* ed. Horst Boog. New York: Berg. 279–297.

———. 1994. "SED, VVN und Juden in der sowjetischen Besazungszone Deutschlands (1945–1949)." *Jahrbuch für Antisemitismusforschung* 3: 282–302.

Groh, Christian. 2000. *Das war das 20. Jahrhundert in Pforzheim.* Gudensberg-Gleichen: Wartberg.

Grossmann, Atina. 1997. "A Question of Silence: The Rape of German Women by Occupation Soldiers." In *West Germany under Construction: Politics, Society, and Culture in the Adenauer Era,* ed. Robert Moeller. Ann Arbor: University of Michigan Press. 33–52.

Grünbein, Durs. 1999. *Nach die Satiren.* Frankfurt a.M.: Suhrkamp.

———. 2005. *Porzellan. Poem vom Untergang Meiner Stadt.* Frankfurt a.M.: Suhrkamp.

Grünberg, Wolfgang. 1997. "'Als das feuer vom Himmel fiel . . .'. St. Nikolai als Gedächtnisort." In *Das Gedächtnis der Stadt. Hamburg im Umgang mit Seiner nationalsozialistischen Vergangenheit,* ed. Peter Reichel. Hamburg: Döling und Galitz. 47–60.

Güntner, Joachim. 1998. "Der Luftkrieg fend im Osten statt." *Neue Züricher Zeitung,* January 24.

———. 2002. "Opfer und Tabu." *Neue Zürcher Zeitung,* February 23.

———. 2005. "Politik der Entschuldung?" *Neue Züricher Zeitung,* March 1.

Haar, Ingo. 2005. "Morden für die Karriere; Eine skandalöse Quelle im geplanten Zentrum gegen Vertreibungen." *Süddeutsche Zeitung,* January 17.

———. 2006. "Hochgerechnetes Unglück." *Süddeutsche Zeitung,* November 14. 46.

———. 2007. "Die deutsche 'Vertreibungsverluste'—Zur Entstehungsgeschichte der 'Dokumentation der Vertreibung.'" *Tel Aviver Jahrbuch für deutsche Geschichte* 35: 251–272.

Haar, Ingo, and Michael Fahlbush. 2005. *German Scholars and Ethnic Cleansing 1919–1945.* New York: Berghahn Books.

Habenicht, Gottfried. 1996. *Leid in Lied. Südost- und ostdeutsche Lagerlieder und Lieder von Flucht, und vertreibung und Verschpleppung.* Freiburg: Johannes-Künzig-Institut für ostdeutsche Volkskunde.

Hadek, Alfred. 1947. *Flüchtlinge im Kampf um eine neue Heimat!* München: Landesleitung der Kommunistischen Partei.

Hage, Volker. 1998. "Feuer vom Himmel." *Der Spiegel,* no. 3, January 12.

———. 2002. "Das tausendmalige Sterben." *Der Spiegel,* no. 6, February 4. 184–190.

Hahn, Eva. n.d. "Das völkische Stereotyp, 'Osteuropa' im kalten Krieg." http://www.bohemistik.de/lemberg.pdf. Accessed October 17, 2007.

Hahn, Eva, and Hans Henning Hahn. 2002. "Wie aus Flüchtlingen Vertriebene wurden." *Frankfurter Rundschau,* no. 171, July 26.

———. 2004. "Peter Glotz und seine Geschichtsbilder." *Zeitschrift für Geschichtswissenschaft* 52: 72–80.

———. 2005. "The Resettlement of the German Population from Eastern Europe in Retrospect. On the New Interpretation of 'Expulsion' as 'Ethnic Cleansing'" (Heb.). *Dapim—Studies on the Shoah* 19: 197–218.

Hahn, Hans-Joachim. 2005. "From the 'German Passion' to the 'People of Victims': The Return of National Anti-Semitic Patterns within German Literature" (Heb.). *Dapim—Studies on the Shoah* 19, 219–240.

"Hamburg, die unverzagte Stadt." 1973. *Hamburger Abendblatt,* no. 172, July 26. 10.

Hamburger Institut für Sozialforschung, ed. 1996. *Vernichtungskrieg. Verbrechen der Wehrmacht 1941–1944. Ausstellungkatalog.* Hamburg: Hamburger Edition.

———. 1999. *Eine Ausstellung und Ihre Folgen.* Hamburg: Hamburger Edition.

Hartewig, Karin. 2000. "Militarismus und Antifaschismus: Die Wehrmacht im kollektiven Gedächtnis der DDR." In *Der Krieg in der Nachkriegszeit: Der Zweite Weltkrieg in Politik und Gesellschaft der Bundesrepublik,* ed. Michael Th. Greven and Oliver von Wrochem. Opladen: Leske & Budrich. 237–254.

Hartman, Geoffrey, ed. 1986. *Bitburg in Moral and Political Perspective.* Bloomington: Indiana University Press.

Hartmann, Christian. 2004. "Verbrecherischer Krieg—verbrecherische Wehrmacht? Überlegungen zur Struktur des deutschen Ostheeres 1941–1944." *Vierteljahrshefte für Zeitgeschichte* 52: 1–75.

Hartog, Arie. 2001. "A Clean Tradition? Reflections on German Figurative Sculpture." In *Taking Positions: Figurative Sculpture and the Third Reich,* ed. Penelope Curtis. London: Henry Moore Foundation. 30–41.

Hass, Frauke. 2002. "Die Menschen haben sich nicht gefreut, dass wir da waren. Die Bundestagsabgeordnete Erika Steinbach über das durch Günter Grass wiedererweckte Thema Vertreibung." *Frankfurter Rundschau,* February 16.

Hass, Gerhart. 1999. "Zum Bild der Wehrmacht in der Geschichtsschreibung der DDR." In *Die Wehrmacht: Mythos und Realitaet, im Auftrag des Militaergeschichtlichen Forschungsamtes,* ed. Rolf-Dieter Müller and Hans-Erich Volkmann. München: R. Oldenbourg Verlag. 1100–1112.

Hastings, Max. 1987. *Bomber Command.* New York: Simon and Schuster.

Haury, Thomas. 2002. *Antisemitismus von Links: Kommunistische Ideologie, Nationalismus und Antizionismus in der frühen DDR.* Hamburg: Hamburger Edition.

Heer, Hannes. 2004. *Vom Verschwinden der Täte: Der Vernichtungskrieg fand statt, aber keiner war Dabei.* Berlin: Aufbau.

Heim, Susanne, and Götz Aly. 1994. "The Holocaust and Population Policy: Remarks on the Decision on the 'Final Solution.'" *Yad Vashem Studies* 24: 45–70.

"Heimatrecht ist ein Teil des Völkerrecht." 1958. *Frankfurter Rundschau*, September 16.

Heineman, Elizabeth. 1996. "The Hour of the Woman: Memories of Germany's 'Crisis Years' and West German National Identity." *American Historical Review* 101, 2 (April): 354–395.

Heller, Edith. 1992. *Macht Kirche Politik. Der Briefwechsel zwischen den polnischen und deutschen Bischöfen im Jahre 1965*. Köln: Treff-Punkt-Verl.

Henke, Klaus-Dietmar. 1995. "Der Weg nach Potsdam: Die Alliierten und die Vertreibung." In *Die Vertreibung der Deutschen aus dem Osten: Ursachen, Ereignisse, Folgen*, ed. Wolfgang Benz. Frankfurt a.M.: Fischer. 58–85.

Henrich, Hans. 1951. "Heil Seebohm!" *Frankfurter Rundschau*, December 7.

Herbert, Ulrich. 1998. "NS-Eliten in der Bundesrepublik." In *Verwandlungspolitik. NS-Eliten in der westdeutschen Nachkriegsgesellschaft*, ed. Wilfried Loth and Bernd-A. Rusinek. Frankfurt: Campus. 93–116.

———. 2000. "Extermination Policy: New Answers and Questions about the History of the 'Holocaust' in German Historiography." In *National Socialist Extermination Policies: Contemporary German Perspectives and Controversies*, ed. Ulrich Herbert. New York: Berghahn. 1–52.

———. 2002. "Liberalisierung als Lernprozeβ. Die Bundesrepublikin der deutschen Geschichte—eine Skizze." In *Wandlungsprozesse in Westdeutschland. Belastung, Integration, Liberalisierung 1945–1980*, ed. Ulrich Herbert. Göttingen: Wallstein. 7–52.

Herbert, Ulrich, and Olaf Groehler. 1994. "SED, VVN und Juden in der sowjetischen Besatzungszone Deutschlands 1945–1949." *Jahrbuch für Antisemitismusforschung* 3: 282–302.

Herf, Jeffrey. 1980. "The 'Holocaust' Reception in West Germany: Right, Center and Left." *New German Critique* 19: 30–52.

———. 1997. *Divided Memory: The Nazi Past in the Two Germanys*. Cambridge, Mass.: Harvard University Press.

Heuss, Theodor. 1940. "Das Groβere Vaterland." *Das Reich*, no. 8, July 14.

———. 1955. *Würdigungen, Reden, Aufsätze und Briefe aus den Jahren 1949–1955*. Ed. Hans Bott. Tübingen: Wuderlich.

———. 1964. *An und über Juden: Aus Schriften und Reden, 1906–1963*. Düsseldorf und Wien: Econ-Verlag.

———. 1967. *Die Grossen Reden*. München: DTV.

Hippler, Fritz. 1994. *Korrekturen: Zeitgeschichtliche Spurensuche, einmal anders*. Berg: VGB-Verlagsgesellschaft.

Hirsch, Helga. 2004. *Schweres Gepäck. Flucht und Vertreibung als Lebensthema*. Hamburg: Edition Körber Stiftung.

"Historiker Irving korrigierte sich." 1966. *Frankfurter Rundschau*, July 8.

"Historikerstreit." Die Dokumentation der Kontroverse um die Einzigartigkeit der nationalsozialistischen Judenvernichtung. 1987. München: Piper.

Hochhuth, Rolf. 1968. *Soldiers: An Obituary for Geneva*. Trans. Robert David MacDonald. New York: Grove Press.

"Hochkomissare protestiere gegen Seebohm Ausführungen." 1951. *Frankfurter Rundschau*, December 5.

Hodenberg von, Christina. 2002. "Die Journalisten und der Aufbruch zur kritischen Öffentlichkeit." In *Wandlungsprozesse in Westdeutschland. Belastung, Integration, Liberalisierung 1945–1980*, ed. Ulrich Herbert. Göttingen: Wallstein. 278–314.

Hofman, Gunter. 2007. "Trübe wege." *Die Zeit*, August 10.

Hoffmann, Dierk, and Michael Schwartz, eds. 1999. *Geglückte Integration—Spezifika und Vergleichbarkeiten der Vertriebenen-Eingliederung in der SBZ/DDR.* München: R. Oldenbourg.

Hoffmann, Dierk, et al., eds. 1993. *Die DDR vor dem Mauerbau: Dokumente zur Geschichte des anderen deutsche staates 1949–1961.* München: Piper.

Hoffmann, Egbert A. 1983. "Sir Arthur Harris' tödliche Rechnung." In "Als der Feuer vom Himmel fiel. Eine Serie." *Hamburger Abendblatt*, no. 162, July 15. 7.

Hoffman, Volkmar. 1964. "Bundesminister Krüger beurlaubt." *Frankfurter Rundschau*, January 23.

Hoffmann-Curtius, Kathrin. 1999. "Sieg ohne Trauer—Trauer ohne Sieg: Totenklage auf Kriegerdenkmäler des Ersten Weltkrieges." In *Trauer tragen-Trauer zeigen. Inszenierungen der Geschlechter*, ed. Gisela Ecker. München: Wilhelm Fink. 259–286.

———. 2002. "Feminisierte Trauer und aufgerichtete Helden Figürlichen Denkmäler der frühen Nachkriegzeit in Deutschland und Österreich." In *Gedächtnis und Geschlecht: Deutungsmuster in Darstellungen des nationalsozialistischen Genozids*, ed. Insa Eschebach et al. Frankfurt a.M.: Campus. 363–394.

Hofman, Gunter. 2007. "Trübe wege." *Die Zeit*, August 10.

Hofmann, Margaret. 1964. "Als Dresden in Truemmer sank." *Die Zeit*, September 25.

Hohlbaum, Robert. 1924. *Die deutsche Passion.* Leipzig: Staackmann.

"Holländische Kritik an Seebohm." 1964. *Frankfurter Rundschau*, May 21.

Holze, Henry. 1992. "Die Botschaft der Stalingrad Madona." In *Die Stalingrad—Madona: Das Werk Kurt Reubers als Dokument der Versöhnung*, ed. Martin Kruse. Hannover: Lutherisches Verlagshaus, pp. 14–20.

Hörning, Erika. 1985. "Frauen als Kriegsbeute: Der Zweifrontenkrieg, Beispiel aus Berlin." In *"Wir kriegen jetzt andere Zeiten": Auf der Suche nach den Erfahrungen des Volkes in nachfaschistischen Ländern*, ed. Lutz Niethammer and Alexander von Plato. Berlin und Bonn: Dietz. 327–347.

"Ilja Ehrenburg der Europäer." 1960. *Deutsche Soldaten Zeitung* 9, May 1. Folge.

"Im Bewuβtsein der Kraft unseres freien Volkes schreiten wir mit Optimismus voran." 1970. *Neues Deutschland*, February 13.

"Inferno—empfunden, aber nicht gestalten." 1953. *Frankfurter Rundschau*, February 10.

Institut für Denkmalpflege in der DDR, ed. 1974. *Gedenkstaetten. Arbeiterbewegung. Antifaschistischer Widerstand Aufbau des Sozialismus.* Leipzig: Urania Verlag.

Institut für Zeitgeschichte, München, 1947. OMGUS Files: POLAD 773/33, report of the American Consulate in Munich on Wilhelm Pieck's speech, March 20.

"An Interview with Julius H. Schoeps: Jede Vertreibung ist zu verurteilen." 2003. *Jungle World*, October 1.

Irving, David. 1963. *The Destruction of Dresden.* London: Macmillan.

———. 1964. *Der Untergang Dresdens.* Gütersloh: Siegbert Mohn.

Jahn, Peter, ed. 1997. *Ilja Erenburg und die Deutschen.* Berlin: Museum Berlin—Karlhorst.

Janowitz, Morris. 1946. "German Reactions to Nazi Atrocities." *American Journal of Sociology* 52, 2 (September): 141–146.

Jarausch, Konrad H. 2002. "Die Krise der nationalen Meistererzählungen." In *Die historische Meistererzählung: Deutungslinien der deutschen Nationalgeschichte nach 1945*, ed. Konrad H. Jarausch and Martin Sabrow. 40–162.

———. 2006. *After Hitler. Recivilizing Germans, 1945–1995*. Trans. Brandon Hunziker. Oxford: Oxford University Press.

Jarausch, Konrad H., and Martin Sabrow. 2002. "'Meistererzählung'—Zur Karriere eines Begriff." In *Die historische Meistererzählung: Deutungslinien der deutschen Nationalgeschichte nach 1945*, ed. Konrad H. Jarausch and Martin Sabrow. Göttingen: Vandenhoeck & Ruprecht. 9–32.

Jaspers, Karl. 1946. *Die Schuldfrage. Ein Beitrag zu dentschen Frage*. Zürich: Artemis.

———. 1965. *Hoffnung und Sorge. Schriften zur deutschen Politik 1945–1965*. München: Piper.

———. 2000. *The Question of German Guilt*. Trans. E. B. Ashton. New York: Fordham University Press.

Jelinek, Yeshayahu A. 1990. "Political Acumen, Altruism, Foreign Pressure or Moral Debt: Konrad Adenauer and the 'Shilumim.'" *Tel Aviver Jahrbuch für deutsche Geschichte* 19: 77–102.

Jelpke, Ulla. 2002. "Vertriebene hoffähig." *Junge Welt*, June 29.

Jessen, Ralph. 2002. "Zeithistoriker im Konfliktfeld der Vergangenheitspolitik." In *Verletztes Gedächtnis. Erinnerungskultur und Zeitgeschichte in Konflikt*, ed. Konrad H. Jarausch and Martin Sabrow. Frankfurt: Campus. 153–176.

Johr, Barbara. 2005. "Die Ereignisse in Zahlen." In *BeFreier und Befreite. Krieg, Vergewaltigung, Kinder*, ed. Helke Sander and Barbara Johr. Frankfurt a.M.: Fischer. 46–73.

Jordan, Maria. 1956. "Die nicht oeffentliche Meinung." *Colloquium*: 16–17.

Jünger, Ernst. 1980. *Sämtliche Werke 3, Tagebücher III: Strahlungen II*. Stuttgart: Klett-Cotta.

Kansteiner, Wulf. 2003a. "Die Radikalisierung des deutschen Gedächtnisses im Zeitalter seiner kommerziellen Reproduktion: Hitler und das 'Dritte Reich' in den Fernsehdokumentationen von Guido Knopp." *Zeitschrift für Geschichtswissenschaft* 51. Jg. Heft 7: 626–648.

———. 2003b. "Ein Völkermord ohne Täter? Die Darstellung der 'Endlösung' in den Sendungen des Zweiten Deutschen Fernsehens." *Tel Aviver Jahrbuch für deutsche Geschichte* 31: 278–297.

"Kanzler beschwichtigt Rom." 1960. *Frankfurter Rundschau*, September 21.

"Kanzler glaubt an Rückkehr der Schlesier." 1953. *Frankfurter Rundschau*, July 27.

"Kanzler verurteilt Seebohm-Rede." 1964. *Frankfurter Rundschau*, June 9.

Kappel, Kai. 2005. "Der Umgang mit Ruinen und Trümersteinen des Zweiten Weltkrieges." In *Architektur der Wunderkinder: Aufbruch und Verdrängung in Bayern 1945–1960*, ed. Winfried Nerdinger and Inez Florschütz. Salzburg-München: Verlag Anton Pustet. 25–31.

Keil, Lars-Broder, and Sven Felix Kellerhoff. 2002. *Deutsche Legenden: Vom "Dolchstoss" und anderen Mythen der Geschichte*. Berlin: Ch. Links.

Keilbach, Judith. 2002. "Von Hitler zu Holokaust. Die thematisierung des Holocaust in den Geschichtsdokumentationen der ZDF—Redaktion Geschichte." In *Nar-*

rative der Shoah: Repräsentationen der Vergangenheit in Historiographie, Kunst und Politik, ed. Susanne Düwell and Mathias Schmidt. Paderborn, München, Wien, und Zürich: Ferdinand Schönning. 127–141.

Kellerhoff, Sven Felix. 2002. "Versenkt, verdrängt, vergessen." *Berliner Morgenpost*, February 5.

———. 2005. "Nur jeder Zehnte kennt das Ausmaβ der Vertreibung." *Die Welt*, November 11.

———. 2007. "Zentrum gegen Vorurteile." *Die Welt*, August 10.

Kempowski, Walter. 1999. *Echolot (Fuga Furiosa): Ein Kollektives Tagebuch Winter 1945*. München: Knaus.

Kershaw, Ian. 1979. "Antisemitismus und Volksmeinung: Reaktionen auf die Judenverfolgung." In *Bayern in der NS-Zeit* II, ed. Martin Broszat and Elka Fröhlich. München: R. Oldenbourg. 281–348.

———. 1981. "The Persecution of the Jews and German Popular Opinion in the Third Reich." *Leo Baeck Institute Year Book* 26: 261–290.

Kessler, Ralf, and Hartmut Rüdiger Peter. 1995. "Antifaschisten in der SBZ. Zwischen elitärem Selbstverständnis und politischer Instrumentalisierung." *Vierteljahrshefte für Zeitgeschichte* 43: 611–632.

Kettenacker, Lothar, ed. 2003. *Ein Volk von Opfern: Die neue Debatte um den Bombenkrieg 1940–45*. Berlin: Rowohlt.

Kirchliches Jahrbuch für die evangelische Kirche in Deutschland 1945–1948. 1949. Gütersloh: Bretelsmann.

Kittel, Manfred. 2007. *Vertreibung der Vertriebenen? Der historische deutsche Osten in der Erinnerungskultur der Bundesrepublik 1961–1982*. München: R. Oldenburg.

"Klärung dringend nötig." 1951. *Neue Zeitung*, December 6.

Klausing, Helmut. 1946. "Deutsche Passion." *Rad. Neuste Nachrichten*, April 25.

Klein, Gotthard. 1997. *Seliger Bernhard Lichtenberg*. Regensburg: Schnell & Steiner.

Klemperer, Victor. 1975. *LTI. Notizbuch eines Philologen*. Leipzig: Reclam.

———. 1995. *"Ich Will Zeugnis ablegen bis zu letzten." Tagebücher 1933–1945*. Berlin: Aufbau.

Knopp, Guido. 2001. *Die Große Flucht: Das Schicksal der Vertriebenen*. München: Ullstein.

———. 2003. A Speech during the Celebration of the 50th Anniversary Jubilee for the Enactment of the Federal Expellees Law (*Bundesvertriebenengesetz* [*BVFG*]). May 6. http://www.bund-der-vertriebenen.de/presse/index.php3?id=45.

Kochavi, Arieh J. 1998. *Prelude to Nuremberg: Allied War Crimes Policy and the Question of Punishment*. Chapel Hill, N.C.: University of North Carolina Press.

———. 2002. *Ha-Derech Le-Mishpatei Nuremburg. Gibush Mediniut Anisha Klapei Poshei Milchama*. Jerusalem: Yad Vashem.

Koennen, Gerd. 2001. *Das rote Jahrzehnt: Unsere kleine deutsche Kulturrevolution 1967–1977*. Köln: Kiepenheuer und Witsch.

Kossert, Andreas. 2008. *Kalte Heimat. Die Geschichte der deutschen Vertriebenen nach 1945*. München: Siedler.

Kössler, Till. 2005. *Abschied von der Revolution. Kommunisten und Gesellschaft in Westdeutschlands 1945–1968*. Düsseldorf: Droste.

Kraft, Wldemar. 1955. "Treu halten ?—Ja! Aber wem?" *Unser Standpunkt. Nachrichten der Gruppe Kraft—Oberländer*. September 21. 2.

Kraushaar, Wolfgang. 1996. *Die Protest-Chronik 1949–1959: Eine illustrierte Geschichte von Bewegung Widerstand und Utopie* I-III. Hamburg: Rogner & Bernhard.

"Kritik an Oberländers Personalpolitik." 1954. *Frankfurter Rundschau,* April 8.

Krockow, Christian Graf von. 1997. *Die Stunde der Frauen: Bericht aus Pommern 1944 bis 1947.* München: DTV.

Krohn, Knut. 2007. "Wer ist Donald Tusk?" *Der Tagesspiegel,* October 21.

Kucklick, Christoph. 2003. *Feuersturm: Der Bombenkrieg gegen Deutschland.* Hamburg: Eller & Richter Verlag.

Kulka, Otto Dov, and Eberhard Jäckel. 2004. *Die Juden in den geheimen NS-Stimmungsberichten 1933–1945 (Schriften des Bundesarchivs* 62). Düsseldorf: Droste.

"Kunst auf dem Wallberg 'fehl am Platz.'" 2004. *Pforzheimer Kurier,* August 25.

Laak, Dirk van. 2002. "Der Platz des Holocaust im deutschen Geschichtsbild." In *Die historische Meistererzählung: Deutungslinien der deutschen Nationalgeschichte nach 1945,* ed. Konrad H. Jarausch and Martin Sabrow. Göttingen: Vandenhoeck & Ruprecht. 163–193.

Lahme, Tilmann. 2005. "Rede an eine Nation vor dem Untergang." *Frankfurter Allgemeine Zeitung,* February 18.

Lau, Jörg. 2003. "Blühende Museumslandschaften." *Die Zeit,* no. 40, September 25. 50.

———. 2004. "Gedenken mit Schmiss." *Die Zeit,* no. 23, March 27.

Laurie, Clayton D. 1996. *The Propaganda Warriors. America's Crusade against Nazi Germany.* Lawrence: University Press of Kansas.

Lemke, Michael. 1993. "Kampagnen gegen Bonn. Die Systemkrise der DDR und die West-Propaganda der SED 1960–1963." *VfZG* 41: 153–174.

———. 2001. *Einheit oder Sozialismus? Die Deutschlandpolitik der SED.* Köln, Weimar, und Wien: Böhlau.

Leonhard, Wolfgang. 1957. *Child of the Revolution.* Trans. C. M. Woodhause. London: Collins.

Leuner, H. D. 1966. *When Compassion Was a Crime: Germany's Silent Heroes, 1933–1945.* London: O. Wolff.

Levkov, Ilya I. 1987. *Bitburg and Beyond: Encounter in American, German, and Jewish History.* New York: Schapolsky.

Löffler, Peter. 1988. *Bischof Clemens August Graf von Galen Akte, Briefe und Predigten 1933–1946.* Vol. 2: 1939–1946. Mainz: Matthias Grünewald.

Longerich, Peter. 2006. *"Davon haben wir nichts gewusst!" Die Deutschen und die Judenverfolgung 1933–1945.* München: Siedler.

"Mahnmal, das kein Mahnmal ist." 1952. *Hamburger Volkszeitung,* no. 175, July 29.

Major, Patrick. 1997. *The Death of the KPD: Communism and Anti-Communism in West Germany, 1945–1956.* Oxford: Clarendon Press.

Mann, Thomas. 1963. *Briefe 1937–1947.* Frankfurt a.M.: Fischer.

———. 1995. *Deutsche Hörer! Radiosendungen nach Deutschland aus den Jahren 1940 bis 1945.* Frankfurt a.M.: Fischer.

Mann, Golo. 2005. "Deutschland in Flammen." *Frankfurter Allgemeine Zeitung,* February 18.

Manoschek, Walter, ed. 1995. *"Es gibt nur eines für das Judentum: Vernichtung." Das Judenbild in deutschen Soldatenbriefen 1939–1944.* Hamburg: Hamburger Edition.

Manske, Beate. 1989. "Auftrag und Botschaft: Mahnmale von Gerhard Marcks." In *Gerhard Marcks 1889–1981: Retrospektive*, ed. Martina Rudolf. München: Hirmer. 271–291.

Marcks, Gerhard. 1988. *1889–1981 Dokumente zu Leben und Werke*. Ausgewählt, bearbeitet und eingeleitet von Ursula Frenzel. München: Prestel.

Margalit, Gilad. 2002a. "German Suffering during WWII: Remembrance in the Two Germanies 1945–1965" (Heb.). *Historia* 10: 91–127.

———. 2002b. *Germany and Its Gypsies: A Post-Auschwitz Ordeal*. Madison: University of Wisconsin Press.

———. 2007. "Grass und das jüdische Alter Ego." In *Literarischer Antisemitismus nach Ausschwitz*, ed. K. M. Bogdal, K. Holz, und M. N. Lorenz. Stuttgart: Verlag J.B. Metzler. 159–170.

Martin, Hans-Werner. 1996. "*. . . nicht spurlos aus der Geschichte verschwinden*": *Wenzel Jaksch und die Integration der sudetendeutschen Demokraten in die SPD nach dem II. Weltkrieg 1945–1949*. Frankfurt a.M.: Lang.

Medicus, Thomas. 2002. "Seismograph. Günter Grass' neues Buch." *Frankfurter Rundschau*, February 5.

"Mehr verdrängt als bewältigt." 1992. *Juden und Deutsche. Spiegel Special* 2: 61–73.

Meier, Kurt. 1968. *Kirche und Judentum: Die Haltung der evangelischen Kirche zur Judenpolitik des Dritten Reiches*. Göttingen: Vandenhoeck & Ruprecht.

Melendy, Brenda. 2005. "Expellees on Strike: Competing Victimization Discourses and the Dachau Refugee Camp Protest Movement, 1948–1949." *German Studies Review* 28, 1: 107–125.

Menzel-Severing, Hans. 1980. *Der Bildhauer Benno Elkan*. Dortmund: Verlag des Historischen Vereins Dortmund.

Merritt, Richard L., and Anna J. Merritt. 1970. *Public Opinion in Occupied Germany—The OMGUS Survey 1945–1949*. Urbana: University of Illinois Press.

Messenger, Charles. 1984. *'Bomber' Harris and the Strategic Bombing Offensive, 1939–1945*. New York: St. Martin's Press.

Michaelsen, Sven, and Volker Hinz. 2002. "Der Ärger muss raus. Interview mit Walter Kempowski." *Stern*, April.

Middlebrook, Martin. 1981. *The Battle of Hamburg: Allied Bomber Forces against a German City in 1943*. New York: Scribner.

"Minister Oberländer unter schwerem Verdacht." 1959. *Die Tat*, no. 39, September 26.

"Minister Seebohm im Gegensatz zur Bundesregierung." 1964. *Frankfurter Rundschau*, May 20.

Miska, Peter. 1954. "Zum Opfer und zur Arbeit erziehen . . . " *Frankfurter Rundschau*, April 24.

Moeller, Robert G. n.d. "Der 'Barde des Zweiten Weltkriegs' und der Zusammenbruch des 'Deutschen Ostens': Frank Wisbar *Nacht fiel über Gotenhafen*." Unpublished ms.

———. 1996. "War Stories: The Search for a Usable Past in the Federal Republic of Germany." *American Historical Review* 101, 3–5: 1008–1048.

———, ed. 1997. *West Germany under Construction: Politics, Society, and Culture in the Adenauer Era*. Ann Arbor: University of Michigan Press.

———. 2001a. *War Stories: The Search for a Usable Past in the Federal Republic of Germany*. Berkley: University of California Press.

———. 2001b. "Deutsche Opfer, Opfer der Deutschen. Kriegsgefangene, Vertriebene, NS-Verfolgte: Opferausgleich als Identitätpolitik." In *Nachkrieg in Deutschland*, ed. Klaus Naumann. Hamburg: Hamburger Edition. 29–58.

———. 2003. "Sinking Ships, the Lost *Heimat* and Broken Taboos: Günter Grass and the Politics of Memory in Contemporary Germany." *Contemporary European History* 12: 147–181.

———. 2005a. "Changing Legacy of 1945 in Germany: A Round-Table Discussion." *German History* 23, 4: 519–546.

———. 2005b. "Germans as Victims? Thoughts on a Post-Cold War History of the Second World War's Legacies." *History and Memory* 17,½: 147–194.

———. 2006. "On the History of Man-Made Destruction: Loss, Death, Memory, and Germany in the Bombing War." *History Workshop Journal* 61: 103–134.

Moller, Sabine. 1998. *Die Entkonkretisierung der NS-Herschaft in der Ära Kohl. Die Neue Wache—Das Denkmal für die ermordeten Juden Europas—Das Haus der Geschichte der Bundesrepublik Deutschland.* Hannover: Offizin.

Mommsen, Hans. 1988. "Was haben die Deutschen vom Völkermord an den Juden gewusst?" In *Der Judenpogrom 1938: Von der 'Reichskristalnacht' zum Völkermord,* ed. Walter H. Pehle. Frankfurt a.M.: Fischer. 176–200.

———. 1991. "The Realization of the Unthinkable: The Final Solution of the Jewish Question in the Third Reich." In *From Weimar to Auschwitz: Essays in German History,* ed. Hans. Mommsen. Oxford: Polity Press. 224–253.

Mönch, Regina. 2007. "Vergleichen ohne aufzurechnen." *Frankfurter Allgemeine Zeitung,* August 11.

Moses, A. Dirk. 1999. "The Forty-Fivers. A Generation between Fascism and Democracy." *German Politics and Society* 17: 94–126.

———. 2007. *German Intellectuals and the Nazi Past.* Cambridge: Cambridge University Press.

Moskowitz, Moses. 1946. "The Germans and the Jews: Postwar Report, The Enigma of German Irresponsibility." *Commentary* 1/2 (July): 7–14.

Mühlhäuser, Regina. 2001. "Vergewaltigungen in Deutschland 1945. Nationaler Opferdiskurs und individuelles Erinnern betroffener Frauen." In *Nachkrieg in Deutschland,* ed. Klaus Naumann. Hamburg: Hamburger Edition. 384–408.

Naimark, Norman M. 2002. *Fires of Hatred: Ethnic Cleansing in Twentieth-Century Europe.* Cambridge, Mass.: Harvard University Press.

Nationale Front des demokratischen Deutschland, ed. 1950. "Dresden kämpf für den Frieden."

Nationalrat der Nationalen Front der demokratischen Deutschland, ed. 1954. *Vom Ersten zum zweiten Nationalkongress. 4 Jahre erfolgreicher Kampf für demokratische Einheit und Frieden* II. Nationalkongress Berlin. May 15–16.

Nawratil, Heinz. 2005. *Schwarzbuch der Vertreibung 1945 bis 1948. Das letzte Kapitel unbewältigter Vergangenheit.* 12. München: Universitas.

Neukirch, Ralf, and Jan Paul. 2009. "Findbild Nummer Eins." *Der Spiegel,* February 21.

Neutzner, Matthias. 2005. "Vom Anklagen zum Erinnern." In *Das rote Leuchten. Dresden und der Bombenkrieg,* ed. Oliver Reinhard, Matthias Neutzner, and Wolfgang Hesse. Dresden: Sächsische Zeitung. 128–163.

"New York gegen Seebohm." 1955. *Frankfurter Rundschau,* June 4.

"Nie wieder Hiroshima—nie wieder Bomben auf Hamburg." 1950. *Hamburger Volkszeitung*, no. 172, July 27. 1.

Niemöller, Martin. 1946a. *Über die deutsche Schuld Not und Hoffnung*. Zürich: Evangelischer Verlag.

———. 1946b. *Die Aufgaben der Evangelischen Kirchen der Gegenwart*. Düsseldorf: Vier Falken Verlag.

———. 1946c. *Die Brücke über dem Abgrund*. Saarbrücken: Buchengewerbehaus.

Niethammer, Lutz. 1990. "Juden und Russen im Gedaechtnis der Deutschen." In *Der historische Ort des Nationalsozialismus: Annährungen*, ed. Walter Pehle. Frankfurt a.M.: Fischer. 114–134.

Niven, Bill. 2003. *Facing the Nazi Past: United Germany and the Legacy of the Third Reich*. London: Routledge.

———. 2006. "German Victimhood at the Turn of the Millennium." In *Germans as Victims: Remembering the Past in Contemporary Germany*, ed. Bill Niven. New York: Palgrave Macmillan. 1–25.

Noack, Hans-Joachim. 2002. "Die deutsche als Opfer." *Der Spiegel*, no. 13, March 25. 36–39.

Noelle, Elisabeth, and Erich Peter Neumann, eds. 1956. *Jahrbuch der Öffentlichen Meinung 1947–1955*, Vol. 1. Allensbach: Verlag fur Demoskopie.

———. 1957. *Jahrbuch der Öffentlichen Meinung 1957*. Allensbach: Verlag fur Demoskopie.

———. 1997. *The Germans: Public Opinion Polls 1947–1966*. Westport, Conn.: Greenwood Press.

Nolan, Mary. 2005. "Air Wars, Memory Wars." *Central European History* 38, 1: 7–40.

Norbisrath, Gudrun, ed. 2000. *Gestohlene Jugend: der Zweite Weltkrieg in Erinnerungen*. Essen: Klartex.

Norden, Albert. 1947. *Lehren Deutscher Geschichte: Zur politischen Rolle des Finanzkapitals und der Junker*. Berlin: Dietz.

———. 1949. "Der amerikanische Imperialismus Deutschlands Todfeind." *Neue Welt* 17, 81 (September): 24–40.

———. 1952. *Um die Nation*. Berlin: Dietz.

Nossack, Hans Erich. 1961. *Der Untergang*. Frankfurt a.M.: Suhrkamp.

"OdF Mahnmal in Frankfurt geschändet." 1949. *Frankfurter Rundschau*, September 12.

Ohliger, Rainer. 2000. "Vertreibungsforschung, Osteuropaforschung, 'Deutschtumsforschung'? Zwei Debatten—ein Konflikt und einige unzeitgemaesse Betrachtungen zu Pfingsten." June 9. http://hsozkult.geschichte.hu-berlin.de/BEITRAG/essays/ohra0600.htm. Accessed October 20, 2007.

"100,000 Dresdner demonstrierten am Jahrestag des USA Terrorangriffs für den Frieden." 1953. *Neues Deutschland*, February 14. 1.

Oppenheimer, Andrew. 2004. "West German Pacifism and the Ambivalence of Human Solidarity, 1945–1968." *Peace & Change* 29, 3/4 (July): 353–389.

Oren, Amir. 2002a. "Germaniyyah 'Orekhet be-Yisra'el Azkarah le-Hallelei Wehrmacht ve-Es-Es." *Ha'aretz*, October 27. 1.

———. 2002b. "Shagrirut Germaniyyah Dahata ha-Teqes le-Hallelim me-ha-Wehrmacht ve-ha-Es-Es." *Ha'aretz*, November 28.

Overesch, Manfred. 1995. *Buchenwald und die DDR. Oder Die Suche nach Selbstlegitimation*. Göttingen: Vandenhoeck & Ruprecht.

Overmans, Rüdiger. 1999. *Deutsche Militärische Verluste in Zweiten Weltkrieg.* München: Oldenburg.

Overy, Richard. 2003a. "Barbarisch aber sinnvoll." In *Ein Volk von Opfern? Die neue Debatte um den Bombenkrieg 1940–45*, ed. Lothar Kettenacker. Berlin: Rowohlt. 183–187.

———. 2003b. "Die Alliiere Bombe-Strategie als Ausdruck des 'totalen Krieges.'" In *Ein Volk von Opfern? Die neue Debatte um den Bombenkrieg 1040–45*, ed. Lothar Kettenacker. Berlin: Rowohlt. 27–47.

Padover, Saul K. 1946. *Experiment in Germany. The Story of an American Intelligence Officer.* New York: Duell, Sloan and Pearce.

Panitz, Eberhard. 1979. *Meines Vaters Straßenbahn. Erzählung.* Halle-Leipzig: Mitteldeutscher Verlag.

———. 1980. *Die Feuer sinken.* Berlin: Militärverlag der DDR.

Papenbrock, Martin. 1998. "Gerhard Marcks: Der Gefesselte. Mahnmal für Osnabrück 1964." In *Symbole des Friedens und des Krieges im öffentlichen Raum: Osnabrück, die "Stadt des Westfälischen Friedens."* Weimar: VDG. 231–246.

Pauer, Jan. 2002. "Das geringere Leid." *Süddeutsche Zeitung*, June 5.

"Pawelka: Preußische Treuhand reicht im Herbst ein." 2004. *Frankfurter Rundschau*, August 4.

Peitsch, Helmut. 1989. "Autobiographical Writing as *Vergangenheitsbewältigung*: Mastering the Past." *German History* 7 (April): 47–70.

Peters, Christian. 2002. *"Glücklicherweise bilden wir eine Ausnahme." Mannhein in den fünfziger Jahren.* Stuttgart: Thorbeck.

Petersen, Thomas. 2005. *Flucht und Vertreibung aus Sicht der deutschen, polnischen und tschechischen Bevölkerung.* Bonn: Stiftung Haus der Geschichte der Bundesrepublik Deutschland.

Petersen, Thomas Peter. 1998. *Der Volkstrauertag—seine Geschichte und Entwicklung.* Bad Kleinen: n.p.

Peukert, Detlev. 1987. *Inside Nazi Germany: Conformity, Opposition and Racism in Everyday Life.* B. T. Batsford: London.

Phayer, Michael. 1995. "The Postwar German Catholic Debate over Holocaust Guilt." *Kirchliche Zeitgeschichte* 8. 426–439.

———. 1996. "The German Catholic Church after the Holocaust." *Holocaust and Genocide Studies* 10, 2 (Fall): 151–167.

Pieck, Wilhelm. 1979. *Gesammelte Reden und Schriften. Vol. 6: 1939 bis Mai 1945.* Berlin: Dietz Verlag.

Pietsch, Herbert, Rainer Potratz, and Meinhard Stark. 1995. *Nun hängen die Schreie mir an . . . Halbe, Ein Friedhof und seine Toten.* Berlin Editon: Hentrich.

Piskorski, Jan M. 2005. *Vertreibung und Deutsch-Polnische Geschichte. Eine Streitschrift.* Osnabrück: Fibre.

Plagemann, Volker. 1986. *"Vaterstadt Vaterland. . . . " Denkmäler in Hamburg.* Hamburg: Christians.

Platthaus, Andreas. 2002. "Don't mention the war crimes." *Frankfurter Allgemeine Zeitung*, November 26.

Podewin, Norbert. 2001. *Albert Norden. Der Rabbinersohn im Politbüro. Eine Biographie.* Berlin: Edition Ost.

"Polen fühlt sich provoziert." 2009. *Frankfurter Rundschau*, February 17.

Portmann, Heinrich. 1957. *Cardinal von Galen*. Trans. R. L. Sedgwick. London: Jarrolds.

Posener, Julius. 2002. *In Deutschland: 1945 bis 1946*. Berlin: Siedler.

Prenzlauer Berg Museum des Kulturamtes Berlin Prenzlauer Berg, ed. 1996. *"Ich schlug meiner Mutter die brennenden Funken ab." Berliner Schulaufsätze aus dem Jahr 1946*. Berlin: Kontext.

"Pro und Contra Vertriebenen-Zentrum." 2005. *Die Welt*, August 6.

Prolingheuer, Hans. 1987. *Wir sind in die Irre gegeangen: Die Schuld der Kirche unterm Hakenkreuz, nach dem Bekenntnis des "Darmstädter Wortes" von 1947*. Köln: Pahl-Rugenstein.

"Propaganda rettet Dresden nicht." 1950. *Wirtzschaftzeitung*, February 25.

Puvogel, Ulrike, Martin Stanowski, and Ursula Graf, eds. 1995. *Gedenkstätten für die Opfer des Nationalsozialismus: Eine Dokumentation* I-II. Bonn: Bundeszentrale für politische Bildung.

Rabinbach, Anson. 1997. *In the Shadow of Catastrophe: German Intellectuals between Apocalypse and Enlightenment*. Berkley: University of California Press.

Rahms, Helene. 1955. "Als Dresden brannte." *Frankfurter Allgemeine Zeitung*, February 12.

Raiser, Ludwig, Klaus von Bismarck, and Carl Friedrick von Weizsäcker. 1962. "Warum wir das Wort ergriffen, Ludwig Raiser, Klaus von Bismarck und Carl Friedrick von Weizsäcker begründen das Memorandum der Acht." *Die Zeit*, no. 10, March 9.

Reichel, Peter. 1995. *Politik mit der Erinnerung: Gedaechtnisorte im Streit um die nationalsozialistische Vergangenheit*. München und Wien: Carl Hanser.

———. 2001. *Vergangenheitsbewältigung in Deutschland: Die Auseinandersetzung mit der NS -Diktatur von 1945 bis heute*. München: Beck.

Reichenberger, Emmanuel J. 1948. *Ost-Deutsche Passion*. Düsseldorf: Westland Verlag.

———. 1995. *Sudentendeutsche Passion. Für Wahrheit und Gerechtigkeit*. Kiel: Arndt.

Reichert, Friedrich. 1994. "Verbrannt bis zur Unkentlichkeit." In Dresdner Stadtmuseum, *Verbrannt bis zur Unkenntlickkeit: Die Zerstörung Dresdens 1945*. Altenburg: DZA Verlag für Kultur und Wissenschaft.

Reifahrth, Dieter, and Viktoria Schmidt-Linsenhoff. 1995. "Die Kamera der Täter." In *Vernichtungskrieg: Verbrechen der Wehrmacht 1941–1944*, ed. Hannes Heer and Klaus Naumann. Frankfurt a.M.: Zweitausendeins. 475–503.

Reimann, P. Augustin. 1954. "Maria in Elend." *Königsteiner Rufe* 6, 9 (September): 258.

Reinhard, Oliver. 2005. "Vom Bodensee bis Guernica. Anfänge des Bombenkrieges—1900 bis 1937." In *Das rote Leuchten. Dresden und der Bombenkrieg*, ed. Oliver Reinhard, Matthias Neutzner, and Wolfgang Hesse. Dresden: Sächsische Zeitung. 10–25.

Reuter, Elke, and Detlef Hansel. 1997. *Das Kurze Leben der VVN von 1947 bis 1953*. Berlin: Edition Ost.

Richter, Horst. 1965. " . . . damit keine Stadt der Welt je wieder leide." *Neues Deutschland*, February 13. 5.

Rieth, Theobald. 1955. "Zum Geleit." In *Versöhnung über den Gräbe: Eine Wegweisung*, ed. Franz Josef Rustige. Köln: Kolping Verlag.

Ritscher, Bodo. 1995. "Die NKWD/ MWD—'Speziallager' in Deutschland. Anmerkungen zu einem Forschungsgegenstand." In *Die geteilte Vergangenheit*, ed. Jürgen Danyel. Berlin: Akademie. 163–180.

Rodenberger, Axel. 1952. *Der Tod von Dresden*. Dortmund: Rodenberger.

Rogalla, Annette. 1998. "Jedem sein Denkmal? Helmut Kohl will den Vertriebenen zu einer Gedenkstätte verhelfen." *Tageszeitung*, September 7.

Rothfels, Hans. 1960. *Bismark, der Osten und das Reich*. Stuttgart: Kohlhammer.

Rubenstein, Richard L., and John K. Roth, eds. 2003. *Approaches to Auschwitz: The Holocaust and Its Legacy*. Rev. ed. Louisville: Westminster John Knox Press.

Ruhl, Klaus-Jörg. 1980. *Die Besatzer und die Deutschen: Amerikanische Zone 1945–1948*. Düsseldorf: Droste.

Salzborn, Samuel. 1999. "'Rückkehr in die alte Heimat'. 50. 'Tag der Heimat' des 'Bundes der Vertriebenen'." *Der Rechte Rand*, no. 61, November. http://www.stade.vvn-bda.de/heimat.htm.

———. 2000. *Grenzenlose Heimat: Geschichte, Gegenwart und Zukunft der Vertriebenenverbände*. Berlin: Elefanten Press.

———. 2003. "Opfer, Tabu, Kollektivschuld: Über Motive deutscher Obsession." In *Erinnern, verdrängen, vergessen: Geschichtspolitische Wege ins 21. Jahrhundert*, ed. Michael Klundt et al. Giessen: NBKK. 17–41.

Sander, Helke, and Barbara Johr, eds. 1992. *Befreier und Befreite. Krieg, Vergewaltigung, Kinder*. Frankfurt a.M.: Fischer.

Schäfer, Hermann. 2006. "Zur Ausstellung 'Flucht, Vertreibung, Integration.'" In *Flucht, Vertreibung, Integration*, ed. Stiftung Haus der Geschichte der Bundesrepublik Deutschland. Bonn: Kerber. 6–13.

"Scharfe Kritik an Seebohm." 1953. *Frankfurter Rundschau*, June 6.

Scheibe, Moritz. 2002. "Auf der Suche nach der demokratischen Gesellschaft." In *Wandlungsprozesse in Westdeutschland. Belastung, Integration, Liberalisierung 1945–1980*, ed. Ulrich Herbert. Göttingen: Wallstein. 245–277.

Schieder, Theodor, et al., eds. 1955. "Die Vertreibung der deutschen Bevälkerung aus den Gebieten östlich der Oder-Neisse." Dokumentation der Vertreibung der Deutschen aus Ost-Mitteleuropa. Bonn: Bundesministerium für vertriebene Vol. I/1.

Schildt, Axel. 1998. "NS-Eliten in der Bundesrepublik." In *Verwandlungspolitik. NS-Eliten in der westdeutschen Nachkriegsgesellschaft*, ed. Wilfried Loth and Bernd-A. Rusinek. Frankfurt: Campus. 19–54.

———. 1999. *Ankunft im Westen: Ein Essay zur Erfolgsgeschichte der Bundesrepublik Deutschland*. Frankfurt a.M.: Fischer.

———. 2007 "Die lange Schatten des Krieges über die westdeutschen Nachkriegesgesellschaft." In *Der Zweite Weltkrieg in Europa*, ed. Jörg Echternkamp and Stefan Martens. Paderborn, München, Wien, und Zürich: Ferdinand Schöningh. 223–236.

Schily, Otto. 1999. "Erinnerung und Gedenken finden ihren Sinn im Willen für eine besser Zukunft." Rede von Bundesinnenminister auf der Festveranstaltung zum 50. Jahrestag des Bundes der Vertriebenen am 29. Mai 1999 im berliner Dom. In *Bulletin der Bundesregierung* Nr. 35-1. June 1.

Schirmer, Wulf, ed. 1988. *Egon Eiermann 1904–1970: Bauten und Projekte*. Stuttgart: DVA.

Schirrmacher, Frank. 1998. "Luftkrieg. Beginnt morgen die deutsche Nachkriegsliteratur?" *Frankfurter Allgemeine Zeitung*, January 15.

———. 2006. "Eine zeitgeschichtliche Pointe." *Frankfurter Allgemeine Zeitung*, August 12.

Schittly, Dagmar. 2002. *Zwischen Regie und Regime: Die Filmpolitik der SED im Spiegel der DEFA-Produktionen*. Berlin: Ch. Links.

Schlant, Ernestine. 1999. *The Language of Silence: West German Literature and the Holocaust*. New York and London: Routledge.

"Schliemmer als die Atombombe." 1953. *Hamburger Abendblatt*, no. 174, July 29. 3.

Schlink, Bernhard. 1999. *The Reader*. Trans. Carol Brown Janeway. Thorndike: G. K. Hall.

Schlögel, Karl. 2002. "Die Sprache des Krebses. Der neue Grass und die Erinnerung an die Vertreibung." *Frankfurter Rundschau*, March 12.

Schmidt, Alfred. 1973. "Waren das Keine Kriegsverbrechen?" *Hamburger Abendblatt*, no. 174, July 28–29. 28.

Schmidt, Marcus. 2006. "Ethnische Säuberung und Völkermord." *Junge Freiheit*, June 9.

Schmitz, Helmut. 2006. "The Birth of the Collective from the Sprit of Empathy: From the 'Historians Dispute' to German Suffering." In *Germans as Victims: Remembering the Past in Contemporary Germany*, ed. Bill Niven. New York: Palgrave Macmillan. 93–108.

Schneider, Ulrich. 1997. *Zukunftsentwurf Antifaschismus: 50 Jahre Wirken der VVN für "eine neue Welt des Friedens und der Freiheit."* Bonn: Pahl-Rugenstein.

Schneider, Wolf. 1965. "Warum musste Dresden sterben?" *Süddeutsche Zeitung*, February 12.

Schoenfeld, Helmut. 2000. *Der Friedhof Ohlsdorf: Gräbe. Geschichte. Gedenkstätten.* Hamburg: Christians.

Schraut, Sylvia, and Thomas Grosser, eds. 1996. *Die Flüchtlingsfrage in der deutschen Nachkriegsgeschichte*. Mannheim: Palatinum.

Schröder, Gerhard. 2004. "Rede anlässlich des Tag der Heimat 2004." http://www.bundeskanzler.de/Reden-.7715.11806/Rede-von-Bundeskanzler-Gerhard-Schroeder-anlaess . . . htm. Accessed August 19, 2004.

Schulze Wessel, Martin. 2006. "Was ein Völkermord ist—und was nicht." *Süddeutsche Zeitung*, May 29.

Schwake, Norbert. 2008. Deutsche Soldatengräber in Israel. Der Einsatz deutscher Soldaten an der Palästinafront in Ersten Weltkrieg und das Schisksal ihrer Grabstätten. Münster: Aschendorff Verlag.

Schwartz, Michael. 2004. *Vertriebene und "Umsiedlerpolitik." Integrationkonflikte in den deutschen Nachkriegs-Gesellschaften und die Assimilationsstrategien in der SBZ/DDR 1945–1961*. München: R. Oldenburg.

———. 2008. "Vertriebene im doppelten Deutschland. Integrations- und Erinnerungspolitik in der DDR und in der Bundesrepublik." *Vierteljahrshefte für Zeitgeschichte* 56: 101–151.

Schwartz, Moritz. 2001. "Schule des Hasses." *Junge Freiheit*, no. 49, November 30.

Schwarz, Herbert. 1959. "Der 'Fall Oberländer.'" *Die Zeit*, October 9.

Schwarz, Rudolf. 1960. *Kirchenbau: Welt vor der Schwelle*. Heidelberg: Kerle Verlag.

Schwinge, Erich. 1978. *Bilanz der Kriegsgeneration: Ein Beitrag zur Geschichte unserer Zeit.* Marburg: Elwert.

Sebald, W. G. 2001. *Luftkrieg und Literatur.* Frankfurt a.M.: Fischer.

———. 2004. *On the Natural History of Destruction.* Trans. Anthea Bell. New York: Modern Library.

"Seebohm dementiert Regierung." 1964. *Frankfurter Rundschau,* May 14.

"Seebohm löst Lodgman." 1959. *Frankfurter Rundschau,* September 21.

"Seebohm muß sich verantworten." 1964. *Frankfurter Rundschau,* May 23.

"Seebohm verteidigt erneut das Münchener Abkommen." 1964. *Frankfurter Rundschau,* May 19.

"Seebohm vor Sudetendeutschen." 1952. *Frankfurter Rundschau,* September 15.

Seewald, Berthold. 2004. "Zwei deutsche Diktaturen, aber welches Erinnern?" *Die Welt,* January 24.

Segev, Tom. 1994. *The Seventh Million. The Israelis and the Holocaust.* Trans. Haim Watzman. New York: Hill and Wang.

Seghers, Anna. 1981. *Erzählungen 1945–1951.* Berlin: Aufbau.

Semler, Christian. 2007. "Verwischte Spurren." *Die Tageszeitung,* August 12.

Semrau, Jens, ed. 1995. *Durchs dunkle Deutschland: Gerhard Marcks—Briefwechsel 1933 bis 1980.* Leipzig: E. A. Seemann.

Shafir, Shlomo. 1987. *An Outstretched Hand: The German Social Democrats and Their Attitude toward Jews and the State of Israel, 1945–1967* (Heb.). Tel Aviv: Zmora Bitan.

Siegfried, Detlef. 2000. "Zwischen Aufarbeitung und Schlussstrich: Der Umgang mit der NS-Vergengenheit in den beiden deutschen Staaten 1958 bis 1969." In *Dynamische Zeiten: Die 60er Jahre in den beiden deutschen Gesellschaften,* ed. Axel Schildt, Detlef Siegfried, and Karl Christian Lammers. Hamburg: Christians. 77–113.

"6 Millionen ermordete Deutsche: Der Massenmord ohne Sühne." 1980. *Deutsche National Zeitung,* August 1.

"Soldatenfriedhof Hürtgenwald eingeweiht." 1952. *Frankfurter Rundschau,* August 18.

"Sollte die erste Atombombe auf Dresden fallen?" 1963. *Frankfurter Rundschau,* February 18.

Speicher, Stephan. 2007. "Falsch ist das nicht. Aber es ist zu wenig." *Berliner Zeitung,* August 11.

Spence, Basil. 1962. *Phoenix at Coventry: The Building of a Cathedral.* London: Geoffrey Bles.

"Spiel mit Zahlen." 1965. *Frankfurter Rundschau,* June 9.

Stargardt, Nicholas. 2007. *Witnesses of War: Children's Lives under the Nazis.* New York: Vintage Books.

Staritz, Dietrich. 1995. "Von der 'schande der Judenpogrome' zur 'zionistischen Diversionsarbeit'. Judenverfolgung und Antisemitismus in der Wahrnehmung der KPD." In *Scwieriges Erbe: Der Umgang mit Nationalsozialismus und Antisemitismus in Oestreich, der DDR und der Bundesrepublik Deutschland,* ed. Werner Bergmann et al. Frankfurt a.M.: Campus. 212–235.

Steinbach, Erika. 1999. "Opfer und Täter." http://www.swg-hamburg.de/Deutschland Journal/opfer-_und_taeter.pdf.

———. 2002. "Die Menschen haben sich nicht gefreut, dass wir da waren." *Die Welt,* February 16.

"Stellungnahme der USA zu den Luftangriffen auf Dresden." 1953. *Neue Zeitung,* February 11.

Stern, Frank. 1990. "The Historic Triangle: Occupiers, Germans and Jews." *Tel Aviver Jahrbuch für deutsche Geschichte* 19. 47–76.

———. 1992. *The Whitewashing of the Yellow Badge: Antisemitism and Philosemitism in Postwar Germany.* Trans. William Templer. Oxford: Pergamon Press.

———. 2005. "A Cinema of Subversive Contradictions: Jews in the Eastern German Features Films." In *Memory and Amnesia: The Holocaust in Germany,* ed. Gilad Margalit and Yfaat Weiss. Tel Aviv: HaKibbutz HaMeuchad. 174–197.

Stickler, Matthias. 2004. *"Ostdeutsch heiβt Gesmtdeutsch." Organisation, Selbstverständnis und heimatpolitische Zielsetzungen der deutschen Vertriebenenverbände 1949–1972.* Düsseldorf: Droste.

Stobwasser, Albin. 2000. *Die den roten Winkel trugen: Zur Geschichte der VVN-Bund der antifaschisten-Hamburg.* Hamburg: Paasch, Gridelhof.

Stölzl, Christoph, ed. 1993. *Die Neue Wache Unter den Linden: Ein deutsches Denkmal im Wandel der Geschichte.* Berlin: Koehler & Amelang.

Stöver, Bernd. 2002. *Die Befreiung vom Kommunismus, Amerikanische Liberation Policy im Kalten Krieg 1947–1991.* Köln: Böhlau Verlag.

———. 2005. "Pressure Group im Kalten Krieg. Die Vertriebenen, die USA und der Kaltekrieg 1947–1990." *Zeitschrieft für Geschichtswissenschaft* 53, 10: 897–911.

Stubbe, Walter. 1950. "Nein! Niemals! Unsere Gedanken zum Tag des Verbrechen von Potsdam." *Pommern-Brief. Mitteilungsblatt der Pommerschen Landsmannschaft* 2, 9 (August 1).

Süβ, Dietmar. 2007. "Luftkrieg, Öffentlichkeit und die Konjukturen der Erinnerung." In *Der Zweite Weltkrieg in Europa,* ed. Jörg Echternkamp and Stefan Martens. Paderborn, München, Wien, und Zürich: Ferdinand Schöningh. 207–222.

Szarota, Tomasz. 1998. *Der deutsche Michel. Die Geschichte eines nationalen Symbols und Autostereotyp.* Osnabrück: Fibre.

Taberner, Stuart. 2006. "Representation of German Wartime suffering in Recent Fiction." In *Germans as Victims: Remembering the Past in Contemporary Germany,* ed. Bill Niven. New York: Palgrave Macmillan. 164–180.

"Tausende protestierten gegen schmutzigen Krieg." 1966. *Freie Presse,* February 12.

Ther, Philipp. 1998. *Deutsche und polnische Vertriebene. Gesellschaft und Vertriebenenpolitik in der SBZ/DDR und in Polen 1945–1956.* Göttingen: Vandenhoeck & Ruprecht.

———. 2003. "Erinnern oder aufklären. Zur Konzeption eines Zentrum gegen Vertreibungen." *Zeitschrift für Geschichtswissenschaft* 51: 36–41.

Thiessen, Malte. 2007. *Eingebrannt ins Gedächtnis: Hamburgs Gedenken an Luftkrieg und Kriegsende 1943 bis 2005.* München: Dölling und Galitz.

Timm, Uwe. 2003. *Am Beispiel Meines Bruders.* Köln: Kipenheuer & Witsch.

———. 2005. *In My Brother's Shadow: A Life and Death in the SS.* Trans. Anthea Bell. New York: Farrer, Straus Giroux.

"Tötet alle Deutsche." 1962. *Deutsche Soldaten Zeitung* 18, May 11. 1.

"Trotz Terror: Wir bleiben hart." 1945. *Der Freiheitskampf Dresdner Zeitung,* February 16.

"Trümmerberg auf dem Birkenkopf." 1954. *Stuttgarter Zeitung,* no. 175, July 30.

"Trybuna Ludu." 1964. *Frankfurter Rundschau,* May 20.

"Tschechiens Ministerpräsident verteidigt Vertreibung." 2002. *Spiegel Online,* May 18. http://www.spiegel.de/politik/deutschland/0,1518,196846,00.html.

Ullrich, Volker. 2002. "Jörg Friedrichs brisantes Buch über den alliierten Bombenkrieg gegen Deutschland." *Die Zeit* 49, November 27.

"Umfrage: Polien zweifeln an Deutschen." 2003. *Frankfurter Allgemeine Zeitung,* no. 246, October 23.

"Umstrittenes Vertriebenenzentrum kommt doch." 2008. *Die Welt,* March 19.

"Und das Heimweh der Leute nach Deutschland." 1966. *Der Spiegel.* May 16, 41.

"Unser Künstlerporträt: Martin Hellberg." 1955. *Neues Deutschland,* January 30.

Undset, Sigrid. 1945. "Die Unerziehung der Deutschen." *Neue Zeitung,* October 25.

"Verbot der Flüchtlingsparteien." 1946. *Neue Zeitung,* August 8.

Verhandlungen des Deutschen Bundestages I. Wahlperiode 1949 Stenographische Berichte. 1951. Bonn. Vol. 6.

"Vertriebenen Bund nominiert Erika Steinbach." 2009. *Frankfurter Allgemeine Zeitung,* February 18.

"Verzeihen aber nicht Vergessen." 1951. *Hamburger Abendblatt,* no. 175, July 30. 3.

Vogel, Rolf, ed. 1967. *Deutschlands Weg nach Israel: Eine Dokumentation.* Stuttgart: Seewald.

Volk, Ludwig. 1978. *Akten Kardinal Michael von Faulhaber 1917–1945.* Vol. 2. Mainz: Matthias Grünewald.

———. 1983. *Akten deutscher Bischöfe über die Lage der Kirche 1933–1945.* Vol. 4. Mainz: Matthias Grünewald.

Volksbund Deutsche Kriegsgräberfürsorge e.V, ed. 1952. *Den Gefallenen. Ein Buch des Gedenkens und des Trostes.* München-Salzburg: Akademischer Gemeinschaftsverlag.

Volksbund Deutsche Kriegsgraeberfuersorge, ed. 1987. *Wir gedenken . . . Reden zum Volkstrauertag von 1951–1987.* Ulm: Ebner.

Volksstimme. 1951. "Nie wieder eine Schreckensnacht!" No. 54, March 5. 1.

"Volkstrauertag—heute wie vor 28 Jahren." 1950. *Kriegsgräberfürsorge* 26, 3 (March): 18.

Vollnhals, Clemens. 1989. *Evangelischen Kirche und Entnazifizierung 1945–1949. Die Last der nationalsozialistischen Vergangenheit.* München: R. Oldenburg.

Vollmer, Antje. 1997a. "Ende der Zweideutigkeiten. Rede der Vizepräsidentin des Deutschen Bundestages in der Karls-Universität Prag, 1997Ä." http://www.antje-vollmer.de/cms/default/dok/4/4336.ende_der_zweideutigkeiten_rede_in_prag_1.html.

———. 1997b. "Rede zur Deutsch-Tschechischen Erklärung im Deutschen Bundestag." http://www.antje-vollmer.de/cms/default/dok/4/4337.rede_zur_deutschtschechischen_erklaerung.html.

———. 2002. "Vertreibung und Nationalstaatsgedanke. Vertreibung und Nationalstaatsgedanke Eduard Benes, ein Kind seiner Zeit." *Neue Zürcher Zeitung,* May 11.

Wachs, Philipp-Christian. 2000. *Der Fall Theodor Oberländer 1905 bis 1998.* Frankfurt a.M.: Campus Verlag.

"Warum ich nach sechzig Jahren mein Schweigen breche." 2006. *Frankfurter Allgemeine Zeitung,* August 12.

"Was Graf Büllow und Ehrenburg verbindet." 2005. *Preußische Allgemeine Zeitung,* October 1.

"Was haben wir uns angetan? An Interview with Joschka Fischer." 2003. *Die Zeit*, no. 36, August 30.
Wasserstein, Bernard. 1982. *Britain and the Jews of Europe 1939–1945* (Heb.). Tel Aviv: Am-Oved.
Webster, Charles, and Noble Frankland. 1961. *The Strategic Air Offensive against Germany, 1939–1945*, vol. 1. London: H. M. Stationery Office.
Weckel, Ulrike. 2000. "Die Mörder sind unter uns oder: Vom Verschwinden der Opfer." *Werkstattgeschichte* 25: 105–115.
———. 2005. "A Failure of a Shock Treatment? On the Impact of the Film *Die Todesmühlen* on the German Public" (Heb.). In *Memory and Amnesia. The Holocaust in Germany*, ed. Gilad Margalit and Yfaat Weiss. Tel Aviv: HaKibbutz HaMeuchad. 282–318.
Weckerling, Rudolf. 1947. "Das Kreuz unter den Kreuzen." *Die Kirche*, March 30.
Wehler, Hans Ulrich. 2002. "Der Weltuntergang kann nicht schlimmer sein." *Süddeutsche Zeitung*, December 14.
Weidauer, Walter. 1946. "Zu 13. Februar." *Sächsische Volkszetung*, February 13. 2.
———. 1949. "Vor vier Jahren sank Dresden in Asche." *Neues Deutschland*, Sonntagsbeilage, February 13.
———. 1965. *Inferno Dresden: Über Lügen und Legenden um die Aktion "Donnerschlag."* Berlin: Dietz.
"Weihnachtsworte an Coventry." 1946. *Neue Zeitung*, December 23.
Weiβ, Hermann. 1995. "Die Organisationen der Vertriebenen und Ihre Presse." In *Die Vertreibung der Deutschen aus dem Osten. Ursachen, Ereignisse Folgen*, ed. Wolfgang Benz. Frankfurt a.M.: Fischer. 244–264.
Weiss, Konrad. 1998. *Lothar Kreyssig: Prophet der Versöhnung*. Gerlingen: Bleicher.
Weissmark, Mona Sue. 2004. *Justice Matters: Legacies of the Holocaust and World War II*. Oxford: Oxford University Press.
Welzer, Harald. 2004. "Schön unscharf: Über die Konjunktur der Familien—und Generationsromane." *Literatur: Beilage zum Mittelweg* 36, 1: 53–64.
———. 2005. "Cumulative Heroization—Turning the Bystanders and Criminals into Anti-Nazi Heroes in the Inter-Generation Discourse" (Heb.). In *Memory and Amnesia: The Holocaust in Germany*, ed. Gilad Margalit and Yfaat Weiss. Tel Aviv: HaKibbutz HaMeuchad. 198–215.
Welzer, Harald, Sabine Moller, and Karoline Tschuggnall. 2002. *"Opa war kein Nazi." Nationalsozialismus und Holocaust im Familiengedächtnis*. Frankfurt a.M.: Fischer.
Wendler, Lisa. 1950. "Der 5. März erfordert verstaerkten Einsatz fuer den Frieden!" *Volksstimme*, no. 55, March 6.
"Wenig beglückt." 1958. *Frankfurter Rundschau*, April 18.
Wenzke, Rüdiger. 1999. "Das unliebsame Erbe der Wehrmacht und der Aufbau der DDR—Volksarmee." In *Die Wehrmacht: Mythos und Realität*, ed. Rolf-Dieter Müller and Hans-Erich Volkmann. München: R. Oldenburg. 1113–1138.
"Wer Adolf will." 1966. *Der Spiegel*, November 28. 34.
"Westmaechte ermutigten Hitler." 1948. *Neues Deutschland*, February 13. 1, 3.
Wierling, Dorothee. 1990. "Is There an East German Identity? Aspects of a Social History of the Soviet Zone/German Democratic Republic." *Tel Aviver Jahrbuch für deutsche Geschichte* 19: 193–208.

———. 2002a. "Erzählungen in Wiederspruch? Der Nationalsozialismus und die erste Nachkriegsgeneration der DDR." *Werkstattgeschichte* 30: 17–31.

———. 2002b. *Geboren im Jahr Eins: Der Jahrgang 1949 in der DDR Versuch einer Kolleltivbiographie.* Berlin: Ch. Links Verlag.

Wimmer, Reinhard. 2002. "Lo Ma'adirim et Zikhram" (letter to the editor). *Ha'aretz,* October 31.

"Wir leben wie Tiere in Erdlöcher." 2003. *Bild,* November 25.

"Wir Toten sind gröβere Heere." 1952. *Westdeutsche Allgemeine,* November 17.

Wittlinger, Ruth. 2006. "Taboo or Tradition? The 'Germans as Victims' Theme in West Germany until the Early 1990s." In *Germans as Victims: Remembering the Past in Contemporary Germany,* ed. Bill Niven. New York: Palgrave Macmillan. 62–75.

Wittstock, Uwe. 2002. "Die weit offen stehende Tabu-Tür." *Die Welt,* February 15.

Wodak, Ruth. 1990. *Wir sind alle unschuldige Täter! Diskurshistorische Studien zum Nachkriegsantisemitismus.* With R. de Cillia, H. Gruber, R. Mitten, P. Nowak, and J. Pelikan. Frankfurt a.M.: Suhrkamp.

Wolffsohn, Michael. 2003. "Vertriebene verdienen Vertrauen." *Die Welt,* August 30.

Wolffsohn, Michael, and Thomas Brechenmacher. 1999. *Die Deutschen und Ihre Vornamen: 200 Jahre Politik und Öffentliche Meinung.* München und Zürich: Diana.

Zekri, Sonja. 2002. "Tiefe Resignation." *Süddeutsche Zeitung,* February 9.

———. 2003a. "Geteiltes Leid." *Süddeutsche Zeitung,* January 22.

———. 2003b. "Bis hierher und nicht weiter." *Süddeutsche Zeitung,* January 23.

———. 2007. "Was bleibt, ist Heimweh." *Süddeutsche Zeitung,* August 11.

Zelizer, Barbie. 1998. *Remembering to Forget: Holocaust Memory through the Camera's Eye.* Chicago: University of Chicago Press.

Zimmer, B. 1949. "Sudetendeutsche Passion." *Karlsbader Heimatbrief Folge,* February 2.

Zimmering, Max. 1954. *Phosphor und Flieder: Vom Untergang und Wiederaufstieg der Stadt Dresden.* Berlin: Dietz.

Zimmermann, Moshe. 2003. "In Deutschland wie in Nahost." *Süddeutsche Zeitung,* July 30.

"Zuschriften aus dem Leserkreis: Opfer des Faschismus." 1945. *Deutsche Volkszeitung,* no. 20, July 5.

INDEX

Page numbers in italics indicate illustrations.

Gilad Margalit is Senior Lecturer in the Department of General History at the University of Haifa, Israel, and deputy director of the Haifa Center for German European Studies (HCGES). Born in Haifa, he studied history at Tel Aviv University and at the Hebrew University in Jerusalem, where he earned his doctorate. He is author of *Germany and Its Gypsies: A Post-Auschwitz Ordeal.* The Israeli edition of *Guilt, Suffering, and Memory* was awarded the Jacob Bahat Prize for the best original book.